ABOVE US OR AROUND US, VOLUME I:

THE STORY OF THE BLOODY EIGHTH

By Jennifer Thompson

Jennifer Thompson

Cover photo: Eighth Indiana Regiment Flag from the collection at the World War Memorial, Indianapolis, Indiana. Courtesy of Jennifer Watson

Dedication

I dedicate this book in memory of my grandfather Jesse Lewis McKay, who gave me a love for history. I also dedicate this book to my first graduate professor Bryan Mark Rigg, who gave me a love for research while writing my first graduate paper, the basis for my four books about this regiment; and to my husband Jerry, who has supported my many years of research on this project.

Too many people have helped with this project for me to thank each one individually. The names of those who provided photographs are in the photo captions. The names of those who provided information are in the Bibliography. I wish to thank all of you for your part in making this book a reality.

TABLE OF CONTENTS

INTRODUCTION

At the beginning of the Civil War, the Eighth Indiana Volunteer Infantry (with 784 men) organized for three months of service (April 25 - August 2). When the war did not end as quickly as expected, the regiment (with 1046 men) reorganized for three years of service. James W. Alexander, a distant relative, enlisted in this three-year regiment.

This book will trace the history of the three-month and three-year Eighth Indiana Volunteer Infantry through letters and poems from enlisted men, official reports from the officers, newspaper accounts, and historical studies from historians. Letters will describe problems faced in the regiment - seasonal campaigns, increasing desertions, and monotonous duty; hazards of duty - bad water, horse stampedes, and swamp dangers; and various aspects of battles - close calls and laying siege. One writer claims this brigade had the honor of being the first into and the last out of the Battle of Port Gibson. A letter and a poem give accounts of the Battle of Cedar Creek, where the army declared James W. Alexander missing and presumed dead and where Ira Hough earned a Medal of Honor for capturing the enemy flag. A letter tells of visiting Washington, D.C., yet failing to see the President. Accounts describe how hometowns honored furloughed men with flag presentations and receptions. Volume Two and Three of the series will also include a biography of each soldier in these two regiments. Volume Four shares newspaper articles about the regiment and the soldiers.

Enlisted letters and poems given the soldiers' viewpoint of military life. The official reports of the officers will evaluate the accuracy of the enlisted accounts. Historical studies generally use official reports as sources. Historians can trace their history through enlisted men's letters, diaries, and poems, which they can compare to official reports and memoirs of the officers and historical studies, to gain a complete regiment history. This book will show the value of enlisted accounts and will give the reader a greater knowledge and appreciation of the Eighth Indiana Volunteer Infantry and its contribution to the Union.

PART I: HISTORY OF THE REGIMENT

Chapter 1: The War Begins and Indiana's Response

"Indiana knows no North, no South, nothing but the Union." State of Indiana Memorial stone placed in the Washington Monument in the 1850s. NPS photo

As tensions grew across the nation prior to the Civil War, Indiana organized several state militia companies including the Cambridge City Grays. These companies disbanded, and many members enlisted when the war began.

After Lincoln's first call for volunteers, Indiana had an overwhelming response with over 12,000 men answering the call in five days. This was three times Indiana's quota of 4,458.[1] The number of soldiers serving from Indiana during the Civil War ranked second among all the Union states.[2] The State divided these first volunteers into six regiments (six to eleven) for three months service. Civil War regiments started with number six to avoid confusion with the five regiments who had recently fought in the Mexican War. The Eighth Indiana regiment consisted of one company from each of the following counties: Delaware, Grant, Hancock, Henry, Madison, Randolph, and Wabash, and three companies from Wayne County.[3] Many of the Cambridge City Grays, organized in 1858, enlisted in Company A of the Eighth Indiana.[4]

An article published in the *New Castle Courier* showed the response in New Castle to soldiers leaving to answer Lincoln's call. Everything shut down and the entire town gathered at the railroad depot, where last farewells and patriotic speeches occurred. "They go forth bearing aloft the flag of our country, to defend this glorious fabric of a government, against which

---

[1] David Stevenson, A. M. *Indiana's Roll of Honor*, Vol. I (Indianapolis: A. D. Streight, 1864), 20.
[2] Emma Lou Thornbrough, *Indiana in the Civil War Era 1850-1880: The History of Indiana*, Vol. III (Indianapolis: Indiana Historical Bureau & Indiana Historical Society, 1965), 124.
[3] Stevenson, 81.
[4] U.Z. Reigle bought a hat from a Cambridge City Gray uniform at the McGrady auction in September 1929. See "Story of a Hat," *The Cambridge City Tribune*, September 12, 1929, 4, https://www.newspapers.com.

traitors have raised their impious hands; and God defend this right."[5] Company B was the first company organized in Henry County and

> was one of the first to reach Indianapolis, after the call for troops had been issued. It arrived there before any kind of adequate arrangements had been made for the reception of troops, as is evidenced, by the fact, that during the first day and a half of its stay at the Capitol City, it was quartered at the Bates House, then the leading hotel of the city, occupying the present site of the Hotel Claypool.[6]

Businesses shut down in Wayne County and the whole town gathered together to listen to speakers and the band playing songs. Judge William P. Benton volunteered his services to the state and urged others to join him. The superintendent of the railroad provided the group of 133 men who signed up free passage by train to Indianapolis the next morning. Those who stayed behind promised to care for their families and started gathering money for that purpose.[7]

Businesses also shut down in Wabash County. Charles S. Parrish and Joseph M. Thompson opened a recruiting office April 13, the day after the attack on Fort Sumter; many men volunteered for service.

> From morning till night each day, troops have been parading our streets, and the sounds of the fife and drum have been so constant that our village wore the appearance of a garrisoned town....It was evident the great heart of the people was stirred, and the signs of the times indicated that a terrible vengeance was about to be taken on the cowardly traitors who were endeavoring to destroy the government.[8]

Valentine Thuma came from Richland County, Ohio, and wrote about joining his company:

> I reached Wabash April 17th intending to enlist in the Wabash Volunteers. Presented myself in the evening for that purpose and was accepted and sworn in. Remained there (expenses all paid) until the company started. On Monday afternoon the Co. organized. It then consisted of 140 members....Name adopted Relief Co. No. 1.[9]

The men of this company, Company K, elected the following officers: Captain Charles S. Parrish, First Lieutenant Joseph M. Thompson and Second Lieutenant Franklin Dailey. All three of these men served the full three-month term and reenlisted into the three-year regiment.

---

[5] "Henry County's First Civil War Volunteers, April 1861," *Henry County Genealogical Services*, accessed February 7, 2012, http://www.hcgs.net/civilvolunteers.html.
[6] George Hazzard, *Hazzard's History of Henry County, Indiana 1822-1906, Military Edition*, Vol. I (New Castle: George Hazzard, 1906), 251.
[7] "A Relic of Soldier Days: Old Wayne to the Fore in '61 as Always Before," *The Richmond Item*, December 2, 1882, 1, https://www.newspapers.com.
[8] *History of Wabash County, Indiana* (Chicago: John Morris, 1884), 163.
[9] Valentine Thuma Diary, August 23, 1861, Special Collections, William Henry Smith Memorial Library, Indiana Historical Society, Indianapolis.

"Several railroad companies, operating in the State, announced that they would carry all regularly enlisted volunteers free."[10] The company left by railroad for Indianapolis, arriving at Camp Morton to find over eight thousand soldiers in the camp. Wabash had sent twenty-five more soldiers than needed for the Eighth Indiana, so these men became part of the Seventeenth Indiana. On April 21, Lew Wallace wrote a military discharge for Levi Bean in Captain Parrish's Company "on account of his being one of the excess in the number of members in said company" because the Secretary of War had reduced the number for a company from eighty-four or one hundred to only sixty-four.[11]

The same day, Captain Vandevender enlisted a full company of one hundred men in Anderson from Madison County's 186 volunteers. They mustered in April 22 for three months and elected the following officers: Captain Hiram T. Vandevender, First Lieutenant John J. Robinson, Second Lieutenant James Fergus, and First Sergeant John D. Johnson.

Reuben Riley and Henry Snow organized a fife and drum corps in Hancock County "to make rounds of the county communities to boost patriotic emotion and volunteer enlistment."[12] Riley organized the Union Guards of Hancock County on April 22, who mustered in as Company G of the Eighth Indiana.

---

[10] W. H. H. Terrill, *Indiana in the War of the Rebellion: Report of the Adjutant General,* Vol. 1 (1869, Reprint, Indiana Historical Society, 1960), 9.

[11] Military Discharge, 21 April 1861, "Eighth Indiana Volunteer Infantry regiment correspondence," Records of Adjutant General of Indiana: Roll No. 3, Indiana State Archives.

[12] Sue Baker, *Hancock County, Indiana Civil War Soldiers Plus Related Facts* (Westminster, MD: Heritage Books, 2006), 1.

Chapter 2: Training for War

This historical marker is located in the 1900 block of North Alabama Street, Indianapolis, Indiana. Photo from Thompson Family Album

Camp Morton was located at the new state fairgrounds, a thirty-six acre tract of land bounded by 19th Street, Central Avenue, 22nd Street, and Talbott Street. This camp, where troops organized, equipped, and trained, would later serve as a prison camp for thousands of Rebels. Ira T. Gregg wrote about his visit to Camp Morton:

> Soon after President Lincoln issued his first call for volunteers (Seventy five Thousand), I visited Camp Morton at Indianapolis, and witnessed the arrival of many troops, fresh from the fields of busy life, who was immediately put under discipline and drill for service in the army. They doffed their Citizens clothes, and donned the army blue, and in a few short days, they were organized into companys and Regiments, and equipped for the war. They soon left their first camping ground, and proudly marched through the Streets of the City to the Union Depot, for transportation, headed by Brass Bands, and waving flags, amid the shouts of thousands of Citizens, who sent up cheer after cheer, as they grandly marched by, soon to be on fields of blood and carnage. I cannot describe the patriotic love I had in my heart for those brave men, who had left home and friends, and went out in defense of our Country's call, to battle for life liberty and freedom, to face the dangers of the battle field, and still more to be dreaded the prison pens of the Southern Confederacy, which no tongue can fully tell, nor pen portray.[13]

---

[13] Ira T. Gregg, "A Brief Sketch of my parents, Stephen and Hannah Gregg; Genealogy and Biography of Ira T. Gregg," Photocopy of unpublished memoir.

The companies swore in April 25. On the twenty-sixth, the companies organized into the Eighth Indiana regiment. The men elected officers: Colonel William P. Benton (who had enlisted April 17 as a captain in Company I); Lieutenant Colonel Silas Colgrove (who had enlisted April 20 as a captain in Company C); and Major David Shunk (who had enlisted April 19 as a captain in Company B). They transformed horse and cattle stalls into barracks. The regiment took up quarters in stalls along the west side of Camp P at Camp Morton. On May 1, the regiment moved their quarters to horse sheds on the north side of the camp, and companies divided into messes of six to eight. "Each mess has a chief selected from the number who draws provisions and details a man each day for cook."[14] Offices became guardhouses and the power hall became a hospital. The men bathed in Fall Creek, a half mile to the north. The regiment spent thirty days in Camp Morton before transferring to Camp McClellan on the east side of Indianapolis near the Irvington neighborhood.

They presented the captain with a brace of pistols on April 27. The men received regular U.S. muskets on May 2, but expected to receive better guns than these smoothbore muskets. On June 4, "We received rifles of Springfield manufacture. They are considered the best kind of guns in general use. We are well satisfied now and are confident of leaving soon."[15] The Springfield rifle, Model M1861, had a forty inch brightly polished barrel and walnut stock. This .58 caliber, single-shot, muzzle-loading rifle measured seventy-four inches from butt plate to muzzle and weighed approximately ten pounds. The rifle used percussion caps and had an eighteen-inch triangular bayonet. The men marched to town for cartridge boxes on May 15. The men did not receive ammunition until June 11:

> the guards had ball and cartridge furnished for their guns today. For the first time. Several rounds of blank cartridge were fired today by our regt. at regt. drill. The verberation of 600 rifles discharged simultaniously is enough to arouse within one all the preconcerted ideas of real battle.[16]

The minié bullet was the type of ammunition used in the Springfield rifle. When fired, gas entered the hollow base of this bullet-shaped lead projectile, forcing the outer side into the rifling of the barrel. This type of bullet improved accuracy and range.

---

[14] Thuma, May 1, 1861.
[15] Thuma, June 4, 1861.
[16] Thuma, June 11, 1861.

On May 18, the regiment went to Indianapolis for uniforms, but found the uniforms would be sent to camp. "There has been some strife between the 8th, 9th, 10th Regts for the suit of uniform we are to have being most coveted because it is of dark gray color."[17] Many volunteers preferred gray, because blue was the color worn by the Regular Army. The men of the Eighth and Tenth Indiana wore gray jackets and trousers with a slouch hat in 1861. The uniforms arrived May 19:

> This afternoon our uniform was distributed. The suit consists of pants and roundabout. The clothes fit very imperfectly and our Captain says they must be made to fit at expense of government or he will refuse them altogether.[18]

The hats arrived May 24. "We received our hats today. They are gray, rough and ready with the left side buttoned up."[19] That same day, General McClellan visited Indianapolis to review the three-month brigade. "The review was the most grand military pageant that had ever been witnessed at the Capital of Indiana. The troops were in fine condition, and eager to be led to the field. They were highly complimented by Gen. McClellan. Their equipment was pronounced complete."[20]

Dr. Ford received one ambulance and a four-horse team to haul his medical supplies. He had to bring his own surgical equipment, and his mother provided "an ample supply of bandages and lint, manufactured with her own hands." Colonel Benton verbally arrested him when he refused to write discharge papers for "a sound, able-bodied man" who "had given offense and was perhaps troublesome." He reported the incident to the Medical Director who ordered Benton to headquarters the next day, leading to Ford's immediate release.[21]

The captain read the U.S. army laws and regiment rules on May 9, giving the order of the day. "Reveille," sounded by drums in infantry units at 5 a.m. in the summer and 6 a.m. in the winter, gave the men fifteen minutes to wash and dress before "Assembly." At "Assembly," the regiment formed by sections for sergeant's roll call. The sergeant presented his company "all present or accounted for" or listed those missing. After the first drill of the morning, the First Sergeant read special orders before dismissing the men for breakfast at 7 a.m. Sick men went to

---

[17] Thuma, May 18, 1861.
[18] Thuma, May 19, 1861.
[19] Thuma, May 24, 1861.
[20] Stevenson, Vol. I, 39.
[21] James Ford, Civil War Correspondence, 1861-1863 between James Ford, U.S. Surgeon, 8th Regiment Volunteer Infantry, and America Holton Ford, Wabash, Indiana. Manuscript published July 2004 for the Ford Family Reunion by the Charley Creek Foundation, 1.

the "infirmary," the surgeon's tent, for sick call at 7:30 a.m. Fatigue call specified details for cleaning up camp, chopping firewood, and performing other chores. At Guard Mounting, at 8 a.m., the First Sergeant inspected the men who would stand company guard for the next twenty-four hours, then marched them to the parade ground for another inspection and assignment by the regiment adjutant and sergeant major. Those not on guard or detail participated in company, regimental, or brigade drills at 5:45 – 6:45 a.m., 8:30 – 9:30 a.m., and 10:30 – 11:30 a.m. Lt. Col. Silas Colgrove drilled Company K on May 14: "Our Lieut Colonel drilled our Company today and pronounced us the best drilled Com. in the Regiment."[22] Free time followed dinner at noon before more drills at 2 – 3 p.m. and 4 – 5 p.m. A formal retreat ceremony occurred at 5:45, which called men to "attention" followed by "retreat." Roll call, inspections, and dress parade were held and official orders, communications, and results of court-martials were read before being dismissed for supper at 6 p.m. "Tatoo," preceded by "Attention" and "Assembly," was the final roll call of the day at 8:30 p.m. Men were ordered to their quarters, and "Taps," at 9:30 p.m., signaled lights out.

The ladies of Indiana presented flags for the soldiers to carry into battle. On April 22, the ladies of Wabash presented a silk flag to the Wabash Volunteers, Company K, who on May 21 elected John R. Wolf, Second Sergeant, as Regimental Ensign. Mrs. R. D. Helen gave a "beautiful tribute to the patriotic spirit that had induced their brave sons, husbands and lovers to offer themselves a willing sacrifice upon their country's altar."[23] The ladies from Greenfield, including Mrs. Permelia Thayer, Mrs. A. P. Williams, Miss Alice Pierson, and Miss Martha Meeks, made a large flag in the home of Mrs. Thayer on the northeast corner of Main and Pennsylvania Streets and presented it to Company G. Seventeen ladies from Marion each sewed a star on the flag they made and each one signed her name on her star.[24] They presented that flag to the Marion Guards of Company B on May 2: "May these stars ever serve as beacon-lights, to direct your minds to the loved ones at home and may it ere long triumphantly wave o'er a peaceful and happy country."[25] Captain Oliver H. P. Carey replied,

---

[22] Thuma, May 14, 1861.
[23] *History of Wabash County, Indiana*, 163.
[24] "Old Flag Is Exhibited," *The Star Press*, June 15, 1909, 2, hpps://www.newspapers.com. This flag is part of the Marion Public Library and Museum Collection. It is extremely fragile, so it cannot be photographed.
[25] David I. McCormick, *Indiana Battle Flags* (Indianapolis: The Indiana Battle Flag Commission, 1929), 48.

> We also pledge you our lives and our sacred honor, to stand by and support it, - and in the beautiful language of Ruth to Naomi, "entreat us not to leave it." Whither it goes, there we will go, until it shall again proudly wave over our country. And should it ever hopelessly trail in the dust, then let us be buried.[26]

On May 7, the ladies from Indianapolis presented a silk banner to Company H. May 17, the *Indianapolis Journal*, told about the Eighth Indiana's regiment flag and motto and spoke of their devotion to the Union:

> The flag borne by Colonel Benton's regiment bears the motto, "above us or around us." That motto indicates the true spirit of the Regiment. They will wave the star-spangled banner over their heads in victory and life, or wrap it around their bodies in defeat and death. Their colors they will never depart.[27]

The company dressed in their newly made uniforms for a special ceremony to receive a flag and banner from the ladies in front of the State House May 22. Thuma described the beautiful flag and banner:

> The flag was of first quality made and presented by Ladies of Indianapolis. The banner was blue beautifully embroidered with an Eagle in centre. It was made and presented by Ladies of Terre Haute. Our colonel replied to the presentation in a glowing speech. He closed by appealing to the 8th Regt to adopt for their watchword in the hour of danger "The Ladies of Indianapolis and Terre Haute," which appeal was responded to by a universal "yes" from the soldiers.[28]

The office of the World War Memorial in Indianapolis has a notebook with pictures of the tattered Eighth Indiana regiment banners and flags stored in their archives.

The *Indianapolis Journal* described the Eighth Indiana regiment in an article May 23, 1861. "The Eighth is an excellent regiment and anxious to get into active service."[29] The long delay in leaving for the field led to discipline problems. May 7, two men faced court-martial for attempting to fight and received the penalty of extra guard duty. The orderly sergeant of Company E attempted to kill his lieutenant and they put him in the guardhouse May 30, awaiting his court-martial. "He has conducted himself very disreputable since in camp and the common opinion is that he will be dealt with without much mercy and at last will be drummed out of

---

26 McCormick,49.
27 McCormick,50.
28 Thuma, May 22, 1861.
29 McCormick, 51.

camp."[30] On Saturday, June 8, many men, supposedly in town drunk, missed dress parade. The colonel ordered that when the absent returned, they should immediately be placed in the Guard House. Penalty for missing dress parade was usually twenty-four hours extra guard duty. Most of the soldiers returned Monday and they placed them under arrest. One company had thirty deserters. The punishment for all these absent soldiers was to dig wells. Violations of Articles of War (drunkenness, insubordination, theft, disrespect, sitting on guard duty, leaving post without authority, absent without pass) led to courts-martial. Punishments varied – digging and filling up latrines, burying dead horses, or helping company cooks. Special courts-martial required a board of the regiment commander and three officers. In non-capital cases, guilty sentences brought loss of one month's pay or one month in prison or hard labor. NCOs (non-commissioned officers) faced demotion. Other punishments included: being bucked and gagged for six to twelve hours, wearing a cannon ball shackled to one leg, standing on a barrel for hours, holding a log on one's shoulders, marching around camp wearing a barrel or marching around with a knapsack full of rocks. Capital offenses required a general court-martial board of five to thirteen officers. Soldiers served time in federal prison for capital offenses. They drummed deserters and cowards out of the service. Extreme cases (murder, mutiny, treason, rape, and desertion) led to death sentences. Thuma discussed why he felt the regiment had so many discipline problems:

> The Regiments will never prosper while remaining here for two reasons. The first and leading cause is a spirit of mutiny at not being called into the field. Most, if not all od [of] us, volunteered with the expectation of going almost immediately into actual service. By remaining here with nothing to stimylate us we naturally lose our enthusiasm and become indifferent. The other reason is the boys are too near home and will steal interviews with friends.[31]

While in Indianapolis, one man from Company K was irregularly discharged, Private William W. Sankey.

---

[30] Thuma, May 30, 1861.

[31] Thuma, June 10, 1861. Author has added brackets to clarify some spelling errors and missing punctuation on several quotations.

This cannon base monument at the Wabash County Memorial Hall honors James H. Emmett, the first Wabash County soldier to die in the Civil War. Photo from Thompson Family Album

June 19, the regiment finally received marching orders to join Rosecran's Brigade, McClelland's Provincial Army of West Virginia. "Yesterday morning about 3 o'clock 8th and 10th regiment were aroused by the welcome cry of marching orders."[32] They marched to Indianapolis and boarded railroad cars to Cincinnati, Ohio. They reached Greensborough (Greensburg?) around noon. The townspeople met the train with food for the soldiers. After arriving at Cincinnati and waiting several hours, the officers called the men into ranks and they marched uptown.

> At the market house a bontiful supper was prepared of which we were urged to partake freely. The hospitalities of our entertainers were unbounded. After eating all we desired we were requested to fill the remainder in our haversacks for future use. Such demonstrations of respect and sympathy bestowed upon our soldiers has a tendency to stimulate them in the cause prized so dearly by the bestowers.[33]

At Chilacothe the next noon, the men received a reception similar to the one at Greensborough. John Smith died while there, shortly after being crushed by railroad

[32] Thuma, June 20, 1861.
[33] Thuma, June 20, 1861.

cars.[34] These receptions and the earlier flag presentations encouraged the men to fight for their loved ones at home. That evening at Marietta, the regiment stowed their belongings and rested in boats for the night. June 21 and 22, they traveled by boats downriver to Parkersburg, where Gen. McClellan and several distinguished persons inspected the troops.

June 23, the regiment traveled by railroad to Clarksburg (West Virginia), and built entrenchments at Camp Carlisle June 24. "This morning early we commenced entrenching and throwing up breast work along the outer edge of the first porch. A wall is built on the outside with stone and dirt is filled on the inside."[35] Eighth Indiana scouts captured four rebels and a Confederate flag on June 25. "They attempted to run, but the scouts fired at them and made them stop."[36] The regiment marched to Camp Buchanan June 29. The army discharged their Quartermaster because he failed to provide supplies. John Polk was angry and wanted to kill him because the Quartermaster had his baggage and owed him money. Dr. James Ford established a hospital here; a number of soldiers suffered from diarrhea.[37]At this brigade camp, the Eighth Indiana called their regiment camp, Camp Conner. Before the end of their three-month enlistments, Governor Morton sent "messengers to all the regimental commanders with letters urging them to re-enlist."[38] While at this camp, Colonel Benton started recruiting for the three-year regiment:

> This evening a test was made by the Colonel to ascertain how many three year men could be found in the 8th Regt. All who desired to return home at the end of the 3 months term were requested to step out of the ranks and form line by themselves. Three year men stand fast. Contrary, doubtless, to the Col's expectation 2/3 of the men left ranks. 30 of our men remained fast, myself among the numbers.[39]

The Union Army followed the retreating Confederate army for several days until July 10, when Rebels made a stand and shot a German Ohio picket guard. The entire

---

[34] James K. Bigelow, *Abridged History of the Eighth Indiana Volunteer Infantry, from its Organization, April 21st, 1861, to the Date of Re-enlistment as Veterans, Januay 1, 1864* (Indianapolis: Ellis Barnes, 1864), 7-8.
[35] Thuma, June 24, 1861.
[36] Jennifer McSpadden, *A Leaf of Voices: Stories of the American Civil War in the Words of Those Who Lived and Died, 1861-65* (Indianapolis: Indiana Historical Society Press, 2014), 123.
[37] McSpadden, 124.
[38] Terrill, Vol. 1, 17.
[39] Thuma, June 24, 1861.

Eighth Indiana regiment stood picket guard that night. A Union sympathizer, David Hart, came into the camp July 10. He told of a secret route around the south spur of Rich Mountain, which would allow Rosecran's Army to flank Pegram's Army. Rosecran's Army (five companies from the Eighth Indiana, Tenth Indiana, Thirteenth Indiana, and Nineteenth Ohio regiments) left at 4 a.m. through the rain, dim light and rough terrain, without any stops. "Many of us had neither supper nor breakfast, but from our eagerness for a battle, and anxiety to make the surprise complete, all was endured without a murmur."[40] They quickly marched fifteen miles to surprise the enemy pickets five miles from the Rebel camp. Skirmishers met the pickets a short distance from the fort:

> The pickets scampered. Our force was considerably behind at the time of the firing and the command was immediately given "Closeup, close up, double quick," And with all the speed our already taxed energies could command up we went, until having reached our point we fell into line of battle, ready for the attack. Just at this moment the rain commenced falling in torrents and continued for about 15 minutes, during which time we stood at secure arms quietly taking the drenching.[41]

After the rain, a battery opened on the regiments hidden in the woods. The Nineteenth Ohio commenced the attack at 2 o'clock, followed by the Tenth Indiana. When the Tenth Indiana received orders to fall back, the Eighth and Thirteenth received orders to enter the battle. "And down we went without the least apparent trepidation or fear. We saluted them with a volley that made the hills reverberate."[42] The Eighth Indiana could see the battery, and totally unmanned and silenced it; "when our boys let into them with their Enfield and Minie rifles I never heard such screaming in all my life."[43] After a period of heavy and constant firing, the colonel ordered the men to charge. "Finally our Col (W.P. Benton) gave the command 'Forward, Charge – take the battery.' No sooner said than done. Eager to engage the rebels inclose the conflict we started full speed, yelling as we went."[44] The Rebels retreated quickly to avoid certain death. "Andrew J. Fuller was color bearer for Company B, 8th Regiment and planted the colors in the enemy's

---

[40] Thuma, July 11, 1861.
[41] Thuma, July 11, 1861.
[42] Thuma, July 11, 1861.
[43] Clarkson W. Weesner, *History of Wabash County Indiana: A Narrative Account of its Historical Progress, Its People, and Its Principal Interests*, Vol. I (Chicago: Lewis, 1914), 265.
[44] Thuma, July 11, 1861.

fortification."[45] The Union Army followed them for a short distance then gave up the chase. At the foot of the mountain, they found a bloody and horrible spectacle of mangled dead and dying men. They took everything the Rebels had left behind.

Three hours had transpired from the battery attack to the Rebel retreat. "Men experienced in war pronounce the battle extraordinary for unflinching bravery and long duration."[46] The Eighth Indiana stationed itself in line of battle along the road in case a cavalry regiment came to rescue the Rebels. McClellan reported twelve killed, fifty-nine wounded, and no prisoners with an enemy loss of 135 killed and between eight hundred and nine hundred wounded and prisoners. This battle freed this portion of Western Virginia from the Confederate Army. July 15, the *Indianapolis Journal* praised the Eighth Indiana and Colonel Benton for their quick building of the entrenchments at Clarksburgh and their brave conduct. "The only banner in the engagement was that of the Eighth, the motto of which was: 'ABOVE US OR AROUND US.'"[47] The army released prisoners of war, much to the dismay of the enlisted men. "Many of our men were highly dissatisfied at their release predicting that they will meet us again."[48] The Eighth Indiana suffered casualties in the Battle of Rich Mountain. Those killed in battle were Private Philander Wiseheart of Co. F, and Privates Joseph Beck and James H. Emmett (Valentine's messmate) of Company K. Emmett was near Dr. Ford when he died. "A 'hot streak' ran up my back into the brain—I was mad, and found myself hunting for a gun to avenge his death."[49] Dr. Ford spent all night caring for the wounded and as he was about to amputate the leg of a wounded Ohio man the next morning, "about twenty-five men rode up, all dressed in officer's clothes, and surrounded me."[50] He continued the surgery without a word and one of the officers, the U.S. Head Surgeon C. Kingsley, Jr., made Ford surgeon of the hospital and promised him all needed supplies. Of the eighteen wounded, Sergeant Marion M. Stephenson of Co. G died July 20. Some wounded soldiers carved inscriptions on nearby boulders; these still lie on the battlefield site

---

[45] Baker, 430-431.
[46] Thuma, July 11, 1861.
[47] *The Soldier of Indiana in the War For the Union*, Vol. 1 (Indianapolis: Merrill and Company, 1866), 55.
[48] Thuma, July 17, 1861.
[49] Ford, Civil War Correspondence, 7.
[50] Ford, Civil War Correspondence, 7-8.

today.[51]Company H from Wabash had one deserter, John Ballinger.[52] On the way into battle, Jeremiah Sullivan, who was a gardener, ran through a flower garden full of "peonas" (peonies). After the battle, he went back and dug up some of the roots and sent them home to have them planted in his garden.[53] On July 17, Colonel Benton sent a telegram to Governor Morton requesting 540 pairs of "pantaloons" as soon as possible because "the boys fought like men they are all ragged."[54]

---

[51] Stan B. Cohen, *A Pictorial Guide to West Virginia's Civil War Sites* (Charleston: Quarrier Press, 2003), 90.

[52] Weesner, 266.

[53] *The Richmond Item*, May 30, 1888, 3, https://www.newspapers.com.

[54] Telegram from Colonel Benton to Governor Morton, July 17, 1861, "Civil War: Governor Morton Telegraph Books and Slips," The Digital Collections of IUPUI University Library, accessed February 3, 2012, http://indiamond6.ulib.iupui.edu/cdm4/document.php?CISOROOT=/Telegraph&CISOPTR=4407&REC=2.

Chapter 4: Home Again

Portrait of Indiana Governor Oliver P. Morton, C106. www.civilwarphotos.net, accessed 23 May 2015.

With the enlistment time nearly up, the Eighth Indiana became eager to return home. "We have had a fight and our time being about out we are anxious to return home."[55] Major General George B. McClellan sent a message to Governor Morton on July 21 directing the Indiana troops to return to Indianapolis. "I can not permit them to return to you without again expressing my high appreciation of the distinguished valor and endurance of the Indiana troops, and my hope that but a short time will elapse before I have the pleasure of knowing that they are again ready for the field."[56] Thuma recorded, "We commenced our march at brisk and elastic pace buoyed with the prospect of soon seeing again the old Hoosier State, there to receive the congratulations and greetings of anxious friends." [57]Upon arrival in Richmond, Indiana, the colonel's hometown, the regiment enjoyed a breakfast prepared at the colonel's request. Governor Oliver P.

[55] Thuma, July 19, 1861.
[56] Terrill, vol. 1, 12.
[57] Thuma, July 22, 1861.

Morton had established a system of receptions to gratify the "loyal heart" of the people, encourage returning soldiers, and stimulate recruiting. "Governor O P Morton always welcomed them, always giving them a public and warm reception, worthy the high honors they had won."[58] Communities planned receptions and announced them the day before. They prepared a public dinner. Music and cannon-fire escorted the regiment or battery to the Capitol grounds or public halls. Officials gave addresses of welcome and congratulations and included a short military history of each unit. A delegation of fair Indianapolis ladies waited on the soldiers as they ate their meal. Singing clubs and individuals presented patriotic and humorous songs. Every Indiana regiment received this honor. On July 26, the Eighth Indiana marched to the West Market House and quickly ate the dinner prepared for them "with a rapidity and earnestness strikingly suggestive of hard biscuits and rusty bacon during the past two months."[59] They marched to the State House Square and William Wallace welcomed them home. Wallace praised them for their accomplishments and how they helped wipe out the unjust blot put upon the state by the Battle of Buena Vista in the Mexican War. [60] Colonel Benton expressed the thanks of the regiment and quickly told the history of the regiment since its departure from Indiana.

> He alluded proudly to their flag presented by the ladies of this city and Terre Haute and said it was, by accident, the only flag at the battle of Rich Mountain, and to it all eyes were turned as the symbol of the cause for which they were perilling their lives. He declared that their flag should never leave the field till that of the nation was respected and obeyed all over the country (loud cheers) and that he and his regiment would re-enlist for the war and stand by the flag until it was over. Here he turned to the men and said, "Do I speak for you, men?" … A universal cry of "Yes," and tremendous cheering was the answer, and a very satisfactory answer, too. [61]

Lieutenant Colonel Colgrove prepared the men to march. Wallace stopped them so he could give Governor Morton's regrets of missing the opportunity to welcome this regiment as he had welcomed all others. Army business had forced him to leave the city. After a round of cheers, the regiment marched to the Circle, where they remained

---

[58] Gregg, "A Brief Sketch."
[59] McCormick, 52.
[60] The Battle of Buena Vista (Mexican War) occurred February 23, 1847. The Second Indiana infantry regiment was ordered forward and became separated from support. Their colonel ordered them to cease fire and retreat. Once the retreat to Buena Vista began, most of the men refused to come back to the field. This action had disgraced Indiana.
[61] McCormick, 52.

awaiting orders about their encampment. "The band, while they were in the Circle, played several patriotic airs very finely, better, we thought, than any band we have heard yet."[62] Since the army would not discharge the regiment or allow men to draw pay until the following week (August 6), the men were free to go home or stay in camp. The Wabash company returned home on July 27 and "were greeted at the depot by hundreds of friends."[63] Thuma returned home to his wife in Ohio. The citizens of Hancock County welcomed their soldiers home on August 5 with "a reception at Pierson's Grove, adjoining Greenfield on the southwest, which was located west of Pennsylvania Street and south of the railroad (Pennsy Trail)."[64] The three-month Eighth Indiana regiment mustered in with 784 men. They lost seven men by death (four killed or mortally wounded and three by disease), fifteen men by desertion, and one man unaccounted.

---

[62] McCormick, 52.
[63] *History of Wabash County, Indiana*, 164.
[64] Baker, 431.

Sergeant Henry Norton (Co. H), Sergeant George W. Harlan (Co. I), and Private William Conde (Co. K) lie buried in this trench grave at Salisbury National Cemetery. Photo from Thompson Family Album

Governor Morton played a key role in recruiting troops and did all he could to support them, even appealing to the women of the state to make and send woolen shirts and drawers, gloves or mittens, and several pairs of socks for soldiers to the Quartermaster with a card listing the donor's name and residence and specific soldier, if desired. With the war continuing, he proclaimed:

> There is no curse like that of a lingering war. If, with the immense superiority in wealth, population and resources of the loyal States, their power was promptly exerted in anything like an equal ratio with the efforts made in the seceding States, this rebellion would be speedily extinguished. Let Indiana set the glorious example of doing her whole duty, and show to the world how much can be accomplished by the brave and loyal people of a single State. To this we are prompted by every consideration of hope, interest, and affection. All that we are, all that we hope to be, is in issue. Our cause is the holiest for which arms were ever taken, involving, as it does, the existence of our government, and all that is valuable and dear to a free people.[65]

[65] Quoted in Melissa Rose, "Indiana and the Civil War," *Indiana and the Civil War* (Mooresville: Mooresville Parks & Recreation District, 1994), 1.

The regiment re-organized August 20. Wabash County provided two companies (F and I). Hancock County said good-bye to their soldiers.

> On Monday last Captain Walls left for Indianapolis with a company of Hancock County boys to enter the service of the United States for a term of three years or during the war. It will be part of the Eighth Regiment as reorganized, and will retain its former position in the regiment. The scene at the depot as the boys passed through, the large number of men, women and children who gathered in from all points of the county to witness the departure, was sad and sorrowful in the extreme. God bless the noble-hearted boys, and preserve and protect them in the patriotic hazardous duties they have voluntarily taken upon themselves! May they all safely return at the expiration of a term of service to receive the warm embrace of mothers, fathers, sisters, brothers and kind friends left behind.[66]

They mustered in September 5, 1861 with Col. William P. Benton in command.

> Retaining the same regimental organization entire, and, with few exceptions, the same company officers, its ranks were completely filled in the brief period of about thirty-three days, and much sooner than any of the six three-months' regiments, excepting the Eleventh....without sending out recruiting officers...or the aid of outside influences....It was significant that the regiment retained so large a number of those who were in its ranks in the three-months' service.[67]

James W. Alexander, a carpenter and distant relative of the author, enlisted in this regiment in Company E. On September 2, the regiment received coats, pants, caps, guns, and accouterments (equipment other than clothing and weapons). They received their shirts, socks and shoes on September 3: "Clothing wool and very Coarse[.] Shoes heavy[.] Sewed not nice."[68] John R. Summers became the regiment sutler that same day. A group of soldiers destroyed items in a home the night of September 9, 1861 and the husband, Hezekiah Bates, filed a list of the damaged item with Madison County Justice of the Peace Abraham B. Canoll on October 3.[69] The regiment marched from Indianapolis September 10, wearing "the new pale blue uniform."[70]

They traveled by railroad to St. Louis, Missouri to join Fremont's army, arriving on September 11. Those in St. Louis expected the Indiana troops to be unruly in the camps and in the city. The *St. Louis Democrat* reported:

---

[66] Baker, 2.
[67] Rev. A. W. Sanford, quoted in *The Soldier of Indiana in the War for the Union*, Vol. I (Indianapolis, Merrill and Company, 1866), 162.
[68] McCormick, 53.
[69] See correspondence located on pages 126-128 of this volume for the list.
[70] *The Soldier of Indiana in the War for the Union*, Vol. I (Indianapolis:, Merrill and Company, 1866), 162.

> The excellent order which has prevailed among the Ohio and Indiana troops since their encampment, both at the fair grounds and at Lafayette Park, is well worthy of mention. In all the regiments we have not heard of a single case of disturbance or disorderly conduct among the soldiers, or improper action towards civilians. This is owing both the general manly disposition of the men, and to strict military discipline.[71]

Samuel Dunbar explained how Illinois and St. Louis received them:

> Our passage thru' Illinois, and our march through St. Louis were marked by demonstrations of congratulation and welcome. In the city, the children, the ladies, and the men, from housetops, windows, and sidewalks, were waving flags, little flags, big ones, fine and coarse ones, and the cry was "Hurrah for the bloody Eighth!" Everybody seemed to have heard about Col. Benton and his "bloody Eighth."[72]

After a few days march, the regiment reached Jefferson City on September 14, where they camped for a week. "Rain fell daily in torrents. The grass was beaten down, and the melancholy, boundless prairie was a sea of black mud."[73] Even though they were wet, tired, and hungry, "nobody grumbles, nobody tho't it a bad time....good cheer continued to reign."[74]

Sickness affected the regiment greatly in Missouri. Several were in the hospital at Jefferson City. The leading killer diseases for Union troops were chronic diarrhea and typhoid fever. Other major diseases were acute diarrhea, chronic dysentery, and acute dysentery. All these diseases were due to contaminated food and water. Some speculated that someone had poisoned the drinking water with bi-chloride of mercury or arsenic, but the town used the same water and they were not ill.[75] "The health of our Regiment is improving although there are quite a number sick yet I do not wonder at either for the water we use is not fit for boys to drink but we cannot do any better now."[76] Dr. Ford tested the water and found no trace of arsenic. He felt the typhoid fever originated from their first camp in Indianapolis on the East bank of the White River near Washington Street where "Southwest winds carried the foul exhalations from decaying animal and

---

[71] *Soldier of Indiana*, Vol. I, 162-163.
[72] Baker, 432.
[73] *Soldier of Indiana*, Vol. I, 176.
[74] Baker, 432.
[75] Bigelow, 31-32.
[76] David S. Scott, Camp Wickline, Kentucky, to his sister Adaline, February 12, 1862, Special Collections, William Henry Smith Memorial Library, Indiana Historical Society, Indianapolis.

vegetable matter in the bed of the stream, the fog and malaria, moved into our camp."[77] Soldiers also suffered from measles, smallpox, erysipelas (an infectious skin disease caused by streptococcus), consumption (tuberculosis), malaria, pneumonia, rheumatism, V.D., and combat fatigue. "The Eighth regiment alone hauled in its rear one hundred and forty who were afflicted with measles."[78] Corporal James A. Brown, of Company E spent time in the hospital with measles; he did recover. The regiment lost over eighty men to disease in Missouri and Iowa. One of the soldiers in the Eighteenth Indiana accidentally shot and killed George Carney when he took the loaded pistol from Henry Griffy's pocket.[79] The regiment also faced problems with guerrillas, who hunted Union men "like wild beasts."[80]

September 22, they marched to Springfield in fourteen days and returned to Otterville in seven days. The army relieved Fremont of command in early November. His successor, Major General Hunter, abandoned gained ground and dispersed the troops. Swain Marshall expressed the Eighth Indiana regiment's feelings about this event:

> Thee wanted to know the feeling of the soldiers in regard to the removal of Fremont; every one without exception that I ever heard say any thing about it, were awful mad about it; and I hear some one say nearly every day that if he had stayed in command that we would not have had this last trip to Springfield; he was superseded when we were at Springfield before and we were ordered to Otterville; instead of following Price up & running him out of Mo. as we would have done.[81]

The regiment faced problems of not receiving all of their supplies. On September 28, Colonel Benton wrote to Governor Morton to request their missing overcoats. He related that General Davis had arrested him for taking 8,000 more cartridges than allowed. He explained that with that 8,000, they only received 26,000 cartridges, instead of the 40,000 they should have received. This arrest "came very near resulting in an open mutiny; the men stacked their arms and refused to march unless I would lead them." He was able to restore order and felt that if the regiment had to retreat because of the lack of cartridges, he would remember "my present imprisonment as the proudest circumstance

[77] Ford, Civil War Correspondence, 10, 16.
[78] *The Soldier of Indiana*, Vol. I, 191.
[79] McSpadden, 163.
[80] McSpadden, 163.
[81] Swain Marshall, January 1862, Special Collections, William Smith Memorial Library, Indiana Historical Society, Indianapolis.

of my life."[82] The regiment lost William Baker on October 20, 1861, when he committed suicide in Syracuse, Missouri. While on the march to Pilot Knob, three men left the ranks and stole a coat, several pictures, and an army discharge from a nearby home. The owner followed them and reported them to Colonel Benton, who courtmartialed them that night. Before the regiment continued the march the next day, the regiments watched the men being drummed out of the service with a warning that others who steal would face the same consequence.[83]

After the resignation and death of Dr. George Edgerly, Dr. James Beck and the people of Henry County started writing letters requesting his appointment as assistant surgeon. The officers unanimously recommended the appointment of Dr. James K. Bigelow because,

> At the hospital on Rich Mountain battle ground no one was so kind and attentive to our wounded men as Bigelow....He is always kind and always willing, the result is we all love him as a brother, and the whole regiment feels that he has fairly earned the vacant place.[84]

Beck became quartermaster general, and Bigelow became assistant surgeon.

In November, two men entered the camp at Georgetown seeking a runaway slave. Colonel Parrish realized they were describing Captain Kenney's contraband cook. He went to Kenney's tent and told the runaway slave to lie down while he covered him with a buffalo robe. By the time the owner came to search the tent, Parrish and Kenney were playing euchre on the buffalo robe table and arguing over a point. He never searched under the card table, so the cook was safe from being returned to his master.[85]

December 17, the regiment marched to Warrensburg and assisted in the capture of 1300 Rebels:

> we have had another long and werisome march since I got a letter from you...we brought about thirteen or fourteen hundred secesh with us. We sent them to st. louis for safe keeping, if they are all as easy taken as these was we will not have any trouble in cleaning Missouri out.[86]

---

[82]Colonel Benton to Governor Morton, September 28, 1861, "Eighth Indiana Correspondence."
[83] William C. Scott to his mother, November 10, 1862, http://bjsgenealogy.com/Scott/WCScottJrCivilWar.htm.
[84] Colonel Benton to Governor Morton, November 21, 1861, "Eighth Indiana Correspondence."
[85] "A Living Card Table," *Burlington Republican*, August 20, 1895, 8, https://www.newspapers.com.
[86] Thomas Melick, camp near Otterville, to uncle (Robert Watson), December 29, 1861, Jacob W. Bartmess Collection, Special Collections, William Smith Memorial Library, Indiana Historical Society, Indianapolis.

The regiment also confiscated slaves in Jefferson City. Against her will, Colonel Benton took Cathy Williams to be a cook for the officers; however, "I had always been a house girl and did not know how to cook."[87] They made her their laundress instead. "For her labor, she probably received a small allowance for necessities…to purchase her own clothes and extra food….received the same monotonous and bland rations…usually slept on the ground" and "would have to endure the same discomforts and deprivations as the 8th Indiana's soldiers."[88]

On December 19, William Taylor Stott, Eighteenth Indiana, found his old friend from Franklin College, Captain Hiram T. Vandevender.[89] The regiment learned the difficulties of a soldier's life during this winter:

> Soldiering is a very nice thing to talk about and is nice in the summer season with pleasant weather and nothing to do, but when it comes to a winter campaign, with forced marches, rain and snow, hail, etc., sleeping part of the time with tents and part of the times without them then you come to the sad reality of a soldiers life in full.[90]

The soldiers did not feel forgotten by Governor Morton or their families at home, nor were they idle during this time. They received boxes of warm clothing and studied math, geology, and French during the winter months.[91] They returned to Otterville on December 22 in the extreme cold. "It being the custom of the soldiers at night to place in their tents their camp kettles filled with live coals to keep them from freezing, a private of Co. A, was poisoned to death, and several others serverally [sic] injured by the generation of carbonic acid gas from the coals, in new, close tents."[92] That soldier's name was Allen Stultz.

The men were not happy with their winter-quarters and being on guard duty instead of out fighting. Samuel Dunbar explained:

---

[87] Phillip Thomas Tucker, *Cathy Williams: From Slave to Buffalo Soldier* (Mechanicsburg, PA: Stackpole Books, 2009), 37.
[88] Tucker, 40.
[89] Lloyd A. Hunter, *For Duty and Destiny: The Life and Civil War Diary of Hoosier Soldier and Educator William Taylor Stott* (Indianapolis: Indiana Historical Society Press, 2010), 86.
[90] William A. Buskirk, on the north side of Osage River, opposite the town of Linn Creek, to his wife Emma, February 1-2, 1862, Special Collections, William Smith Memorial Library, Indiana Historical Society, Indianapolis.
[91] *The Soldier of Indiana*, Vol. I, 195-196.
[92] Bigelow, 11.

> Our log huts, which were to be our shelter, and in which we had indulged dreams of enjoying so much comfort, safe from the storm and raging tempest without, have not been built. Sibley tents, furnished with stove and pipe, which were promised us, instead of the huts, have not come, and we have about concluded to let them go the way of the houses. We still possess our old tents, which serve us as well as possible, *but we are expecting they will be taken from us and given to the Missouri Home Guards*.
> Indiana troops are composed of such metal as makes them terribly opposed to being used as guards for bridges, railroads, and other property of cowardly Missourian. Our Commander probably knew this aversion of the Hoosiers, therefore he said that Otterville was a convenient place for a camp, and that we should build and live in comfortable winter-quarters, that we should rest from the fearful fatigue and hardships that we have, during the last four months, undergone, and that here we should "sweetly live." It is not surprising that the fact that we were guarding the Lamine bridge and railroad, was to us unrevealed. Indianians are hard to kill, I know, and harder to scare, but they know when they are used right.[93]

During this Missouri campaign, seven men of the Eighth Indiana fell wounded. Because the company only had one wagon to haul the sick and supplies, those who were sick or wounded had to try to keep up with the regiment during a march. "Some drop behind, running the risk of being captured, as six of our boys were on our last march, who have not yet been heard from."[94] They became prisoners of war: Recruit Richard Haipsler of Company A; Private Elijah H. Tyner of Company B; Sergeant Henry Norton of Company H; Sergeant George W. Harlan of Company I; and Privates William Conde and John Lyons of Company K. Norton, Harlan, and Conde died as prisoners in Salisbury, North Carolina.

Salisbury was located close to the railroad. The Confederacy purchased Maxwell Chambers Factory in November 1861 and quickly made repairs to house prisoners in the four-story building. They also built a high wall around the prison with a trench just inside the wall for the deadline. Prisoners who died before the fall of 1864 lie in separate graves. Norton, Harlan, and Conde lie buried in one of the trenches, "four feet deep, about six feet wide, and extending about sixty yards. Naked bodies of the dead were placed side by

---

93 *The Hancock Democrat*, January 15, 1862,1, https://www.newspapers.com.
94 Ibid.

side until the space was filled up, and another row began with one body placed on top between every two."[95]

In December 1861, the Army of the Southwest formed under the command of Brigadier General Samuel R. Curtis. On December 28, Colonel Benton requested and received a leave of absence to attend to his large law practice back in Richmond to "secure a considerable amount of money which would otherwise be lost."[96] Doctor Ford reported the regiment was "about the happiest set of fellows you ever saw."[97] Chaplain Arthur Sanford remarked that the regiment's moral status was "improving. Profanity is either decreasing or is practiced at a greater distance from my presence. Gambling…is prohibited by regimental order, rigidly enforced by the company officers, and the men seem resigned to, if not pleased with, the prohibition."[98]

The Eighth Indiana regiment, as part of the Third Division, joined Curtis on his advance to Springfield January 25, 1862 and pursued Price to Cassville, Arkansas. "In one of these running fights Sergeant John A. Edwards, of the Eighth, was shot through the arm, the bone of which was broken; he had two horses shot under him, mounted a third, and was shot through the thigh, before he left the field."[99] Pay Agents followed regiments to collect and send money from the soldiers to their families. Soldiers gave their money to the agents and wrote the amount they wanted to send home on blank drafts, which the agents sent to the family members. The agents took the money to the bank at home, and family members took the drafts to the bank to collect the money. "It took several months to introduce the new system; the soldiers did not understand it, and the Paymasters, upon whom it imposed new duties, were for a time specially averse to it."[100] On January 26, General Stone "collected $7,000 of the Eighth Regiment at Otterville, Missouri and brought it with him."[101]

---

[95] Louis A. Brown, *The Salisbury Prison: A Case Study of Confederate Military Prisons 1861-1865* (Wilmington: Broadfoot Publishing Company, 1992), 141.
[96] Tucker, 42.
[97] McSpadden, 172.
[98] Chaplain Arthur Sanford, January 8, 1862, Transcribed letter published January 14, 1862 in the *Indianapolis Daily Journal*.
[99] *The Soldier of Indiana*, Vol. I, 198.
[100] Stevenson, Vol. I, 29.
[101] Terrill, Vol. 1, 435.

On January 27, it stormed and poured rain all night. "Many of the tents had been pitched in little hallows which soon filled, and many a poor fellow had to make his bed on rails, logs and coarse brush, or lie half submerged in water."[102] The next day, the rain continued off and on causing "mud nearly deep enough to mire an ox" and made it difficult for soldiers to light cook fires with "the continent of mud and water around them."[103] On February 13, the regiment continued the march to Springfield, expecting soon to meet the enemy. "There were no faces bleaching with fear—no muscle quivering, save with eager anxiety for the fray."[104] That night the regiment suffered through a fierce winter storm. The next day, they found Springfield abandoned and reached Wilson's Creek, the scene of a battle six months earlier. Animals and floods had exposed the skeletal remains of the men buried there. The army marched so quickly that they outpaced their supply wagons, and many went to bed hungry. On February 17, the Army of the Southwest crossed the state line into Arkansas as their bands played patriotic tunes. Rather than risk losing his army to battle or starvation or allowing Price to return to Missouri, Curtis chose to keep the enemy at bay in northwest Arkansas. He requested reinforcements, but only received 10,000 pairs of pants, no men, or horses.

---

[102] Sanford, February 27, 1862, Transcribed letter published March 11, 1862 in the *Indianapolis Daily Journal*.

[103] Sanford, February 27, 1862, Transcribed letter published March 11, 1862 in the *Indianapolis Daily Journal*.

[104] Sanford, February 27, 1862, Transcribed letter published March 11, 1862 in the *Indianapolis Daily Journal*.

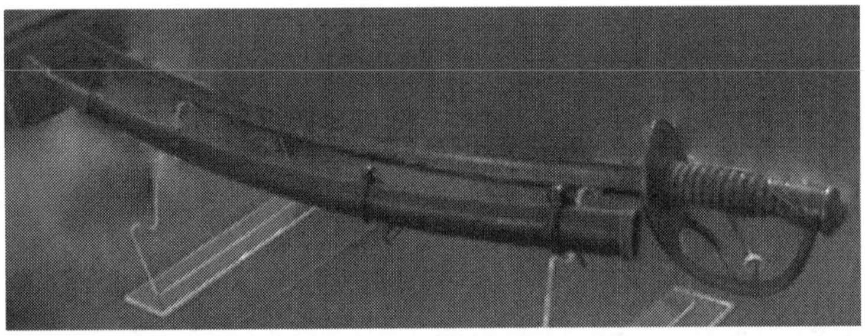

Colonel Benton received at least two engraved swords during his Civil War service. The top sword is in the hands of a private collector. He received this sword while in Richmond in 1861. James M. Starr presented this sword to Benton with a sash. The sword handle is engraved "Presented to Col. Wm. P. Benton by the citizens of Richmond." The bottom sword was on display at the Indiana State Museum in 2015. He received the second sword in 1862. The sword and scabbard are engraved "Genl. W. P. Benton, from Eighth Ind. Vols." Both photos from Thompson Family Album

The Third Division spent the beginning of March preparing defensive works in Little Sugar Creek Valley. Residents called the land, between Little Sugar Creek Valley and Cross Timber Hollow, Pea Ridge. Elkhorn Tavern was at the head of Cross Timber Hollow. On March 6, Curtis ordered the Third Division to the top of steep bluffs on the north side of the creek, where they constructed two redoubts (breastworks) for artillery on either side of Telegraph Road. Corporal Samuel Herrington of Company D described his trench sixty feet above the valley floor: "We had a fine place, the best Position any wheres along the road."[105] The army cut down hundreds of trees along the face of the bluff and in the valley, and burned Enoch Trott's store, so the Rebels could not use trees or the store for cover.

On March 7, Curtis ordered Benton to send half of the Eighth Indiana to Elkhorn Tavern. Lt. Col. Shunk and five companies of the regiment followed Captain Klauss and the First Indiana Battery (with three six-pounder rifled guns) to Elkhorn Tavern. Lieutenant James R. Smith fell wounded in the leg during the march and urged his comrades to leave him,

> which they reluctantly did. The Regiment had no sooner passed on, than the rebels occupied the ground on which the Lieutenant fell, and upon coming up to him they brutally pierced his neck with a bayonet, and stripped him of his boots, and of whatever else he had that was of any value to them.[106]

Benton and the rest of his regiment stayed to guard Telegraph Road in case of an attack from the south. The fiercest fighting of Pea Ridge occurred at Elkhorn Tavern. Carr sent Shunk's battalion to support Dodge at Clemon's Farm. The men marched at double-quick and found themselves exposed to enemy fire until they reached the woods, where they joined the Third Illinois Cavalry. Sigel noted the withdrawal of one of the heavily engaged batteries exposed the infantry on the right.

> One of the regiments—I think it was the 22d or the 8th Indiana—was thrown into momentary disorder by this surprise, and the men fell back toward an eminence on the right of the road on which I was halting. I assisted their brave commander to rally them, which did not take long, and spoke a few words to them, saying that if the right could hold out for half an hour, assistance would come, and all would be well.[107]

The two groups fought against twice as many Confederates, who forced them back toward Vandever's line. The battle ended in a draw. During the night, hundreds of soldiers wandered the battlefield helping the wounded and stealing from the dead. Choctaw, Cherokee, and Chickasaw Indians had fought with the Confederates. General Curtis complained "the Indians had violated the usages of war by 'tomahawking, scalping and otherwise mangling the bodies of the dead and wounded, many Federal dead thus

---

[105] Quoted in William L. Shea and Earl J. Hess, *Pea Ridge: Civil War Campaign in the West* (Chapel Hill: The University of North Carolina Press, 1992), 68.
[106] Bigelow, 13.
[107] Franz Sigel, "The Pea Ridge Campaign," *Battles and Leaders of the Civil War: Grant-Lee Edition*, Vol. I, Part I (New York: Century Co., 1884-1887. Reprint, National Historical Society, 2005), 328.

shamefully treated having been found on the field.'"[108] The Third Division secured the Leetown battlefield and retrieved the wounded. Curtis ordered the Third Division to reinforce the Second and Fourth Divisions on Telegraph Road. They marched so quickly that few men were able to get their overcoats and blankets. They suffered greatly from the cold, but they were able to have food and water that night.

The next morning, the Third Division formed a shallow V on Telegraph Road; the Eighth Indiana was on the east side crouched behind piles of fence rails, which proved to be unsafe shelter. The men were moved back to a second line of fences at the edges of Cox's and Ruddick's fields. Curtis ordered them back to their original positions. All four divisions formed a line from Cox's field to woods southwest of Ruddick's field. The entire Army of the Southwest advanced shortly after 10 a.m. "For what may have been the only time in the Civil War, an entire army was visible in line of battle from flank to flank."[109] Brig. Gen. Sigel, who previously had been a problem for Curtis, ordered the First and Second Divisions forward and blasted the Rebels on the west side of Telegraph Road with case shot and canister. The Third Division assaulted the Rebels on the east side of the road. Herrington described this attack:

> On the right into line double quick. Lord but how we made things hum. Forward quick time guide right. Marched in on an open space. Halt make ready take aim fire. After first shot load at will....Our guns a booming. The battery howling. Wounded groaning. Some excited, I might say all. But we was going forward.[110]

When the Third Division advanced into the woods, they met Rebel fire, but the Rebels soon retreated. The Third Division reached Huntsville Road on the east side of Clemon's field and waited there for orders. Curtis rode up Telegraph Road shouting victory, causing the troops to rejoice. During the afternoon, the Third and Fourth Divisions secured the battlefield, gathered wounded and collected prisoners. "Both during and after

[108] "Civil War Fifty Years Ago Today," *The Indianapolis Star*, March 8, 1912, 6, https://www.newspapers.com.
[109] William L. Shea and Earl J. Hess, 239.
[110] Quoted in William L. Shea and Earl J. Hess, 247.

the battle, Cathy Williams might well have helped to attend to some of the wounded soldiers of the 8th Indiana."[111]

March 9, officers assigned details to bury the dead. Herrington described this task:

> Our men are burying the dead as fast as they can today posibly do it. Just dig a hole and throw them in and cover them up. Always wrap their blankets around them. It looks horrid but they dont know any thing about it poor fellows.[112]

The Eighth Indiana lost five men on March 7: Privates John Coburn, Henry Hardbarger and John Stiles of Company F, and First Sergeant James R. Smith and Private Samuel Harter of Company H. Twenty-six men fell wounded. Four of these men died from their wounds: Corporal Thomas C. Webb and Privates James Malcolm and William Salisbury of Company G and Private William A. Garrison of Company I. Colonel Benton praised the regiment in his official report.

> I cannot close this report without honorable mention of the promptitude and fidelity with which each member of the regiment executed every order given. Officers and men, comprehending the magnitude of the task to be accomplished, all were eager to bear their part. And when the order came for a part of the regiment, the question was not which part would have to go, but which be compelled to remain—a question which was decided by lot.[113]

Franz Sigel summarized the importance of the Battle of Pea Ridge.

> It was not a "great" battle, like that of Gettysburg or Chattanooga; it was not of such preponderating national importance; it did not "break the backbone of the Rebellion," but it virtually cleared the South-west of the enemy, gave peace to the people of Missouri, at least for the next two years, and made it possible for our veterans to reinforce the armies under Buell, Rosecrans, Grant, and Sherman.[114]

Five of the men, William Morgan, Elijah Tyner, William Branson, William Short, and Samuel Dunbar, caught smallpox on March 25.

> We were moved to a lonely house on a lonely road in a lonely little hollow shut in by two immense hills. This place we agreed to name and forever remember as

---

[111] Tucker, 46.
[112] Shea and Hess, 272.
[113] Sanford, March 9, 1862, Transcribed letter published March 19, 1862 in the *Indianapolis Daily Journal*.
[114] Quoted in Michael A. Hughes, "A Forgotten Battle in a Region Ignore…Pea Ridge, or Elkhorn Tavern Arkansas – March 7-8, 1862: The Campaign, the Battle, and the Men Who Fought for the Fate of Missouri," *Blue & Gray Magazine* 5, no. 3 (January 1988), 32.

> "Small-pox Hollow." There the regiment's medical aid left us to live or die, as fortune and the smallpox should decree. Here we remained suffering all the pain, horror and loathsomeness of the disease until the 23d of April.[115]

George Dixon and Charles Dippery volunteered to care for the sick men. Every five days, one of them would ride a horse they named "Hollow" to Cassville to get provisions. A neighboring widow lady from Indiana provided milk, butter, and other delicacies until Rebels drove her from her home. The Rebels avoided the sick house because of the smallpox, but the men decided to move to Cassville to finish recovering from the disease. Morgan had a mild case of smallpox and was the first one to return to the regiment. Tyner and Branson returned on May 15. Dixon caught the varioloid (a mild case of smallpox) and Dippery caught it April 15. They all returned to the regiment in late May.

The regiment spent the next month in camp at Cross Timbers. On April 3, Benton, Shunk, and Parrish assembled in a little log hut as part of the officer detail for a court-martial of General Sheridan, who Curtis charged with disobedience of orders, "on account of delays in moving his supply train, which delays the General thought were unnecessary and in violation of orders."[116] Before Sheridan appeared, nearby firing ended the proceedings and they quickly transformed the log hut into a barricade. Judge-Advocate C. H. Frederick sent all the paperwork to St. Louis and Sheridan soon received a transfer to another command. On April 14, George Harland and Erastus Burgett visited the Fourth Iowa Infantry looking for someone who could repair their watches. A man repaired Harland's watch and charged him a dollar, but he lacked the watch hands needed to repair Burgett's watch.[117] On April 20, Stott again visited Vandevender; "the special object was to get supper, and I got it. We talked of the old College times. He was surprised that I came into the service as a private."[118] They moved to Forsynthe, Missouri. At the camp on Fox Creek, Doctor Ford reported, "Our men are very ragged, barefooted, and dirty; yet the poor fellows are cheerful, and crack jokes about their nude condition....our digestion is good and sharp."[119] The army began discharging sick men

---

[115] *The Hancock Democrat*, June 18, 1862, 2, https://www.newspapers.com.
[116] "Gen. Sheridan," *Chicago Daily Tribune*, December 23, 1881, 5, https://www.newspapers.com.
[117] Erastus G. Burgett, April 14, 1862, "Diaries, 1862," SC 2701, Manuscript Collection, William Smith Memorial Library, Indiana Historical Society, Indianapolis.
[118] Quoted in Hunter, 163.
[119] McSpadden, 176.

who are off duty for two months, sending wounded men home as soon as possible, and listing those who leave the company for six days as deserters. "The sick man could be of no use in or out of the army; in short, the latter are a class of men in whom no confidence can be reposed, and should at once be officially decapitated."[120] The men received a large wagon train of supplies including new pants, which made them much happier. The regiment crossed country to Batesville, Arkansas, and halted at Sulphur Rock for about two months.

Colonel Benton received a commission as brigadier general on May 13 and sent recommendations to Governor Morton. "The old 8th, the 'Bloody, Old 8th, as the boys call her have ever been faithful to me. I shall always remain true to her best interests."[121] The regiment felt happy with his promotion.

> The General bears his "blushing honors" very gracefully, is always accessible to everybody, ever ready to make every effort for the comfort of his men; and, should opportunity offer, will most assuredly justify the confidence of the Government evidenced by his commission, by his disposition and bearing on the field of battle.[122]

James W. Alexander received a promotion to corporal May 15, 1862.

In June, the Eighth Indiana received another regiment flag. James Brown described this event:

> the Ladies of Terrehaute have presented the 8th Reg with a beautiful silk Banner with Rich Mountain inscribed on one Corner and Pea Ridge on the other. also the 8th has presented Gen Benton with a sword which cost nearly two hundred dollars. Gen Benton and Col Shunk are two [of] the best men that walks on top of ground. at least I think so any how.[123]

The officers of the Eighth, Eighteenth, and Twenty-second Indiana regiments had collected money to purchase the sword. Chaplain Sanford purchased it while on sick leave in Indiana. By the time he returned, the Twenty-second Indiana had transferred to another division, so the "Old Eighth" presented it to Benton. "The regiment being formed on its 'parade,' was marched to the General's headquarters, and properly disposed, when Col. Shunk, who prefers a hard fight to a long speech, presented the sword, with a few

---

[120] McSpadden, 176.
[121] Brig. Gen. Benton to Governor Morton, May 13, 1862, "Eighth Indiana Correspondence."
[122] Sanford, June 9, 1862, Transcribed letter published June 27, 1862 in the *Indianapolis Daily Journal*.
[123] Erich L. Ewald, "War at the Crossroads," *Indiana Magazine of History* 92, no. 4 (December 1996): 353.

plain direct, and well timed remarks, worth of the man, and befitting the occasion."[124] Benton promised to keep the sword for life, "and dying, bequeath it to his son, never to be drawn but in defense of his country's honor—never sheathed while a foreign or domestic foe, in arms threatened her existence or integrity."[125] The Eighth Indiana had now proven themselves worthy in two battles.

[124] Sanford, June 16, 1862, Transcribed letter published June 27, 1862 in the *Indianapolis Daily Journal*.
[125] Sanford, June 16, 1862, Transcribed letter published June 27, 1862 in the *Indianapolis Daily Journal*.

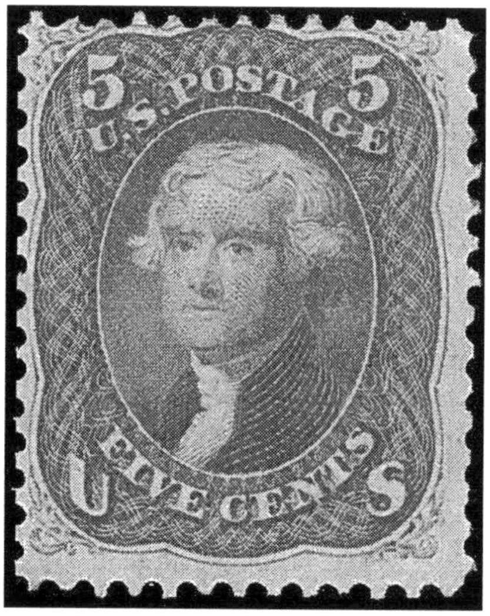

Thomas Jefferson, 1861 stamp. QuickiWiki.

During the summer of 1862, Indiana constructed a "Soldiers' Home and Rest," near White River north of the Terre Haute Railroad, to provide a place of rest for returning soldiers. The building had sleeping quarters, a dining hall, and a kitchen. This building proved too small, so in the fall, they added a separate dining hall, able to seat one thousand soldiers. The Sanitary Commission and citizens provided needed expenses, food, books, writing material, and "the Postmaster of Indianapolis, Hon. A.H. CONNER, donated a quantity of postage stamps, not the least important contribution to men far away from home and friends."[126] In 1863, they added a hospital building and the state found and furnished a "Ladies' Home" on South Illinois Street south of the Union Depot, where families could stay safely while visiting their soldiers who were staying in the "Soldiers' Home." In 1864, they built two more sleeping quarter buildings so "the 'Home' could lodge about 1,800 men, and feed 8,000 every day. But even yet, General STONE says, there were occasions when one half the men requiring accommodations could not have them."[127]

Curtis moved his supply base to Helena, Arkansas. "While on this march, the command suffered so severely for want of provisions—the daily ration consisting frequently of four ears of corn and a small allowance of meat per man each day—as to

[126] Terrill, Vol. 1, 456.
[127] *Indiana in the War of the Rebellion: Indiana Historical Collections*, Vol. XLI (Indianapolis: Indiana Historical Bureau, 1960), 456-457.

illy fit them for the duties imposed."[128] Hundreds of former Arkansas slaves started to follow the army "wandering around the camp as thick as blackberries."[129] The army ordered Cathy Williams and other freed slaves to go to Little Rock to learn how to cook. "Then after gaining her culinary skills, she spent some time cooking for the occupation forces in the city, where hundreds of other ex-slaves provided menial service to the Union soldiers."[130] "Helena was not an agreeable post....The Eighth, upon its arrival at Helena was so nearly exhausted with hunger, fatigue, and the excessive heat of the weather, that in a short time nearly half of them were sick and unable to do duty."[131] Nearly all recruits got diseases from the nearby swamps, and over half of them died. The camp tents were twenty feet from the river, and Dr. Ford told General Benton that everyone would be sick with cholera morbus because of the unhealthy location and the nightly fogs from the river. Three days later, Dr. Ford found himself vomiting into the river and Benton called to the other officers, mocking "Dr. Ford demonstrating his *Theory*!" They did not find it funny. A few days later, Benton was vomiting into the river from the same sickness. Ford called for the other officers and told him, "You are demonstrating my *Theory*, General." Benton started to curse him. "The hard tack that had been eaten the day before was on it[s] way to the Mississippi, and blocked the road so the sentence was never finished. The completeness of the demonstration, however, was never called in question again."[132] A few days later, Benton ordered him to find a healthier location for the camp. Ford chose a location one-half mile west, and within two weeks, "the men never were in finer spirits, and in better trim for duty."[133]

On July 4, Laban Garner and a comrade went two miles down the river and requested dinner at the Reiff home. While waiting for its preparation, a rebel, who was hiding nearby and who was involved in the attack on the transports at St. Charles Bluff, came into the home and asked Mrs. Reiff for a gun.

On being told there was none, he came out and seized an axe, which he drew on Garner,

---

[128] *History of Wabash County, Indiana*, 166.
[129] Tucker, 51.
[130] Tucker, 54.
[131] *The Soldier of Indiana in the War for the Union*, Vol. II (Indianapolis: Merrill and Company, 1869), 251.
[132] Ford, Civil War Correspondence, 53-54.
[133] Ford, Civil War Correspondence, 57.

> demanding his surrender, and calling on Reiff to secure his comrade. Reiff declined. Garner seized the axe with one hand and Bland's throat with the other, and his comrade having wrenched the axe from Bland, Garner pitched into him and beat him so nearly dead with his fist, that when he released him he staggered to the river bank and tumbled in and drowned.[134]

On that same day, companies A and B and a cavalry battalion, searching for Rebels, found their abandoned camp and a concealed military wagon train. They took "equipage and provisions" from the camp and "good things fixed up by special friends for palates of the traitors" on the five wagons.[135] At three o'clock that afternoon, the band from the Eighteenth Indiana Infantry called the troops together to celebrate the day. Reverend Sanford opened in prayer. General Benton presented an "excellent speech. His voice was drowned several times by the deafining cheers which rang from the merry group of soldiers." General Hovey and Colonels Bussy and Washburn also spoke. After they finished, "we all give three long loud cheers for Union & three for each speaker. I have been to several Fourth of July celebrations but I never enjoyed myself as well before."[136]

On July 7, the Confederates fought back at Hill's Plantation. The Eighth Indiana regiment, as part of Gen. Benton's force, received orders to that area to protect Colonel Hovey's flank. "Gen. BENTON pursued the fleeing foe five or six miles toward Des Arc, killing several and taking prisoners. All along the route he found the houses filled with dead and wounded. Curbstones were wet with blood, and in one case even the water of the well was crimsoned with gore."[137] By sunset, they completely routed the enemy. None of the Eighth regiment was lost in this conflict. Chaplain Sanford praised Colonel Benton for his willingness to take himself and his regiment into action. "Still, with all his impetuous daring, I know of no other commander who takes more pains, or displays more coolness in arranging everything for the safety and comfort of his men, in the battlefield, on march and in camp."[138] Dr. Ford complained that too many soldiers and officers were going home "without furloughs or leaves of absence, that the regiment is almost in a state of anarchy." The men received their pay and could now buy new clothing. "They are

---

[134] Sanford, July 5, 1862, Transcribed letter published July 21, 1862 in the *Indianapolis Daily Journal*.
[135] Baker, 434-435.
[136] Burgett, July 4, 1862.
[137] "Operations in the Southwest," *The New York Times*, August 4, 1862, 3, https://www.newspapers.com.
[138] Sanford, July 14, 1862, Transcribed letter published July 21, 1862 in the *Indianapolis Daily Journal*.

better dressed now than they ever were."[139] On July 31, the Eighth and the Forty-seventh Indiana found themselves in the same camp. "They met like a band of brothers…Their faces looked familiar, and make us feel like being at home, to see them all at once."[140] Ford complained that homesickness and leaving without orders continued to be a major problem. "Indeed insubordination never manifested itself to such an extent in the 8th Regiment before us as at this time."[141] On August 13, the regiment presented a sword to Colonel Shunk.[142]

Another skirmish occurred at Austin, Missouri on August 24; Private Jacob Powell of Company E lost his life there. The murder of John W. McCarthey occurred on September 16 when "a private of Co. C, named Samuel Edwards, brutally shot a private of Co. K."[143] A group of soldiers went foraging without permission on September 27.[144] October 6, the Eighth Indiana regiment traveled by steamer to Sulphur Hill near St. Louis, then marched to Ironton October 11. They marched and countermarched throughout southeast Missouri until the following March. James W. Alexander received promotion to sergeant October 20, 1862. Colonel Shunk supervised prisoners building a bridge at Black River. "The work was tedious, but was enlivened by the constant presence of Shunk, who could make a joke and tell a story."[145]

Dr. Burke, the acting Medical Director at the St. Louis General Hospital pushed to have Dr. Bigelow mustered out of service in November "for bringing a lot of sick men of the 1st Brigade from Sulphur Springs to St. Louis," but he "was acting under orders of General Wm. P. Benton in the matter."[146] The army mustered him out of service and forced him to forfeit four months pay.

The regiment camped on Black River in Wayne County, Missouri until ten days of rain caused the river to rise quickly on December 15. E. G. Burgess (Erastus G. Burget) described this event:

---

139 Ford, Civil War Correspondence, July 28, 1862 letter to wife, 58.
140 McSpadden, 246.
141 Ford, Civil War Correspondence, August 10, 1862 letter to wife, 61.
142 Hunter, 181.
143 Bigelow, 15.
144 These men are not identified, but the Adjutant General's Report lists Alonzo Taylor, Henry Kirsman, James H. Reister, and Jacob Sheets as deserting that day.
145 *The Soldier of Indiana*, Vol. II, 254.
146 Colonel Shunk to Colonel Lazarus Noble, November 7, 1862, "Eighth Indiana Correspondence."

> After going to bed we all slept sound until two in the morning, when we were roused by the alarm that the river was rising, and would soon sweep us away if we did not get out of there. I was so sleepy that I did not care much, but I got up and stuck my head out of the tent. Sure enough [t]he water was within a few feet of us on every side. We had to wade knee-deep to get out with our things. Ugh! But the water was cold! In a few minutes the water was all over the spot where we had lain wrapt in sleep, not dreaming of danger. About daylight the water commenced falling, and it wasn't long till the river was inside its banks again. Colonel Shunk hunted out another camp, and we…were soon fixed as comfortable as ever.[147]

Chaplain Skinner felt, "It was amusing to hear the wit and fun perpetrated by the boys amid this scene of darkness and confusion….'all ready, cast off now,'…'what are you fishing for?'…'you must be thirsty, take a drink.'"[148] After moving the camp to dry ground, several of the officers, including General Benton, "thought it proper to dampen the internal so became drunk. Capt. Vandervender, who was once an earnest seeker after conversion of his soul, was drinking with the rest."[149] A few days before this, General Benton married a widow Mrs. Pettit while drunk. "He saw her first a month ago….A soldier told me that the General had never gone to see her sober."[150]

On December 7, Major Thomas Brady read a circular from Governor Morton to the soldiers, which "struck a chord in the heart of the volunteers" and aroused their emotions.[151] Guerrillas captured some of their militia on December 9, so "Colonel Shunk mounted a lot of our boys on mules….It was rather a cold-looking sight – the boys all mounted, some with saddles and some without, with the long Minie rifle strapped over their shoulders."[152] Guerrillas attacked the Eighth Indiana's forage train Wednesday, December 24, and captured a lieutenant and several other soldiers. The forage train had another skirmish on Saturday, and a few men fell wounded. January 1863 brought heavy snow and more difficulties with moving the provision train. On Friday, January 13, the regiment camped on a Rebel Lieutenant's farm "and General Benton has given us the

---

[147] Quoted in *The Soldier of Indiana in the War for the Union* (Indianapolis: Merrill and Company, 1869), 256.
[148] McSpadden, 253.
[149] Stott quoted in Hunter, 195.
[150] Stott quoted in Hunter, 196.
[151] Major Thomas Brady to Governor Morton, December 7, 1862. "Eighth Indiana Correspondence."
[152] Eratus Burgett quoted in *The Soldier of Indiana*, Vol. II, 257.

privilege of burning the rails."[153] The next day, they had oak rails to burn, but on January 29: "They won't allow us to burn rails. I suppose they think a Union man lives here."[154] The Union Army was not to molest Union sympathizers. On February 6, 1863, guerrillas killed Private Franklin Williamson of Company K near Rolla, Missouri. Benton, now a brigadier general, tried to get the Eighth Indiana transferred to the eastern army.

---

[153] Quoted in *The Soldier of Indiana in the War for the Union* (Indianapolis: Merrill and Company, 1869), 256.

[154] Quoted in *The Soldier of Indiana in the War for the Union* (Indianapolis: Merrill and Company, 1869), 256.

"Admiral Porter's Fleet Running the Rebel Blockade of the Mississippi at Vicksburg, April 16th 1863." Currier & Ives, New York, 1863. http://www.americancivilwar.com/tcwn/civil_war/Navy_Ships/Union_Blockade_run_Vicksburg.html, accessed 23 May 2015.

Vicksburg was vital to the Union. Lincoln remarked, "See what a lot of land these fellows hold, of which Vicksburg is the key. The war can never be brought to a close until that key is in our pocket."[155] The regiment left West Plains on February 7 and marched for two weeks, heading to Vicksburg. Swain Marshall described that difficult journey:

> Our reg't. had charge of a provision train and as the roads were almost impassible, We had a hard time. The mules were worked down and dying every day. So we had to push the wagons through the mud. We got here night before last, and are going to draw clothing & then start down the river. Col. Shunk said we would stay here four or five days, and he said that any man that would run off now and go home was a coward.[156]

---

[155] Quoted in Terrence J. Winschel, "Unvexing the Father of Waters: The Fall of Vicksburg," *Hallowed Ground* 5, no. 3 (Fall 2004), 21.
[156] Swain Marshall, camp near the Knob, to his parents, February 22, 1863.

On February 21, Colonel Shunk gave a verbal order that "every man was to get drunk. And in quite a measure it was obeyed."[157] When General Benton arrived on March 15, he "ordered a salute of 11 guns in honor of his arrival!"[158] The Eighth Indiana regiment traveled on the steamer *City of Alton* from St. Genevieve to Milliken's Bend. The regiment reorganized at Milliken's Bend, Louisiana and became part of the Thirteenth Army Corps. Benton was now in command of the First Brigade of the Fourteenth Division, and Shunk, now a colonel, was in charge of the Eighth Indiana. The Thirteenth Army Corps "camped all the way down the River to Youngs Point is nearly opposite Vicksburg."[159]

On April 16, seven gunboats (the flagship *Benton*, *Lafayette*, *Louisville*, *Mound City*, *Pittsburg*, *Carondelet*, and *Tuscumbia*) and three army transports (*Forest Queen*, *Silver Wave*, and *Henry Clay* - barricaded with cotton bales) ran the blockade at Vicksburg. The Confederates attacked them when they passed Vicksburg. They hit every vessel, but the transport *Henry Clay* was set afire and sunk. Swain spoke of the boats needing repairs:

> The gun boats that run the blockade are here also the two transports. We came about four miles across a bayou on one of them. It beat all the boat riding that ever I heard of. The most of the way was through the woods. Couldn't go more than two rods without running against a tree but they kept dodging and pulling around until they got through. They are repairing the Lexington and Benton. They were damaged considerable. The Benton was hit six or seven times and the Lexington nine times.[160]

Grant sent the troops to the bank opposite Grand Gulf.

The Eighth Indiana was about two miles from the camp of the Forty-seventh Indiana. On April 17, Captains John Polk and Joseph Thompson and Lieutenant Dick Smith visited their friends in the Forty-seventh Indiana. Stock Campbell reported, "They are looking well and represent the health of their regiment as good."[161] Campbell ate Sunday dinner with Thompson and Lieutenant Bob Torrence and met some of the other officers, including the quartermaster and chaplain. "The 8th Indiana is commanded by

---

[157] Stott, quoted in Hunter, 203.
[158] Stott, quoted in Hunter, 206.
[159] David Scott, Milicans Bend, Louisiana, to his future wife Kate, April 10, 1863.
[160] Swain Marshall, Carthage, Louisiana, to friends at home, April 22, 1863.
[161] McSpadden, 51.

officers, who are not only an honor to the regiment, but also the noble State which they represent."[162] Henry Whipple, Twenty-ninth Wisconsin Infantry, recorded in his diary a frightening event that occurred in camp at Dawson's Plantation, Louisiana, on April 19. "Two men of the 8th Indiana killed by alligators. We saw the alligators, and saw the boys go down, but never saw the bodies again. There was great excitement for a while as we were nearly all of us in the water."[163] Adjutant General reports and other records fail to identify these two men.

Grant planned to have the navy silence the guns at Grand Gulf April 29, to allow troops to cross over by transports and barges and to overtake the city. After four or five hours of fighting, the batteries on the high bluff proved too strong. The men returned to Hard Times and marched to a point on the opposite side of the river three miles below Grand Gulf; "each stout-hearted fellow trudging along under the broiling sun with a cracker box, a hundred pounds in weight, on his shoulders."[164] On this march, a bullet hit one of the men of the Eighth Indiana in front of Captain George Smith, Thirty-third Illinois Infantry:

> I believe one of the 8th Indiana stopped a ball for me. We were just coming up the hill and filing in rear of the 8th who were in line. Just as I got up the hill a man on the left of the 8th exactly in front of me was struck and would have fallen on me had I not stepped aside involuntarily. The ball struck him right in the face and he was so close that the "clinck" made one shiver. I thought he was stone dead but he got up in a few minutes and walked off with the help of his comrade.[165]

Private Henry C. Brandon of Company G fell wounded on this march; he died of his wounds May 5. Grant described his movement of the troops:

> The troops marched across the point of land under the cover of night, unobserved. By the time it was light the enemy saw our whole fleet, iron-clads, gunboats, river steamers and barges, quietly moving down the river three miles below them, black, or rather blue, with National troops.[166]

---

162 McSpadden, 54.
163 Henry P. Whipple, *Henry P. Whipple's The Diary of a Private Soldier* (1906: Wisconsin Historical Society, 2011) accessed May 15, 2014, http://content.wisconsinhistory.org/cdm/ref/collection/quiner/id/24846.
164 *The Soldier of Indiana*, Vol. 2, 298.
165 *Voices of the Civil War: Vicksburg*, ed. Paul Mathless (Alexandria: Time-Life Books, 1997), 41-42.
166 Ulysses S. Grant, *The Civil War Memoirs of Ulysses S. Grant*, ed. Brian M. Thomsen (New York: Tom Doherty Associates, 1992), 159-160.

It took most of the day to move the Thirteenth Corps and one division of the Seventeenth Corps across the river to Bruinsburg, eight miles below Grand Gulf.

The army advanced on Port Gibson at four o'clock. The road to Port Gibson divided and followed two ridges before uniting again just outside of town. The Eighth Indiana marched on the right-hand branch. The left-hand branch suffered some loss and command sent one brigade from the Eighth Indiana to support that division. The morning of May 1, the Confederates engaged the Union forces. "Maj. Brady 8th Ind took command of our skirmishes and maneuvered them superbly....The 8th and 18th rushed through the first strip of woods and in climbing the next hill were met with a withering fire....We kept up a heavy musketry fire on each side for an hour or more."[167] Although seriously ill, Lieut. Col. Parrish "gallantly led the charge which gained us the strongest rebel position on our right."[168] The Confederates were unable to stop the Union advance and left the field in the evening. They evacuated Grand Gulf May 2. Daniel Roberts described the Battle of Port Gibson to his family as the battle: "In which our brigade had the honor of being the first into, and the last out."[169] Roberts's division went ahead to take possession of a bridge eight miles away, while the rest of the regiment received rations. "The General said we had done without any thing to eat for a week and we could do it again if there was any chance for a fight."[170] Alfred Wilson, although wounded in the head by grape shot, refused to leave his gun behind when taken to the hospital. Amos Neagle captured the Fifteenth Arkansas flag and colorbearer. Although wounded and unable to shoot, George Black carried water to the others during the battle. After skirmishing all night, the company charged the Louisiana Tigers and Mississippi Tigers (who had never been defeated until this battle). The Rebels evacuated Grand Gulf May 2: "we captured all the artillery they had but one piece and run them 10 miles, there was 4 killed in our regiment and 29 wounded but none of our company."[171] Brigadier-General George F. McGinnis, of the Twelfth Division, praised the Eighth Indiana for their willingness to aid his division during this engagement:

---

167 Stott, quoted in Hunter, 212.
168 Bigelow, 18-19.
169 Daniel Roberts, to mother and sisters, May 6, 1863, Special Collections, Indiana State Library, Indianapolis.
170 Roberts, May 6, 1863.
171 Roberts, May 6, 1863.

> Having no regiment of my own command unemployed, I called upon General Benton for the required assistance, who generously tendered the services of the gallant Eighth Indiana, Colonel Shunk, and, although they were short of ammunition, they went in with a will and rendered the necessary relief, and fought gloriously and victoriously during the remainder of the engagement.[172]

General Carr also praised the conduct of the Eighth Indiana, stating, "Indiana continues to be glorified in her sons."[173] Four men of the Eighth Indiana died in the Battle of Port Gibson: Private William D. Hess of Company C, Private Joseph Conklin of Company D, Private James Hampson of Company F, and Private John Duck of Company H.

On May 8, the Eighth Indiana regiment marched through Raymond and camped nearby. The regiment now was short of supplies and rations. Henry C. Leeson complained, "We have no tents, but few cooking utensils and but scant provisions to cook in them there is no wagons allong only Ammunition and what we capture."[174] On May 13, they marched to Clinton to be in supporting distance of the forces capturing Jackson. On May 15, the Union and Confederate armies camped within four miles of each other. That night, the Eighth Indiana regiment slept without tents in a deluge of rain. Skirmishing began the next morning at 7:30 a.m. By 11 a.m., the Union army had captured some ground; by mid-afternoon, the Confederate army was in peril. Sanborn, a spy, informed Dodge of the available Confederate forces during the battle of Champion's Hill, aiding in the Union victory. The Eighth Indiana regiment as part of Benton's Brigade remained held in reserve until late afternoon. Another member of the Brigade, Private Edward H. Ingraham, Thirty-third Illinois, complained "For four hours we stood there listening, waiting and wondering why we were not put into the fight."[175] Commanders ordered them to the south side of Raymond Road, where they advanced and captured several prisoners. The Rebel ammunition train, which had been set on fire, fell into the hands of the Eighth Indiana. The men were able to uncouple several cars and push them away, saving much ammunition. Grant's army prevented Pemberton's left wing from uniting with Johnston's army. Losses were heavy for both armies. Major General J. F. C. Fuller, British military historian, and Edwin C. Bearss, Nation Park

---

[172] *The War of the Rebellion: A Compilation of the Official Records of the Union and Confederate Armies* Vol. 24/1, no. 12 (Washington: Government Printing Office, 1880), 607.
[173] *The Soldier of Indiana in the War for the Union,* 303.
[174] Quoted in Hunter, 137.
[175] Timothy B. Smith, *Champion Hill: Decisive Battle for Vicksburg* (New York: Savas Beatie, 2004), 290.

historian and Civil War authority, declare this battle one of the most decisive battles of the Civil War.[176]

Pemberton retreated to Big Black River Bridge. He ordered his men to guard the bridge from the Union army. The morning of May17, the two armies clashed again at the river. Leeson described the heavy fighting. "I lay as close to the ground as I could get…One Shot would have hit me if I had been Standing but my nose was in the ground."[177] Carr's Division led McClernand's Corps. The Eighth Indiana was at the head of Benton's Brigade in the advance of Carr's Division and formed a line on the south side of the railroad. After a general assault and the capture of their fortified position, the Rebels began to withdraw across the railroad bridge and steamboat dock. As soon as they crossed, they set fire to the bridges, abandoning some of their soldiers. Confederates captured Eighth Indiana Recruit William B. Pruett of Company I at Black River Bridge. The Union Army captured many Rebel soldiers, left on the wrong side of the river. Many tried to escape and some of those drowned. To see if the river was passable, four men from the Eighth Indiana, while under fire, swam across the river and back. Mrs. Emma Balfour described the return of Pemberton's army to Vicksburg:

> I hope never to witness again such a scene as the return of our routed army!...From twelve o'clock until late in the night the streets and roads were jammed with wagons, cannons, horses, men, mules, stock, sheep, everything you can imagine that appertains to an army being brought hurriedly within the entrenchment….What is to become of all the living things in this place…shut up as in a trap…God only knows.[178]

The Union army built three new bridges and crossed the river on the eighteenth. Marshall described this battle and the capture of the Rebels:

> I will begin now with the Black River fight where I left off in my letter this morning; as I said we made the attack about Six in the morning and after about four hours hard cannonading, we charged on their breast works. When all but three or four regiments (which we captured), broke and run across the bridge and fired it, we took twenty seven pieces of cannon and about three thousand prisoners. Out of the twenty seven pieces our brigade took seventeen; when we came up to the riflepits there was one regiment laying in there a cussing them that run they said that they could have whipped us if it had not been for some Mississippi regiments that run. The most of our prisoners we had taken are Mo.,

---

[176] Herb Phillips, Champion Hill! (Clinton, Mississippi: Phillips, n.d.), 4.
[177] Quoted in Hunter, 146.
[178] Quoted in Winschel, "Unvexing the Father of Waters: The Fall of Vicksburg," 26.

> Ark., and Louisiana troops. Our pioneers built a brige across the river that night and next day we crossed over and came within three miles of Vicksburg, laid over till morning.[179]

The regiment advanced in front of the enemy's works at Vicksburg and formed to the left of Smith's Division. Grant ordered an assault on Vicksburg on May 19.

> All were fully convinced that it was a mad move, and that we would meet slaughter and defeat. Nevertheless, at the appointed hour, we fell into line and moved forward. The column had been in motion but a few moments, when the enemy opened upon it from rifle pits and forts, with musketry, grape, shell and schrapnel. Confusion at once began---Men fell dead and wounded at every step. Many being wounded were afterward killed, and the slaughter was terrible.[180]

On May 20, General Pemberton reported to General Joseph Johnston that, "The enemy assaulted our entrenched lines yesterday at two points, center and left, and was repulsed with heavy loss....At this time 8 1/2 a.m. he is briskly cannonading with long range guns."[181] Several soldiers lost their lives during the assault. Recruit Charles W. Canaday of Company H died May 20. Corporal Richard Lamb of Company B and Sergeant Isaac A. Blakely of Company F died May 21. "As the westerners closed in upon the Hill City, their minds were more focused on their stomachs" but they "laughed and cheered and ate heartily that night when supply wagons delivered the promised provender."[182]

They attempted another assault on May 22. The Eighth Indiana and the Thirty-third Illinois were part of the second assault. "Herrington observed two men of the Eighth Indiana who 'went up in the bushes got down on their knees & prayed that they might be spared in this terrible charge.'"[183] A. G. Walden was thirteen when he joined the army with his brother A. P. Walden and cousin Minor Walden. They "went into this charge eating pie." A. G. had stolen "two pies from the commissary and had divided them with his brother, cousin and a friend. While they were eating the pie the order to advance was

---

[179] Swain Marshall, camp near Vicksburg, to his friends at home, May 29, 1863.
[180] S. H. Dunbar, "Army Correspondence," *The Hancock Democrat*, June 11, 1863, 3, https://www.newspapers.com.
[181] David M. Smith, ed. *Compelled to Appear in Print: The Vicksburg Manuscript of General John C. Pemberton*. (Cincinnati, Ohio: Ironclad Printing, 1999), 180.
[182] James R. Arnold, *Grant Wins the War: Decision at Vicksburg* (New York: John Wiley & Sons, 1997), 246.
[183] Hunter, 149.

passed along the line."[184] Benton's Brigade attacked the Second Texas regiment, who were defending the Second Texas Lunette north of the railroad.[185] Captain Pat White of the Chicago Mercantile Boys wrote about this assault in his memoirs:

> At 3 a.m. the cannonading began from the land side. Every available gun was brought to bear on the works. It was the most terrible bombardment during the seige [sic], and continued until nearly 11 o'clock, while our sharpshooters kept up such a galling fire that the rebel cannoneers could seldom rise to load their pieces. The artillery of McClernand's 13th Corps had succeeded in breaching several points of the enemy's works, silencing five or six guns and exploding four caissons. At ten a.m., the columns moved to the assault.[186]

Benton's Brigade advanced on Baldwin's Ferry Road. This position exposed them to enemy fire, and they sought protection where they could. At night, they slipped away. During one of these unsuccessful assaults, "the Eighth Indiana was the first to succeed in planting its colors on the enemy's battlement, but they were later repulsed."[187]

Dr. Bigelow, Chaplain Skinner, and Dr. Orr, Twenty-first Iowa stayed up all night caring for the wounded. "They were laid on raw cotton, under China trees, where they remained until they had their wounds operated upon, and disposed of in a different manner."[188] The Eighth Indiana lost seventeen men that day. Company A lost Captain Andrew O'Daniel, Corporals Andrew Ridenour and George Craw, and Recruits John Slake and Sylvester Tripplett. Company B lost Privates Franklin May and John B. Scotten, and Company D lost Captain Frederick S. Wysong, Private William Smith, and Recruit Lewis Swartz. Company E lost Privates Henry Good and Andrew J. Phillips, and Company F lost Private John A. Rhodes. Company G lost Private William M. Chaffin; Company H lost Privates William Price and Amos Stevens, and Company I lost Private Thomas S. Smith. The eight wounded men later died from their wounds. Private Albert Whitman of Company A died July 26 at Evansville. Recruit Anthony Mincer of Company G died June 7. Private Thomas Melick of Company H died July 13 at St. Louis. Privates Warren Blackman died May 28, John M. Benbow died July 22, Elijah R. Scott

---

184 "Went Into Charge Eating Stolen Pie," *Wichita Daily Eagle*, May 23, 1912, 5, https://www.newspapers.com.
185 Edwin C. Bearss, *Fields of Honor: Pivotal Battles of the Civil War* (Washington, D.C.: National Geographic, 2006), 241,
186 Quoted in Richard Brady Williams, "Chicago's Battery Boys," *Hallowed Ground* 5, no. 3 (Fall 2004), 37.
187 Thornbrough, 154.
188 Bigelow, 22.

died June 5, and David J. Williamson died June 1, all members of Company I. Captain Hiram T. Vandevender of Company K died May 23. Flagbearer John Swafford, fell mortally wounded, and either, his son, Daniel D. Swafford, or Sergeant Samuel Webb grabbed the colors in his place.[189]

They called a brief truce Sunday afternoon to allow time to recover and bury the dead. "When we went under a flag truce to bury the dead we found three wounded still living, they had lain all the time under a burning sun with nothing to eat or drink." [190]

---

[189] According to *The Soldier in the War for the Union*, Corporal Swafford fell mortally wounded on May 22; however, according to the *Report of the Adjutant General*, Vol. 4, Private John L. Swafford was killed May 24. According to *The Soldier in the War for the Union,* Sergeant Samuel Webb grabbed the colors, but according to *Indiana at Vicksburg*, Swafford's son (Daniel D. Swafford) grabbed the colors and "held them up through the storm of shot and shell."

[190] Swain Marshall, camp near Vicksburg, to friends at home, May 29, 1863.

Vicksburg Monument and closeup of left side plaque "INDIANA 1ST BRIG. 14TH DIV. 10TH CORPS 8TH INFANTRY, COLONEL DAVID SHUNK, MAJOR THOMAS J. BRADY, ENGAGED: PORT GIBSON, MAY 1; CHAMPION'S HILL, MAY16; BIG BLACK RIVER BRIDGE, MAY 17; ASSAULT, MAY 22; SIEGE, MAY 23 – JULY 4. CASUALTIES: KILLED 27, WOUNDED 133, MISSING 1, TOTAL 161, CAPTAINS ANDREW O'DANIEL, FREDERICK S. WYSONG AND HIRAM T. VANDEVENDER KILLED." NPS photos

After these two failed assaults, Grant decided upon a regular siege, which lasted forty-eight days. Engineers constructed mines, tunnels, and batteries. During this time, Governor Morton continued to send supplies, nurses, and doctors to the troops. During 1863, he sent seven missions down the Mississippi River using different steamers, who returned to Indiana with wounded soldiers aboard. The Eighth Indiana stayed in the right center of the corps line on the right of the railroad leading to Jackson during the siege. Samuel Herrington remembered how wanting a second plate of beans saved his life:

> We were sitting in our tent eating dinner one day and I was just leaning over to dish out a second plate of beans when a ball passed through the tent, taking a large piece of our center pole with it. We were quite nervous over it, you may be sure. One of the boys traced the course of the ball through the tent and it was found that, if I had been sitting in a natural position instead of leaning over, the

ball would have struck me at the base of the brain. That made me more nervous than ever. I always have given the beans credit for saving my life.[191]

Marshall described the dangers of the siege:

> there is bullets whisling over our heads all the time, but we are protected by a hill so that it is only a few stray shot that gets low enough to hit us here, one of our company boys was hit in the leg this morning while he was in bed; yesterday our company was in the pits a shooting I got some bully shots at the rebs heads when they would poke them up to shoot; late in the evening I got struck in the wrist bone with a spent ball it swelled up and is pretty sore this morning but will be all right before many days. it was lucky for me that it was not going with much force, for it would not have taken but little more force to have broken my wrist.[192]

Each day the Union army shelled the city, waiting for hunger to conquer the enemy. Thomas Bailey described the shelling,

> slowly ascends the monster shell, twinkling and sparkling in the star-lit dome of heaven. Then gracefully it curves, and gently it glides down until almost lost beneath the horizon; then a flash, a crashing and whizzing sound, tell that its mission of death and destruction is finished.[193]

More soldiers lost their lives during the siege. Private William T. Beck of Company E and Corporal Jacob Ogan of Company I died May 23. Privates George W. Eby and James F. Neal of Company A and Private Alfred Lowder of Company B died May 25. Recruit Israel Shaffer of Company A died May 27. Private Joseph P. Dempsey of Company C died May 29. Private William H. Hoke died June 2. Recruit Joseph B. Gossett of Company E died June 6.[194] "By mid-June they were down to half rations. The Eighth Indiana, like many regiments had a daily allowance of only a little meat and four ears of corn for each soldier."[195]

Both armies had a mutual understanding between the pickets during the siege. There was no firing after dark and general conversation and trading (coffee for tobacco) was permissible. Daniel Roberts wrote about the pickets: "We are digging rifle pits still closer to them every night, our pickets are close enough to talk to each other but we have

---

[191] "Tells War Events," *The Indianapolis Star*, April 7, 1912, 20, https://www.newspapers.com.
[192] Swain Marshall, camp in rear of Vicksburg, to sister, June 8, 1863.
[193] McSpadden, 223.
[194] The adjutant reports list Gossett's death as June 6, 1863. Footnote 12 of Erich L. Ewald, ed., "A Letter from the Front: Vicksburg, 1863," *Indiana Magazine of History,* 91, No. 3 (September 1995) 320-325 lists his date of death as June 16, which Vicksburg National park historian Terrence J. Winschel verified in a letter to the editor April 15, 1993.
[195] Hunter, 109.

orders not to fire unless they advance; and they say they have the same orders."[196] On June18, they bombarded the mortar boats. Roberts described one of the bombs as:

> a livid flash like summer lightning from a cloud beneath the horizon....a glim spark like a meteor half aglow...slowly climbing the sky, momentarily visible, and as often disappearing...then begins to descend slowly at first but acelerating its velocity till it shoots into the earth with the speed of lightening. At the same time you hear a rushing sound, broken somewhat like that of a locomotive in the distance, and ceasing with a sudden thump.[197]

During the siege, some soldiers visited friends and family members in other regiments. On June 22, William M. Macy, Ninety-ninth Illinois, visited his cousin. "Came off Picket this morning at eight. Went up on the lines today to the 8th Ind. to see my cousin Swain Marshall. found him in Co. G. returned in evening by sunset."[198]

On the morning of July 3, three Confederates rode to the Union army with a white flag. Grant required an "unconditional surrender." At 3 p.m., the Rebels reluctantly agreed to surrender. That evening, eight to ten men from a Texas regiment came over the trenches and spent a couple hours with the Eighth Indiana. On July 4, the army formally surrendered, as they marched out and stacked arms. When Herrington saw the Confederate flags go down that morning, he jumped up and was the first Union soldier to enter the city after the surrender. Roberts wrote home of the surrender:

> I now sit down to let you know the good news; Vicksburg is ours, they surrendered about an hour ago. Yesterday at 10 o'clock they came out with a flag of truce, offering to surrender on terms, which Grant would not accept, saying it should be unconditional. And they have been running back and forth with flags of truce ever since; till now they have raised the white flag on every fort and are now coming out and stacking their arms as fast as they can.[199]

July 5, the Eighth Indiana regiment marched to Jackson, in pursuit of Johnston's Army. After a brief skirmish, the Eighth Indiana regiment spent the next forty-eight hours digging rifle-pits to protect themselves. On the morning of July 17, they found the enemy had evacuated Jackson. On the eighteenth, the Eighth Indiana regiment marched south to the New Orleans and Jackson Railroad, and tore up and burned the track as far south as

---

[196] Daniel Roberts, the battleground in the rear of Vicksburg, to his mother and sisters, June 19, 1863.
[197] Roberts, June 19, 1863.
[198] William M. Macy, "The Civil War Diary of William M. Macy," *Indiana Magazine of History* 30, no. 2 (June 1934), 185.
[199] Daniel Roberts, in the rear of Vicksburg, to his mother and sisters, July 4, 1863.

Byram Station, ten miles south of Jackson. They returned to Jackson on the twentieth, and the next day headed back to Vicksburg. Benton recommended Col. Shunk for promotion to brigadier-general because of his actions at Jackson:

> Col. David Shunk, of the Eighth Indiana Volunteer Infantry, commanding First Brigade, was particularly distinguished by taking the advance of his line of skirmishers and himself first examining the contested ground over which he proposed to take his men; also by his sleepless energy in constructing earthworks, with a half dozen spades and two picks and one foot adze, which won the encomiums of both Generals Ord and Sherman, the corps and expeditionary commanders. In my judgment, his promotion to be a brigadier-general is one eminently fit to be made, and has been abundantly earned.[200]

Benton stated the Fourteenth Division lost one man by disease, four killed in battle, and thirty-two wounded. The Adjutant Report stated Private Samuel Robinson of Company B died July 1863 in Vicksburg. Swain Marshall and his cousin William M. Macy visited each other again on July 24. During this time, Cathy Williams continued to serve the regimental officers as their cook and laundress.[201] The regiment stayed in Vicksburg until August 20. Part of the regiment furloughed home for twenty days. July 28, James W. Alexander furloughed home for thirty days.

---

[200] *Official Records*, 24/2, No. 33, 609-610.
[201] Tucker, 56.

Chapter 10: Operations in Louisiana and Texas

City of Madison (steamboat). http://mjcpl.org/rivertorail/ageofsteam/the-city-of-madison-disaster, accessed 23 May 2015.

August 19, Private David Potts of Company C was on guard duty when he was killed in an explosion on the Steamer *City of Madison*, when someone "dropped a box of shells into the hold, which ignited the entire cargo, exploded, killing and wounding a large number."[202] The regiment traveled by the Steamer *North America* on August 20 to Carrollton, Louisiana, arriving August 23. The army reorganized August 31 and the Eighth Indiana (Lt. Col. Charles S. Parrish) became part of First Brigade (Col. David Shunk), First Division (Brig. Gen. William P. Benton), Thirteenth Army Corps, Department of the Gulf. The men complained about the swampy conditions of Louisiana:

> For the first ten miles, along the river, the country was very nice but from there on it is a perfect swamp with a few houses scattered along in the highest places. The balance is inhabited by moccason snakes, alligaters and musquitoes, the latter in particular are very bother-some to soldiers, coming out in the evening. We could see them sitting on the tops of the trees whetting their bills, ready to pounce down upon us as quick as they found out where we were going to camp; they sometimes;...well I guess hardly ever carry men off.[203]

Isaac Elliott remarked "that the soldiers of the First Brigade 'first made acquaintance with alligators,' and some of the 'young saurians were pets in the regiment.'"[204] On September 3, the regiment moved across Algiers River and traveled by the New Orleans

---

[202] Bigelow, 23.
[203] Daniel Roberts, Camp Bayou, Beriff, LA, to his mother and sisters, September 9, 1863.
[204] Quoted in Hunter, 243.

Opollooses and Great Western Railroad to Berwick Bay. The regiment experienced another flood from another torrential rain. "Around us was a vast sea of water, and shouts, and cheers, and oaths, and jokes, and calls for help, came up from every part of the camp."[205]

They became part of the "Teche" campaign under General Banks, passing through Franklin, New Iberia, St. Martinsville, and Vermilion to Opelousas, Louisiana. During the march from Brashear City, they passed several plantations owned by French citizens. The regiment was angered that one of those citizens, Sorrel, claimed the French government would protect his elegant property. They felt they would soon be fighting the French "with a fury never before seen."[206] The army arrested Colonel Shunk on October 13 because he allowed foraging.[207] Chaplain Skinner learned the army had acquitted him; "we are anxiously looking for his return in a few days, and the boys will make the welkin ring when they see our old Colonel come into camp again."[208] During this fall, Sergeants Cyrus Hanes and Elijah Tuttle and four others took an oyster boat into the interior of Louisiana and safely accomplished a secret mission.[209] The regiment stayed there until October 26 and returned by the same route to Berwick Bay. James W. Alexander was in General Hospital at New Orleans from October 15 – December 2. Dr. Beck again applied to Governor Morton for the position of assistant surgeon on October 18. His son had died in May at Vicksburg from a mortal wound: "I said mortally would not have been so with a little attention, a Spent grape shot struck him between the Ankle & knee no bones broken the ligature Sloughed off and he was left to bleed to death."[210]

On November 12, the regiment with other troops left Berwick City on the steamship *St. Mary* for Texas. On November 14, they faced rough seas from a "Northerner" storm; few slept that night and many became very seasick. On November 17, the regiment surprised and captured the garrison at Aranzas Pass on Mustang Island. "The troops took 103 prisoners and three siege guns, on Mustang Island without firing a

---

[205] McSpadden, 255.
[206] S. H. Dunbar to Mr. Andrew Wilson, October 7, 1863, "Eighth Indiana Correspondence."
[207] Hunter, 265.
[208] McSpadden, 265.
[209] Baker, 439.
[210] Dr. James Beck to Governor Morton, October 18, 1863, "Eighth Indiana Correspondence."

gun."[211] That evening, a "Norther" began that lasted for three days. "The sand flew like fine snow in a gale, blinding us, and filling our ears, hair, throat and clothing."[212] The men suffered greatly since their blankets and camp equipment remained on the boats. They also lacked enough wood for a good fire. "Things got so bad that, on November 19, smaller boats anchored off shore were tossed about, even landing on sandbars. On one of them, Chaplain Henry C. Skinner, Eighth Indiana, 'offered up a Prair that they might all be spaired.'"[213] On the twenty-third, the regiment crossed Aranzas Pass, traveled up St. Joseph Island, crossed Cedar Bayou on rafts on the evening of November 25, and marched up Matagorda Island the next two days. They arrived near Fort Esperanza on the twenty-seventh. That night, the army dug a rifle pit 210 yards long (large enough for a regiment) parallel to the enemy's works. The next morning, they drove in the pickets and took part of the works with no trouble. The Seventh Michigan battery dropped shells into the fort, and the infantry moved forward the morning of the thirtieth: "it was an awful cold morning for this country and every feller had a blanket around him. We...layed there all day a sharpshooting, had not tasted a mouthfull of any thing since the morning before."[214] By evening, four companies of the Eighth Indiana were in the sand hills 275 yards from the fort. At midnight, the Confederates spiked the mounted guns and blew up the gunpowder magazines in the fort, prior to their evacuation. The Union Army rushed in to save as much as possible and captured six of the rear guard:

> it was not many minutes 'til our reg't. was in the fort to see what they had left. We got plenty of flour and corn meal, and soon had fires built and were cooking breakfast, had the best meal I had eat since we left Lousiana. After we got to the fort three more magazines blew up killing one more and wounding two or three.[215]

Adjutant McPherson, as he entered the fort,

> discovered a line of torpedoes on the outside, with strings extending inside, to be exploded beneath our feet in an attempt to take it by storm. We carefully cut the strings and ordered the prisoners to dig up and remove them, which was done without accident, and thus valuable lives were saved.[216]

---

[211] Daniel Roberts, Matagorda Island, December 1, 1863.
[212] McSpadden, 316.
[213] Hunter, 252.
[214] Swain Marshall, Matagorda Island, Texas, to Friends at home, December 16, 1863.
[215] Swain Marshall, Matagorda Island, Texas, to Friends at home, December 16, 1863.
[216] *Daily Journal* news clipping of letter dated December 10, 1863, "Eighth Indiana Correspondence."

When they started to pursue the Confederates, the Union Army discovered they had cut the ropes on the floating bridge; they had also started to burn the bridge.

The Eighth Indiana regiment lost two men at Fort Esperanza: Private Joseph Gregory of Company H (November 29) and Musician Henry Williams of Company F (December 6). The army occupied this fort until December 23. The First Brigade (the Eighth and Eighteenth Indiana) sailed to Indianola. "Quartered in deserted houses, the troops at Indianola passed the winter with its frequent 'Northers' quite pleasantly. Good shelter, oysters and sea breezes secured universal health…"[217]

[217] *The Soldier of Indiana in the War for the Union*, 517.

Bronze relief depicting Oliver P. Morton giving a speech to a troop. This relief is located on the north side of the east entrance to the Indiana Statehouse. Photo courtesy of Cindy Kreegar

On December 18, Benton wrote to Governor Morton requesting that those who re-enlisted be organized into an artillery regiment because they preferred "their muster rolls show they have marched on foot over four thousand miles in the service, and some of them complain, they are worn out from marching, and therefore greatly prefer to ride here after."[218] On January 1, 417 of the 515 in the regiment re-enlisted, including James W. Alexander and Swain Marshall. Veterans who re-enlisted for three years received one month's advance pay, a thirty-day furlough, a bounty of $402 (which was paid even if the war ended before the end of the three year term or to the family of those who died during service), and were entitled to wear badges "of honorable distinction, 'service chevrons.'"[219] While the veterans were on furlough, the army temporarily assigned those

[218] W. P. Benton to Governor Morton, December 18, 1863, "Eighth Indiana Correspondence."
[219] Terrill, Vol. 1, 33.

who did not re-enlist to the Sixty-ninth Indiana.[220] Marshall wrote about this re-enlistment:

> I thought awhile that I would not reenlist until my old term was out, and see how things looked then, but when the order came for veterans, I knew that the regiment would go and I could not think of leaving the old eighth and going in some other reg't, so I was one of the first to put my name down, and should I have to serve three years more I will do it faithfully and willingly, trying to do my duty to my country. There was about one hundred of the reg't that did not reenlist – they have been transferred to the 69th, they look like stray sheep; there is some one comes back nearly every day and enlists.[221]

Prior to this re-enlistment, the regiment lost forty-eight killed in action; thirty-two died from wounds, and 137 died from disease, making a total loss of 217 men. During this time, Chaplains Henry C. Skinner and John S. Donaldson, Eighteenth Indiana held temperance meetings three times a week. Marshall reported, "eight hundred from our brigade and the third have signed the pledge…not to drink any intoxicating drink while in the United States Service."[222] Philander Smith signed the pledge on January 4. He also made the decision to become a Christian and attended nightly meetings held by the U. S. Christian Commission.[223]

Governor Morton required three-fourths of a regiment to re-enlist before the men would go home on furlough. They sent one NCO or private from each company to recruit more soldiers. The private earned a promotion if he recruited the required minimum. All of these recruiters had to report to the governor. One of the new recruits was Ira Hough of Company E. In April, the veterans returned to Indianapolis for a one-month furlough. The community delayed the welcoming reception until May 28, since the men were so anxious to return home to their families. On May 28, they fired the cannon at 8 a.m. to signal the ladies at the Soldiers' Home to prepare the meal. E. Anne Butler wrote about this dinner in a letter to her son Scot in the Thirty-third Indiana.

> The 8th Ind Reg. had a dinner and reception yesterday. They arrived from the front about a month ago but owing to the impatience of the men to get home it was deferred until they passed through on thier return to the field, yesterday was a

---

[220] Henry C. Adams, Jr., *Indiana at Vicksburg* (Indianapolis: Wm. B. Burford, 1911. Reprinted.Lexington, KY: Forgotten Books, 2012), 205.
[221] Swain Marshall, Indianola, Texas, to Father, February 18, 1864.
[222] Quoted in Hunter, 258.
[223] "Letter from Philander Smith to Sarah Smith," January 4, 1864, Philander Smith Papers, MSS 216/ PSC 225, Box 1.

> delightful day, clear & cool after a week of showery weather. This winds up the dinne[r]s and receptions of the Veterans until the war is over the Eight being the last of the reenlisted regiments.[224]

The regiment lined up at 10 a.m. and marched to the State House yard at 2 p.m. where several gave speeches in their honor. Mayor Cavin welcomed them home and spoke of their two flags: "not as yet been baptized in the smoke of battle" and the two old flags "all seared and rent and faded."[225] True to their motto, the old flags had remained above them or around them:

> in peace, an angel of good will to all mankind….in war, an eagle of vengeance….amid the storm and smoke of battle, its stars lighting up the pathway to victory….floating proudly and defiant in the hour of triumph, and if fallen, then around you – a winding sheet around your bloody form."[226]

The blot against Indiana because of the disgrace at Buena Vista had been:

> washed away in blood. Indiana stood redeemed and more than redeemed. Instead of that stain upon her flag you have written an inscription that will grow brighter with time, and that inscription is this: "Among the states in the war for the Union, Indiana first upon the roll of honor."[227]

Colonel Shunk thanked the ladies, the Governor and the Mayor for the reception. Although the men of the Eighth Indiana were from farms and workshops, he felt there were "no better in the army."[228]

---

[224] Barbara Butler Davis, *Affectionately Yours: The Civil War Home-Front Letters of the Ovid Butler Family* (Indianapolis: Indiana Historical Society Press, 2004), 84.
[225] McCormick, 54.
[226] McCormick, 54-55.
[227] McCormick, 55.
[228] McCormick, 56.

"Major-Gen. Sheridan riding along the lines after the Battle of Fisher's Hill, Va.," Frank Leslie's Illustrated Newspaper, October 15, 1864, 56. House Divided: The Civil War Research Engine at Dickinson College. http://hd.housedivided.dickinson.edu/node/43347, accessed 23 May 2015.

They returned to their regiment as part of the District of LaFourche, Department of the Gulf at New Orleans in late June. The regiment guarded the railroad - three companies at Terre Bonne Station; one company at Boutte Station; two companies at Chucahoula; one company at Bayou Des Allemands; one company at La Fourche Crossing; and one company at Tigerville. Marshall discussed this duty and his feelings about the swampy conditions again:

> We are doing the most low lifed business that they could put a soldier at guarding the N.O. and Brashear City Railroad. We are sixty six miles from N.O. our company and F. are stationed here. The rest of the regiment is stationed at different places along the road between the city and here…I was on picket last night spilt some of my best blood in my country's cause or rather the musketoes cause don't think I ever suffered more in my life. They are so thick and savage that a fellow cannot keep them off. We have musketo bars in the tents or we could not sleep any here.[229]

[229] Swain Marshall, Tigerville, Louisiana, to friends at home, July 4, 1864.

On July 28, the regiment engaged the Rebels at Atchafalaya, Louisiana. Two men fell wounded and one man became a prisoner: Private John W. Goodlander of Company F. Goodlander wrote home to his parents on October 4, "I am a prisoner of war…We have been treated…just as good as they could treat us."[230] He wrote again a few days later about his capture, "They threatened to shoot me…I have been robbed of everything I had."[231] They took him to Camp Ford prison camp in Tyler, Texas.

After this battle, the regiment traveled by steamer to Washington, D.C. They were off the coast of Cape Hatteras in a storm and many became seasick, including Swain Marshall. The next day, they traveled up the Chesapeake Bay and anchored close to Fort Monroe. On the first, they arrived at Alexandria and took a ferryboat to camp. Marshall described their march August 2 through Washington, D.C., on their way to a supper at a convalescent home near the Baltimore and Ohio Depot: "Where we landed we marched through the city, passed by the Capitol and White House did not get to see Old Abe. Think that if he had known that it was the 8th passing, that he would have come out and saluted us."[232] The regiment spent two weeks in defense of Washington, cutting bushes in front of the forts. On the fourteenth, "a man hung as a rebel spy til he was dead."[233] The regiment marched to Berryville, Virginia. On August 22, Dr. Beck again wrote to Governor Morton requesting appointment as assistant surgeon.

Now assigned to the Nineteenth Corps, they joined Sheridan's Shenandoah Valley Campaign. At sunset on September 3 as the Union army went into camp, the Nineteenth Corps clashed briefly with the Rebels and captured about three hundred prisoners. By dark, the Union drove the Rebels back toward Winchester. On September 5, B and D company skirmishers drove Rebel skirmishers from behind a stone fence:

> While we were firing at them behind the wall I saw about a dozen men come up a hill in a field to the left of where we were firing. I thought at first that they were our men as they had blue clothes on, but I saw that some of them had grey pants. I got up and went towards them to see for certain whether they were our men or not, as some of the boys were going to shoot at them. I did not have to go far before I found what they were, just as I got to edge of the woods they commenced whistling bullets too close to my head to be comfortable so I gave them a volley

[230] McSpadden, 112.
[231] McSpadden, 113.
[232] Swain Marshall, Washington City, D.C., to friends at home, August 13, 1864.
[233] Abner Vanmatre diary, on display at Colonel Eli Lily Civil War Museum, Soldiers' and Sailors' Monument, Indianapolis, Indiana.

> and retreated back to the company. I took good aim at the pile but as they all dodged down I could not tell whether I plugged one or not. All of our regiment and the 28th Iowa was deployed for skirmishers and we advanced, the rebs breaking and running without much more opposition.[234]

Although the Eighth Indiana regiment could not go home for the presidential election, the men took a poll of how they would have voted. "The vote stands for Lincoln two hundred and ninety four McClellan twenty five Fremont six, majority two hundred and sixty three, very well but not as good as I wished for."[235]

On September 18, Chaplain Skinner held joint religious services in the morning and evening with the Twenty-eighth Iowa in a hollow to the rear of the regiment.[236] The next morning, the Nineteenth Corps attacked Early's Army on the Berryville pike at the crossing of Opequon Creek from early morning until 5 o'clock in the evening.

> At twenty minutes before mid-day, the line moved across the open to the belt of woods opposite, where the flashes of the enemy's cannon had told of his presence. No sooner had the infantry gone forward than the battle became at once deadly, and so continued throughout the day, being fought without field-works.[237]

Miss Rebecca Wright, a member of the Society of Friends and teacher of a small private school, was a Union spy and told the locations of Kershaw's infantry and Cutshaw's artillery. This knowledge contributed much to the Union success at this battle of Opequon (Third Winchester). Early's forces were separated, which led to his defeat. Shunk's brigade was on the extreme left. B. F. Hubbard, Second Vermont, wrote, "The 8th and 19th Corps on our left, made an advance, and after a desperate fight the Rebs were forced back."[238] Grant was thrilled with this victory. "We have just sent them whirling through Winchester, and we are after them tomorrow. This army behaved splendidly."[239]

Losses were heavy on both sides. The Eighth Indiana lost two men killed in battle – Private Benjamin F. Bock of Company E and Private John T. Jenkins of Company G – and one prisoner of war Private Daniel Duffee of Company F. The Confederates took

---

[234] Swain Marshall, camp near Berryville, Virginia, to friends at home, September 7, 1864.
[235] Swain Marshall, camp near Berryville, Virginia, to friends at home, September 7, 1864.
[236] McSpadden, 228.
[237] George E. Pond, *Campaigns of the Civil War XI: The Shenandoah Valley in 1864* (Reprinted Edison, NJ: Castle Books, 2002; First published in 1883), 160.
[238] B. F. Hubbard, letter to Julia, September 21, 1864, near Strasburg, in *Letters Home IV: Life at the Front, Original Civil War Soldiers' Letters & Photographs* (Gettysburg: Alan Sessarego Collection, 2003), 29.
[239] Pond, 167.

Duffee to Libby Prison and Belle Isle until they paroled him on October 8. He complained, "they came near to starving us....they took everything away from us except the suit of clothes that was on our backs….took all the money they could find."[240]

Sheridan's Army pursued the enemy to Fisher's Hill and attacked them again September 22. The Union Army swarmed over the breastworks and routed Early's Army, capturing twenty pieces of artillery, 1,100 prisoners of war, and much ammunition. The chase continued all night, but Sheridan was unable to catch Early. "Fisher's Hill was the corollary of Winchester. It was a hurricane battle, totally unlike the one delivered three days before: and the Union troops were as palpably inspirited by their previous triumph as the Confederates were unnerved from the same cause."[241] Chaplain Skinner, the Sanitary Commission, and others provided blankets and clothing for the wounded to make them comfortable. "The sight of gaping wounds and scenes of suffering and destitution, can never be described."[242] Cathy Williams had traveled with the Eighth Indiana to the Shenandoah Valley, but here she received a new assignment "to serve as cook and laundress for General Sheridan and his staff at the headquarters of the Army of the Shenandoah" at Belle Grove.[243]

---

240 McSpadden, 114-115.
241 Pond, 182.
242 McSpadden, 231.
243 Tucker, 61.

Chapter 13: The Battle of Cedar Creek

Belle Grove – the Battle of Cedar Creek occurred all around this home. The only damage to the home was a bullet hole in the pillar to the right of the stairs. Photo from Thompson Family Album

On October 10, Sheridan's Army moved to Cedar Creek. They built rifle pits in the front of the line. General Grant expressed a wish to have Sheridan cut the Virginia Central Railroad at Gordonsville and Charlottesville. Major-General Halleck turned the wish into an order to Sheridan on October 12. Secretary of War Edwin M. Stanton became involved and he ordered Sheridan to Washington October 13 for a consultation. Sheridan left with the Cavalry Corps on October 15. Wright sent him an urgent message about a Confederate signal flag message from Longstreet to Early. "Be ready to move as soon as my forces join you, and we will crush Sheridan."[244] Sheridan had planned to raid Charlottesville, but decided to order the Merritt's and Custer's cavalry back to Cedar Creek with the following message: "make your position strong…Close in Colonel Powell, who will be at this point…. be well prepared."[245] Powell's cavalry received orders to stay at Front Royal until Sheridan returned from Washington. They ignored the

---

[244] Pond, 213.
[245] Philip Sheridan, *Civil War Memoirs* (New York: Bantam Books, 1991), 270.

order to close in Colonel Powell. Sheridan had hoped to return to his men on the eighteenth, but:

> Colonel Alexander was a man of enormous weight, and Colonel Thom correspondingly light, and as both were unaccustomed to riding we had to go slowly, losing so much time, in fact, that we did not reach Winchester till between 3 and 4 o'clock in the afternoon, though the distance is but twenty-eight miles.[246]

They spent the night at Winchester.

The enemy spent the evening of the eighteenth flanking Sheridan's Army. They removed all metal from their uniforms to insure silence; heavy fog at 4 a.m. enabled them get into position unseen. The army had delivered a large amount of mail to the Union soldiers that day, so many spent the evening reading letters, while a group of Ohio boys sang songs of home and a homesick soldier played his flute.[247] The Nineteenth Corps, encamped on an elevated plain near Belle Grove House (now Sheridan's headquarters), was under orders to be alert at 4 a.m. Reveille was heard at 3:30 and the pickets from Shunk's brigade were roused and put under arms. At 4:00, the enemy had a brief skirmish with Custer's sentinels. Some men woke up, but most rolled over and went back to sleep. Kershaw's men crossed Cedar Creek at 4:30 and heard early risers talking in their tents. In a letter to his wife, Taylor Peirce, Twenty-second Iowa Infantry, wrote, "The Eastern sky had just begun to show signs of approaching day....when all at once as if from every hill and every valley there arose such a rattle of Musketry as I have ever heard."[248] Kershaw's men attacked at 5 a.m. with a thundering volley on the right for fifteen minutes. Then Gordon's men opened a volley on the extreme left. They caught each group unawares. Some fought briefly but most ran for safety. Marshall told of a rumor that went around camp:

> The rebels dressed in our uniform had relieved their picketts, and the first firing we had heard was the enemy firing from our breast works into the 8th Corps Camp. A more disgracefull surprise has not happened during the war; and it came very near causing a "skedadle back to Washington."[249]

---

[246] Thomas A. Lewis, *The Guns at Cedar Creek* (New York: Laurel, 1988), 262.
[247] General A. B. Nettleton, "The Famous Fight at Cedar Creek," in The Annals of the War Written by Leading Participants North and South, Originally Published in the *Philadelphia Weekly Times* (Philadelphia: Times, 1879; reprint, National Historical Society, 2012), 658-659.
[248] Richard L. Kiper, ed., *Dear Catherine, Dear Taylor* (Lawrence: University Press of Kansas, 2002), 288.
[249] Swain Marshall, camp on Cedar Hill, to friends at home, October 23, 1864.

General Horatio G. Wright, commander of the Sixth Corps, was in charge of the Army in Sheridan's absence. He discounted the rumor of Rebels relieving the pickets in Union uniforms: "It was reported in camp that he first relieved a part of our lines by his own men dressed in our uniform, but I have never been able to confirm this rumor."[250]

Rebels then attacked the Nineteenth Corps, guarding Cedar Creek Bridge. Since they were the last group attacked, they had more time to prepare, but also had to deal with the fleeing masses of their fellow soldiers. They soon joined the retreat:

> We held our ground till the enemy moved around our left, and came very near surrounding before we were ordered back they had taken all the artillery belonging to the 8th Corps and had turned it on us, and were closing in our three sides hollering halt you Yankees – but I for one was not round halting.[251]

Marshall grabbed his knapsack on his way past his tent, but most men lost their possessions. Many of the Confederate soldiers were barefoot, wearing ragged clothing, and hungry.

> In passing through Sheridan's camp they had a great temptation thrown in their way; many of the tents were open, and in plain sight were rations, shoes, overcoats, and blankets!...some of the men stopped, secured well-filled haversacks, and as they investigated their contents, the temptation to stop and eat was too great, as they had had nothing since the evening before, and they yielded. Others tried on shoes, others put on warm pants in place of the tattered ones, others got overcoats and blankets, articles so much needed for the coming cold![252]

Sheridan awoke to the sound of gunfire and rushed back to Cedar Creek with Powell's cavalry. They met a panic-stricken army. When the men saw him, they stopped, cheered, turned around, and followed him to the front. "Hope took the place of fear, courage the place of despondency, cheerfulness the place of gloom. The entire aspect of things seemed changed in a moment. Further retreat was not longer thought of."[253] By 10:00, Rebels were looting the camp to replenish their tattered uniforms:

> While they left the field they stripped all the dead and robbed the wounded. Sergt. Webb of our Co. wounded (since died) was robbed of everything he had, even the ring off his finger. Cap. Watson of Co. "A" left dead on the field had every stitch

[250] *Official Records,* 43/1, No. 11, 160.
[251] Marshall, October 23, 1864.
[252] John H. Worsham, *One of Jackson' Foot Cavalry* (New York: Neale Publishing Company, 1912. Reprint, Time-Life Books, 1981), 276.
[253] Nettleton, 661.

of clothing taken off but the man that stripped him met a just fate he was found dead on the field with Watsons clothes on.[254]

Sheridan arrived at 10:30 and reformed the line to attack at 1:00. "The magnitude of his fiery energy electrified the army with a kindred spirit, and they fought with just that desperate valor that was needed to turn the tide of affairs in our favor."[255] Sheridan began a counterattack at 4:00 and drove the Rebels in confusion to Fishers Hill. At a small bridge near Spangler's Mill in Strasburg, the bridge broke or a wagon fell off the edge, creating a bottleneck, enabling the Union Army to recapture their guns and much of their equipment: "In the last fight our regt. captured thirty five prisoners and a battle flag."[256]

A Connecticut officer described the battlefield. "Here and there were splashes of blood, and zigzag trails of blood, and bodies of men and horses…I never on any other battlefield saw so much blood as on this of Cedar Creek. The firm limestone soil would not receive it, and there was no pitying summer grass to hide it."[257]

Sheridan downplayed his role in this victory; however, Lincoln sent a message of congratulations and Grant praised him as a hero: "Turning what bid fair to be a disaster into a glorious victory stamps Sheridan what I have always thought him – one of the ablest generals."[258] Sheridan was riding his favorite black horse, Rienzi, which the Second Michigan Cavalry presented to him in Rienzi, Mississippi in 1862. This horse bore him into nearly all the remaining battles after Cedar Creek. When Rienzi died in 1878, at the age of twenty, its body was stuffed and put into a museum on Governor's Island, where veterans decorated it with flowers each Memorial Day. The victory and Sheridan's ride, so enraptured the North, that poems and stories told about this event. C. A. Savage of Company K wrote a poem describing this battle, which the G.P. Hardwick Music Company published some time after the war. Although considered the author for many years, his name is not on the original writings. According to the Cedar Creek

---

[254] Swain Marshall, camp on Cedar Hill, to friends at home, October 23, 1864.
[255] Gary W. Gallagher, ed. The Shenandoah Valley Campaign of 1864 (Chapel Hill: University of North Carolina Press, 2006), 109.
[256] Swain Marshall, to brother, October 24, 1864.
[257] Earl J. Hess, *The Union Soldier in Battle: Enduring the Ordeal of Combat* (Lawrence: University Press of Kansas, 1997), 38.
[258] Horace Porter, *Campaigning with Grant* (New York: The Century Co., 1897; reprint, Time-Life Books, 1981), 308.

Battlefield Foundation, Private Robert Tracey Hixon, First Massachusetts Cavalry, wrote the original ballad. Thomas Buchanan Read wrote "Sheridan's Ride" on November 1, 1864, after viewing the picture "Sheridan's Ride to the Front" in the *Harper's Weekly*.[259] This poem was in northern school textbooks and was part of patriotic events and veteran reunions for decades. Herman Melville wrote "Sheridan at Cedar Creek."[260] This victory helped re-elect Lincoln and earned Sheridan a promotion to major general in the Regular Army. Private Ira Hough, a new recruit in Company E, captured an enemy flag. On October 26, he received the Medal of Honor for this gallant action.

The Eighth Indiana regiment lost four men in this battle: Captain William D. Watson of Company A; First Lt. George W. Quay of Company C; Recruit Daniel Stickler of Company F; and Private John Lytle of Company H. Of the wounded, Lt. Col. Alexander J. Kenny died of his wounds November 26. The Confederates captured ten men: Recruit William G. Beeth, Company A; Private Cyrus Hane (Hanes), Company B; Recruit William H. Hopkins, Company D; Privates Joseph McVicker and John Watson (later supposed dead), Company F; Private Kennedy C. Hollingsworth and Recruit Alexander Jordan, Company G; Private William V. Harvey, Company H; and Privates Joseph T. Hale and Ezra Hunnicut, Company I. The army originally listed Private James W. Alexander missing in action and later declared him killed in action. Cathy Williams had fled with the troops during the Battle of Cedar Creek, but after the battle, she rejoined the regiment.

---

[259] Henry Howe, LL.D, *Historical Collections of Ohio in Two Volumes*, Vol. II (Cincinnati: C.J. Krehbiel, 1908), 392-393.

[260] These four poems can be found in Part Two of this book.

"Fortress Monroe, Old Point Comfort, & Hygeia Hotel, VA in 1861 & 1862. The Key to the South." Lithograph & print by E. Sachse & Co., 1862. Library of Congress

The Eighth Indiana went into winter quarters at Martinsburg. Duty was very boring this winter, as Charles Lawson complained: "I am at loss to [k]now how to pass of the monotony of camp life I cannot get any books or papers and the time passes very slow."[261] The regiment was consolidated into the Fourth Brigade, Second Division, Nineteenth Army Corps. Over the course of the enlistment, many officers had resigned.[262] This resignation problem upset Swain Marshall:

> What few officers we have left are going to resign on account of the reg't. being consolidated; our Captain sent up his papers to day. I think it is a mean trick in them getting us to reenlist and then leave us – they promised to stay with us until

[261] Charles Lawson, camp in Virginia, to friend Jennie Davis, December 28, 1986, Special Collections, Indiana State Library, Indianapolis.

[262] In 1861, First Lt. George W. Parkinson resigned December 30. In 1862, the following officers resigned: Chaplain Amos W. Sanford (August 14); Second Lt. William P. Goolman, Company D (September 27); Second Lt. Milton R. Dungan, Company E (July 16, later amended to an honorable discharge March 6, 1863); First Lt. Franklin Dailey, Company F (November 29); First Lt. Charles S. Ellis (September 25) and Second Lts. John Banister (February 5) and Noble Morris (September 6), Company I; and Second Lt. George H. Dula, Company K (December 7). In 1863, more officers resigned: Surgeon James Ford (June 5); Asst. Surgeon George W. Bruce (January 26); Captain George W.H. Riley (March 4), First Lt. Jesse W. Way (November 13), and Second Lt. Allen O. Neff (June 18) of Company G. Resignations continued in 1864: Adjutant Joseph P. Wiggins (December 28); First Lts. John R. Pearce (February 23) and Cyrus Vanmatre (December 4), and Second Lt. Samuel Mitchell (February 28) of Company E; Second Lt. William W. Mather of Company H (February 8); and First Lt. John H. Hicks of Company K (January 30).

> the thing was settled. I do not know how it will be about the new officers whether they will be appointed by the Major, or elected by the different Companies. don't care much – there will be about thirty non-commissioned officers mustered out of service, I have been trying to get them to muster me out, but the Major says he would rather not let me go. That is what I get for always being at my post – all the good for nothings, will get out, think I shall go to playing off too. They have been trying to get me to take orderly ship but I tell them "I cant see it." I would rather as the saying is, Be a private with a privates pass – than to be an orderly sergeant to kiss the Capt. A—[263]

Later, Marshall did accept a promotion to First Lieutenant on July 19, 1865.

January 9, the Eighth and Eighteenth Indiana and a New Hampshire regiment left Baltimore on the steamer *Ariel*. The rest of the brigade left on another ship. The fog was so heavy; they spent the night at anchor in the bay. They anchored off Fort Monroe a few days later, to take on fifteen days of rations. Marshall wrote about this trip:

> I hear that we will remain here a day or two, have to take on fifteen days rations; that looks like a long spell of Sea-Sickness. I do not know where we are bound for… – don't care much which, any place where it ain't so thundering cold as it is here…. Our Company is in the cabin every thing is as nice as a parlor we have nice bunks to sleep in…I saw Ft. McHenry while at Baltimore, except Ft. Monroe it is the best Fort I ever saw; it is about forty feet higher than the water in the Bay.[264]

The regiment arrived in Savannah, Georgia, January 16 and remained on duty there as part of the District of Savannah, Second Division, First Brigade. Their camp was near Laurel Grove Cemetery. Chaplain Skinner held services every Sabbath afternoon at the Post Hospital Chapel, "here we had Union and Rebel seated side by side, united in the exercises and attentively listening to the truths of the Gospel."[265] They were assigned provost duty (military police):

> We are now at the city (Savannah) on provost duty a soft thing you can immagen for yourself, we are seeing the best of times and every thing is prospering well it is the supposition that we will remain her[e] this summer but you have been a soldier long enough to now that is uncertain[266]

---

[263] Swain Marshall, Camp Russell, Virginia, to friends at home, December 27, 1864.
[264] Swain Marshall, anchored off Fort Monroe, to friends at home, January 12, 1865.
[265] McSpadden, 283.
[266] Henry C. Conley, Savannah, Georgia, to cousin Robert G. Conley, March 3, 1865, Special Collections, William Smith Memorial Library, Indiana Historical Society, Indianapolis.

The news of Lincoln's assassination left the soldiers "terribly exasperated, and it would have needed but a hint from the right quarter, to lay the city in ashes….the officers had to interpose all their persuasion and authority to prevent it."[267]

The regiment mustered out in Savannah on August 28. At the time of their discharge, all soldiers were to receive two copies of their discharge certificates. The paymaster endorsed the amount of their final payment on the back of the certificate and kept one copy of the discharge. Lt. Col. Polk had ordered each company to turn in muster-out rolls to Captain Thompson before they left Darien, Georgia. Thompson would turn these records over to the chief mustering officer of the State at Indianapolis. In 1866, Adjutant General Terrill wrote letters to each company commander requesting these records. Several replies to him in March of 1866 indicated that the rolls were not in their possession. Captain Hughes of Company A had turned his muster roll over to Captain Thompson. Captain Adams of Company D also stated he had turned over all records to Captain Thompson. He had also given four copies to the asst. commander of muster, Second Division, Nineteenth Army Corps, at Winchester in September 1864. Two copies were for the Pay Master General and one copy was for each of the adjutant generals (U. S. A. and Indiana). Captain Vandevender's widow reported that she did not have possession of the muster out rolls for Company E. Captain Widaman of Company G said that he had turned in his muster out rolls to Brig. Gen. Pitcher, Chief Commissary of Musters, State of Indiana; when they did not turn up, he wrote them out by memory in March 1866. Captain Thompson of Company I claimed he had never received a copy of them from the officer who mustered out his company. Fourteen officers and 245 NCOs and enlisted men arrived in Indianapolis September 17, under the command of Lt. Col. John R. Polk. After Governor Morton publicly received them on behalf of the state at the Capitol grounds, the army finally discharged the regiment. "The 8th Indiana Infantry Regiment continues today as a part of the 152 National Guard Regiment."[268] Total enrollment was 1,672 men and officers, with losses of seven officers and eighty-four enlisted killed or mortally wounded, and five officers and 166 enlisted by disease (a total loss of 258 men). Cathy Williams traveled with the regiment to Indiana and continued on

---

[267] McSpadden, 287.
[268] Baker, 439.

west. "I was sent from Virginia to some place in Iowa" and then "to Jefferson Barracks."[269]

When the regiment returned home, the community welcomed them with a reception at the State House. The ladies prepared an outstanding dinner. General Mansfield welcomed them. "The General's remarks were short, pithy and soldierly, and were well received by the men to whom they were addressed."[270] Governor Morton's words of welcome and praise were brief as he was recovering from health issues. They responded with applause. Major General Grose mentioned the possibility of the defeat of the Union. "Had history recorded such an humiliation, he would have been ashamed of himself, of his country, and of his fellow-men."[271] General Washburn, Colonel Brady, and Indiana Attorney General Williamson welcomed them with short speeches. Chaplain Lozier presented two songs. The first one was "in the shape of a humorous, rhythmical history of the meeting of a Johnny Blue-coat, and a regular Southern female, high-strung, high-blooded, and awfully 'snuffed up';" the second song was "his 'Loyal Dixie.'"[272]

---

[269] Tucker, 67. Late in 1866, she would become a Buffalo Soldier under the name of William Cathay until her true identity was discovered two years later.
[270] "Histories of the Regiment," Undated newspaper article, "Eighth Indiana Correspondence."
[271] "Histories of the Regiment," Undated newspaper article, "Eighth Indiana Correspondence."
[272] "Histories of the Regiment," Undated newspaper article, "Eighth Indiana Correspondence."

Chapter 15: Grand Army of the Republic and Memorials

The Soldiers' and Sailors' Monument on Monument Circle, Indianapolis. Photo from Thompson Family Album

After the war, Indiana continued to honor her Civil War veterans. When Dr. Benjamin Franklin Stephenson, a former major and surgeon in the Fourteenth Illinois infantry, founded the Grand Army of the Republic (GAR), Governor Morton encouraged the organization and Indiana became the unofficial national Headquarters for several months. Indianapolis was the site of the first national encampment November 20-21, 1866. Indianapolis held other encampments in 1881, 1893, 1920, 1921, 1942, 1946, including the final encampment (with only six members) in 1949. Marshall enjoyed attending the national encampment in San Francisco in 1886, "I am much pleased with our reception. Your climate and the products of your soil are surprisingly excellent. I am favorably impressed by San Francisco, especially by its architecture and cable cars."[273] The veterans from Wabash named Post 6 in honor of James H. Emmitt, the first soldier from Wabash County to die in the Civil War. Marion named Post 23 in honor of Gen. Shunk. Greenfield named Post 92 in honor of Samuel H. Dunbar. Middletown named Post 119 in honor of George W. Rader. Pendleton named Post 230 in honor of Major

[273] "Veteran Views," *San Francisco Chronicle*, August 7, 1886, 1, https://www.newspapers.com.

Samuel Henry. Jonesboro named Post 409 in honor of Wick Spence (It was also called Magnolia Post.). This was the last GAR Post in Indiana in 1949.

In 1909, the Sixty-ninth Indiana Reunion Association nominated Capt. M. M. Lacey for Indiana GAR department commander "as a loving surprise and in recognition of his long service as secretary of the reunion association."[274] The GAR helped veterans in need. In 1883, "Comrade Justin B. Hodge, Colorado Springs, Colo., writes us that Post No. 22, of that place, has recently sent Captain Tompkins, an old veteran, though not a member of the G. A. R., back to his home at Montrose, Iowa, where he desired to go."[275] In January 1886, Joshua Richardson arrived in Neodosha, Kansas, "destitute of money or means to carry himself farther. Some of the G.A.R. boys took him in hand, made up a purse for him at the installation on Wednesday night kept him until Thursday and sent him, thankful, on his way to Piedmont where he has some relatives."[276] They also helped them get their pensions. The General Pension Law in 1862 allowed only soldiers who could prove combat injuries or diseases while in service to receive a pension based on their rank and level of disability. Pensions for widows or dependents used only the deceased veteran's rank. These pensions changed in 1890 with the Dependent Pension Act. George Graham Post at Seneca, Kansas voted a resolution to demand Congress pass "the service pension bill introduced in the house by Representative Cheadle and in the senate by Senator Ingalls."[277] They felt it was unfair that bondholders received interest payments nearly four times the amount veterans receive in pensions. The bondholders controlled financial legislation, so the veterans felt they should unite to ask for the pensions needed by so many veterans. This allowed pensions for any veteran who became disabled. "By 1906 old age alone became sufficient justification to receive a pension."[278] In 1912, pensioners had to show their pension certificate when they signed their check in front of two witnesses. The pension number on the check and certificate had to be the same. These witnesses also signed a certificate on the back of the check.

---

[274] "To Head the State G.A.R.," *The Indianapolis News*, February 20, 1909, 21, https://www.newspapers.com.
[275] *The National Tribune*, July 12, 1883, 6, https://www.newspapers.com.
[276] "G.A.R. of Kansas," *The Topeka Daily Capital*, January 28, 1886, 2, https://www.newspapers.com.
[277] "Justice: A Service Pension Demanded by the Nation's Defenders," *The Topeka Daily Capital*, March 25, 1890, 5, https://www.newspapers.com.
[278] "Civil War Pensions," accessed March 22, 2012, http://www.civilwarhome.com/pensions.htm.

Southern states provided pensions for their veterans, who did not want to become dependent on the Federal government.

Comrades actively recruited to increase their post memberships and observed Decoration Day (Memorial Day) each year. Some of the veterans liked to use their pensions to bring joy to others. In 1910, William Cochran "celebrated his Christmas by giving to the kindergarten children of the orphans' home, in East Washington street, three dozen apples, three dozen oranges, three dozen bananas, ten pounds of candy and seven pounds of nuts. Mr. Cochran paid for these out of his pension."[279] Marshall Frazier joined the Winfield Scott Post No. 73 in New Jersey. Their cemetery in 1914 had the only concrete flagpole in the country. "The flag pole of which we speak is made of reinforced cement, 60 feet high, 16 inches tapering to 8 inches in diameter and rests on a base 5 feet in diameter."[280]

April 1, 1862, the *Indianapolis Daily Journal* printed a letter to the editor suggesting that: "a monument be erected in Circle Park to all from Indiana who fell in defense of the Union."[281] Governor Morton was the first to support this idea, and suggested Crown Hill Cemetery as the location. In 1875, a reunion of Civil War veterans at Indianapolis, formed the "Monument Association," and raised $1,000 for the monument. Governor Morton died in 1877. In 1882, the GAR raised $1,500 for the monument. In 1887, the legislature granted $200,000.00, chose Circle Park (where all troops had stayed on their way to camps) as the location, and appointed a Monument Commission to choose the design and sculptors. Garrett Shover built the special heavy wagons with wide treads pulled by twelve horses that carried the stones used to build the monument.[282] August 22, 1889, they laid the cornerstone at the northeast corner of the Soldiers' and Sailors' Monument. William H. Short was one of the marshals of the parade that day. He was badly injured when his horse threw him; he died two days later.[283] It took thirteen years to build the monument, which the state dedicated May 15,

---

[279] "Pension for Christmas Cheer," *The Indianapolis News*, December 24, 1910, 2, https://www.newspapers.com.

[280] *The Cambridge City Tribune*, June 11, 1914, 1, https://www.newspapers.com.

[281] Ernestine Bradford Rose, *The Circle: "The Center of Indianapolis"* (Indianapolis: Crippin Printing Corporation, 1971), 43.

[282] E. M. Haas, "Shover Family Prominent Here in Civil War Time," *Palladium-Item*, May 10, 1927, 11, https://www.newspapers.com.

[283] "Sympathy From the President," *Chicago Tribune*, August 30, 1889, 9, https://www.newspapers.com.

1902. This monument was the story of the War Between the States, and was "the first in the nation to be dedicated to the common soldier."[284] The Colonel Eli Lily Civil War Museum opened inside the monument October 1999. The diary of Abner Vanmatre of Company E is on display in this museum. Counties throughout Indiana erected other monuments to honor their deceased soldiers, listing their names and places or battles where they died.

The Soldiers' and Sailors' Monument was designed to honor Civil War veterans, but now honors all veterans from wars prior to World War I. An infantryman stands on the left and the cavalry scout stands on the right. The entrance to the Colonel Eli Lily Civil War Museum is around the corner from the infantryman statue. Photo from Thompson Family Album

Indianapolis also has the distinction of having the first Congressional Medal of Honor Memorial, which was dedicated May 28, 1999. The name of Ira Hough of Company E appears on this memorial.

[284] Rose, 48.

The Medal of Honor Memorial, on the Canal, in Indianapolis. The author is pointing to the location of Ira Hough's name in the second panel from the top. Photo from Thompson Family Album

Ira Hough's marker on the Medal of Honor Memorial. Photo from Thompson Family Album

Hough's name also appears on an Indiana Medal of Honor Memorial inside the World War Memorial at Indianapolis.

The Hoosier Medal of Honor shrine in the World War Memorial, Indianapolis. Photo from Thompson Family Album

The author is pointing to Ira Hough's marker on the Hoosier Medal of Honor shrine. Photo from Thompson Family Album

Reunion Ribbons from the Eighth and Eighteenth Infantry and Second Indiana Battery from the author's private collection. From left to right: Fourteenth, held at Franklin on October, 17, 1889; Eighteenth, held at Indianapolis on September 6, 1893; Twenty-third, held at Bloomington on October 19, 1898; Twenty-fifth, held at Franklin on October 19, 1900; Thirtieth, held at Franklin on October 19, 1905; Thirty-third, held at Middleton on October 20, 1908; Forty-fifth, held at Lafontaine on October 19, 1916; Forty-fourth, held at Franklin on October 18, 1919; and Forty-seventh, held at Winchester on October 19, 1922. Photo from Thompson Family Album

The "Old Brigade" (Eighth and Eighteenth Indiana Infantry and First Indiana Battery) held yearly reunions around Indiana starting in 1876. Many reunions occurred on October 19, the anniversary of the Battle of Cedar Creek.[285] At least three reunions occurred in September: the tenth reunion at Franklin on September 18, 1885; the eighteenth reunion at Indianapolis on September 6, 1893; and the nineteenth reunion at the Winchester Opera House on September 19, 1894. The third reunion occurred at Indianapolis in 1878. The thirteenth reunion occurred at Newcastle on October 19, 1888. The fifteenth, thirty-fifth, and forty-fifth reunion occurred in Richmond on October 16 in 1890 and October 19 in 1910 and 1920. The twenty-first reunion occurred October 23, 1896 at Wabash. The twenty-second reunion occurred on October 19, 1897 at Marion. The twenty-third reunion occurred on October 19, 1898 at Bloomington. The thirty-first reunion occurred October 19, 1906 at Pendleton. The thirty-second reunion occurred at

[285] A private collector owns a number of the reunion ribbons. The twenty-second reunion occurred at Marion in 1897. The twenty-fourth reunion occurred at New Castle in 1899. The twenty-ninth reunion occurred at Greenfield in 1904. The thirty-fourth reunion occurred at Fortville in 1909. The thirty-fifth reunion occurred at Richmond in 1910. The forty-first reunion occurred at Lafontaine in 1916.

Wabash on October 18, 1907. The thirty-third reunion occurred at Middletown on October 20, 1908. At the fortieth reunion at Marion on October 19, 1915, Salathial Bowers was the only veteran still alive who had attended all of the reunions. The forty-first reunion occurred October 19, 1916 in Lafontaine, Indiana. The forty-seventh reunion occurred on October 19, 1922 in Winchester. The fourth, fourteenth, twentieth, twenty-fifth, thirtieth, thirty-fourth, and forty-fourth reunions occurred in Franklin in 1879, 1889, 1895, 1900, 1905, 1909, and 1919. Their twenty-sixth reunion held in Cambridge City on October 17, 1901, had ninety veterans in attendance. "The weather was decidedly favorable and the coming together of these honored old comrades afforded them a day full of many pleasures. Our city wore the American colors and everybody assisted in making the visit of the boys in blue one not soon to be forgotten."[286] They ended the day with a campfire program with music, readings, and other entertainment. George DuBois read an account he wrote about the Battle of Cedar Creek and the Women's Relief Corps provided the meals for the day. Companies also held reunions in their hometowns. Family members also attended these reunions. The daughter of Captain Fred Wysong, Mrs. J. H. Winter, attended the reunion in 1904.[287] That reunion held at Greenfield, had 135 veterans in attendance.

Re-enactors help keep the memory of the Eighth Indiana alive at Civil War reenactments at the various battlefields. On July 25, 1976, Mike Estes portrayed Philander Wisehart, the first Henry County soldier killed in the Civil War, at the reenactment of the Battle of Rich Mountain, staged "as a part of Middletown's Bicentennial celebration."[288]

---

[286] "Soldiers' Reunion," *The Cambridge City Tribune*, October 24, 1901, 2, https://www.newspapers.com.
[287] *The Cambridge City Tribune*, October 20, 1904, 3, https://www.newspapers.com.
[288] "Civil War Reenactment Depicts First Casualty," *Anderson Herald*, July 15, 1976, 9, https://www.newspapers.com.

Reunion of members of Eighth Indiana Infantry, Co. I on October 10, 1886. Seated: unknown child, Joseph Moran Thompson, Jackson G. Stober, Joshua Tucker, unknown, and James Elliott; Standing front row: unknown, William V. Lucas, John H. Lefforge, unknown, Milton Tyner, Dr. Thomas Clement Kimball, Tobias H. Miller, unknown, Henry Gardner, Andrew Jackson Robinson, Oscar A. Wickersham, and David Coble; Standing back row: William F. Lines, Christopher C. Mikesell, Lewis Teal, Erastus Burgett, unknown, Thomas Bridges, Flavius Brewer. Photo courtesy of Eric Lowman

Prior to the war, Congress established the U.S. Naval Asylum in 1811, the U.S. Military Asylum in 1851, and the Government Hospital for the Insane in 1852. Congress established the National Asylum (later changed in 1873 to Home) for Disabled Volunteer Soldiers in 1865, eventually consisting of eleven branches across the country in 1929. A Board of Managers consisting of the president, secretary of war, chief justice, and nine members appointed by Congress "was responsible for establishing the branches, inspecting the sites, monitoring the finances, and reporting to Congress annually."[289] This new system began with four branches: the Eastern Branch in Togus, Maine; the Northwestern Branch at Milwaukee, Wisconsin; Central Branch at Dayton, Ohio; and Southern Branch at Hampton, Virginia. They established National Cemeteries next to

[289] "History of the National Home for Disabled Volunteer Soldiers," Veterans Affairs National Home for Disabled Volunteer Soldiers, accessed April 27, 2012, http://www.nps.gov/nr/travel/veterans_affairs/History.html.

each of these homes. The Eastern branch used the buildings at a former health resort; the other branches built their facilities. Some of these buildings included barracks, icehouse, slaughterhouse, boiler house, conservatory, gas works, bakery, kitchen, dining hall, hospital, greenhouse, laundry, wagon and blacksmith shop, printing plant, fire department, storehouse, carpenter shop, hay barn, cattle barn, gatehouse and sentry box, and homes for the branch's farmer and treasurer. These facilities had training programs for disabled veterans, so some of them could return to private life and earn a living. At first, the homes only admitted veterans who could prove service-related disabilities. This policy changed in the early 1880s to include all disabled veterans. "Many deserving men, the Board held, could not prove a link between their disability and their military service, even though aging and loss of supportive family members might be exacerbating conditions that indeed had their roots in war action."[290] This created a need for more branches: the Western Branch in Leavenworth, Kansas, and the Pacific Branch in Sawtelle, California. States, both in the North and the South, established state homes, but these still could not accommodate all the veterans. Congressman George Steele promoted the establishment of the Marion Branch at Marion, Indiana in 1888. Congressman Joseph Cannon promoted the establishment of the Danville Branch at Danville, Illinois in 1897. Congressman Walter Brownlow helped establish the Mountain Branch in Johnson City, Tennessee in 1901. The mild climate and higher elevation helped those with respiratory problems; it became a tuberculosis sanitarium after WWI. In 1902, they created the Battle Mountain Sanitarium in Hot Springs, South Dakota. This medical facility with its mineral springs provided treatment for those suffering with rheumatism and other diseases. "Men were allowed to remain at the sanitarium only as long as they were benefitting from treatments offered there. They were discharged or transferred to one of the other branches when treatments were no longer necessary or helpful."[291] In 1929, the New York State Soldiers' and Sailors' Home in Bath, New York, established in 1876, became the Bath Branch. Later, a branch also opened in Roseburg, Oregon. Each of these homes is still in existence today as part of the VA system. No Eighth Indiana soldiers entered the homes

[290] Suzanne Julin, "National Home for Disabled Volunteer Soldiers: Assessment of Significance and National Historic Landmark Recommendations," 21.
[291] Julin, 57.

at Bath, Roseburg, or Togus. Most of the soldiers entered the Marion Branch or Dayton Branch, and several soldiers entered more than one branch.

Many veterans applied for admission in the military home of their choice. They could also request transfers or discharges. Admission was a lengthy process.

> When an application for admission is made, a blank is sent to the applicant who is required to fill it out. This is returned to the Home Surgeon, and if, in his opinion, the disability of the applicant entitles him to admission the application is approved by him and referred to the local manager, who passes on the question of admission. If the application is approved by him the veteran is notified and given transportation to the home. On his arrival another examination is required to remove all doubt as to his right to be admitted. Should the Home be filled when the application is approved, it is placed on a waiting list, and the veteran is given a number. As soon as room can be made for him he is notified. [292]

At first, only Union veterans could enter the homes. In 1871, Congress allowed admission of War of 1812 and Mexican War veterans, who did not fight against the Union; in 1900, they added Spanish American War veterans. African American veterans could enter the homes, but the homes kept them segregated. Women entered the homes after 1928. They prohibited Confederate veterans, so the southern States established their own homes.

The homes, organized using a military structure with officers and companies, allowed furloughs, but dropped members who were absent without leave or failed to renew furloughs over sixty days.

The homes issued blue uniforms to the men and loosely followed army regulations. Upon

> admission, each veteran was given a member number and assigned to a company. A company sergeant oversaw each company. The days were regulated with bugle calls waking the men in the morning, calling them to the dining hall, and putting them to sleep at night.[293]

Each home kept records of the veterans in registers, listing their military, domestic, and home history and included other remarks.

---

[292] "Many Applying For Admission Into the National Soldiers' Home at Marion," *The Cincinnati Enquirer*, June 20, 1897, 24, http://www.newspapers.com/image/33298357/.

[293] Trevor K. Plante, "Genealogy Notes: The National Home for Disabled Volunteer Soldiers," *Prologue* 36, no. 1 (Spring 2004), accessed April 27, 2012, http://www.archives.gov/publications/prologue/2004/spring/soldiers-home.html.

> The veteran's military history gives the time and place of each enlistment, rank, company, regiment, time and place of discharge, and nature of disabilities when admitted to the home. The domestic history provides information about the veteran such as birthplace, age, height, various physical features, religion, occupation, residence, marital status, and name and address of nearest relative. The home history provides the rate of pension, date or dates of admission, conditions of readmission, date of discharge, cause of discharge, date and cause of death, and place of burial. General remarks contain information about papers relating to the veteran, such as admission papers, army discharge certificate, and pension certificate. Information was also entered concerning money and personal effects if the member died while in residence at the branch.[294]

Each time a veteran came back to a home, he received the same member number, but if he switched homes, he received a different member number for that home. They originally called members inmates but dropped that term in the 1880s. The early pages in the registers for the Bath National Home lists the pages as "General Register of inmates admitted to the NY State Soldiers' and Sailors' Home."[295]

At first, veterans had the choice to send some of their pension to their wives and children; that changed in 1899 when Congress required they send half their pension home. Veterans could request passes to leave for the weekend or a short time period. Homes punished veterans for deeds of misconduct (drunkenness, being absent without leave "AWOL," or disorderly conduct such as cursing, urinating in public, or exposing themselves). Homes fined veterans, made them serve thirty days labor without pay, or discharged them from the home. Drunkenness became a major problem; trains struck inebriated veterans who were walking on nearby railroad tracks, and veterans visited taverns near the homes. "'And this is not to be wondered at,' the Board's report stated, 'when it is recalled that many of those who find themselves in such destitution as to ask admission to the Home, have been brought to that extreme by the habit of strong drink, in many cases amounting to a disease.'"[296] William Sailors was intoxicated when he died of exposure near the Marion Home on March 1, 1903. The homes changed their no alcohol policies to allow the sale of beer on the grounds, but this ended in 1907 when an appropriations bill denied funding if they sold liquor. The Homes were open to the public

[294] Plante.
[295] "U.S. National Homes for Disabled Volunteer Soldiers, 1866-1938." *Ancestry*. http://search.ancestry.com/search/db.aspx?dbid=1200.
[296] Julin, 27.

and established home bands consisting of members and civilians. "Local citizens enjoyed listening to the regular band concerts as well as picknicking and strolling on the well-kept grounds of the branches, boating or fishing on the lakes, and attending concerts and theatrical productions at the theaters."[297]

[297] Julin, 28.

Chapter 17: Family Ties, Claims to Fame, and Tragic Endings

Many soldiers were relatives. One hundred and ten sets of brothers enlisted in this regiment: Andrew and John Alyea; David, George, and Philip Anshutz; Elias, Levi, and Stephen Bagley; Lewis and Thomas Baxter; Collins and William Bedford; Jacob and James Beroth; Alpheus and Warren Blackman; Benjamin and John Bock; Benjamin and Pelatiah Bond; Flavius and Joel Brewer; Hiram and William Bromagem; Jefferson and Solomon Brown; Thomas and William Burchett; Benedict and John Burkart; Henry and Johnson Burris; Henry, James, and John Bush; Joel and Theodore Butler; George, Richard, and William Craw; Abner and Robert Crosley; Daniel and Joseph Dempsey; Alexander and James Derry; George and Larkin Dula; Alfred and Samuel Edwards; Beniah and William R. Fleming; Burden Fuqua and James L. Fugate; Alfred, Eli, and William Gapen; John W. and William A. Garrison; John C. and Ner Gaunt; John F. and Thomas W. George; Isaac G. and Thomas Gillum; Joseph B. and William Gossett; Thaddeus C. and Thomas B. Greene; John, Marion, and William Griffy; George, John, and Mark Haines; Joseph and Richard L. Hankins; Jacob and John Harnish; Jeremiah, John and Samuel Hicks; Kennedy and Thomas Hollingsworth; Henry and Joseph Hubbard; John and Leander Hummel; David, Thomas W., and William H. Huston; James M. and Oliver Irish; John and William Irwin; John and Richard Jenkins; Avery and Gary Jester; Alexander, Benjamin, and Wesley Jordan; Daniel and George Keene; Albert W. and William H. Keller; Ira J. and William M. Knight; Peter and Richard Lamb; Edwin, Francis, and James Lewark; Adam, Alfred, James, and William Lowder; John and William Lucas; John, Newton, and Stanford Lytle; Samuel and Seth Marsh; Charles, Clifton, and Robert McCallister; Corydon, James, Lorenzo, and William McCallister; George and James McGraw; John and Richard McNew; Adam and Andrew Melrose; Benjamin, Samuel, and Washington Milgrim; Alexander and Simon Miller; George, John S., and Levi Miller; Barney and Elias Mills; Samuel and William Mitchell; Lewis and Uriah Mock; James and Seth Nation; Samuel and William Newbold; James and William Parker; George and William Parkison; George and Thomas Paxson; John and Jasper Newton Pope; Abel, Edward, and James Pugh; John Puderbaugh and William Puterbaugh; Duria and Frank Riddle; Joseph and Robert Rigdon; George and Reuben Riley; Benjamin and Edward Roney; Jesse and William Rooks; Henry, Jasper, and Perry

Rutherford; Ebenezer, John, and William Scotton; Jesse and John Shimer; Frederick and Henry Sittloh; Aaron and William Sleeth; Levi and Wilson Slifer; George and Richard Steele; Eli and Ruel Stephens; John and Joseph Stiles; Henry and Jackson Stober; Curtis and Tilghman Stone; David and Samuel Strahan; James and Jeremiah Sullivan, Junior; Thomas and William Sutton; Albert and John Titherington; Abraham and William Trout; David and John Ulrey; Martin and Reuben Van Buskirk; Abner and Cyrus Van Matre; Henry and Michael Voris; George and Noah Warner; David Wertz and William Werts; Benjamin, Pennel, and William West; Ira and John Wharton; John and Lawson Wiggins; Joseph and William Wiggins; Benjamin and Edward Williams; Alfred and Samuel Wilson; James and Zachariah Windsor; and John and William Yost. Some soldiers were half-brothers: Elijah and George Barrett; Anthony and Thomas Leakey; Abraham and Cephas Reeve. Some were cousins: John and Thomas Carmin; George and Henry Rader; Alfred and Avery Riggs; Isaac and William Study; and Henry and John Wyman. Artemus Bond was the cousin of Benjamin and Pelatiah Bond. David Craw was the cousin of George, Richard, and William Craw. Andrew J. Fleming was the cousin of Beniah and William R. Fleming. John McCallister and the two sets of McCallister brothers were cousins. Charles A. Fleming was the second cousin of Andrew J., Beniah, and William R. Fleming. Nelson Parkison was the cousin of George and William Parkison. Levi Shoemaker was the cousin of Henry Shoemaker. Lafayette Slifer was the cousin of Levi and Wilson Slifer. Isaac and William Study were the cousins of Fernando and Lorenzo Study. David Dove was the uncle of William Dove. Dr. James Ford was the uncle of William Wallace Ford. Abner and Cyrus Van Matre were the uncles of Cyrus Pittser. Jesse Scott was the uncle of William C. Scott. John Showers was the uncle of John, Samuel, and Jeremiah Hicks. Some soldiers were father and son. Silas Colgrove was the father of Theodore Colgrove. Merrick Conklin was the father of Joseph Conklin. John Farra was the father of William A. Farra. Grimes Holcom was the father of James Holcom. Thomas W. Huston was the father of John B. Huston. Abner Leach was the father of Marshall Leach. William Rutherford was the father of Henry, Jasper, and Perry Rutherford. George Sharp was the father of Wilkerson Sharp. Jeremiah "Jerry" Sullivan was the father of James and Jeremiah Sullivan, Junior. John Swafford was the father of Daniel Swafford. Ethan Taylor was the father of Alonzo Taylor. Some soldiers became relatives by marriage. Hiram Brattain married Philander Wisehart's older sister before the war. Charles Gunn married John Alyea's sister before the war. Joseph M. Thompson married a daughter of Dr. James Ford before the war. John A. Griffey married the sister of the Butler brothers before the war. The sister of Corydon, James, Lorenzo, and William McCallister married Hiram Vandevender before the war. William R. Myers married the daughter of William H. Mershon before the war. James Cummings married William Cummings' daughter during the war. Lewis G. Kiess married the sister of Francis Mosbaugh during the war. After the war, John Anderson married the sister of the Bush brothers. George Harrison Black married the sister of John S. Welling after the war. Lee O. Harris married the sister of Thomas Benton Foster. Frank Swiggett married the sister of Frank Mosbaugh after the war. Benjamin Williams married a daughter of Dr. James Ford after the war.

Several soldiers had a connection to Indiana's famous poet James Whitcomb Riley. John Anderson and his wife Mary lived a few blocks down the street from Riley's home in Greenfield. Lee Harris was Riley's favorite schoolteacher. George Riley was his uncle. Reuben Riley was his father. Riley read the poem listed in this book to the veterans at their reunions. One soldier, Archibald Harrison, was the grandson of President William Henry Harrison and the brother of future president Benjamin Harrison. James and Seth Nation were related to Carrie Nation. She married their brother David.

Patriotism was important to these men. When flag bearer John Swafford fell mortally wounded at Vicksburg, his son Daniel or Samuel Webb grabbed the flag, planted it on the ramparts of the fort, and carried it for the rest of that conflict. Ira Hough captured a battle-flag during the Battle of Cedar Creek and received the Medal of Honor for this deed on October 26, 1864. Andrew Fuller, who had served as flag bearer for the regiment at Rich Mountain, had the honor of raising the flag for a Boy Scout parade and program on May 6, 1917. Reuben Riley read Lincoln's Second Inaugural Address to the crowds waiting for Lincoln's funeral train to pass through Greenfield, Indiana.

For three months in 1861, John H. Popp served in Governor Morton's Secret Service. During the summer and winter of 1864, Thomas Elliott served as one of Governor Morton's Secret Detectives, keeping him informed of the activities of the Sons of Liberty, until their conviction at the Treason Trials. Silas Colgrove served as president of the Indianapolis Treason Trials commission in 1864. Reuben Riley served as judge advocate general and was in charge of several cases involving members of the Knights of the Golden Circle. Frank Kerlin was in the party of soldiers who captured John Hunt Morgan.

Collins Bedford was a self-made man; he became a well-known physician and professor in Indianapolis and was active in many organizations. He also started "the only Physio-Medical Wholesale Drug House in the United States," the "C.T. Bedford Drug House," which did wholesale business across the country.[298] Noah Hutton and his brother built the first thresher in Indiana.[299]

David Potts died in the explosion of the Steamer *City of Madison* on August 19, 1863. Martin Frazee and Albert Lemon survived the explosion of the Steamer *Sultana* on April 27, 1865. Thaddeus Greene survived the war without injury; however, he became severely injured when a cannon he was firing during a Republican rally in 1866 exploded, which led to the amputation of both hands. He wore artificial hands with special holes in the palm to hold eating utensils and learned to write again.

Several soldiers in this regiment committed suicide. William Baker committed suicide using his gun on October 20, 1861 in Syracuse, Missouri. Charles O. Howard took 1 1/2 ounces of laudunum to commit suicide on November 22, 1869 in Milwaukee. Caleb Squires hung himself on October 1, 1880. Caleb Garrett threw himself under an electric streetcar to commit suicide in Tacoma, Washington on December 8, 1892. John Morris hung himself in an outhouse in May 1894. George Travis blew his stomach out with a shotgun on September 28, 1903. Colonel Charles S. Parrish took an overdose of morphine in September 1906. John Zent shot himself in the head while living in the Marion National Home and died May 8, 1907. George Osborn drank carbolic acid to commit suicide in his home on December 14, 1908. John Alyea had been in declining health for several years. His youngest son had died in 1899 and his wife had died in 1910. He cut a gash in his arm above the wrist but failed to sever a major blood vessel. His daughter-in-law arrived at the home with food and found him bleeding at 3 o'clock on

---

[298] George Hazzard, *Hazzard's History of Henry County, Indiana 1822-1906, Military Edition*, Volume I (New Castle: George Hazzard, 1906), 272.

[299] "Noah Hutton, 83, PIONEER TELEPHONE MANAGER, DIES," *The Indianapolis News*, July 30, 1928, 3, http://www.newspapers.com.

February 20, 1915. She ran home to get her husband, but before they made it back to his home, Alyea shot himself in the head with a 22-calibre rifle. He died at 6 o'clock. "The mind of the deceased had been noticeably affected for several days, it is said."[300]

Several soldiers experienced poisoning. William Bankhead drank poisoned water while in the service and died October 26, 1861. Darius Riddle drank poisoned water at Georgetown, Missouri in the fall of 1861 and received a disability discharge. John Confair and William Walker drank poisoned water at Sulfur Rock, Missouri, but they recovered. John Jackson died of poisoning while in the service in 1863. Absalom Antrim died a very painful death when muriatic acid entered a scratch on his leg in 1884. He had been moving a pile of bricks saturated with the acid.[301] Francis Oldaker and his family became violently ill after eating a meal of pork and beans in 1890. He had grown the beans on his farm and the family and others had eaten them before. The doctor did not arrive until early the next morning and he died within a few minutes of his arrival. The rest of the family had taken emetics (medicine to cause vomiting) and recovered. The coroner sent his stomach to Indianapolis for analysis, but it appeared to be an accidental poisoning.[302]

Several soldiers drowned. Dennis Guiney fell off a steamboat and drowned on September 16, 1862 at Helena, Arkansas. Thompson McCune missed his step crossing between steamers near Island 26 and drowned on April 8, 1863. William Wiggins was returning from a furlough the summer of 1863 to rejoin his company at Helena, Arkansas, when the boat snagged and sunk in two minutes. He drowned and the army fired siege guns to raise his body, so his father could take him home for burial. John A. Jennings, Wilford Massey, and Francis Miller drowned on March 13, 1864 in Saluria Bayou, Texas and Matagorda Bay, Mississippi. While on a furlough home, William Hill walked off the upper deck of the steamer Mississippi and drowned on June 3, 1864. Alfred B. Cook was lost at sea when the steamer *Gen. Lyon* sank off Cape Hatteras on March 30, 1865.

---

[300] "Man Past Eighty Shoots Himself: John A. Alyea Made Two Attempts to End Life and Last was Successful. The Bullet Went Though [sic] His Head," *Greenfield Daily Reporter*, February 22, 1915, 1, https://www.newspapers.com.
[301] "Local Notes," *The Herald-Despatch*, September 6, 1884, 3, https://www.newspapers.com.
[302] *Cambridge City Tribune*, April 17, 1890, 3 and April 24, 1890, 3. https://www.newspapers.com.

Lightning hit Levi H. Miller's barn in July 1873 and destroyed the barns, corn, hay, tools, and three horses. While unhitching his horses, Charles Hartner was hit by lightning in 1877, killing one horse and fracturing his jaw; he survived. A tornado blew Charles Fleming's store off its foundation and wrecked his home on April 1, 1887. He rebuilt the store and started over. A massive tornado struck in Kansas on May 1, 1895 and destroyed everything in its eighteen-mile path, including the home of William Armstrong, killing him, and leaving his wife seriously injured. Two storms with large hail on July 6, 1907 injured Charles W. Wynn and damaged the roof of his home and three roofs of an outbuilding. A bad storm with high winds in Chicago on May 7, 1908 knocked down and caused the death of John Lucas, who also suffered from heart disease. Cornelius F. Harrison died in a railroad accident near Lafayette, Indiana in October 1864. Virgil A. Cook was uncoupling railroad cars in Kansas, when he fell under the wheels and died on November 20, 1891. Daniel Duffee died in a hotel fire in Council Bluffs, Arkansas in 1876. The Pension office declared Henry Garrison dead by mistake in June 1901. He died in a house fire on January 29, 1929.

Several soldiers were involved in murders. Samuel Edwards shot and killed John W. McCarthey on September 16, 1862 at Helena, Arkansas. A fellow soldier shot and killed Alpheus Davis on January 18, 1865 at Pulaski, Tennessee. Charles Peirson Clinton (alias Pinson W. Clanton) killed his first wife on March 25, 1872, when they got into a drunken fight. He spent two years in jail and six years in the Tennessee Penitentiary before receiving a pardon from the governor. John Little was drinking when he was fatally stabbed by a friend during a quarrel on August 13, 1873. Thomas Benton Foster was the victim of a baffling murder case. Someone murdered and robbed him as he slept in the back of his store in Tuscola, Illinois on April 6, 1913.

The Eighth Indiana regiment deserves great honor for its role in the Civil War. Led by capable officers, brave men who fought for their loved ones at home filled its ranks. Lizzie Pollock, sister of Joseph W. Pollock of Company C, wrote about a speech made in Richmond in August 1863:

> Gen. Grant is praised highly for the victory won at Vicksburg. A great many soldiers from that department are here on furloughs. Col. Bennett of the 69th is also here, he made a political speech on main street last Saturday evening. He is

> not in favor of the officers claiming all the honor. He says the honor and bravery belongs to the privates, I think he is about right on that score don't you?[303]

The study of any regiment's history requires more than official reports of officers and historical studies. Enlisted men's writings should play a part in telling the story of the regiment, since they are the ones who did the fighting in those battles. Any of these records can have errors, but careful study and comparison of all of these sources can lead to a better understanding of the history of the regiment.

---

[303] Lizzie Pollock, Richmond, Indiana, to Robert S. Conley (Nineteenth Indiana Regiment), August 24, 1863, Robert S. Conley correspondence, Special Collections, William Smith Memorial Library, Indiana Historical Society, Indianapolis.

Part II: POEMS ABOUT THE BATTLE OF CEDAR CREEK AND BY JAMES WHITCOMB RILEY

Sheridan's Ride. Battle of Cedar Creek by Alfred R. Waud. Library of Congress

"Battle of Cedar Creek, Oct. 19, 1864"
By C.A. Savage, Co. "K", 8th INDIANA

Old Early camped at Fisher's Hill,
Resolved some Yankee blood to spill;
He chose his time when Phil. was gone,
The Yankee camp to fall upon.
At night, like thief, of sense bereft,
He marched his troops around our left,
With orders strict unto his boys,
To nothing take t' would made a noise.

Get out of the way, says Gen. Early,
I've come to drive you from the Valley.

While they were on their mission bent,
We Yanks were sleeping in our tents;
Until the Rebs, with rousing volley,
Warned us that sleep was death and folly.
Old Early carried out his plan,
Surprising Crook and his command,
Who had not time their lines to form,
So sudden came the rebel storm.

"Battle of Ceader Creek"
By Robert Tracey Hixon, 1st MA Cav.

Old Early camped on Fisher's Hill,
Resolved some Yankee Blood to spill.
He chose his time when Phil was gone
The Yankee Camp to fall upon.

Get out of the way says Gen Early
I've come to drive you from the Valley -
All night like a theaf of sence bererft
He mached his troops around our left
With orders strict unto his men
To nothing take t'would make a noise.
While thay were on there mission bent
We Yanks were sleeping in our tents
Untill the Reb's with a rousing volley
Warned us to sleep was death and folly
Old Early carried out his plan
Supprising Crook and his comand
Whou had not time there ranks to fill
So sudden came the Rebel storm
Now the Ninth corps all had run

Now, at the rising of the sun,
Old Early thought it jovial fun;
But Gen. Grover, (God bless his name)
Said he would help them play the game.
He formed a line the pike along,
To check old Early and his throng;
And here he held the rebs at bay,
'Til he was flanked from every way.

This gave the Sixth Corps time to form,
Who bravely faced the leaden storm;
'Til the other Corps' had time to rally,
To stop the rebels in the Valley.
The Johnnies thought the victory won,
And their usual pillaging begun;
Robbing the dead and wounded too,
As none but Southern bloods can do.

Now when the day was almost lost,
God sends a reinforcing host;
The host he sends is but a man,
But that's the noble Sheridan.
On, on he comes with lightning speed,
Crying, who hath done this awful deed;
He'd better fare 'neath Southern skies,
Who dares my sleeping camp surprise.

Get out of the way says Phil. to Early,
You've come too late to get the Valley.

Ah, there another sound is heard,
And Liberty's the rallying word;
And every heart is filled with pride,
To see their gallant leader ride.
Saying "Form quick – the fight renew,
And see what right with wrong can do;
By night our camp we will regain,
And vengeance have for those that's slain."

Then orders flew from left to right,
And glorious was the evening sight;
The rebels fled 'mid cannon's roar,
Losing all they'd gained & thousands more.

Old Early thought it joviel fun
But Gen Grover, God bless his name
Said he would help them play the game.
He formed a line the Pike along
To check Old Early and his throng
And here he held the Rebs at bay
Till he was flanked from every way.
This gave the sixth corps time to form
Whou Bravely faced the Rebel storm
Till the ninthed corps had time to Rally
To stop the Rebels in the Valley
Now the Rebs thought the victory won
And there usual Pillageing begun
Robbing the dead and wounded to
As none but Suthern Bloods can do
Now the day was almost lost
But God sent ous a reinforceing host
The host he send is but a man
But thats the noble Sheridan
Now turns tune say's Phil to Early
You come to late to get the Valley.
On on he came with lightning speed
Crying who hath done this awfull deed
He better fare neath southern skys
Who dars my sleeping camp supprise.
Get out of the way say's Phil to Early
Youve come to late to get Valley
Ah there is sound is herd
And liberty is the rallying word
And every heart is filed with pride
To see there gallant leader ride.
Saying form quick the fight will renew
And see what right with rong can do
By night our camp we will regain
And vengance have for those that slain
The orders flew from left to right
And glorious was the evening sight
The Rebels flew mid canons roar
Losing all thay'd and thousands more[304]

[304] Robert Tracey Hixon, "Battle of Ceader Creek," Cedar Creek Battlefield Foundation.

Round their flank brave Custer flew,
As other Cavalry ne'er could do;
Capturing guns, well nigh three score,
Including those we'd lost before.

Three cheers for Emory, Crook and Wright,
Torbett, Merret, and General Dwight;
Three for Custer and his command,
Our Union and General Sheridan.
God bless our Nation and her sons,
And may this bloody war be done;
May North and South, United stand,
As once they were a happy band.[305]

[305] C.A. Savage, *Battle of Cedar Creek, Oct. 19, 1864*, Special Collections, William Smith Memorial Library, Indiana Historical Society, Indianapolis.

Sheridan's Ride

By Thomas Buchanan Read

Up from the South, at break of day,
Bringing to Winchester fresh dismay,
The affrighted air with a shudder bore,
Like a herald in haste, to the chieftain's door,
The terrible grumble, and rumble, and roar,
Telling the battle was on once more,
And Sheridan twenty miles away.

And wider still those billows of war
Thundered along the horizon's bar;
And louder yet into Winchester rolled
The roar of that red sea uncontrolled,
Making the blood of the listener cold,
As he thought of the stake in that fiery fray,
With Sheridan twenty miles away.

But there is a road from Winchester town,
A good, broad highway leading down;
And there, through the flush of the morning light,
A steed as black as the steeds of night
Was seen to pass, as with eagle flight;
As if he knew the terrible need,
He stretched away with the utmost speed;
Hills rose and fell, but his heart was gay,
With Sheridan fifteen miles away.

Still sprang from those swift hoofs, thundering South,
The dust, like smoke from the cannon's mouth;
Or the trail of a comet, sweeping faster and faster,
Foreboding to traitors the doom of disaster,
The heart of the steed and the heart of the master
Were beating like prisoners assaulting their walls,
Impatient to be where the battlefield calls;
Every nerve of the charger was strained to full play,
With Sheridan only ten miles away.

Under his spurning feet, the road
Like an arrowy Alpine river flowed,
And the landscape sped away behind
Like an ocean flying before the wind;
And the steed, like a barque fed with furnace ire,
Swept on, with his wild eye full of fire.
But, lo! He is nearing his heart's desire;
He is snuffing the smoke of the roaring fray,

With Sheridan only five miles away.

The first that the general saw were the groups
Of stragglers, and then the retreating troops;
What was done? what to do? A glance told him both.
Then striking his spurs, with a terrible oath,
He dashed down the line 'mid a storm of huzzas,
And the wave of retreat checked its course there, because
The sight of the master compelled it to pause.
With foam and with dust the black charger was gray;
By the flash of his eye and the red nostril's play,
He seemed to the whole great army to say,
"I have brought you Sheridan all the way
From Winchester down to save the day!"

Hurrah! hurrah for Sheridan!
Hurrah! hurrah for horse and man!
And when their statues are placed on high,
Under the dome of the Union sky,
The American soldier's Temple of Fame,
There, with the glorious general's name,
Be it said, in letters both bold and bright,
"Here is the steed that saved the day,
By carrying Sheridan into the fight,
From Winchester, twenty miles away!"[306]

[306] *The Columbia Book of Civil War Poetry*, Richard Marius, ed., (New York: Columbia University Press, 1994), 184-186.

Sheridan at Cedar Creek
By Herman Melville

Shoe the steed with silver
        That bore him to the fray,
When he heard the guns at dawning—
        Miles away;
When he heard them calling, calling—
        Mount! nor stay:
                Quick, or all is lost;
                They've surprised and stormed the post,
                They push your routed host—
Gallop! retrieve the day.

House the horse in ermine—
        For the foam-flake blew
White through the red October;
        He thundered into view;
They cheered him in the looming,
        Horseman and horse they knew.
                The turn of the tide began,
                The rally of bugles ran,
                He swung his hat in the van;
        The electric hoof-spark flew.

Wreathe the steed and lead him—
        For the charge he led
Touched and turned the cypress
        Into amaranths for the head
Of Philip, king of riders,
        Who raised them from the dead.
                The camp (at dawning lost),
                By eve, recovered – forced,
                Rang with laughter of the host
        At belated Early fled.

Shroud the horse in sable—
For the mounds they heap!
There is firing in the Valley,
        And yet no strife they keep;
It is the parting volley,
It is the pathos deep.
        There is glory for the brave
        Who lead, and nobly save,
        But no knowledge in the grave
Where the nameless followers sleep.[307]

---

[307] *The Columbia Book of Civil War Poetry*, 187-189.

A Summer Sunrise
By James Whitcomb Riley

AFTER LEE O. HARRIS
The master-hand whose pencils trace
This wondrous landscape of the morn,
Is but the sun, whose glowing face
Reflects the rapture and the grace
Of inspiration Heaven-born.

And yet with vision-dazzled eyes,
I see the lotus-lands of old,
Where odorous breezes fall and rise,
And mountains, peering in the skies,
Stand ankle-deep in lakes of gold.

And, spangled with the shine and shade,
I see the rivers raveled out
In strands of silver, slowly fade
In threads of light along the glade
Where truant roses hide and pout.

The tamarind on gleaming sands
Droops drowsily beneath the heat;
And bowed as though aweary, stands
The stately palm, with lazy hands
That fold their shadows round his feet.

And mistily, as through a veil,
I catch the glances of a sea
Of sapphire, dimpled with a gale
Toward Colch's blowing, where the sail
Of Jason's Argo beckons me.

And gazing on and father yet,
I see the isles enchanted, bright
With fretted spire and parapet,
And gilded mosque and minaret,
That glitter in the crimson light.

But as I gaze, the city's walls
Are keenly smitten with a gleam
Of pallid splendor, that appalls
The fancy as the ruin falls
In ashen embers of a dream.

Yet over all the waking earth
        The tears of night are brushed away,
And eyes are lit with love and mirth,
And benisons of richest worth
        Go up to bless the new-born day.[308]

[308] James Whitcomb Riley, *The Complete Poetical Works of James Whitcomb Riley* (Indianapolis: The Bobbs-Merrill Company, 1937), 80. This poem was written in honor of Lee O. Harris.

Father William
By James Whitcomb Riley

A NEW VERSION BY LEE O. HARRIS AND JAMES WHITCOMB RILEY

"You are old, Father William, and though one would think
All the veins in your body were dry,
Yet the end of your nose is red as a pink;
I beg your indulgence, but why?"

"You see," Father William replied, "in my youth -
'Tis a thing I must ever regret -
It worried me so to keep up with the truth
That my nose has a flush on it yet."

"You are old," said the youth, "and I grieve to detect
A feverish gleam in your eye;
Yet I'm willing to give you full time to reflect.
Now, pray, can you answer me why?"

"Alas," said the sage, "I was tempted to choose
Me a wife in my earlier years,
And the grief, when I think that she didn't refuse,
Has reddened my eyelids with tears."

"You are old, Father William," the young man said,
"And you never touch wine, you declare,
Yet you sleep with your feet at the head of the bed;
Now answer me that if you dare."

"In my youth," said the sage, "I was told it was true,
That the world turned around in the night;
I cherished the lesson, my boy, and I knew
That at morning my feet would be right."

"You are old," said the youth, "and it grieved me to note,
As you recently fell through the door,
That 'full as a goose' had been chalked on your coat;
Now answer me that I implore."

"My boy," said the sage, "I have answered you fair,
While you stuck to the point in dispute,
But this is a personal matter, and there
Is my answer - the toe of my boot."[309]

---

[309] James Whitcomb Riley, *The Complete Poetical Works of James Whitcomb Riley* (Indianapolis: The Bobbs-Merrill Company, 1937), 73. James wrote this poem with Lee O. Harris.

Decoration Day on the Place
By James Whitcomb Riley

It's lonesome—sorto' lonesome,—it's a *Sund'y-day* to me,
It 'pears-like—more'n any day I nearly ever see!
Yit, with the Stars and Stripes above, a-flutterin' in the air,
On ev'ry Soldier's grave I'd love to lay a lilly thare.

They say, though, Decoration Days is giner'ly observed
'Most *ev'rywheres*—espeshally by soldier-boys that's served.—
But me and Mother's never went—we seldom git away,—
In p'int o' fact, we're *allus* home on *Decoration Day*.

They say the old boys marches through the streets in colum's grand,
A-follerin' the old war-tunes they're playin' on the band—
And citizuns all jinin' in—and little childern, too—
All marchin', under shelter of the old Red White and Blue.—

With roses! roses! roses!—ev'rybody in the town!—
And crowds o' little girls in white, jest fairly loaded down!—
Oh! don't THE Boys know it, from theyr camp acrost the hill?—
Don't they see theyr com'ards comin' and the old flag wavin' still?

Oh! can't they hear the bugul and the rattle of the drum?—
Ain't they no way under heavens they can rickollect us some?
Ain't they no way we can coax 'em, through the roses, jest to say
They know that ev'ry day on earth's theyr Decoration Day?

We've tried that—me and Mother,—whare Elias takes his rest,
In the orchurd—in his uniform, and hands acrost his brest,
And the flag he died fer, smilin' and a-ripplin' in the breeze
Above his grave—and over that,—*the robin in the trees*!

And *yit* it's lonesome—lonesome!—It's a *Sund'y-day*, to *me*,
It 'pears-like—more'n any day I nearly ever see!—
Still, with the Stars and Stripes above, a-flutterin' in the air,
On ev'ry soldier's grave I'd love to lay a lily thare.[310]

[310] James Whitcomb Riley, *The Complete Poetical Works of James Whitcomb Riley* (Indianapolis: The Bobbs-Merrill Company, 1937), 471. Riley published this poem in *Neighborly Poems* in 1883. Riley delivered this poem to the Civil War veterans at GAR gatherings.

Lee O. Harris
Christmas Day - 1909
by James Whitcomb Riley

O SAY not he is dead,
        The friend we honored so;
Lift up a grateful voice instead
        And say: He lives, we know ---
We know it by the light
        Of his enduring love
Of honor, valor, truth and right,
        And man, and God above.

Remember how he drew
        The child-heart to his own,
And taught the parable anew,
        And reaped as he had sown;
Remember with what cheer
        He filled the little lives,
And stayed the sob and dried the tear
        With mirth that still survives.

All duties to his kind
        It was his joy to fill;
With nature gentle and refined,
        Yet dauntless soul and will,
He met the trying need
        Of every troublous call,
Yet high and clear and glad indeed
        He sung above it all.

Ay, listen! Still we hear
        The patriot song, the lay
Of love, the woodland note so dear ---
        These will not die away,
Then say not he is dead,
        The friend we honor so,
But lift a grateful voice instead
        And say: He lives, we know.[311]

---

[311] James Whitcomb Riley, *The Complete Poetical Works of James Whitcomb Riley* (Indianapolis: The Bobbs-Merrill Company, 1937), 758-759. James wrote this poem after the death of Lee Harris.

Part III: CORRESPONDENCE

8th Indiana Volunteer Infantry regiment correspondence
Roll No. 3
Records of the Adjutant General of Indiana
Indiana State Archives
Indianapolis, Indiana

(Some letters on this microfilm reel belong to other regiments but are included in this transcription since they were on this reel.)

Adjutant General's Office,

INDIANA VOLUNTEER MILITIA,
INDIANAPOLIS, __________ 1861/

This is to certify that John Ruess was Elected Capt. Co H 8th Regt. Vice Cary Promoted
Luther H. Harmon 1st Lieut. Co. H 8th Regt Vice Ruess Promoted
James R. Smith 2nd Lieut. 8th Regt Co H Vice Harman Promoted

Benj. F. Elwood was elected Capt of Co ( ) 8th Regt. Vice Tykle Resigned
Henry Rader 1st Lieut. Co. ( ) 8th Regt.Vice Elwood Promoted

David Shunk
Lieut. Col. 8th Regt. Ind Vols.

[back] John Ruess and others

* * * * *

Me, the sword Judges and Clerks in our election held in the Court House in Muncie, Delaware Co. Ind. by the Military Company styled "The Delaware Guards," to fill offices of Captain, 1, 2, & 3 Lieutenants, do hereby certify that at said election held on the 16th April, 1861, at place aforesaid, that Tom J. Brady receiving a majority of all the votes cast, was duly elected Captain of said Company, And that Geo. W. Edgerle received a majority of the votes for the office of 1 Lieutenant: – William Fisher for 2 Lieutenant: - and John H. Harlan for 3 Lieutenant.

And that, in every respect, the election was conducted as authorized by the Laws of Indiana:

Geo. W. Edgerle }
Jos. Shipley } Judges
Jno. H. Harlan }

Cyrus M. Newcomb }
Clark M. Armstrong } Clerks

Muncie Delaware Co. Ind.
April 16th, 1861

(State of Indiana } SS

Delaware County } I John H. Ellis an acting Justice of the peace within and for said county do certify that the above named Judges and Clerks were severally sworn to as the law directs Prior to the holding of the Said election
Attess. April 16th, 1861 John H. Ellis. J.P. {Seal}

[back] 3 mos. 8th Regt
Delaware Guards
Co. "D"
Com…ed 16 April
to
Thomas J. Brady Capt.
Geo W. Edgerle 1st L
Wm Fisher 2d
John H. Harlan 3d

* * * * *

Roll of Members of Delaware Guards

Geo. W. Edgerle
Tom J. Brady
John McConnell
John H. Ellis
David Nation
Joseph Kirk
John C. Taylor
Clark W. Anthony
John H. Harlan
Edward Pugh
James Pugh
Abel Pugh
William Berry
John Ridge
John Randal
Joseph Brown
George Darracott
Charles Morehouse
John Mattox
Andrew O'Daniel
Thomas Paxon
Joseph Gessell
John Kirk
Richard M. Martin
John Irwin
John C ---cle
John Shafer
George W. Taylor
William Hatfield
John A. Gilbert
Samuel Sullivan
Cyrus W. Newcomb
James Ennis
William Fisher
Miles Smith
Emanuel Aldridge
Henry Smith
I. W. Ellis
James Brice
Asbury Kirwood
James Cummerford
Robert Galbraith
Joseph Shipley
S. Peterman
Isaac Shoe
Andrew Ridenour

* * * * *

Butler Sears
Geo. W. Eastman
Isaac Wittimire
John E. Williams

George Taylor
Clermont C. Smith
John Turner
Jeremiah Thomas
Alex. Wasson
David Sloniker
Samuel Miller
Samuel Williams
John Charles
Isaac Cowgill
Reuben Conner
Allen Miller
Michael Mattox
John H. Walker
Samuel Carmine
Elijah Carmine
Wm. H. Harvey
Charles Miller
Jacob Pierpont
C-------f Kigrice
Matthew Hughes
Tom Corbet
George Coffin
Henry Klossimire
George H. Harlan
Uriah Harrold
John Fulhart
Alfred Rhodes
Edward Smith
Nathan Branson
Thomas Gilbert
Nathan Branson
Sidney Jewett
James Brown

* * * * *

Wabash Ind. April 17th 1861.

Sir,

I send herewith, by Samuel G. Thompson, M.D. a muster roll, rank and file of Relief Guard number one of Wabash County.

It will be impossible for the corps to report themselves at your rendezvous, ready for service before Saturday night 20th inst.

If it is absolutely necessary that they report themselves before that time we must disband. If not, advise me by telegraph.

We would prefer to have further time, if consistant with the service, say until wednesday next week. At all events please be kind enough to give <u>definite postitive</u> orders in the premises.

In haste, but very
Respectfull to [---------   -------------]
Charles S. Parrish

To Lew Wallace
Adj. Genl.
Ind. Militia

[back] 36
Capt. Parrish

* * * * *

Head Quarters of the "Marion Guards"
Marion April 18th 1861

To his Excellency
Gov. Morton,

The undersigned duly elected to act as Judge and clerk of an election held by the members of the Marion Guard a volunteer Military company, at Marion Grant County Indiana, for the purpose of electing one Captain, one first Lieutenant, and one second Lieutenant for said company, do certify that, David Shunk was duly elected captain, Oliver H.P. Cary was duly elected 1st Lieutenant and John Ruess was duly elected 2d Lieutenant.

In witness whereof I have hereunto set our names this 18th day of April 1861, - the same day of said election.

D.S.T. Cogin Judge
J. A. Stritch Clerk

[back] 3 mos. 8 regt.
Marion Guards
Co. "B"

* * * * *

Greenfield Ind April 19, 1861. [------ -----]

To His Excellency Gov. Morton,

This will certify that at a meeting of the Union Guard of Hancock County, volunteers under the call of the President of the United States, held at the Court-House in Greenfield, on Friday, April 19, 1861, the following gentlemen were duly elected as officers of said company, to wit.

Reuben A. Riley, Captain
Henry G. Rariden, 1st Lieutenant
Geo. W. H. Riley, 2nd "
Wm. R. Walls, Sr. 3rd "
E.S. Duncan Orderly Sargent
L. O. Harris 2nd "
P. Bond 3rd "
M.M. Stevensen 4th "
Arthur V. Brown 5th "
The corporals to be appointed by the Captain

William Mitchell, Secretary.

A.K. Brankane (?), Capt.
Chairman

[back] Union Guards
Greenfield

* * * * *

State of Indiana:
Randolph County:

We the undersigned Clerks of the Election of the Randolph County Guards, certify that the following gentlemen were elected as officers for said company, to wit,

Silas Colgrove, Captain
E. M. Ives 1st Lieutenant
Allen O. Neff 2nd "
R. W. Hamilton 3rd " (this was crossed out)

In testimony whereof we hereunto set our hands, this 20th day of April A.D. 1861.

Thomas J. Lee
A. O. Neff

I Joseph A. Kirk, do certify that the foregoing is a true copy of the certificate reported to me.

Joseph A. Kirk
Colonel

[back] 3 mos. 8th Regt.
Capt. Silas Colgrove
Co. C.
Cert. of election of Officers

Camp Morton
April. 20th 1861

I do hereby certify that Thomas J. Lee was this day unanimously Elected Captain of the Randolph County guards.

Silas Colgrove

* * * * *

[one side] 8th Regt.
Capt. Silas Colgrove
Co. D
Cert. of election of Officers

Camp Morton
April 27th, 1861

We hereby certify that Thos J. Lee was duly elected Captain of Randolph Co. Guards this Morning by a vote of 44 to 29.

Attess
A.O. Neff
E. M. Ives
(to fill Colgrove vacancy)
Lieuts of Camp

[back] 3y
Randolph County Guards
C---------
April 20/61

* * * * *

Newcastle Ind April 20th/ 61
L. Wallis Adj. Gen Sir

I have the honor to present to you the Muster Roll and Organization of my Company the Company Organized by Electing the following Officers for Commission

Captain	Frederick Tykle
First Lieutenant	Henry Ray
Second Lieutenant	Joseph W. Connell

[back] 3 mos. 8th Regt.
Capt. Fredk Tykle's
Co. H

* * * * *

Camp Morton
April 24th 1861
It is hereby Certified that John Ruess Was unanimously Elected ensign of the Marian Guards now in Camp.

David Shunk Captain
O H P Carey 1st Lieut

[back] 3 mos. 8th Regt
Marian Guards
Grant Co.
Co. "B"

* * * * *

MILITARY DISCHARGE

This is to Certify, That Levi Bean
private in Captain Parish's Company
of INDIANA VOLUNTEERS, has been HONORABLY DISCHARGED from the service, on account of his being one of the excess in the number of members in said company, the call by me being in the first place for eighty-four or one hundred in a company, and Secretary of War reducing the same to sixty-four.

Witness my hand, this 21 day of April 1861
Lew Wallace
Adj. Gen.

[back] Levi Bean.

* * * * *

Camp Morton – April 26th 1861

The Captains of the 8th Regiment make the following unanimous recommendation for their Regimental officers –

For Col. William P. Benton

For Lieut Col. Silas Colgrove
For Major David Shunk
1. R.A. Riley Capt. (----) Guards
2. Tom J. Brady Capt. Del. Guards
3. J. Widaman Capt. Wayne Guards
4. C. O. Howard. Capt. M.S.G.
5. H. T. Vandevender M.S.G.
6. (------------) Capt. M. Guard
David Shunk Marian Guard
7. Charles S. Parrish, Relief Guard Wabash
W.P. Benton, I.R.G.
S. Colgrove R.C. Guards

[back] His Excellency
O. P. Morton
Recommendation
of Captain ---

8th Regt.
8th

* * * * *

Adj't. Gen. Office
Indianapolis, Apr. 27th, 1861
It is hereby Certified that John Ruess was duly elected first Lieutenant of the Marian Guards.
David Shunk Company Comd

[back] 3 mos. 43 8th Regt
Marian Guard
Rand. Co.
Co. B
Filed Apr 30

* * * * *

Adj't Gen. Office
Indianapolis, Apr. 27th, 1861
It is hereby Certified that Oliver H.P. Carey was duly Elected Captain of the Marian Guards to fill the vacancy occasioned by the Promotion of Capt. D. Shunk
David Shunk Capt.
Marian Guards
(-----------) 27th 61

[back] 3 mos. 43 8th Regt.
Capt. Carey

Marian Guard
Co. "B"

* * * * *

To his Excellency,
Gov. Morton
Sir,

I have again to appeal to you for the appointment of Dr. Edgerlee of Muncie to the position of Surgeon to the 8th Regiment of Indiana Volunteers, not because or personal friendship, however; - but that it is the strenuous desire of my Company, and the earnest wish of the parents of the boys I command, who know they will suffer not under the care of Dr. Edgerlee. His skill as a Surgeon no one will doubt who have his acquaintance, and his sympathetic nature (--------) qualifies him for the position he asks. Will you not give it him?

I have sought no favors for myself – I expect to fight my way through. Yet I think myself justly entitled to some consideration – for I was among the first to respond to your call. But all I ask my boys be satisfied as only the appointment of Dr. Edgerlee can satisfy them.

Truly,
Your friend
& obt. Servant.
Tom J. Brady
Capt. Del. Guards

April 27th, 1861.
[back] Capt. T.J. Brady
Geo. W. Edgerlee.

* * * * *

Adj't. Gen. Office
Indianapolis, April 29th 1861
This is to certify that at an Election this day held by the Richmond Guards Erwin Harrison was duly Elected First Lt. and M.M. Lacy was duly elected Captain.
W.P. Benton
Col. 8th Regt. Ind. Vol.

Indianapolis April 20th 1861,
This is to certify that at an Election duly held by the Richmond Guards James Conner was duly and legally Elected Ensign of said Company.
W.P. Benton
Col. 8th Reg.

* * * * *

[back] Apr 30

[top appears to be the same as first half of above, but is blocked by bent page]

Indianapolis, May 2/61

Ensign Jas. Conner has my permission to go to Richmond Ind and return tomorrow evening, duly ch—the written consent of the Governor

W.P. Benton
Col. 8th Reg.

[back] 3 mos. 8th Regt.
Election of Officers
"Richmond Guards"
Co. "I"
Filed Apl

* * * * *

Camp Morton

May 1st, 1861.

This certifies that Joseph Kirk of the Delaware Guards was unanimously chosen by said company to fill the vacancy in its First Lieutenancy, caused by the detachment of Lieut. Geo. W. Edgerlee for the medical staff of the 8th Regiment, and that he is entitled to receive a Commission as such.

Tom J. Brady
Capt. Del. Guards
& Nathan Branson
Ensign

[back] Delaware Guard
Certif Election
May 1st

* * * * *

(------- ---------) Noble

Sir – My friend Hickman Kirby a private in Comp G 8th Regt. has been active as Steward in City Hospital during all of my connection with it and deserves more than any other our man who proposes to serve his County – Could you pass him to Muncie & return

very truly

City Hospital
June 20th /61

Geo. W. Edgerle asst. Surgeon
8th Regt. Ind. Vols.

[back] Hickman Kirby

* * * * *

Parkerburg Va June 21st /61

This is to certify that Lieut. A.J. Kenny has been appointed by me and elected by Co. F. Captain of Said Company to fill the vacancy occasioned by the promotion of Capt. C.O. Howard.

W.P. Benton
Col. 8th Regt. Ind.

C.O. Howard
Adjutant

[back] 3 mos. 8th Regt.
Alex. J. Kenny to be
Capt. Co. H.
Vice Chs. O. Howard
Appt. Adjt.
Certf. Of. Col. Benton

* * * * *

N. H. Richardson

Dublin, Aug. 21st, '61

Sir

I am desirous of entering a cavalry company. I have been in the 8th Regt. for three months. – Capt. Widamans Company (A)
Is there a chance to get in a cavalry company if so I am ready with a good horse and a determination to see the Stars and Stripes wave over all before I return. Please give me the necessary information in regard to equipment pay (….) and Oblig

Yours truly
N. H. Richardson
Dublin, Ind.

Agt. Gen. (Laz Noble?)
Indianapolis

* * * * *

Lee Yarzan
Adjt
8th Regt
Indianapolis, Ind.
April 27, 1861
(--------) Morton
Dear Sir
First my compliments. Second kindness.
Lee Yarzan Esq has been speaking to me about the position of Adjutant; I give it to you as my opinion – that his would be an appointment fit to be made. I am under no obligations (------) Yarzan but I think the cause of our Common County would be (-------) by his promotion therefore I recommend it.

W.P. Benton
Col. 8th Ind.

* * * * *

Adjutant General's Office

INDIANA VOLUNTEERS
Indianapolis, Aug. 2nd, 1861.

His Excellency O.P. Morton
Governor of Indiana

Dr. John W. Davis with whom I was most pleasantly associated for some months at the City Hospital desires reappointment as surgeons mate to one the reorganizing volunteer Regts. –

Doctor Davis is the man for the place

Geo. W. Edgerle
Surgeons Mate 8th Regt. Ind.Vols.

[back] John W. Davis
Surgeon

* * * * *

Greenfield Ind. Aug. 15th. 1861

I hereby certify, that upon the re-organization of Company B of the 8th Regt. of Ind. Vols. that notice was duly given that at the hour of two oclock P.M. on ---day, said Company would re-organize by the Election of Officers; that at the hour of two oclock P.M. on said 15th day said members of said Company, called to attention, that Reuben A. Riley was chosen chairman and Samuel Durban Secretary.

That 1st Lieut William R. Walls was unanimously Elected Captain of said Company.

That Solomon T. Kauble was unanimously Elected 1st Lieut. of said Company.

That Samuel H. Dunbar was unanimously Elected 2nd Lieut. of said Company.

R.A. Riley Chairman
Late Capt. of Co. B. 8th Regt. Ind.Vols.

[back] Certificate of Election
of
Company B
William R. Walls
Filed Augt 19, 1861.

* * * * *

[on side of paper] 8th Regt.
Commission of 8th
Regt. Ind. Vols.

Commission (?) dated
20 Augt. 1861.

Filed Sept. 9, 1861.

List of officers elected in the 8th Regt. Indiana Vols. to whom Commissions have not been issued. to wit –

Comp. A.	Luther H. Harmon	2nd Lieutenant
Comp. B.	Jesse Way	2nd Lieutenant
Comp. C.	Benjamin Elwood	1st Lieutenant
	Milton R. Dungan	1st Lieutenant
Comp. E.	George H. Dula	2nd Lieutenant
Comp. F.	Joseph M. Thompson	Captain
	Charles S. Ellis	1st Lieutenant
	John Bannister	2nd Lieutenant
Comp. G.	Jesse E. Scott	1st Lieutenant
	John A. Caho	2nd Lieutenant
Comp. H.	Fredrick Wysong	Captain
	George W. Adams	1st Lieutenant
	William P. Goolman	2nd Lieutenant
Comp. K.	George Parkerson	1st Lieutenant
	Andrew O'Daniel	2nd Lieutenant

the foregoing list e------s all of the officers of my Regt that have been chosen by their respective Companies to which Commissions have not yet been issued

Wm. P. Benton
Col. 8th Regt. Ind. Vols.

[back] 8th Regt. 3 mos.
Kerney, Poke, Vandevender, Tykle, Riley, Walls
Com filed Aug 2-, 1861.
Wilson

* * * * *

This is to certify that JR Polk has been Elected Captain. Franklin Daily 1st Lt & Richard M. Smith 2nd Lt in the 8th Regiment.
Richard Smith 2nd Lt.

W.P. Benton
Col. 8th Regt.

CO Howard
Adj.

* * * * *

Camp Morris Aug. 20th 1861.
This is to certify that George H. Dula was duly Elected 2nd Lieutenant of Com K 8th Regt Ind Vol

H. T. Vandvender Command
Co. K 8th Reg Ind Vol

* * * * *

Camp Benton
Aug 21st 1861

I Elijah Mackleinan Clerk of the Election held at Camp Benton certify that the following Officers were Elect in Company ( ) Wabash Rangers to wit:

8th Reg.

Capt.
Joseph M. Thompson

1st Lieutenant
Charles S. Ellis

2nd Lieutenant
John Banister

attest
E Mackleinan
Clerk

[Back] 8th Regt.
Election return
Filed Aug 21, 1861

* * * * *

Adjutant General's Office,
INDIANA MILITIA
Indianapolis, Aug. 26th 1861

Sec of State.

Will put Commission to George H. Dula, 2nd L Company E, 8th Regt. Ind. Vols.

(Laz?) Noble
Adjutant

[Back] George H. Dula

* * * * *

Wabash Ind
August 28th 1861

Hon. O.P. Morton
Governor

Dear Sir;

I am informed that Lt. Col. Colgrove will most likely be promoted & thereby create a vacancy in the 8th Reg.

If this should occur, we of the Upper Wabash, would be very much gratified to see Capt. C.A. Parrish succeed Lt. Col. Colgrove –

I am aware that you must be very much annoyed with applications & recommendations for appointments – I had occasion to request of you, as early as last winter to remember Capt. Parrish, if there should be any military service required I have not attended to the subject to since – But since time, Capt. Parrish has both seen & done some service at the Battle of Rich Mountain –

The manner in which He has sustained diversely in the 8th Reg. enables me to ask for his promotion with some degree of confidence.

It may be according to military usage that Major Shunk, should succeed Lt. Col. Colgrove; and in that case, we should be satisfied with the appointment of Capt. Parrish Major.

Yours Respectfully
J.D. Conner

P.S. Our enlistment in the Cavelry Co. is progressing rapidly, - will be completed next week.

[back] 8th Regt
Chas. S. Parrish
Major Lt. Col.
Recommendation of
J.D.Conner of
Wabash

* * * * *

STATE OF INDIANA
Executive Department.
Indianapolis Sep. 2, 1861

Secretary of State

Will issue Commissions to David Shunk as Lieut. Col. of 8th Regiment Ind. Vols. and Charles S. Parrish as Major of the same regiment.

O.P. Morton Gov.

[back] Field 8th Regt.
Order for
Commission

* * * * *

Camp Morris, Sept. 2nd, 1861

I, J.R. Polk do hereby certify that at an election held this P.M. for officers of Co. F. 8th Regiment, Indiana Volunteers. That John R. Polk received the highest number of votes and was duly elected Captain of said Company. That Franklin Dailey received the highest number of votes and was duly declaired elected as first Lieutenant of said Company – Further, that Richard M Smith received the highest number of votes and was duly declaired elected Second Lieutenant of said company.

Given under my hand this 2nd day of September 1861,

Lt. John R. Polk
Co. H. 8th Regt
Ind. Vols.

J.D. Conner}
A.M. Smith} --------
Capt. J.M. Thompson clerk

[back] Co. F, 8th Regiment
Certificate of Election
John R. Polk.

Filed Sept. 3, 1861.

* * * * *

Head Quarters 8th Ind
Camp Morris
Sept 3, 1861

This is to certify that John R Summers has been duly recommended by the proper authority and has been appointed Sutler of (this?) Regiment so far as I have the authority to make the same

William P. Benton
Col. 8th Ind. Regt.

[back] Jno. R. Summers
Sutler
Appt by
Col Benton

* * * * *

[side] Andrew Wines
[8]

Cambridge O Sept. 12th, 1861

Gov Morton
Dear Sir

When the 8 Indiana (three months) regiment passed through our place, I recognized a wounded soldier, whom I had formerly known at the battle of Rich Mountain on the 11th July. He received three wounds one slight, two very severe – at the time I first saw him he was laboring under secondary haimharage from the sloughing of an artery & the limb on the point of mortification. I proposed to the surgeon to take him off the car & take care of him, as I did not think he would be able to make Indianapolis alive, of which proposition he gladly availed himself, as he concurred in opinion. He has so far reversed, as to be about some by the aid of crutches.

I write you, because we have written twice to the surgeon of the regiment & have received no answer. The soldiers name is Andrew Wines private in Company B (Capt Carey) 8th Regiment commanded by Col. Benton. Ind. Vol. Inf.

Will you be good enough to hand this to the proper person to inform us what provision is made to pay the bills of a wounded soldier under such circumstances. What vouchers are necessary etc. He has recd no pay except $5 paid by the state since he entered the service. Will he be entitled to pay until he gets well & is mustered out of service, & can a person having a power of attorney to act for him draw his pay for him.

Pleas answer soon – we can pay his bills here by contribution, but as the general Government will no doubt ultimately pay all – It is proper that each state should take care of her own

Respectfully Yours
V. Haynes

* * * * *

[side] 34
Jas Beck
Asst. Surgeon

Mechanicsburg Henry Co. Indiana
To his Excellency Sept 27th 1861
O.P. Morton
Sir

I was at Indianapolis some two weeks for the purpose of getting an Asst Surgeon's place in the 8th Regiment to which was attached a number of my acquaintances, who wished me to apply and try to obtain the situation in that Regiment, but Ford & Edgerly had been with them in the 3 months service, but many of the three months men did not like them, was the reason of their wanting me to make application, Mr. Frank Murphey said he would attend to it, you had so many persons to attend to when I was there, and appeared to have more than any one man could possibly attend too, that I gave up calling on you, I would like to have the situation of Asst. Surgeon in the 34th Regiment forming in Anderson I would refer you to F. Murphey or Milton Murphey or Milt Robinson as respect to my Character those men I am persuaded you are acquainted with, I had given up the Idea altogether of making any further application untill I was solicited by a number belonging to the Regiment, as they had understood that a young man by the name of Markle had made application he is a young man that studied about 3 or 4 months with a Physician who had never entered a Medical Colledge or went through any regular study himself for what time he did read was with my Cousin Dr. J.C. Beck of Cadiz, and this young man had received his Medical education from him, and if he is practicing I do not know it and he is living only 5 miles from here and those that have spoke to me in the Reg don't feel like trusting their lives in his hand, I would merely state I have been practicing Medicine some fifteen years and of that time in this part of Indiana some 8 years, I should be pleased to have the appointment, and if the Situation is filled, I understand there is another Regiment to be formed at Anderson and perhaps, if that should be raised you could confer a situation there, it is not necessary to add more, hoping you will give this a favourable consideration

I remain your
Obedient
Servant
James Beck

* * * * *

[Side] 8th Regt
Col Benton
Sep. 28, 1861.

Overcoats
Cartridges
& etc.

Georgetown Pettis Co. Mo
Sept 28th 1861

To his Excellency
Gov. O.P. Morton

Things are in considerable confusion here, to say the least of it. And I am satisfied we will never get our overcoats, unless you send a special messenger with them. If you could send Halloway with them we will get them: we are only three miles from the terminus of the rail way; but there is a regular game of grab being played all along the road from St Louis here.

It was unfortunate that we did not get enough catridges at Indianapolis. For Gen Davis has me under arrest for taking, as he alleges, 8000 rounds more than was intended for us. Including the 8000 we only got 26000 when we should have had 40,000. The worst feature of the arrest was that it came very near resulting in an open mutiny; the men stacked their arms and refused to march unless I would lead them. I restored order by assuring them, that I would lead them to battle, whether ordered under arrest or not. I am still under arrest but supposed I will be released tomorrow, as I have done nothing intentionally to warrant it: As I understood Gen. Davis that I was to have the very identical catridges in controversy. If the gallant 8th has to retire before the enemy for the want of catridges I shall refer to my present imprisonment as the proudest circumstance of my life.

The enemy is about 50 miles from us in great numbers, between thirty & forty thousand with 18 pieces of artilery. I think we will have a fight within ten days. And since Gen. Seigel has arrived here a general feeling of doubt and doom has given away to one of hopefulness, if such confidence, as to the result.

The health of our men though not good is improving Yours W.P. Benton

* * * * *

The following is a Schedule of the property belonging to Beulah Bates destroyed by the Soldiers of the 8th Indiana Regiment on the night of the 9th day of September 1861

1 Fine Bureau	15.00
1 Dining Table	5.00
1 Centre Table	7.00
1 Stand	3.00
1 Large Mantel Looking Glass	4.00
1 " Bureau do do	4.00
1 " Looking Glass	2.00
1 Common " "	1.00

6 Windsor chairs		6.00
3 common chairs		1.50
1 Cake plate		2.50
1 Large Heating Stove		10.00
6 Irish Linen fancy Table Cloths		6.00
6 Diaper Towels Supposed to be not ( )		2.00
1 Brass Clock		5.00
16 lbs. Cream Nuts	10c	1.60
32 lbs. Almonds	16	5.12
1 doz Lemons	50	.50
½ Box Tobacco		12.00
1000 Common Cigars	40	4.00
300 Principe Cigars	125	3.75
2 hams Dried Beef	100	2.00
8 lbs. Bologne Sausage	1	.80
1 lb. Nutmeg	110	1.10
1 lot allspice	100	1.00
36 Jars Candies	10	3.60
36 Jars glass	20	7.20
1 Counter FairBanks Scales	2.50	2.50
1 Barrel of Vinegar	44 gals 20	8.80
20 Bottles	6	1.20
½ large cheese	150	1.50
½ Barrel Crackers	200	2.00
1 Market Basket	20	.20
Sundry articles	100	1.00
1 large Box Matches	50	.50
9 Window Curtains	.25	2.25
1 Map of the World 7ft by 7		5.00
1 Razor not Supposed to be worth		.75
1 do Strap " " " "		.25
1 Spectacles & case " " "		1.00
9 Window Sash & glass		36.00
3 pair Window Shutters		14.00
1 Large Door window & Shutter		14.00
3 Panel Doors		12.00
1 Board Door		2.00
4 Rooms Lath. Lathing and Plastering damage		15.00
1 Stair Banister		4.00
1 Common Bench		1.00
1 Counter		12.00
1 Show Case		12.00
½ BBL Sugar 100 lbs 9 cts.		9.00
1 Sack Coffee 50 lbs 16 ½		8.16

1 Box raisins	350	3.50
1 " Tea 20 lbs.	75	15.00
1 " Candles 42 lbs.	20	8.40
2 Boxes Soap 30	.6	2.40
1 Bed Tick Sheet & quilt	3.00	3.00

State of Indiana
Madison County

Before me, the undersigned a justice of the peace within and for said county personally came Hezekiah Bates, who being by me duly sworn, declares that the above is a true schedule of the property destroyed by the soldiers of the 8th Indiana regiment on the night of the 9th day of September, 1861.

Hezekiah Bates

Subscribed and sworn to before the 3d day of October, 1861.

Abraham B. Canoll, Seal
Justice of the peace

State of Indiana
Madison County

We, the undersigned, appraisers of the above schedule of property, do swear that the amount set opposite each and every item, is a true cash value of the same, as we verily believe.

Subscribed and sworn to before me, the 3d of October 1861
A.B. Canoll, Seal
Jus P.

{John D. Johnson
{William Carter
{TR Diven
{ V.R. Franks Appraisers

[back] 10-3-61

* * * * *

The undersigned Judges and Clerks of an election held at Richmond Ind. on the 12th day of October, 1861, for our Captain, one first Lieutenant and one Second Lieutenant of a Company of Eighth Infantry Volunteers, certify that the following persons were elected to fill said offices, by a majority in each case of all the votes cast, the No. of votes cast in each case being 40.

John S. McGraw, Captain
Joel J. Finney, 1st Lieutenant
Joseph L. Marsh 2d Lieutenant

Given under our hand this 12th day October 1861.

John M. Grubbs }
W. Yanzy ? } Judges
Clerk

[back]
John S. McGraw

Joel J. Finney
Joseph L. Marsh

2-12

* * * * *

Head Quarter 8th Ind
Otterville, Mo
Oct. 6th, 1861

Gov. O.P. Morton
Dear Sir
Will you please commission Benjamin F. Elwood Captain and Henry Rader 1st Lieutenant of Company "H" They have been duly elected. Elwood elected to fill vacancy created by the Resignation of Capt Tykle. Rader to fill vacancy created by promotion of Elwood.

W. P. Benton
Col. 8th Reg. In. Vols.

C. Howard
Adj.
[back]
B.F. Elwood
&
Henry Rader

* * * * *

Middletown Henry County Ind. Oct 28th / 61
Gov. O.P. Morton
[S]ir
We have sons brothers and friends in the 8th Reg. Indiana volunteers, and we have heard with regret that some of the surgens in that region it are not the kind of men that our friends that are entrusted to them in sickness are treated right, They are intemperate and neglect them --- and think more of a bottle of whiskey than they – do of the souldier lives, some of them with very slight diseases, such as Diarrhea Ague &c, suffer for weeks, and those in a weakened condition are ordered on long marching fall by the way and lay on the prairie all night subject to rebel violence as is often the case that such characters follow in the rear of the army, to murder our men, that so give out by weakness and if those surgeons knew their duty they would see who were able to stand it and who were not
We wish respectfully to call your attention to this matter, believing that you have the interest of the souldiers from Ind. at heart as much so as any Governor in the U.S. Capt Tykle said he had reported Edgerly some ten days before he resigned his position in the regiment. Dr. James Beck was solicited strongly by the privates in that regiment of the three months men, and by one whole company from this District. We would be happy if you would appoint him as an assistant in that regiment All the letters from our sons breathe that spirit to have Dr. James Beck sent to them. He was in camp with them at Indianapolis and a number of the soldiers were sick he prescribed for them and had them

able for duty before he left their camp while 4 or 5 that the regiment surgeons, attended with the same diseases, went or had to be brought back and were under the charge of our physicians, some weeks. These are facts and cannot be denied. Dr. James Beck had been practicing and still has a very good
practice Some 9 years he has been a citizen and physician in this part of the county. With the hope that you will attend to this immediately and oblige many friends. Dr. Beck has a son in that regiment and that would make his interest greater he has practices in the family of nearly every member of one of the companies that went from this township, which ammounted to some 60. We hope to meet with favorable response to our petition and with due respect remain

Yours
Resp. Henry Bowers
Thos. Ginn
Thos. C. Swain
W.A. Rader
H.B. Brattain – in service –
in W. Virginia
&
others

[back]
8th Reg
James Beck
Complaint of Phy-
sicians and rec-
commending Dr.
Beck

Letter from relatives
of soldiers
Middletown
Henry Co.
Ind.

* * * * *

8 Regt
Dr. James Beck
Surgeon
Dr. Beck's letter

Mechanicsburg Henry Co Ind
Nov 16 1861

Hon Gov Morton
Dear Sir

I have written to you several times trying to obtain a Situation in the 8th Regiment Ind Volunteers I discover in looking over the Journal of yesterday that the Asst Surgeons place has become vacant by the death of Dr. George W. Edgerle. I have many friends besides a Son in that Regiment that have solicited me to apply for the situation and as I am the oldest applicant, I hope you will favour me with your influence as I am confident it will be acceptable to many in that Regiment, hoping to hear from you shortly, I remain

Resp.

Yours

James Beck

* * * * *

Syracuse, Mo

Nov 18th 1861

To His Excellency

Oliver P. Morton

Gov of Indiana

Dear Sir

Enclosed please find a recommendation Signed by all of the officers of My regiment for the appointment of Doct James K. Bigelow Assistant Surgion of the regiment. to fill the vacancy Occasioned by the death of Doct Edgerle I would further Say that the appointment of Doct Bigelow will meet the almost unanimous wishes of the entire regiment.

Very Truly Yours

Wm P. Benton,

[back]

8th Regt

James K. Bigelow

M.D.

* * * * *

Syracuse Mo.

Nov. 18th 1861

To His Excellency,

Oliver P. Morton,

Governor of the State of Indiana,

The Undersigned Officers of the 8th Regt Ind. Vols. respectfully petition your Excellency to appoint Doct. James K. Bigelow, assistant Surgeon for our Regt. in place of Doct. Edgerle, decd. Doc.t. Bigelow is now with the Regt. and was also with us in the three months Service in Western Virginia. Where he rendered important medical aid to our sick and wounded.

W. P. Benton Col.

David Shunk Lieut. Col.

John Ruess Capt.

Luther H. Harmon, Lieut.

James R. Smith, Lieut.

Geo. W. Tarkleson Lieut.
Geo. W.H. Riley Capt. Co. G
Jacob Widaman Lt. Co. G
Jesse W. Way , 2nd Lt. Co. G
C. O. Howard, Adjutant
B.F. Elwood Capt. Co. E
M.R. Dungan "
Samuel H. Dunbar Lieut. Co. B
F.S. Wysong Capt Co. D
John A. Caho Lieut Co. C
Arthur [? Amos] W. Sanford Chaplain
John R. Polk Capt. Co. F
F. Dailey 1st Lt. " "
R. M. Smith 2nd " "
Charles S. Parrish Major

Joseph M Thompson Capt. Co. I
Charles S. Ellis Lieut Co. I
John Banister Lieut Co. I
H.T. Vendevender, Capt. Co. K
L.D. McCallister, Lieut,
G.H. Dula, "
A.J. Kenny Capt. Co. C
J.E. Scott Quartermaster
Wm. R. Walls Capt. Co. B
Solomon T. Kauble 1st Lieut. Co. B

* * * * *

Camp 8th Regt Ind Vol. Militia
Syracuse Mo. Nov. 19th 1861

To his Excellency
Gov. O.P. Morton
Indianapolis Ind

We the undersigned Officers, non-commissioned Officers and privates of Co. B, 8th Regt. Ind. Vol. Militia join in most earnestly recommending to you Dr. J.K. Bigelow for appointment to the Assistant Surgeonship of said Regt. made vacant by the death of Dr. Geo. W. Edgerle of Muncie Delaware Co. Ind.

Wm. R. Walls Capt.
Solomon T. Kauble 1st Lieut.
Sml. H. Dunbar 2nd Lieut.
William G. Hill 1st Sergt.
W. H. Short 2nd "
J. S. Chittenden 3rd "
Elijah Tuttle 4 "
Philander Smith 5 "
Aaron Smith Corporal
Richard Leamon "
James Hawkins "
Thomas M. Martin "
Wm. Branson "
William Gapen "
David M. Dove "
Isaac T. Jones "

Privates
W. W. Alexander
John B. Anderson
Henry Bush
John Bush
James Bush
Jacob Bowers
Ahijah Bales
S.S. Brooks
Noah Bixler
Charles Clapper
Levi Collins
C.C. Deppery
Wm. C. Dove
James Derry
Alexander Derry
Jacob Dinkle

Thomas Dinkle
Nicholas Miller
John F. Wiggins

George W. Dixon
George M. Davidson
John Dorman
Saml. H. Dillman
J.S. Davis
Joseph Davis
Frederick H. Ellsberry
Amos Everson
A.J. Fuller
Ira B. Fountain
Andrew F. Gilbert
Eli Gapen
Thomas J. Hutson
Cyrus Hanes
John A. Jennings
S.A. Jones
John Jackson
I.E. Lineback
Peter Lamb
Albert H. Lake
Adam Lowder
William Lowder
James Lowder
Alfred Lowder
H. McCorkhill
Harrison Morgan
Emanuel Morris
F.M. Miller
I.C. McGee
Wm McConnell
Clark McDonald
Franklin Mays
Henry J. Mann
Wm B. Martin
Jacob Martin
A.M. Nixon
Marion Philpott
Samuel Robinson
Edward H. Roney
Benjamin A. Roney
Nicholas Reamshart
C. Redmire
Geo. W. Smith
G.W. Smith
C.H. Smith
William H. Siplinger
Peter Sellery
John B. Scotten
A.H. Scott
Louis Schnell
William T. Snider
Eli Stevens
Wm. H.H. Seely
E.H. Tyner
John M. Underwood
James N. Underwood
John Ullery
Lawson Wiggins
Ad. F. Wilson
Alfred Wilson
William W. Welling

I hereby certify that the above names were written by the members of Co. B or by there request
Wm. R. Walls Capt. Co. B 8th Reg. In Vol

[back]
Dr. Bigelow

Petition

* * * * *

Camp 8th Regt Ind. Vol. Militia (?)
Syracuse Mo. Nov. 19th (?) 1861 (?)

To His Excellency
Gov. O.P. Morton
Indianapolis, Ind.

We, the undersigned, officers, non-commissioned officers, and privates of Co. A, 8th Regt. Ind. Vol. Militia, join in most earnestly recommending to you Dr. J.K. Bigelow for appointment to the Assistant Surgeonship of said Regt., made vacant by the death of Dr. Geo. Geo. W. Edgerle of Muncie, Delaware Co. Ind.

Tom J. Brady Capt.
Geo E. Parkison 1st Lieut.
Andrew O'Daniel 2nd Lieut.
Wm. D. Watson 1st Sergt.
Matthew Hughes 2 Sergt.
Sam. C. Williams 4th Sergt.
William Hamilton 5th Sergt.
James H. Adams 1st Corp.
Geo. W. Thompson 2nd Corp.
3rd ".
A.G. Ridenour 4 Corp.
Thomas Carmin 5 "
William Gates Corp.
George V. Tilson Drumer
W. P. Wagoner
Joseph Zink
Robert Galbraith
Abner Sanders
George W. Albin
George W. Thompson
Miles Thornburgh
Jacob Swain
Abner S. Sanders
Lewis Wilson
J. W. Rigdon
T.H. Smith
Henry Garrison
George Needler
John Smily
Robert H. Clift
William M. Boyce
Lewis N. Rumsey
James F. Neal
Frank Deeren
George Keen
Brice Powers
William Dick
William Fisher
Harvey Berry
George Paxson
David Craw
John Hewey

Jacob Hertzler
George Cummins

Henry W. Jack
Jacob Shafer
Joseph Giek
John Carmin
Ner Gaunt
Emasiah Gerrard
George Taylor
John Winzer
John Hensly
Jo McFarlan
John Slife

I certify the above is the strength of Co. A. in camp at this time – the remainder being sick in Hospts., temporarily detached & absent,

Tom J. Brady
Capt.

R.W. Rigdon
George W. Eby
William Cooley
Martin L. Bron (?Milton Brown?)

[back]

Dr. Bigelow
Petition

* * * * *

Camp. 8th Regt. Ind. Vol. Militia
Syracuse Mo. Nov. 19th 1861

To His Excellency
Gov. O.P. Morton
Indianapolis Ind.

We, the undersigned, Officers, noncommissioned Officers and privates of Co. F. 8th Regt. Ind. Vol. Militia join in most earnestly recommending to you Dr. J.K. Bigelow for appointment to the Assistant Surgeonship of said Regt. made vacant by the death of Dr. Geo. W. Edgerle of Muncie Delaware Co., Ind.

Capt. John R. Polk
1st Lt. Frank Dailey
2nd Lt. Richard M. Smith
Sergt. W.A. VanBuskirk
" Isaac A. Blakley
" G.W. Furrow
" Stephen Wolf
" August Rhoades
Corporal A. Crum
" Samuel Mitten
" John O'Brian
" D.P. Swab
" E.S. Jenks
" F.P. Sayre
"
Private T. Leatherland
" W. Hardbarger
" M. Wolf

(?)
(?)
D. Duffee
William (?)
(?)

W.H. Bell
Jesse Vanduyne
J.A. Peek
Wm. R. Snediker
Robert D. Hite
Reed Meeks [? Irvin R. Meek]
T. P. Duncan
J. Repp
J.S. Wilson
J. Beaumont
T. Bailey
G. Craig
G. Carney
J. Coburn
C. Fountain
W. Case
H. Degering
J. Elms

(?)

C. Stone
(?) J. Long
J. McVicker

D. Hartsell
D. Harvey
O. D. Johnson
J. Kendall
F. Engle
J. Roberson (?)
J. Stuttler
S. Harter
O.B. Johnson
W. King
Newburger M
Geo Patten
J.A. Rhoads
G.C. Kline
Z. Hesford
W. Moore
C. Kramer
J.C. Musselman
W. Roberson
D. Vanduyne
J. Watson
W. Laflin
D.R. Long
J. Swafford
D. Swafford
(?)
L. Parrot
T. Stone
H. Williams

Dr. Bigelow

Petition

* * * * *

Camp 8th Regt. Ind. Vol. Militia
Syracuse Mo. Nov. 19th 1861

To his Excellency
Gov. O.P. Morton
Indianapolis Ind

We, the undersigned, officers, non commissioned officers and privates of Co. G 8th Regt. Ind. Vol. Militia, join in most earnestly recommending to you Dr. J.K. Bigelow for appointment to the Assistant Surgeonship of said Regt. made vacant by the death of Dr. Geo. W. Edgerle of Muncie Delaware Co. Ind.

J. Widaman 1st Lt.
M.W. Bly
John Harvey (?)
John Gunckle
Alexander Bever
Geo. Bartholomew
Ben. Jourdan
Clark Predmore
R.E. Jenkins
18. Geo. Starbuck
19. Slv. White
20. John F. George
21. K.C. Hollingsworth
22. John Baker
23. Sam. Bumpas
24. Geo. W. Dubois
25. Wm. Salisbury
26. James Malcom

Isaac Gillum
Hisekiah Williams
Jas. P. Light
Rodney McClave
Edw. Reilly
L.E. Garner
John Ford
Lewis Mock

27. Wm. Dubois
28. Wm. Burchett
29. John Lewis
30. John Knapp
31. Kirk Pickering
32. Chris Cleveland

[Back]
Dr. Bigelow
Surgeon

Petition

* * * * *

Camp 8th Regt. Ind. Vol Militia
Syracuse Mo. Nov. 19th 1861

To his Excellency
Gov. O.P. Morton
Indianapolis, Ind.

We, the undersigned, officers, non-commissioned officers and privates, of Co. D, 8th Regt. Ind. Vol. Militia join in most earnestly recommending to you, Dr. J.K. Bigelow for appointment to the Assistant Surgeonship of said Regt. made vacant by the death of Dr. Geo. W. Edgerle of Muncie Delaware Co. Ind.

(?)
(?)
(?)
(?)
(?)
(?)
J.B. Hubbard
(?)
Corpls
Jacob G. Harnish
Henry Miller
Samuel Herrington
Jacob Oldaker
Joseph Pritchard

(?)
(?)
(?)
(?)
(?)
(?)
(?)
(?)
Jacob S. Miller
John Whartton
Leander Starr
M. Van Buskirk
Farris Zimmerman
John Oldacre
John Paten
John Hervey
F. M. Oldaker
R. D. Commons

Benjamin F. Binkley

Noah B. Matthews
William Armstrong
All Izor
Ira Izor
Jerry Sullivan
John M. Tout
(?)
(?)
(?) Wright
William H. Newbold
Christian B. Messner
John Messner
Wm. Smith

[on side]
Dr. Bigelow

Petition

* * * * *

{Camp 8th Regt. Ind. Vol. Militia
{Syracuse Mo. Nov. 19th 1861

To his Excellency
Gov. O.P. Morton
Indianapolis, Ind

We, the undersigned, Officers, noncommissioned Officers and privates of Co. C, 8th Regt. Ind. Vol. Militia, join in most earnestly recommending to you Dr. J.K. Bigelow for appointment to the Assistant Surgeonship of said Regt. made vacant by the death of Dr. Geo. W. Edgerle of Muncie Delaware Co. Ind.
[across this letter is written: Dr. Bigelow Petition]

A.J. Kenny, Capt
John A. Caho
Jesse Scott

Seargents
David Fleming
J.W. Lemon
W.S. Griffy
Oliver P. Posey

Corporals
Joseph S. Powell
Geo. W. Brittain
Caleb S. Garrett
Jos. Spealman
John Sinex

James Harrison Reister
Geo F. Kimball
Simon. C. Moreland

Privates
Enoch W. Roberts
Ed? Schaffter
Alpheas Davis
Amos C. Sweezey?
Robert S. Knode
Denis Buckley
E. Brothers
Edward Anible
Sylvester L. Thorne
William D. Hess
Fred Hoffschnaeder
Lewis Korseman

Stephen V Cooper
Geo W. Tivis
Isaac Goodwin

Octvous Potter
Henry A. Helmer
William H. Reppeto
Wm. H. Study
Lewis B. Baxter
E. L. Semans
D. Dempsey
T. Davis
Henry C. Conley
Fernanco Study
William B. Pierce
James T. Ellis
Fredrick H. Fink
John A. Griffy
George W. Green
Hamilton Asborn
Carna Parsons
James W. Buhl
D. C. Kitchel
Edwin Haitson
Erastus Church 45
Nathaniel C. Potter
Lorenzo D. Study
David S. Hamilton
Wm H. Calentine
Wm A. Medearis
James Grass
Daniel Grass
Alonzo Taylor
Justin Hodge
M.M. Pixley
Daniel Potts
Samuel Reynolds
John G. Rockafield
Wilkerson Sharp

* * * * *

{Camp 8th Regt. Ind. Vol. Militia
{Syracuse Mo., Nov. 19th 1861

To his Excellency
Gov. O.P. Morton
Indianapolis, Ind

We, the undersigned Officers, noncommissioned Officers and privates of Co. E 8th Regt. Ind. Vol. Militia, join in most earnestly recommending to you, Dr. J.K. Bigelow, for appointment to the Assistant Surgeonship of said Regt., made vacant by the death of Dr. Geo. W. Edgerle of Muncie, Delaware Co., Ind.

Benjamin F. Elwood Capt.
Henry Rader First Lieut
Milton R. Dungan 2nd Lieut.
Chauncey S. Burr 2nd Sgt.
Samuel Mitchell 3rd "
Cyrus Vanmatre 4th "
Wm Terry 4th corporal

A. J. Phillips	6th "
Wm Mitchell	7th "
Dan Hardman	8
James Alexander	Privates
E. J. Barret	
G. W. Barrett	
Wm T Beck	
Collins Bedford	
F.M. Berry	

Thos Bell Private
Ben Bock
John Bock
A Bole
Geo Brown
John Brown
Josh Clevenger
John Clevenger
Sam Craig
Joel Cummings
Robt Crosly
Wm Davis
Ellis Evans
Wm Fleming
A J Fleming
Beniah Fleming
Good Henry
Richard Hawkins
John M Gray
Joel Hendricks
John T. Hendricks
John Hodson
Gary Lester
James Jones
Cyrus Kunkle
Wm Lemond
John May
J L Moore
R McNew
John McNew
A McCallister
T W McCune
Geo Morris
W Nelson
Joel Osborn
Geo Osborn
A M Painter
A J Perdue
A Perdue
C Pitser
S A Preston
Dan Rent
Jesse Rosier
Jonathan Runyan
Perry Shoemaker
Henry Shoemaker
Wm Skinner
John Stout
J K Swain
Geo Tarkleson
A Vanmatre
Jas Windsor
John Whitworth

[on back]
8th Regt
Dr. J.K. Bigelow
Surgeon

Recommendation

* * * * *

Camp 8th Regt Ind Vols
Syracuse, Mo Nov 20th 1861

To his Excellency
Gov O P Morton
Indianapolis Ind

We the undersigned officers noncommissioned officers and privates of Co K 8th Regt Ind Vols Join in most earnestly recommending to you Doct James K Bigelow for appointment to the Assistant Surgeonship of Said Regt made vacant by the death of Doct Geo W. Edgerle of Muncie

Names

Cap H T Vandvender
Lieut L D McCalister
" George H Duley?
J. H. Hicks
(?)
(?)
(?)
(?)
(?)
Samuel (?)
James G McCallister
Francis M Leuark
James Black
Daniel Roberts?
Daniel Hulbert?
Joseph L Huston/Lanaham?
(?)
C A Savage

Sergt. L. K. Helvie
Sergt. R. Fry
A. E. Lemon
Wm. H. Bowers
Corp. John M. Hunt
A. F. Kraner, Drummer
Daniel R. Hurlbut
John Lyons
PA Keller
A Whitecotten
I Shirts
W Scott
Charles Wm Wynn
Simon Cumins
J. T Manifold
A Crosley
J. J. Pence

Henry S. Wyman
R. A. Brown
William G. Houston
Frank Williams
Frederick Purget
W H McCallister
William Scott
(?)
(?)
(?)
C. S. L?

William H. Huston?
William Conde

Owen Williamson
James McGuire
E. Basicker?

[on back]
8th Regiment
Dr. Bigelow

Petition

* * * * *

Camp 8th Regt Ind Vols
Syracuse Mo Nov 20th 1861

To his Excellency
Gov O.P. Morton
Indianapolis Ind

We the undersigned officers noncommissioned officers and Privates of Company (I) 8th Regt Join in most earnestly recommending Doct James K Bigelow for appointment to the assistant Surgeonship of Said Regt made vacant by the death of Doct Geor W Edgerle of Muncie Ind.

Joseph M Thompson	Capt.
Charles S Ellis	1st Lieut
John Banister	2d do
Robt Torrence	1st Sergeant
Jas D Taylor	2 " "
Adam Miller	3 " "
Elias B McPherson	4 " "
George H Harlan	5 " "
Chris Mikesel	Corporal
James K Darby	" "
Wm V Lucas	" "
Thomas Bridges	" "
Grimes Holcom	" "
Wm H. Noakes	" "
Josias F Austin	Private
Joel V Brewer	" "
Flavius J Brewer	" "
James M Busby	" "

[written on side of this]
The Signatures heare to attached was Signed by the Capt with the Consent of each
Joseph M Thompson
Capt

1-16

George Brower	Private	Levi P Lilly	Private
Warren Black	" "	James C Lessig	" "
Erastus G Burget	" "	Joseph C Milliron	" "
John M Benbow	" "	John B Morris	" "
Daniel Coble	" "	Wm H Maudlin	" "

Joseph Cockson “ “
Wm H Cockran “ “
David M Coppock “ “
Darby Samuel C “ “
Jonathan Dillon “ “
George Esmond “ “
John M Evans “ “
James F Elliott “ “
George W Forney “ “
Wm Forney “ “
George M Gates “ “
Henry Gardner “ “
Wm. H. Humphrey “ “
Simon. Houser “ “
John Hardin “ “
George W Haines “ “
Mark W Haines “ “
Green W Hughes “ “
Ezra Hunnicutt “ “
Ignetz Follmer “ “
Ezra Kryder “ “
Thomas Kimball “ “
James P Loyd “ “
Lewis Lines “ “

Wm H Minnier “ “
Tobias H Miller “ “
George H McNiel “ “
Wm E McNiel “ “
Thomas P McNiel “ “
David W Pond “ “
John M Puderbaugh “ “
Jesse D Quick “ “
Andrew I Robinson “ “
Wm H Robinson “ “
Joseph Root “ “
Perry Rutherford “ “
George F Shackelford “ “
Thomas S Smith “ “
Elijah R Scott “ “
Lewis Summers “ “
Joshua Tucker “ “
Milton Tyner “ “
Wm H Whitcomb “ “
James A Williams “ “
Oscar A Wickersham “ “
Benj F Wimer “ “
John F Whiteside “ “
Amos York “ “
Thornton York “ “

[sideways over list]
Dr. Bigelow
Petition

* * * * *

Camp 8th Regt Ind Vols
Syracuse Mo Nov 20th 1861

To his Excellency
Gov O P Morton
Indianapolis Ind

We the undersigned officers noncommissioned officers and Privates of Company (H) 8th Regt Join in most earnestly recommending Doct James K. Bigelow for appointment to the assistant Surgeonship of Said regt made vacant by the death of Doct Geor W Edgerle of Muncie Ind.

John Ruess Capt.
(?)
James R. Smith 2nd Lieut.
(?)
(?)
Benj Williamson “

William (?)
John Brock
Wm Clevenger
Thomas Mesler
John C Nottingham
Ira J. Knight

(?)
(?)
John E Hodge Corp
Benjamin P. Williamson Corp
John W. Bates Corp
Stanford Lytle Corp
Charles Trentleman Corp
David Scott Corp
George H. Williams Corp
William (?)
John Miller
Jesse Rooks

John Lytle
(?)
Cephos Reeve
Samuel Blinn
William Rutherford?
John P. Finkle
William H Knight
Samuel Horne
Samuel Bechtel
(?)
Samuel Harter
William ?
Cyrus L. Pemberton
William Conner
Daniel Conner
William Joy
Joseph Douglas
Jesse Lezenby
Simon Malott
Abner Leach
Marshal Leach
John Duck
Wm Tremain
J Dolman
William L. Joy
Ruben R. Miller
Geo. W. Miller
John H. Miller

A. Reeve
Hiram L. Lawrence
Daniel M C Ross
R. P. Pilling
M. Wroan
Thomas C Webb
Solomon Maples
Samuel Woods
John Humel
Thomas Milak
Robert Ruggles
Williams Edwards

Edward H. McFarland
John P. Stanley
Jonas Meyers
I. V. Acker
Richard Barry
Dennis Ginney
William Conner

The foregoing are all members of my company ? in Camp. The remainder are either on detached duty or sick in Hospital

Wm. Ruess
Capt. Co. H. 8th Regiment

[on side of paper]
Dr. Bigelow
Petition

* * * * *

Camp 8th Regt Ind Vols
Syracuse Mo Nov 21st 1861

To his Excellency
Gov. O.P. Morton

The undersigned Officers and members of the Brass Band of the 8th Regt. join in most earnestly recommending Doct James K. Biglow for appointment to the assistant Surgeonship of said Regiment made vacant by the death of Doct Geo. W Edgerle of Marion Ind.

Morgan Zeller Leader.
Edward Guenin? "
M. L. Reed
John Hug
John Sheets
Thomas B. Foster
Wilson Adams
E. H. Shaw
H L Dawson
Pet. Memur?
August Huning
E. F. Ordelheide
Penn West
Richd Hartman
Wm Moreland
Wm. D. Eastman
F. C. Eastman
H. C. Rantz
Jacob Jolliff
J. W. Stout
David Bowman

[on back]
Dr. Bigelow
Petition

* * * * *

Syracuse Mo. Nov 21 1861
Gov. O.P. Morton
Dr Sir

Enclosed you will find a recommendation from every officer and man of the 8th Regt. in behalf of Doctor Bigelow for <u>Surgeon's Mate</u> in the place of Dr. Edgerly deceased. Knowing you and knowing <u>what</u> Dr. Bigelow had done for the 8th, I feel assured if you knew all the facts you would appoint him to the place. At the hospital on Rich Mountain battle ground no one was so kind and attentive to our wounded men as Bigelow In a word from the day the 8th was organized to the present moment he has performed the principal work in the medical department of the Regt. And for a month past he has been the only doctor we have had, and is to day, both the others being absent sick. I cannot forget his kindness to the boys on the long and exausting march, forced part of the way, from Otterville to Springfield and back. When a poor fellow would drop by the way side overcome with fatigue or sickness, Bigelow always had a kind and encouraging word for him. He is always kind and always willing, the result is we all love him as a brother, and the whole regiment feels that he has fairly earned the vacant place. The Gentlemen whom the telegraph informs us has been appointed no doubt, is well qualified and you can doubtless provide for him elsewhere. If you do not I shall be satisfied I have failed to fully portray the facts. Yours very truly W.P. Benton.

[on back]
Gov. O P Morton
Dr. Bigelow
Surgeon
Recommendation
By W P Benton Col

* * * * *

Syracuse Mo. Nov. 20th 1861

Sir

I have the honor to state that in the discharge of my duty in this Division, I have had occasion to remark the efficient conduct of Dr. J.K. Bigelow stewards of 8th Indiana Regt. now Act. Asst. Surgeon. During the absence of both medical officers he has been entrusted with the entire charge of the sick of this Regt. and, has performed his professional duties to the perfect satisfaction of his officers, patients & myself. His appointment to the office of Asst. Surgeon would be exceedingly gratifying to me, as well as beneficial to the public service

I have the honor to be
Very Respectfully
Yr. Obt. Sert.
S. W. Everety?
Brig. Surg. Act. Surg. 2nd Div.

To his Excellency
Gov. O.P. Morton
Indianapolis, Ind.

[on back]
J. K. Bigelow
M.D.

Recommendation
of Division Surgeon

* * * * *

Muncie Ind.
Dec. 5th 1861.

Hon. Laz. Noble.
Adjt. Gen. (?)}

Sir: Will you be so kind as to give me information as to the following subjects, being on furlough and that nearly out, how must I proceed to have it reviewed as I am still unable for duty? My furlough being from Gen. Curtis of St. Louis, should I report myself to him, or to my Regiment when able for duty? Does the pay of a non-commissioned officer continue while on furlough?

By answering you will confer a great favor on

Your very obt Servt

Will. R. Irwin

2d Clas. Sergt. 8th I.V.

[on side]
Dec 5th 1861

* * * * *

HEAD QUARTERS, DEPARTMENT OF THE MISSOURI,
St. Louis, Mo, Dec. 21, 1861

SPECIAL ORDERS, }
No. 95 }

The resignation of 1st Lieut. Solomon T. Kauble, 8th Ind. Volunteers, is hereby accepted to take effect this day.

BY ORDER OF MAJOR GENERAL HALLECK

H. Kielon?

Assistant Adjutant General.

Govr of Indiana

[on back]
8th Regt
Co. B.
Resignation of
Lieut. Kauble

Dec 28th

* * * * *

(most of this page is illegible)

William R. Walls

Capt. Co. B 8 Regt Ind Vols

In my judgment both of the above are good selections

W P Benton

Col 8th Ind

[on back]
8th Regt.
Promotions Co. "B"
Co B 8

* * * * *

Camp Lamine? Mo. Jan 10th 1862

To his Excellency:

Gov. O.P. Morton

Indianapolis

Ind.

Sir,

Agreeably to "Gen. Order, No. 22, Dept. of the Missouri," I have the pleasure of recommending to the vacancy occasioned by the resignation of 1st Lieut. Geo. W. Parkison, Co. 8th Ind., accepted the 30th December, 1861, -

Andrew O'Daniel, present 2d Lieut. said Company.

To the vacancy occasioned by the promotion of Lieut. O'Daniels, -

William Irwin, present Quarter Master Sargt. of said Regt.

I may add, in addition, the gentlemen named are the choice of the Co. for the several positions.

I am, very truly,

Your most. obt. servt.

Tom J. Brady Capt.

Co. A. 8th Ind.

Approved

David Shunk

Lieut Col 8th Rgt Ind Vols

Refer to Love and Mable

[Back of paper]

8th Regt.

Promotions

* * * * *

Adjutant General's Office,

Washington, January 2d, 1862.

To His Excellency,

The Governor of Indiana,

Sir:

I have the honor to report, that the following named Officers of the Volunteer forces from the State of Indiana have resigned, to take effect at the dates set opposite their respective names, viz:

First Lieut. Solomon T. Kauble. 8. Regt. December 26, 1861

Second Lieut. Leonidas Thrasher. 3. Battery. December 26, "

I am, Sir,

Very Respectfully,

Your Obt. Servant,

Geor. Ruggles.
Asst. Adjt. General.

[Back of paper]
<u>Resignations:</u>
Lieut. Kauble – 8
" Thrasher – Battery.

* * * * *

Head Quarters of the Army,
Adjutant – General's Office,
Washington, D.C., Feby 4th, 1862.

His Excellency O.P. Morton,
Governor of Indiana,
Indianapolis, Ind.:

Sir, -

In reply to your letter of the 3d inst. I have the honor to inform you, that, except by the direction of the War Department, a Major-General, or General in command of a Division has not the authority "to cashier or dismiss from the service a Major, Captain, or any officer duly commissioned by the Governor of a State, and mustered into service of the United States, for absence without leave, incompetency, or any other cause, without notice to the officer and without trial."

I am, Sir,
Very Respectfully,
Your Obt. Servant,
L. Thomas,
Adjutant – General.

* * * * *

Washington, D.C.
Feby. 4, 1862.

S. Thomas
A. General
to
Gov. O.P. Morton
of Indiana.

No Maj. General or General Comdg. Division can muster out of service any duly commissioned Officer tc, unless by direction of the Secy. Of War & -
Copy retained

officers "<u>mustered out</u>" at the Gn Mo & Miss Depts. have already been <u>notified</u> by a certificate of muster out of service, but not with trial. Don the with in prohibition a----- G.O. 14 (H qr Dept Miss) of 20 Apl 1862?

W. Scott Ketchum
Brig Gnrl
Acty (?)

H qr Dept Miss }
30" Ap'l 1862}

* * * * *

Private Simon D. Brady Co. G. 8th Regt. Ind Vol, having made application for a furlough I do hereby certify that I have carefully examined the private & do find he has had pneumonia & in consequence thereof he is in my opinion unfit for duty. I do further declare that in my opinion he will not be able to resume his duties in a less period that twenty days
Dated at Otterville Mo. this 9th day of Feb. A.D. 1862
W.J. McKim
Surgeon

* * * * *

Sick furlough for 20 days for S.D. Brady a private Co. G. 8th Regt Ind Vol.
Application granted for days twenty from Feb. 8th 1862
By order of Brigadier General Pope
Robt. Jos. Kertiz
Brigade surgeon & Act. Med. Director

* * * * *

Camp Sugar Creek Ark
February 19th 1862
Sir.

I have the honor to respectfully recommend Robert E. Torrence, Orderly Sergt. for appointment and commission as Second Lieutenant of Company "I" 8th Regt Ind Vol. to fill vacancy occasioned by resignation of Second Lieutenant Bannister. Ordered and accepted February 8th 1862.

Joseph M. Thompson
Capt. Co. I 8th Regt.

Ind Vol
To. L.Z Noble
Ad'jt Genl
8 _______ Ind

The above is respectfully forwarded with the following suggestions; as I understand the late order, it says that "the next in line" shall be promoted. On the very first page of the Army Regulations the
[next page is almost faded away and is hard to read]

* * * * *

[this page is too faded to transcribe here]

[side note]
8th Reg.
Promotion of N. Morris previously made
Co. I

* * * * *

Cleveland Indiana
March 3rd 1862

Laz. Noble Esq.
Adjt Genl.

Sir, I am a private in Capt Walls Co. 8th Regiment Ind Vol. I came home on a furlough from Missouri which furlough expires on the 11th day of this month. Since I left Missouri I understand that the 8th Regiment has gone far in to Arkansas and I do not now see how I shall get to my regiment,

I now desire you to give me such information as you think proper Concerning my Case. as I want to know in time what I must do. to know in time what I must do. my Captain I understand is now in Rolla Missouri & I understand he promised to inform all of these on furlough when they could go to their regiment but I have not yet from him. Please let me hear from you by letter, should you decide for more to try to go through, can you furnish me with a pass!

Yours Truly
John S. Davis
Cleveland P.O.
Hancock Co. Indiana

[Back of page]
John S. Davis

* * * * *

Head Quarters 8th Regt New Jersey. Vols
Camp Lower Potomac Md.
March 14th, 1862.

To all whom it may concern
The bearer of this Lieut. P.H. Langstaff is well known to me. I consider him one of the best posted Infantry tacticians in the country He is throughly familiar with the whole system of the U.S. Tactics. and I doubt not his proficiency is as through in respect to other arms of the Service as I have found it to be in Infantry

A. J. Johnson
Comdg 8th Regt N.J.V.

Joseph Trawin
Lieut. Col. 8th

N.J.V.
A true Copy
From the Original

I have served as a 1st Lieut. in a Cavalry regiment

P.H. Langstaff

* * * * *

8 Regt.
Capt. Brady
for Major

Muncie April 2d, 1862

Hon. O.P. Morton

Dear Sir

It has been noticed in the papers that Col Benton has been nominated for a Brigadier Genl with others. This it is supposed will cause some promotions to be made in the 8th regiment. While not wishing to interfere in the organization of the army, or to embonop(?) you in the discharge of the delicate duty of making selections & promotions the friends of Capt Brady here desire that his name will not be forgotten in connection with the position for major.

They say he will be very strongly recommended by their regiment if final action will be delayed until their communication can reach Indianapolis.

What of strategy? As it is not nearly played out.

There certainly, has been ample time to learn that the south means war & nothing but downright – fighting will even bring them to their senses.

Yours truly
Walter March

* * * * *

Camp Cross Lincoln (?) Ark
April 2nd 1862

Col. Wm. P. Benton

Comdg. 8th Regt. Ind. Vol.

In accordance with Special Order No. _______ issued from the office of the Adjutant General of the state of Indiana. I recommend 1st Sergeant William W. Mather to appointment to be appointment Second Lieutenant of Company H. from Regiment to fill the vacancy occasioned by the death of Lieut. James R. Smith killed in the battle of Pea Ridge on the 7th of March 1862.

Dated April 2nd 1862

Capt. John Ruess

Com'dg Co. H. 8th Ind. Vols.

[Back of paper]
Recommended and respectfully forwarded April 2, 1862

Wm. P. Benton
Col. 8th Ind.
D. Shunk
Lieut. 8th Ind.
C. S. Parrish
Maj. 8th Ind.
(Co. H.)

* * * * *

8th Regt
Clothing
Mechancsburg Henry Co Indiana
Mr. J.H. Vajen (?) April 4, 1862
Q.M. General
Dear Sir

I hope you will excuse me for approaching you with a few remarks, you may perhaps think I am medling with that which I have no business with I do not look at in that light, and hope you will not consider it in any other way than feeling for the Soldier, without making any further apologies, I will state the circumstance, I saw two or three letters one I received myself from members of the 8th Reg Ind Volunteers encamped now near Bentonville, one of them says you thought the boys that came back looked hard but if you were to see us you would think they were gentleman beside us, we were ragged and our toes out of our boots and shoes and no chance to get any that is the amount stated, I do not know whether your Department has anything to do with it, but from what little correspondence I have had with you believing you to be a Gentleman, you will know where to apply to remedy this matter, the Sutler belonging to the Regiment is going on with articles and I have no doubt knowing their necessities they will no doubt take advantage of them, I hope Mr. Vajen you will give this your attention, I have felt like I would like to have been in the Army as an assistant Surgeon when there was so many sick and Dying and I tried to get a situation from the commencement of the enlisting for the three years men, but there has been since I first made application an hundred perhaps – appointed if I had not felt myself qualified I should never applied to Governor Morton, but I had confidence in my ability, and have been solicited for med from Soldiers in Different Regiments that were acquainted with me, and sent it to them and cured them, and many have felt a great desire for me to try and get in their Regiments, I had no friend to urge my claims, except what Lawer Bufkin tried, he was acquainted with me as a Physician, and Governor Morton I was not personally acquainted with, I felt a willingness to go into the Army in a position where I could be the most useful, this matter I wish to be confidential, It is true I would like to have your Influence, and had I a portion of that kind you would never have any reason to regret that your Influence obtained it for me, I hope you will make enquiry about the condition of the Reg I spoke of about their necessities, for I believe there is clothing at Indianapolis to meet their wants, by attending to this I shall ever look upon you with a grateful heart that you have been the means of having them made comfortable with those remarks I remain

Resp Yours

Q.M. General James Beck
H.I. Vajen

* * * * *

8th Regt
Capt. Tom Brady
Field Officers

Muncie April 9, 1862

Hon. O. Ridleton

Dear Sir,

It has been noticed in the papers that Col. Benton of the 8th will with others, be made Brigadier. In that event it is suffered that there will be a grade of promotions in the Regiment. --- The friends of Capt. Brady without desiring to interfere in the organization of the army, or to embarrass you in the discharge of the delicate & disagreeable duty of making privations wish to have him remembered in filling the vacancies.

I am told that a strong recommendation in his favor will be presented from the regiment.

I know that one of the infernal curses of this war is that there is a general scramble for a share of the spirit either for gain a political, capital, hereafter – carried so far that is would make the Jews who cast lots for the garments at the cross blush with shame but – Tom has a natural taste for a military life, is a brave fellow & I would like to see him, advanced as far as his merits & the public good will justify.

Yours truly

Walter Moret (?)

* * * * *

Camp on Flat Creek, Mo.
April 8th 1862

Gov. O.P. Morton

Sir. There is a question in dispute amongst the Captains of the Eighth Regt. as to who is the ranking Captain of said Regt. – Now sir the facts are these, I was 1st Lt. In Co. I in the 8th Regt. in the three months Service – I made up and took to Indianapolis on the 19th of August a Co. of 145 men, recieved my commission from you on the same day as Captain of Co. I in the 8th Regt. – went into Camp Morris one day ahead of any other company in the Regt. – had my 47 surplus men transferred to different companies for the purpose of filling up and getting the Regt. in Field – two were accepted and started commanded by the "Bravo Benton" as the only three months Regt. in the West Supposing our gallant soldier would be commander at least of the Post at Jefferson ______ but all a mistake – the rank was disputed on the grounds that the 8th Regt. was not accepted till after all the other Regiments were in the field in the west. If that decision is just – I have no claim to press, if not Sir I claim to be the Ranking Captain of the Eighth Regt, from the fact that a commission in the three months Service according [this section faint and hard to read] _______ ______________ ________ to exist, and is not considered valid in the three years Service.

Sir your decision in the matter will _____ _______ satisfaction to him and you will confer a favor in making it known to me. –

Sir we are not accquainted and I am Sorry to Say so and you may not know me at all but – I request you Sir to call on it above all other Ind. your __________ ___________ your County as Co. A. Riley of Hancock

Sir I remain your humble Servant

William R. Walls

Capt. Co. B. 8th Ind. Regt.

* * * * *

[back of paper]
8th Regt.
Capt. Walls
(Co. B)
In relation to Rank.
Respectfully referred to
Adj. Genl. Noble
O.P. Morton
Gov.

* * * * *

Camp "Good News" Near Forsyth
Mo. April 12th 1862.

To His Excellency O.P. Morton
Gov of the State of Indiana.

Dear Sir

The undersigned commends to you Lieut. Charles S. Ellis, for appointment as Assissant Surgeon of the 8th Ind. Regt. (Vice Dr. G.W. Bruce, who tendered his resignation)

Lieutenant Ellis has been serving with the Regiment ever since its re-organization in September last fall as an officer in the line and as a physician, and in each capacity has given perfect satisfaction to the officers and men of this command.

Hoping that you will find it consistant with the public service to grant our request, in the premises, we? remain Governor.

Very Respectfully your
Obedient Servants,

W.P. Benton	Col. 8th Ind.
D. Shunk	Lieut Col. 8th In
Chas. S. Parish	Maj. 8th "
James Ford	Surgeon 8th Regt. Ind. Vol.

[back of paper]
Lt. Chas. S. Ellis

For Asst. Surgeon

Recommendation of
Field Officers

* * * * *

Camp "Good News" Near
Forsyth Mo. April 12th 1862,
Gov. Morton

Dear Sir,

Enclosed please find letter of recommendation for Dr. Ellis urging his appointment as assistant Surgeon of my Regiment. The applicant is _________, and qualified. Dr. J.K. Bigelow whom the regiment recommended in place of Edgerlee, ______ has been provided for having received position of assistant Surgeon of the 8th Mo. Cavalry.

Very Truly Yours
W.P. Benton
Co. 8th Regt.

[Back of page]
8th Regt.
Lt. Chas. S. Ells
Asst. Surgeon
Vice Dr. Bruce

Letter from Co. W. P. Benton

Letter from Col. W. Benton

* * * * *

Capt. Joseph M. Thompson of Co. I. 8th. Regiment Ind. Vol. having applied for a certificate on which to ground an application for lack of absence, I do hereby certify that I have carefully examined the officer, and find that he has chronic Rheumatism, and Varicose veins about the ankle and postital? space of the left leg. This officer served in war between the U.S. and Mexico. This disease had its origin in the marches of this campaign, and has troubled him more or less ever since. He has not made a march on his leg for a month past, and he is, in my opinion, unfit for duty. I further declare my belief that, he will not be able to resume his duties in a less period than forty days.

Dated at Camp Good News, Mo. this 12th day of April, 1862.

James Ford Surgeon
8th Regt. Ind. Vol.

* * * * *

April 12th, 1862

Capt. H. E. Curtis
___ Adj. Gen.
Sir respectfully ask for leave of absence for forty days grounded on the written certificate
Respectfully your obedient Servant
Joseph M. Thompson
Capt. Co. I 8th Regt. Ind. Vol.

* * * * *

T#23# Forsyth 1862

Joseph M. Thompson
Capt. Co. I
R____ ______ to Brig
8th Ind Vols
Gen Ketchum to muster
this officer out of service
__ __ Kellon(?)
Ap. 23. 62
mustered out of service to take effect 21 Apl 1862 & notice given to all concerned
W. Scott Ketchum
Brig.Genl
Actg ____________

H________ ________
22 Aprl 1862

Dept. Mississippi
April 22, 1862
Approved and respectfully forwarded
W.P. Benton
Col. 8th Ind. Regt.

Respectfully forwarded
approved. April 12, 1862
Thos. Pattison Col.
Com. __ __ Br. 3rd Div.

Respectfully forwarded
Jef C. Davis
Col. C____
3d Div.

[The following was marked out]
___ ___ Army of the S.W.
Forsyth April 14th 1862

Respectfully returned the within certificate not being accompanied either by request for leave of absence, or resignation. It would seem this officer should resign.

By order of Maj. Gen. Curtis

H.E. Curtis

Maj. Genl.

* * * * *

_________ ________ Army of the South West

Forsyth Mo. April 14, 1862

Special Order

No 142

VII ____ Seven Days Leave of Absence is upon Surgeons Certificate, granted to Capt. J.M. Thompson Company "I" 8th Indiana Regt. and he is referred to Department Head Quarter St. Louis for further orders

By commend of Maj. General Curtis

H. E. Curtis

Asst Adjt Genl.

{Capt. J.M. Thompson }
{Company I 8th Regt. Indiana}
{Thro comdg officers }

The above is a correct copy of a leave of absence granted by Maj. Gen. Curtis to me.

J.M. Thompson

Capt. Co. I 8th Reg Ind Vol

* * * * *

Forsyth, Mo.

April 14, 1862

Special Orders

No. 142

H.E. Curtis

As Ad Genl.

Granting leave of absence for 7 days to Capt. J.M. Thompson, 28th Ind. Regt. and is referred to Dept. H.S.

Grs.

* * * * *

Head Quarters 8th Regt.

Camp Sulphur Rock, Arkansas

May 21st 1862

Gov. Oliver P. Morton

Dear Sir,

Having been unofficially informed that Capt. Thompson of Company I 8th Regt, has been mustered out of the service by Order of Genl Halleck. And that Said Charles S. Ellis of said Company and Regt. has been appointed assistant Surgeon – which position under the circumstances he respectfully declines to accept . Therefore if Capt. Thompson is permanently taken from the company, I take pleasure in recommending Lieut. Charles S. Ellis to the Captaincy of Said Company (I) 8th Regt and Orderly Robert Torrence to the 1st Lieutantcy of Said Company (I) And further if there Should be a Vacancy in the Assistant Surgeon's place I would recommend Doct. James K. Bigelow for that position as he will gladly resign his present position in the 6th Missouri for a place in our regt and the regt would Most happy to name him as assistant Surgeon.

Very Respectfully Your
Obt Servant
David Shunk
Lieut Col Comdg 8th Regt In Vols

[on back]
8th Regt.
Col. Shunk
For promotion vice Capt.
Thompson mustered out.

* * * * *

Camp Morton Ind April the 23th 1862
Governor Morton

Dear sir as I have A 1 wife & two litle Children left with out enny Protector from Deceace of her father I though I would rite you A few lines to see if would not let me have A chance to take the oath & return home to them as I Live in 16 miles of Paducah. & I will pay my tax. & I have Bin sick ever since I have bin in the service & am tired of fighting and and am tired of being A prisoner if you will grant me this request you will answer this I yours truly

R..A.. Lewis
Co. E. 8th Ky
[back of paper]
R.A. Lewis

* * * * *

hold over until Monday, 28th April.
Union City Ind April 24, 1862
Ajt. Noble

Sir Mr. Hout of our Regiment having been at your Office. he informs me that an order has been issued giving no one a pass that has been absent from Camp (or Regt) 60 Days. I have been been from the Regiment ever Since 4th of February and am not yet able for duty. I wish to know wether I shall have to go to camp or not as I will doubtless be discharged should I go there having Sent by Mr. Hout for myself & Wm. Bromagen – and got none I thought it best to ask for information as my time of furlough is out the 1st of May. you will please inform us of our duty and if we Shall have to go to camp you will please Send us each a pass.. so the Regt. and oblige ours...

Respectfully
Isaac Sutton
Private
8th Reg. Ind. Vol.

(Disease 1st poisoned at Georgetown then took the Musels after which I have the chronic Direa ever since)

address Isaac Sutton
Union City, Ind.

[back of paper]
Isaac Sutton
Union City

An. Apr 30, 1862

* * * * *

Adjutant General's Office,
INDIANA VOLUNTEER MILITIA
INDIANAPOLIS, April 24th 1862
Brig. Gen. W. Scott Ketchum
Acting Insp. General.
St. Louis Mo.
Dear Sir

Some of the ___ inst. Certifying to Capt. Jos. M. Thompson muster out of the service came duly to hand. The Capt. called on me today asking for an explanation of the summary proceeding and showing a leave of absence Copy of which I send you.

Some similar cases occurred some months ago which were submitted to the Secry. Of War and his answer received a copy of which I send for your inspection.

As your action is the premised scene to be directly a conflict with the decision of the War Dept. His Excellency Gov. Morton deems it to be due to the officers commissioned by him and summarily mustered out by you that a hearing should be allowed them.

Very respectfully
Yours
Laz Noble Adj. Gen.

[back of paper]
1862
8th Regt.
Indianapolis
April 24, 1862
Laz. Noble
Adj. Gl.

To Brig. Genl. Ketchum

Regarding the muster out of Service of Capt. Jos. M. Thompson ___
Send a copy of communication from Secy of War ____

8th
Capt. Thompson
Summary Muster out

* * * * *

Wabash, May 10th, 1862.

My dear Sir:

Capt. Jos. M. Thompson, late commanding Compy. I, 8th. Regt. Ind. Vols. being absent from home temporarily, his family have placed your letter covering Brig. Genl. Ketchum's reply, in my hands, requesting me to acknowledge it.

Genl. Ketchum's reply sets at rest unfavorable references we had drawn against Col. Benton's fair dealing in regard to Capt. Thompson being mustered out of service, and this frank act of justice is cheerfully rendered to above officer. But the reply does not meet your distinct proposition submitted to Gen. Ketchum, "that a Major General or General in command of a Division was not competent to muster out of service any officer commissioned by the Governor of a State , <u>for any case whatever</u>, without notice to the officer and without trial." Capt. Thompson is not prior to any act of the officer in Superior command, touching his case, subsequent to delivering the Surgeon's Certificate to his Colonel, for there he leaves it, and the paper goes forward by routine, and he does not accompany it. He, therefore, gives no assent whatever to the cruel act of his military superiors, in mustering him out of service. He may be pre Turned to give his consent to all he is privy to, namely, asking a furlough. Whatever, in the act complained of, Exceeds this, was an abuse of the just principle avowed in the letter of Secr. Stanton to Gov. Morton. The summary of the matter is, that Captain Thompson, against his wishes and consent, is now outside of the army in disgrace.

Gen. Kechtum's answer seems to leave this matter, where it cannot be reached. Our apprehension was, that instead of an explicit reply, the subject might, is the first instance, be referred to Gen. Halleck, who in turn, would refer it to the War Department, and that in delaying justice, injury would be as substantially done to Capt. Thompson, as in denying justice. But Genl. Ketchum's letter seems to make the case complete, and to leave no question of functilio[?] in the way of presenting the case at once to the War Department. This seems to belong to the State Executive, thro the influence of your office. The Governor's prompt action heretofore, in obtaining the confession of this principle from the War Dept. leaves no doubt it will be done again to protect a worthy officer, and I feel no doubt that this wrong like all other wrongs in the lower ranks of the army, will find its quick remedy, where it can only be found, in the active protection of the head of the Department. If the principle of the Department cannot be made practical, it is obsolete, and worse than obsolete, because while it avows the only just principle of removal, it would then confess itself impotent to prevent its violation, and become a party to the injustice.

I should be pleased for Capt. Thompson's sake, and I know it is his wish, if you would present this case to Secr. Stanton, and invite his prompt attention to it.

I am Very Truly,
Your friend & Servant,
John M. Pettit.

[back of paper]
8th Regt.
John M.? Pettit, Esq. Relative
to case of
Capt. Thompson, muster
out of service.

* * * * *

Camp at Sulphur Rock Ark
May 13, 1862

His Excellency
Gov O.P. Morton

Sir, Having (?) today, ______ a commission as Brig. Gen. a vacancy has occurred in the office of Col. Of the 8th Ind. It affords my pleasure to recommend Lt. Col. David Shunk for Colonel. Major Chas. Parish for Lt. Col., and Capt. Tom J. Brady of Co. A. for Major. They are "next in line" and their promotion is perfectly satisfactory to the regiment, and is expected by it as a matter of course. While each of these officers is my warm personal friend, at the same time if I know myself, I would not recommend their promotion in the gallant old 8th if I did not believe them worthy and qualified for their respective position. The old 8th, the "Bloody, Old 8th" as the boys call her have ever been faithful to me. I shall always remain true to her best interests.

I have the honor to be your very obedient Servant
W.P. Benton
Brig. Gen. Vol.

[back of paper]
Brig. Genl. W.P. Benton
Camp Sulphur Rock
Arkansas
May 13, 1863

Recommending
Lt. Col. Shunk for Col.
Maj. Parrish for Lt. Col.
Capt. Brady for Maj.

* * * * *

His Excellency
Gov. O. P. Morton

Indianapolis, Ind.

Sir,

In retiring from the Command of Co. A. I would ___ have to recommend the following changes and promotions, viz. –

To the Captaincy of Co. A, Lieut. Andrew O'Daniel, present 1st Lieut, said Company.

To the 1st Lieutenancy Co. A, Lieut. W.R. Irwin, present 2d Lieut, said Company.

To the 2d Lieutenancy Co. A. Seargt. William D. Watson, present 1st Seargt. Said Company.

All of whom I present to you as worthy soldiers.

Their commissions, I suppose will date from the period of my commission as Major.

I am, very truly,
your obt. servt.
Tom J. Brady
Maj. 8th Ind.
D. Shunk
Col. 8th Ind.

Camp Sulphur Rock. Ark.
May 26th, 1862
Chas. S. Parrish
Lt. Col. 8th Ind.

[back of paper]
8th Regt.
Co. A.

* * * * *

Milton Ind, May 30th, 1862

To His Excellency Gov. Morton

We the undersigned residents of Milton, Ind., certify that the bearer Franklin Stobaugh enlisted in Cap'tn Widiman's Company in the 8th Regiment Indiana Volunteers for the three months service – That he was dangerously wounded at the battle of Rich Mountain since which time he has been closely confined to his bed until quite recently – That his mother is a poor widow and that neither have any means to subsist on except as they earn it or receive it from public bounty. That he is anxious to enter the service again as a private but his wound is not yet in a condition to permit him to do though it is fast healing up – and in the mean time he wishes to do something by which he can earn his living at least. In view of all these facts respectfully yet earnestly, & urgently recommend his appointment to some post of light duty {if any such there be} by which he may be enabled to earn his living and yet not retard the healing of his wound – We believe he will make a faithful and trusty guard, or be reliable in any position to which he might be appointed.

Any assistance you can render in giving or securing him some suitable situation will be gratefully remembered by him and us.

Respectfully Yours,
E.B. Newman

J. Pennington
Edward Roberts
Jos. Shiosler (?)
____ Marsen
Wm. S. Jones
John Callaway
David G. Kern
John Shifsler

S.S. Gregg
[back of paper]
8th Ind.
Franklin Stobaugh
Wounds
Wants some light duty.
2-30

* * * * *

[side of paper]
Private Brady
8th Reg.

Mansfield, Ohio
2d June, 1862

To His Excellency }
Gov. Morton }

Dear Sir,

Simon D. Brady a private of Capt. Riley's Co. G. 8th Ind. Vols. was sent home from Otterville, Mo. on sick furlough in Feb. last; at the expiration of his furlough it was renewed on the recommendation of his attending physician.

Since that time he has herd nothing of his Regt. though he has forwarded two application for renewal of furlough & two reccommendations for discharge sworn to by his attending physician who says it is doubtful whether he will soon be able to perform military duty. He has always expressed a desire to rejoin his Regt. at, the earliest opportunity but if he was now physically able he has not the means to do so with as he is a day laborer & has been able to do nothing since his return.

He is afraid, that he may have been declared a deserter from the fact that he has been able to hear nothing from his Capt. for the last three months.

He has desired me to write you this statement that he may be governed by your advice. Enclosed I send a copy of his furlough

Yours Respectfully
H. Shellenbarger

4-7

* * * * *

Salem Ark. June 14th (?) 1862
To his excellency
Hon. O.P. Morton
Dr. Sir

It affords me great pleasure to commend to your favorable consideration my friend and former classmate Dr. G.W. Bruce Assistant Surgeon 8th Regt. Ind. Vols. He has been for some time on detached service at the Post Hospital West Plains, Mo. where I spent a week with him, and permit me to assure you that his patients were more kindly cared for and the hospital in a better condition than any hospital I have visited in this Department out of St. Louis. He is worthy of promotion and it would only be the reward of merit to make him the Surgeon of a Regiment at the earliest opportunity.
Excuse me for writing you but the Kindest feelings toward a meritorious friend, one who I regard an honor to the profession of his State have prompted me to do so.

Sincly yours
Isaac Casselberry

Hon. O.P. Morton

[back of paper]
8 Regt 244
Dr. G.W. Bruce
Asst. Surg.
Recommended
for promotion on
account of faithful
Service by Dr.
Isaac Castleberry
2-31

* * * * *

[8]

Camp at Sulphur Rock Ark
June 14, 1862.
His Excellency
Gov. O.P. Morton

We the undersigned Officers of the 1st Brigade 1st Division Army South West take great pleasure in recommending to your Excellency for promotion William H. Keller of Co. G 8th Regt Ind. Vol. Formerly a resident of Cambridge City in "Old Wayne" Mr. Keller bears the scar of a wound received at "Rich Mountain" Va. He is a soldier and a gentleman in the fullest meaning of the terms; and will honor the proud young State of Indiana, which we all love so much in any position which you may please to assign him. He is now principal clerk of the A.A.Gen's office of this Brigade.

W. P. Benton
Br. Gen. Comdg. 1st Brig. 1st Div. ASW
David Shunk

Tom J. Brady Col. 8th Rgt Ind. Vol.
Maj. 8th Inf.
C.O. Howard, Adjt. 8th Ind.
Gr. (?) S. Marshall A.D.C.
C. Towshemell (?) A.D.C.
C.S. Parrish Lieut. Col. 8th Rgt.

[back of paper]
8th Regt.
Wm. H. Keller
For promotion
These papers transferred to 8th Regiment at his request.

* * * * *

Head Quarters 8th Ind. Reg
Sulphur Rock Ark, June 15th
To His Excellency
Gov. O.P. Morton
Indiana
Sir

I have the honor to recommend for the position of Adjt. of ____ the 8th Ind. Regt. made vacant by the transfer of Adjutant C.O. Howard to a Captaincy in the regular army Lieut and Act. Adgt. Joseph P. Wiggins with the rank of 1st Lieut to date from the date of Captain C.O. Howard's Commission (April 28th 1862).

I may add in Justice to Lieut. Jos. P. Wiggins his qualifications and services with said regiment justly entitles him to said promotion.

I am Sir
Your Most Obt. Servt.
David Shunk Co. 8th
Charles S. Parrish Lieut Col. 8th
Tom. J. Brady Maj. 8th Ind.

[back of paper]
8th Regt.
Lt. Jos. P. Wiggins
Recommended for
Adjutant ___
C.O. Howard
____

* * * * *

Camp at Sulphur Rock Ark
June 18, 1862
To O.P. Morton
Indianapolis, Ind.

Sir,

The undersigned officers of the 1st Brig. 1st Div. Army of the South West, would respectfully report to His Excellency that Capt. Joseph M. Thompson of Co. I 8th Regt. Ind. Vol. was informally mustered out of service by order of Major General Halleck under the impression that he was physically incompetent for the duties of his office, while his qualifications as a gentleman and efficient officer stood unimpeached and unassailed. We are satisfied that the General was mistaken, and the matter now is under going a regular and formal investigation which we have no doubt will result in reinstating the Capt. But we are on the frontier and by the time the matter will go through the circumloqution? process of getting to head quarters back the war will be over. We therefore respectfully ask that you will recommission Capt. Thompson the commission to date from the day he was thus mustered out.

W.P. Benton

Brig. Gen. Comdg at Sulphur Rock Ark.
David Shunk
Col. 8th Regt. In Vols.
Chas. S. Parrish
Lt. Col. 8th Regt. Ind. Vol.
Tom. J. Brady
Maj. 8th Ind.
James Ford A. Brig. Surgeon 1st B 1st
division Army S.W.
A.W. Sanford Chaplain 8th Ind. Vols
C.S. Ellis 1st Lieut, com. Co. I 8th Regiment Vol.
Andrew O' Daniel, Capt., Co. A., Ind. Vol.
William D. Watson, 2nd Lieut. Co. A, 8th Ind. Vol.
William R. Walls Capt. Co. B 8th Ind. Vol.
William G. Hill 2nd Lieut Co. B 8th Ind.
Samuel H. Dunbar 1st Lt. Co. B 8th Ind.
John A. Caho, 1st Lt, Comdg Co. C. 8th Ind.
F.S. Wysong, Capt. com D 8th Ind.
Lieut. Geo. W. Adams, Co. D, 8th regt. Ind. Vol.
John R. Polk Capt. Co.F. 8th Regt. Ind. Vol.
Frank Daily 1st Lt. Co. F 8th Ind. Vol
J. Weisman, 1st Lt. Co. G 8th Regt. Ind. Vol.
Benj. F. Elwood Capt. Co. E 8th Ind. Regt.
L.D. McCallister
1st Lieut, Co. K, 8th Reg. Ind. Vols.
William W. Mather 2nd Lieut Co. H. 8th Ind. Vols.
George H. Dula 2nd Lieut Co. K 8th Ind. Vols.
John Ruess Capt. Co. H, 8th Ind.
Joseph P. Wiggins Adjt. 8th Ind. Regt.
Capt.
George W. Riley Capt. Co. G. 8th Ind. Regt.
Jesse Way, 2nd Lt. Co. G. 8th Ind. Regt.
Will. R. Irwin 1st Lt. Co. B. 8th Ind. Reg

C.O. Howard, A.A. Ind. 8th Regt.

[back of paper]
8th Regt.
Capt. Jos. M. Thompson
of Co. I
Camp Sulphur Rock Ark.
June 18, 1862
The officers of the Regt.
petition that Capt. T.
be re-commissioned &
restored to his command
he having been mustered
out of the service by order
of Maj. Genl. Halleck

* * * * *

July 3, 62
Col. Simonson
as to Capt. Pitcher's
appointment as Colonel.

[8]
Indianapolis, Ind.
July 4th, 62

General

I enclose herewith a telegram from Capt. Thos. G. Pitcher of the 8th Infantry in which he inquires if he can get command of an Indiana Regt. This is respectfully referred to yourself and the Governor – please answer – I can add that Capt. Pitcher is a native Indianan is the Son of John Pitcher I think of Posey county – is a graduate of West Point Academy – an officer of high standing in the army and of distinguished Service in the Mexican War.

Very respectfully,
Your Obt. Svt.
I.S.Simonson

Gen. L. Noble
Adj. Genl. Ind.

Please send back the telegram and answer
I.S.S.

Copy of telegram

Middletown 3d July, 1862

Col. Simonson
U.S.A.

Can't I get an Indiana Regiment please answer
T.L. Pitcher

Capt. 8th Infy

* * * * *

Wabash, July 7th, 1862.

Gen. Laz. Noble,
Indianapolis,
Dear Sir,
I have the honor to acknowledge your favor of the 2nd inst. Mentioning that Gov. Morton has reappointed Capt. Jos. M. Thompson to his place in the 8th Regiment. He is now with the Regiment, (Curtis' South Western Division,) where he went some three weeks ago, and where I have written him, I should request you to forward his commission to the care of Col. Shunk. This, though not complete justice, is the only practicable act of justice within the Governor's power, to a very worthy officer, and it gives me pleasure to remember it. At the same time, on your suggestion in a former letter, I have already asked W. Shanks to place the matter before the War Department.

We notice, of the new regiments to be organized, one is to make rendezvous here. We feel that this district (the 11th) will meet the call with but little delay, and our citizens will cheerfully do any thing, if your wishes are known, to forward them, and make the men comfortable.

Very Truly Yr. Obt. Servt.
John W. Pettit.

[back of paper]
John W. Pettit
Wabash, Ind.
July 17, 1862

* * * * *

HdQuarters, 4th Div.
Army of the Miss.
______, Miss
July 12, 1862

Colonel –

I desire respectfully to recommend the Claims of Lieut. Nate Branson to his Excellency's consideration for promotion –
Lieut. B. is the Regt. Qr. Mr. of the 8th Regt. Ind. Vol. & has performed the duties of Division Qr. Mr. in my Div. Since Jan. last – his duties have been very _____ throughout he has proved precisely equal to them.

At the battle of Sugar Creek he volunteered to lead the Cavalry Charge & won the admiration of every participant for his closing conduct (over) though faithful show working in the performance of his duties as Qr. Mr. I am satisfied his qualifications are better adelapted? To the service of the time.

I will vouch for him doing hard fighting & plenty of it as a major – I hope the Governor will give his claims a consideration in his appointments for the new Regts. now being raised.

Very resty
Your obt. Svt.
Brig. Gen.
Cowl? Davis

Col. Laz. Noble
Adjt. Gen. Ind. State
Indianapolis

[back of paper]
20 47
8th Reg.
Brig. Gen. Davis
Nate Branson
Recommends Qr. Mr. Branson for promotion

* * * * *

Head Qrs. 1st Brig. 1st Dvi
Helena, Ark, July 16th 1862

His Excellency Gov. O.P. Morton:

Sir:

The position of 2d Lieutenant of Co. "G", 8th Ind. Reg't. has just been vacated by the resignation of its former incumbent, and at the same time intelligence was received from the Orderly Sergeant, who was at home sick, announcing that he had been discharged on account of "physical disability" – whereupon the Captain immediately called an election to fill the vacancies. The result was the election of the 4th Sergeant, as 2d Lieut, a man whom Col. Wood refused to muster in as <u>an officer</u> on account of his disgraceful conduct in the three months service, and the 3d Sergt. elected as Orderly Serg't. I was assigned to the company, upon its organization, as <u>First</u> duty Sergeant, by Col. W.P. Benton, and have held the position up to the present time; therefore, in accordance with General Orders, No. 1, issued by Adj't. Gen. Noble, I am entitled to the position.

In regard to my competency and fitness to fill the position, I respectfully refer you to a letter of recommendation, of myself, written to your Excellency, by Gen. Benton, some weeks since, or to any of the citizens of Cambridge City my former place of residence.

I am respectfully
Your ob't servt
William H. Keller

[back of paper]
Wm. H. Keller

As to the
Appt. as 2d Lt.
See inside!

* * * * *

Helena Ark. July 22, 1862

To Gov. O.P. Morton

Dear Sir

It is with unreserved pleasure that we recommend to your favorable consideration, Captain Alexander J. Kenney, for appointment and commission, as Lieutenant Colonel in one of the new regiments now forming in Indiana.

During the past fifteen months, Captain Kenney has been serving in the "Eighth Indiana" as a Company Commander, and has deservingly obtained an enviable reputation among his brother officers and the men under his command as an affable and courteous gentleman, a strict disciplinarian and a brave soldier.

Ever active, energetic and discreet, we doubt not Governor, should the appointment sought for be tendered to the Captain, you would find him very useful and efficient in recruiting the regiment to which he might be assigned; while his fine abilities for command – his knowledge of military tactics and habits of strict discipline, would enable him to take, and maintain his position in his regiment with credit to himself – to the benefit of the army and signal good to the cause in which he is fighting.

Believing Governor, that the interest, of the country would be subserved by making the appointment thus solicited – we hope you may find it consistent with your public duties in the premises, to issue the commission asked for.

Very truly Your Friends
and Ob't Servants
D. Shunk
Col. 8th Ind. Infy
Charles S. Parrish
Lt. Col. 8th " "
[hard to read this line] Henry D. Washburn Col. 18 Regt. Ind. Vol.
D. O. Thomas Lt. Col. 18 Regt. Ind. Vol
[hard to read this line] G. N. ? Col. 24 Ind. Vol.
W. L. S? Col. 24th Ind. Vols.
A.W. Sanford Chaplain 8th Ind.

[back of paper]
Capt. Alex. J. Kenney
of 8th Regiment

recommend for
Colonel

* * * * *

[8]

To His Excellency

O.P. Morton

Gov. of Indiana

Sir,

We the undersigned Officers of Indiana Regiments attached to the Army of the South West know Captain William R. Walls of Co. B, 8th Ind. Infty, and believing men of merit deserve promotions and make most efficient officers, we take pleasure in recommending him for promotion in any regiment forming or to any regiment former in which there is a vacancy. Capt. Walls, is competent to fill position of a Field Officer, he has been a faithful and efficient soldier and indured without a murmur, the vicissitudes through which the Army of the South West has passed. He was in the ranks and served throughout the Mexican Campaign, also the three months campaign in Virginia, in which latter service he was 1st Lieut. Of Company I. Hoping that this Officer may receive your favorable consideration, and receive promotion, for which he is qualified and deserving.

Helena, Ark. July 25 1862

Charles S. Parrish	Lt. Col. 8th Ind. Infy
Tom J. Brady	Maj. 8th Ind.
Saml. H. Dunbar	Adjt. 8" Ind.
Andrew O'Daniel	Capt. Co. A. 8th Ind.
William D. Watson	1st Lieut. Co. A, 8th
Henry G. Washburn	Col. 18th Regt. Ind. Vol.
D. O. Thomas	Lt. Col. 8th Regt. Ind. Vols.

[back of paper]
Wm. R. Walls
Capt. 8th Regt.

Field Officer

* * * * *

[side of paper]
F. N. Scott
Richmond
Ind.
August 6, 1862
8th Regt.

Richmond Ind. Aug 6, 1862
L. Noble A.A.G A.S.W.
Indianapolis
Dr. Sir
I am connected with the Q.M. Dpt. Of Genl. Benton's Brig. & intend returning to the army of Monday next & think I can get a few recruits for the 8th Ind. Reg. I wish to ascertain if I can get transportation for myself & the recruits & if so what will be requisite for me to do – can I have them sworn in here & will it be necessary stop at the capitol to

get the necessary papers ___ please inform me immediately. I think there are several persons here who will be willing to enlist for the 8th if they can get free transportation to the reg. who are not inclined to go into the new Reg. & it is conceded on all hands that one recruit in the old is worth two in the new one -----.
I should be pleased to hear from you soon as my time is getting short.

Yours truly
F.N. Scott

* * * * *

To his Excellency
O.P. Morton
Gov. State of Indiana,

The undersigned citizens of Delaware County, Indiana, hereby recommend the Appointment of John Taylor as Second Lieutenant for the recruiting service for the purpose of recruiting a company of volunteers for the military service of the United States of America. Mr. Taylor has seen service as a member of the 8th regiment Indiana Volunteers – three months troops – and is we think, well qualified for the position

August 7th, 1862
C. Gample ?
G. Brimer?
Leon Marks Ho ?
Herman Short
L & W. Shick
E. C. Anthony
Wilson & Hibbits
David Kilgore
W.J.H. Cassady?
W.B. Williams
J.W. Rop?
W.H. Stewart
M Cassady
D. Nation

A.M. Klein
R. Ridbury?
illegible
John Galbraith
W.C. Willard
Chas. F. Willard
Maddy & Sons
Marcus C. Smith
John Brady
Fred. E. Puhicue?
John W. Kirby
W. P. Howell
John W. Dungan
C.E. Shipley
Sam. F. Brady

[back of paper]
John Taylor
Muncie, Ind.
Recommend for
Lieutcy.

* * * * *

[side of paper]
8th Regt.
John H. Bock
Private

8th

Sulphur Springs, Ind. Aug. 11th 1862,
To His Excellency, Gov. O.P. Morton of Indiana, and all to whom it may concern, we take pleasure in recomending , to your consideration the bearer, John H. Bock – a member of the 8th Ind. Regt. Vol. we recomend him as a young man of good moral habits and well drilled in the military service, having been in the service, one year – should he apply for any situation in the service, above his present position, we think his service merits reward.

Albert N Zant?
Jacob Good
Dr. W. K. Hendricks

B. Benbow, P.N.
R.W. Scott
W. S. Jost
H.C. Murphy

Benjamin Benbow
Richard D. Dunbar
Benjamin Harvey
W. Yost
Levi Riddar?
H.T. Vandevender, 8th Reg. Capt. Ind

* * * * *

Helena, Ark, Aug. 18th, 1862

To his Excellency,
Gov. O.P. Morton
Indianapolis, Ind.
Sir: -

We, the undersigned, would respectfully suggest the name of Capt. B.F. Elwood, Co. E. 8th Ind., as a suitable person upon whom to bestow promotion. He has served with the 8th from its organization for the "three months" service, and from the ranks has gone steadily on from one promotion to another, displaying equal ability in the discharge of the duties incumbent and signal fidelity and earnestness. As a soldier we know him to be brave and faithful, as a man we believe him to be true, and worthy [two words crossed out here] with which you may choose to deck? Him.

We are, with respect –
D. Shunk, Col 8th Regt.
C.S. Parrish Lt. Col. 8th Ind.

Tom J. Brady Maj. 8th Ind.
W.P. Benton
Brig. Gen. Comdg
1st Brig 1st Div.?

[Back of paper]
Capt. B.F. Elwood
8th Regt.
Promotion
?
?

* * * * *

Headquarters 1st Div. A.S.W.
Camp at Helena Ark
Aug. 29, 1862

To his Excellency
Gov. O.P. Morton
Dr. Sir:

It affords me pleasure to bear honorable testimony of the merits of Capt. Wysong of Co. H. 8th Ind. He was in the three month service & in the 6th. And has been in the 8th from the commencement of the war service. The Captain & his company are always for duty, and he will fight – there is no mistake, I have seen him tried. He will do honor to himself and the State in any location? to which you may assign him in the troop, now being raised. And in my opinion you ought to have at least one of the old officers among the field officers of every regiment sent out. I have no interest in the matther but what is common with you the glory of the Great State of Indiana.

I have the honor to be
Respectfully your old --- W.P. Benton
Brig. Gen 1st Div. A.S.W.

[next page]
David Shunk
Col 8th Reg Ind. Vols.
C.S. Parrish Lt. Col.
8th Ind. Infy
Tom J. Brady
Maj. 8th Ind.
[back of paper]
8th
Capt. Wysong
Of Co. D. 8th Ind.

For Promotion
in New Regt.

Genl. Benton

* * * * *

Head Quarters 8th Ind.
Helena Ark.
Aug. 30th 1862.

To his Excellency,
Gov. O.P. Morton
Indianapolis, Ind.
Sir –

We would respectfully ask you to commission Dr. J.K. Bigelow of Grant Co., Ind., ---- Hospl. Steward of the 8th Ind., and Asst. Surg. of 6th --- Cav. more lately, junior or second Asst. Surgeon of our Regt. – I need scarcely add he is the choice of the Regt., rank and file, commissioned and noncommissioned, for any position in the Surgeon's Dept. that may be vacated. We once unanimously recommended him for the Asst. Surgeoncy. Dr. & friend Ellis of Wabash declines the commission of Sec. Asst. Surgeon, and Dr. Bigelow being once more foot-loose we respectfully urge his appointment.

-----, Governor

Tom J. Brady
Maj. 8th Ind.

With much respect -
David Shunk Col 8th
C.S. Parish Lt. Col. Comdg.

[back of paper]
8th Regt.
Dr. J.K. Bigelow
of Grant Co.
For asst. surg.

Recommendation
of Field Officers

Appt.

* * * * *

Helena Ark August 30th 1862
O.P. Morton
Gov. Indiana

Sir, I have the honor to respectfully decline accepting the commission as assistant surgeon of the 8th Ind. Regt. issued by your Excellency
April 25th 1862

Respectfully yours C.S. Ellis

PS and would respectfully recommend the appointment of J.K. Bigelow to that Position
C.S. Ellis

* * * * *

Camp Wayne Sep. 2nd 1862

To His Excellency, O.P. Morton Gov. of Ind.

The petition of the undersigned, company officers of the 84th Regt. Ind. Vol. respectfully represents that they were not in camp, when the petition, for the appointment of Lycurgus L. Boblet, as Major of said Regiment was circulated, and were consequently deprived of the privilege of signing said recommendation. They therefore adopt this method of expressing their preference, by soliciting the appointment of said Boblet as aforesaid, believing him to be eminently qualified for the position of Major of the Regt., being acquainted with his reputation, and having witnessed evidence of his abilities as a Drill Master and Tactician, besides his having seen actual service in the field.

Capt. J.M. Fellows
1st Lieut Frank Fullige (?)
2 Lieut/Frank? C. Liat?
Cap. M. Kisby
1st Lieut M.B. Gregory
H.T. Warren 2 Lieut

[back of paper]
84th R. I. Vols.
Lycurgus L. Boblet
Major
Additionaly Recommendn
of Company Officers
Other ---- on file

* * * * *

HEAD QUARTERS, DEPARTMENT OF THE MISSOURI,
September 3, 1862

SPECIAL ORDERS,
No. 315

The resignation of Chaplain A.W. Sanford, 8th Regt. Indiana Inf. Volunteers, is accepted to take effect August 14th 1862.

BY ORDER OF MAJOR GENERAL HALLECK.
L.M. Preston
Assistant Adjutant General.

Chaplain A.W. Sanford reported as belonging to the 81st Regt.. Should be the 8th

Governor of Indiana
Indianapolis
Indiana

[back of paper]
8th Regt.
Rev. A.W. Sanford
Chaplain resignation

* * * * *

Camp at Helena, Ark.
Sep. 6th 1862

To his Excellency
Gov. O.P. Morton

We undersigned take pleasure in recommending to your Excellency for a Commission in the Engineer Corps, Sergeant William A. Van Buskirk of Co. F. 8th Regt. Ind. Vol. He has had much experience both in civil life and in the field. He had been the only engineer on Gen. Benton's staff since the organization of the

Regiment And more than that, he had followed the fortunes of the old 8th Ind Regt from its organization in April 1861 to the present time.

W.P. Benton
Brig. Gen. Comd'g 1st Div. Army S.West

David Shunk
Col. 8th Regt. Ind. Vols.
C.S. Parrish
Lt. Col. 8th Ind. Inf.
[back of paper]
66
Sergt. W. A. Van Buskirk
of 8th Regt.

* * * * *

Indianapolis, Sept. 22d, 1862.

Gov. Morton

I cheerfully recommend to your favorable notice Sergt. Stanton J. Peelle, of Co. G 8th Regt. Ind. Vols., as a man well worthy of promotion. He has been in the service thirteen month, and, on every occasion, has performed his duty as becomes a true soldier. He acquitted himself with credit at the battle of Pea Ridge, Ark., and on all occasions since. He thoroughly understands the various drills – is a strictly sober man, and will if promoted, honor any position to which he may be chosen.

I am Sir,
Your obt. Servt.
G.W. Riley
Capt. Co. G 8th Ind. Infty.

* * * * *

Head Quarters 8th Regt Ind Vols.
Camp at Helena Ark Sept. 26th, 62

Oliver P. Morton
Governor of Indiana

Dr. Sir.

Being officially informed of the resignation of the first and Second Lieutenants of Company (I) of My Regiment I would respectfully recommend as worthy of promotion to fill the vacancies of Said Company the following named persons
Orderly Robert Torrence for 1st Lieutenant vice Lieut. C.S. Ellis Resigned
Sergeant Elias B. McPherson for 2nd Lieutenant vice Noble N. Morris Resigned
both of which vacancies occur in Company (I) 8th Rgt. Ind. Vols. and if Consistent with the interest & usage of the Service would like their commission dated back to Sept. 6th the date at which their discharges takes affect.

Respectfully yours &co?
David Shunk Col
8th Regt. Ind. Vols.

[back of paper]
8th Regt.
Co. I
Promotion

* * * * *

Head Quarters 8th Ind.
Helena Ark, Oct. 1st 1862

Gov. O.P. Morton
Indianapolis
Ind.

Dear Sir –

We take much pleasure in recommending to your favorable consideration Seargt. Stannton J. Peele, of Co. G 8th Ind. Inft. He is a ---- of much merit, prompt in the performance of every duty, energetic, brave, and, withal?, an excellent officer. In any position to which you may feel disposed to place him we feel assured he will give you, and those with whom he may associate, entire satisfaction.

We are, with much respect,
your obt. servts.
W.P. Benton Brig. Gen. Vols
David Shunk Col 8th Rgt
Tom. J. Brady
Maj. 8th Ind.
Charles S. Parrish
Lt. Col. 8th Ind.
G. W. H. Riley Capt. Co. G Infy

2-35

[back of paper]
8th
Stannton J. Peele
Promotion
File among drafted? Papers

* * * * *

Head Quarters 8th Regt.
Camp at Helena Ark. Oct 2nd 1862

Oliver P. Morton
Gov. of Indiana

Dr Sir

Being officially notified of the acceptance of the resignation of the 2nd Lieutenant Wm. P. Goolman of Company (D) 8th regiment 2nd vols. – I take pleasure in recommending for Promotion 1st Sergeant Isaac N. Smith to fill Said vacancy he being next in line in Said company and fully qualified to discharge the duties of Said office.

I am very truly
Your obt. Srvt
David Shunk
Col. 8th Rgt. Ind. Vols.

[back of paper – very faint, hard to read]
8th Regt.
Co. D. prom.
?

* * * * *

Surg. Med. Mills. Nst????
"Chief Medical Director"
Sir

I need not remind you of the vast amount of Suffering and inconvenience, which the absence of Regmtl. Medical officers had occasioned our Army during its Stay in the Sickly & trying climate of Helena, Arkansas, but, I would now respectfully write your attention to the case of these very men, who succeeded in obtaining a Sick leave of absence for twenty days and have far exceeded that leave without proper authority, and are now returning to their Regmts after Spending the Sickly Season North, this to the detriment of the Service, injustice to the Sick, and an imposition on the few and faithful Surgeons who remained "true to their post"

I shall first present the case of Asst. Surg. Bigelow late of the 6th Missouri Cvly who on or about the 23d of August, while Serving with the Army of the South West "1st Div" at Helena, Arkansas, did willingly, and without cause, abandon his Regmt. at a time when Medical officers were Scarce, and Sickness, and Suffering, had existed among the troops. more especially in the 6th Mo. Cavly., that Said officer has not to my Knowledge accounted for the Hospital Stores and property which he from time to time recd. through the Medical Purveyor. Secondly, that his course was a violation of order & discipline, a bad example to officers and men.

I have in my return of Medical Officers ASW for the month of September, already, reported this officer as absent without leave, but the present occasion calls forth a Special report on his case, after an unaccountable absence of Several weeks Dr. Bigelow returns to the Command, but not to the Regiment which he shamefully abandoned, thus having abused the honor conferred on him by the Gov. of Missouri. He returns with a fresh honor in the Shape of a commis. From Gov. Morton Indiana "who I suppose was not aware of the record which he "Dr. B." had left after him in the 6th Mo. Cavly, "and is now doing duty with the 8th Indiana Regmt.

This very unaccountable proceeding of Dr. B's in deserting his Regmt when his services are most required and leaving his Sick without proper medical officer to care for them is Known to most of the Surgeons of the command, and if such a precedent as this remains unpolitical or unpunished, the good and industrious officers can expect by little reward for their toil & energy.

I have the honor to be
Your obdt Sevt.
G. Wall Burke

Surgn of Volunteers
Senr. Surg. of Genl. Steels Army

[back of paper]
HdQrs Genl Steeles Army
Pilot Knob
Oct 18th 1862
R. Noel Burke
Medical Union
Surg -----
Complains of Regt. Surgeons &
Asts being absent Musters
the case of Ast Surgeon
Bigelow
Medical Directors Office
St. Louis Missoui
Oct 22nd 1862
Respectfully referred to
Col. Laz Noble Adjt Genl
State of Indiana Requesting
that if Dr Burke's statement
be true Ast. Surg. Bigelow
be removed from his position
By order Medical Director
Peter? V Schenck
Ast Surg USA
Recd. M.D.O. Oct – 21st 1862

Dr. Bigelow's
Case

Asst. Surgeon

Complaints

* * * * *

His Excellency Oliver P. Morton

In making appointments of Regimental officers for the Regiments formed and being formed in the State, I earnestly recommend to your favorable consideration Capt. Geo W.H. Riley of the 8th Regiment.

He has been in the service since the commencement of the rebellion – was at Rich Mountain, Pea Ridge, with Genl Curtis in his memorable march through Arkansas, and has, under all circumstances, shown himself to be a brave and accomplished officer. He understands militia tactics thoroughly, and will make an efficient and popular officer. I notice with pleasure that your Excellency has been promoting officers who have seen service, and I believe there are few in the army who are more deserving such an honor than Capt Riley.

Hoping a favorable consideration of his merits,
I am
Your friend
Tho. M. Browne

Winchester Ind
October 26th 1862
[back of paper]

Capt. Geo. W.H. Riley
of 8th Regt.

For Regimental
Officer in New Regt.

* * * * *

Col Williams

I certify that I have mustered into the US? Service in and for the 8th Ind Vol
David S. Bowman   Daniel T. Reynolds
Oct 30 1862

Charles A. ----?
Capt. 18? Infy

[back of paper]
8th Indiana

* * * * *

Fort Curtis, Ironton, Mo
Oct 27th 1862
To his Excellency
Gov. O.P. Morton

We the undersigned Officers who are personally acquainted with Corp Joseph S. Powell of Co. C, 8th Ind Infy, and know him to be well qualified to fill any position as an Officer of the brigade? Cheerfully recommend him to you for a commission as a fine officer.

W.P. Benton
Brig Genl Vol.

David Shunk Col
8th Reg In Vols
A. O'Daniel Capt. Co. A, 8th Ind
Wm D. Watson 2nd Lt Co. A 8th Reg
Wm. R. Walls Capt. Co. B
Wm. G. Hill 2nd Lt. Co. B 8th Ind

A.J. Kenny Capt. Co. C 8th Ind. Infty
Comd'g at Fort Curtis
J.A. Caho 1st Lt Co. C 8th Ind

Geo. W. Adams 1st Lt, Co. D 8th Ind.
I. N. Smith 2nd Lt., Co. D 8th Ind.
J.R. Pearce Commanding Co. E
Frank Dailey 1st Lieutenant C
John Ruess Capt. Co. H 8th Ind.
William Mather 2nd Lt. Co. H
Robert E. Torrence 1st Lieut Co. I
Jesse E. Way Co. G 8th [hard to read]
H.T. Vendevender
Capt. Co. K 8th

[back of page]
Oct 27 62
Sergt. Jos. S. Powell

Co. C. 8th Regt. Ind. Vols.

Reccomd for appointment

Jos. S. Powell
Co. C. 8th Regt.
Captain

* * * * *

B Fleming	T. W. McClure
Wm Mitchell	P -----?
Wm Perry	G Brown
D. Coffman	J. Clevenger
	J. Hankins
James A. Brown	A. Riggs
Joel Hendricks	H.P. Thomas
G.H. Berry	J. Maning
S. Bowers	J. McNew
W. Nelson	H. Graham
B. Tarkleson	S. Craig
D Kent	J. Hankins
I.T. Thounburg?????????????	A.J.E. Purdue
Job Ginn	Wm Roberts
John K. Swain	Wm Vanmatre
	H. Shoemaker
William R. Fleming	C. Pitser
Gary Jester	A Oard
	C.T. Bedford
B.S. West	W.T. Beck
J. R. Stout	O.P. Hays
	J.M. Windsor
Henry Good	A. O. Neff
Daniel Hartman	Z. Windsor

[this half of the page is very faint and hard to read]
------ 1863
---- Gov. O.P. Morton
Executive Department
Indianapolis, Indiana

----

the undersigned would like bring attention your honor to appoint -----
Jas. Beck ---------------- Henry Co.

We are acquainted with him as a Physician and Citizen. And would be willing to trust to his abilities to treat us when Sick. Character of Dr. Jas. Beck is known as a temperance

man, and we feel an assurance that we will not be neglected on 6 Oct? his being ------------ ----------- ----------- from ----------------------------------for ------------------------------------
[this section is harder to read, so I did not try to type it]
Names Names
R. S. Moore names could be had but think it unnecessary from the ranks or privates of the 8th Regt. Ind. Vols.
[this section upside down]
8th
Dr. Jas. Black

Henry Co.
Asst Surgeon.

* * * * *

Head Quarters Med. Dep. 8th Ind Infty

Col. Noble
Adj. Genl

Sir, this morning we received from your hand to Burkes labored article of charges against me – notwithstanding his protestation that he was in no wise endeavoring to have me mustered out of the service. For the correctness of my reply I refer the authorities to the Records of the 8th Ind. and 6th Mo. Cavly especially Dr. McConagly – 14th Mo. Vols, Dr. Nixon 4th Mo. Cavly, Brig. Surgeon Otterson Gen. Curtis Staff 8th Mo Infty.

1st I was never commissioned asst. Surgeon 6th Mo. Cavly I was in the commencement of this war mustered into the 8th Mo. Infty as Hospital steward and have never been transferred from that Regt. which the Records will show.

My action in the 6th Mo. Cavly was ordered by my superior officers, and all I done in was under orders from Dr. Otterson Med. Director and Gen. Curtis, and was simply command because it was in the enemies country and needed a surgeon and we were removed so far from Head Quarters at St Louis as to be impractible to have an asst. appointed by the authority I remained with the Regt. and did my duty to the best of my ability and flatter myself to the entire satisfaction of my officers

In reference to the change of "absence without leave" I have only this today that upon Helena, the extra amount of duty I had nec------ undergone during the campaign had so reduced my health and strength that I was compelled to take my bed upon which I remained for five consecutive marks with Continued fever and inflammatory Rheumatism – which so prostrated me that I requested a furlough to go home – and applied to Dr. Burke then acting Med. Director for a certificate upon which to found an application for leave of absence - Dr. Burke refused me on the ground that Med. officers were scarce. And I could not go. I argued that I was unable for duty but the Dr. treated me with great disrespect and did not examine my case but was utterly refused to grant me a certificate.

The Post Surgeon at Helena on the same day saw me inquired if I was able to go to Gen'l Hospital in charge of sick. I accepted the care of the sick and proceeded to Mound City Ills. Gen'l Hospital and from there upon the advise of surgeons there in charge went on to

Indiana for the purpose of recovering my health – and while there was Commissioned Asst. Surgeon of 8th Ind. At the instance of the officers of my Regt. and not by my own expanded desire. I returned at once to my Regt. which was under marching orders and I accompanied them to this place. The 6th Mo. Cavly was all the time in the interior on scouting duties and it was impossible for me to – since the Med. Director an in---- of the Meds & Supplies which were under my control in the Regt. I procured the services of a competent surgeon to accompany the 6th Mo. cavly – and for whose acts I am responsible – and will report the condition of the supplies of that Regt. when the proper time comes in I have only to add further that the cause of my present difficulties with Dr. Burke is not on account of my absence or neglect of duty because as I before said I had done five marks before I left Helena and was not able entirely for duty when I returned to Helena from ----- afterwards – but is on account of the following -

Upon our arrival at Sulphur Springs I was ordered by the Gen. Comdg. to proceed to St. Louis with the sick for Gen'l Hospital – Upon my arrival there I met Dr. Burke - Med. Director who instead of being with the command as he should be to determine who should go the Genl. Hosp.was then and ordered my sick and starving men back to their Regiments to which proceeding I objected and finally succeeded in getting my men into Hospital by the timely interposition Dr. Schank Asst. Surg. U.S.A., after which Dr. Burke attacked me in the Public Reading Room of the Planters House in St. Louis and there called me "A Dam'd ---- - A Dam'd Scoundrel" &c &c – which I felt was unbecoming a gentleman and Officer – and so signified to Dr. Burke Who repeated his epithets and abuse until I was enraged and resented his insults and refer to the gentlemen present if I was not entirely justifiable. It is well to state also in my opinion Dr. Burke was so intoxicated as to be unable for duty – without any doubt the above altercation was the imediate cause of the charges preferred against me.

I have the honor to be ---

J.K. Bigelow

Asst. Surg. 8th Ind. Infty

[back of paper]

<u>8th Regt. Ind.</u>

Dr. Ja. K. Bigelow

<u>Asst. Surg.</u>

Statement of facts relating to his difficulty with Dr. Burke Med. Dir.

* * * * *

Headquarters 8" Ind. Infty

Camp at Patterson Mo.

Nov. 7" 1862

Col. Laz. Noble

Adjt. General State of Indiana

D Sir:

Your favor of the 3rd inst. enclosing statement of Doct. Burke against Dr. James K. Bigelow asking for a statement of the facts in the case came to hand to day. And in reply have the honor to say: that herewith you will please find statement of Dr. Bigelow, together with a copy of <u>Remonstrance</u>, sent to Dr. Burke. These will explain fully the situation of Dr. Bigelow in this matter and our views upon the subject. My opinion is that Dr. Burke is endeavoring to have Bigelow mustered out of the service, because he (Burke) became enraged at Bigelow for bringing a lot of sick men of the 1st Brigade from Sulphur Springs to St. Louis. The sick belonged to the 8", & 18" Indiana Regiments and 1st Indiana Battery. Dr. Bigelow was acting under orders of General Wm. P. Benton in the matter. You will see from his endorsement upon copy of remonstrance referred to that he says, he is not endeavoring to have Dr. Bigelow mustered out of the service, nevertheless he sends up to you a labored argument to that effect which is conclusive evidence to me that there is some malice at the bottom of all of it. If Dr. Burke was half as energetic in some other matters to which I have twice called his attention, it would be much better for the regiment. I refer to the case of Doct. G.W. Bruce. I have twice represented him to Dr. Burke Medical Director Also, as being incompetent to fill the place he is to occupy. He also went home on a 70 days leave granted at Helena Arks, on the 23rd day of August A.D. 1862, and that he was able while at home on such sick leave to visit persons eighty miles distant from his home to. Yet the Medical Director Doct. Burke, takes no notice of this, while in Bigelow's case, he seems to manifest undue anxiety. My desire is to retain Dr. Bigelow. As for Doct. Bruce, I care not how soon you take him away. Bigelow was never commissioned Asst. Surgeon of the 6" Mo. cavalry, but has been hospital steward of the 8" Indiana Regiment. But was sent to that cavalry to do, and did do a surgeons part and was promised commission in said regiment but never received it. In conclusion would say, that his place cannot in my opinion be supplied. In the 8" Ind. all know him well and his efficient services rendered to us when others in better positions, failed, have endeared him to the entire command. Respectfully

David Shunk Col. said 8" Ind.

[back of paper]
8th
Col. D. Shunk
In relation to case
of D. Bigelow

Recd. Nov 10.

* * * * *

Head Qur. Medical Dept.
Patterson Mo. Camp Steel Nov. the 15 1862
Adj. Gen. Laz. Noble

Hon. Sir

I have the honor of addressing you

I was informed to day by James Ford Surgeon of the 8 Reg. Ind. Vol., that I had been reported by the officers of the 8 Reg. as resigning my position as assitt. Surgeon of the above Reg. Such is not the case, I tendered my resignation on the th17 of April last am it was not excepted but sent back disapproved by <u>Gen. Curtis</u>. and I have not resined Since that time I am very sure and I hope you will correct the mistake. I have been with the Reg. and have have change of the Medical department of the Reg. the greater part a lone.

I have the honor to be your obedient cervant

Geo. W. Bruce assist

Surgeon of th 8th Reg. Ind. Vol.
[back of paper]
8" Regt.
Dr. Geo. W. Bruce

Reports his presence for duty etc.

Vacancy exploited on Apl, and another appointed
Noble
ans @

* * * * *

Camp Steele Patterson Mo.

November 14th 1862.
To Charles S. Parrish
Lt. Col. Comdy 8th Ind. Infty.

Sir,

The undersigned field & company officers on duty with such Regiment, respectfully petition that you appoint the Rev. H.C. Skinner as Chaplain of said Regiment, to fill vacancy occasioned by resignation of Rev. G.W. Sanford.

Thos. J. Brady Maj. 8th Ind.
H.T. Vandervender Cap. Co. K
L.D. McAllister 1st Lt. K. IN
E.B. McPherson 1st Lieut. Co. I. 8th Regt.
Robert E. Torrence 1st Lieut Co. I 8th Regt.
John Ruese Capt. Co. H 8th Ind.
William W. Mather 2nd Lt. Co. H 8th Ind.
L.H. Harman 1st Lieut. Co. H Ind.
Jacob Widaman [hard to read]
Jesse W. Way [hard to read]
John R. Polk Capt. Co. "F"
Frank Daily 1st Lt. Co. F
J. R. Pearce 2nd Lieut. Co. E [over]
F.S. Wysong Capt. Co. D
Geo. W. Adams 1st Lieut.
Isaac N. Smith 2nd Lt. Co. D
A.J. Kenny Capt. Co. C
John A. Caho Lieut " "
D. Fleming " " "
Wm. R. Walls Capt. Co. B 8th Ind. Inf.
Andrew O Daniel Capt. Co. A

W.D. Watson 2nd Lt. Co. A. 8th
Joseph M Thompson Capt. Co I 8th Ind.
[back of page]
8th
Revd. Henry C. Skinner
Chaplain

Commissioned

* * * * *

[8]

"To Whom it may Concern."

Whereas the undersigned having been petitioned, by a majority of the Field and Campany Officers, now on duty with the Eighth Regement Indiana Infantry, to appoint the Rev. Henry C. Skinner, as Chaplain of said Regement, vice Rev. A.W. Sanford, resigned.

Now therefore in performance of said petition, and by virtue of the 9th section of the act of Congress, approved July 22d 1861, I hereby constitute and appoint him the said Henry C. Skinner as Chaplain of said Regement, To serve and be respected as such.

Mr. Skinner will report, without delay, to any officer of the United States army, stationed at St. Louis, Mo. for the purpose of being mustered into the service of the United States, in pursuance of Genl order No. 126.

Given at Camp Steele, Patterson, Mo this 18th day of November 1862.

} Charles S. Parrish Lt. Col.
Wm. Hill Ad'jt } Com'dg 8th Ind. In'fy

* * * * *

Camp on Blackman, Mo.
Nov. 26th, 1862

Gov. O.P. Morton,

Dear Governor,

Permit me to make a statements of facts, pertaining to the case James K. Bigalow. At the time you commissioned him Assist. Surgeon of the 8th Ind. Infantry, he was acting as Assist. Surg H. in the 6th Mo. cavalry by order of Gen. Curtis, but had no commission as an officer in the medical staff anywhere. By your authority (being sworn in) he entered on duty in the 8th Ind. Vol. Dr. Burk, the division Surgeon, and he, has some difficulty and Burk reported him as "Shamefully neglecting the sick of the 6th Mo. Cavalry", when he Burk, must have known that Dr. B. was acting under your commission in the 8th Ind. Infantry.

Dr. B. is not only mustered out of service, but some four months pay is forfeited to the government. He is poor, and cannot well afford to loose his just earnings.

He is an efficient officer, well beliked by all the men and officers of the Regt., any favors you may be disposed to extend toward him in restoring him to his command, will be highly appreciated by all his numerous friends, and, especially, by your humble servant.

James Ford Surg. 8th Regt.
Ind. Infantry

[back of paper]
8
Dr. J.K. Bigelow
Statement of Surgeon Ford as to Dr. B's dismissal

* * * * *

Head Quarters, Department of the Missouri
St. Louis, Mo., December 7, 1862.

Special Orders, }
No. 72 } Extract

1. Second Lieut. Geo. H. Dula of Co. "K," 8th Indiana Infy. Vol. having tendered his resignation on account of ill health, is hereby honorably discharged the Service of the United States.

By command of Major General Curtis
H.Z. Curtis
Assistant Adjutant General

Adjutant General,
State of Indiana

[back of paper]
8th
Lt. Dula
Resigned

* * * * *

Camp on Black River,
Wayne Co. Mo. Dec. 7th 1862.

Gov. O.P. Morton
Indianapolis
Ind.

Dear Sir –

By order of Col. Shunk I this evening upon "Dress-parade" had the pleasure of reading to the Regiment your admirable petition on behalf of the soldier. Permit me to assure you, you have struck a chord in the heart of the volunteers that will vibrate long after the occasion which has called him to the field is passed and gone. The vociferous cheering that greeted the persons, continued when companies were dispersed, attests the emotions you have roused. Go on as you have begun and the thanks received of the soldiers will be yours, in the present of a distracted country and remembered in the future of a reunited and happy people.

I am, sir, your friend
and obt. servt.,
Tho. J. Brady
Maj. 8th Ind. Inft.

[back of paper]
8th
Maj. T.J. Brady
effect of circular read to troops

* * * * *

Executive Department of Indiana
Adjutant General's Office
Indianapolis ________ 186_

Adjutant Generals Office
Washington, Dec. 17th, 1862.

George H. Dula 2nd Lieut.
Co. "K" 8th, Regt. Ind. Vols.
Resignation accepted, to take effect from Dec. 7th, 1863.
[back of paper]
Second Lieutenant
Geo. H. Dula

Resignation accepted
Dec. 7th, 1862

Extract
Original filed with 6th Regiment

* * * * *

Camp near Black River Mo.
Dec. 18th, 1862.
To his Excellency,
O.P. Morton
(Gov. Indiana ? hard to read – most of letter is very faint)
(hard to read)
_______ _______ of the resignation of 1st Lt. F. Daily of Co. F 8th Ind. Inft. a vacancy exists and ?in light of the? fact that John R. Polk, Capt. of said Company has intimidated his intention to ?recommend? for 1st Lt. a Sergt. of said company our sec. Lt. Richard M. Smith who is not only ______ ____ to but is _________ qualified to fill said Position with __________ ____________________.

We therefore the privates and non-commissioned officers of Co. F 8th Ind. Inft. do hereby recommend Richard M. Smith 2nd Lt. for promotion as 1st Lt. of said company believing that in doing so you will not only do justice to a brave officer, but will a qualified in the undersigned.

Names	Names
William H. Hoke	Clifton Brown
James C. Musselman	Thomas Leatherland

Joseph McVicker
Eugene Sullivan
John S. Dubois
W. H. Moore Corporal

Names
George F. Cox
William H. Long
John Long
John A. Rhodes
Robert D. Hite
William M. Wright
Francis M. Wright
John W. Goodlander Crpl.
Irvin R. Meek Corpl.
Curtis Stone
Wm. H. Case
Isaac A. Blakely 1st Sergt.
John Elms
Isiah Landis
Jesse Vanduyne
John Vanduyne
Wm. Snediker
William W. King Corpl
James A. Peak
Joseph Repp
Joseph Beaumont
John S. O'Brien, Sergt
David Vanduyne
Kenny? Rutherford
(can't read)
George C. Karney

James A. Wilson
Jonathan S. Hiatt
Zenas Hesford
John H. Grochenour

Names
John H. Roberson
Daniel D. Swafford
Elias Bagley
Jonas Pudderbaugh
William J. ? Roberson
Matthias Wolf
Ezra B. Hale
W. B. Ridgeway
William Laughlin
Aug. Rhoads
Stephen Wolf, Sergt.

* * * * *

Camp on C_________ River
December 20?th 1862
Adjutant General
of the State of Indiana

To fill the vacancy of 2nd Lieutenant Company K 8th Regt. Ind. Volunteers, caused by the resignation of George H. Dula, I hereby recommend, 1st Sergeant John H. Hicks, company K 8th Ind. to fill vacancy.

Hiram T. Vandervender
Capt. Co. K 8th Regt. Ind. Vol.

David Shunk

Col. 8th Ind. Infty
[back of paper]
8th Regt.
Promotion Co. K.
E

* * * * *

Head Quarters 8th Ind. Infty
Camp Alton Mo.
January 21st, 1863
To his Excellency
O.P. Morton
Gov. Indiana
Sir.

Captain William R. Walls of Company B 8th Indiana Infantry having resigned his commission of Captain of said company (official notice of the acceptance of which having been received at Regimental Headquarters) we take pleasure in recommending to fill the vacancy thus made Samuel H. Dunbar, 1st Lieutenant of that company. For 1st Lieutenant, William G. Hill now 2nd Lieutenant of said company. For 2nd Lieutenant, Sergeant Philander Smith. Richard Leamon the 1st Sergeant of the company is physically incompetent, not having performed any duty since July 1st, 1862, and at this time being at his home in Indiana and authentically represented as much reduced and probably never be able to perform the duties of a soldier.

Yours Very Respectfully

David Shunk
Col. Cmdg 8th Ind. Infty

Charles S. Parrish
Lt. Col. 8th Ind. Inf.
P.S. Capt. Walls commission was accepted January 17th 1863
[on side of paper]
8th Regt.
Prom. Co. B
E

* * * * *

HEADQUARTERS , DEPARTMENT OF MISSOURI,
St. Louis, Mo. January 26, 1863
SPECIAL ORDERS,
No. 23
4 The following named Officers, having for good cause tendered their resignations: are herby honorably discharged the service of the United States, to wit:
Asst. Surgeon: Geo. W. Bruce 8th Indiana Infty Vols.

Adjt State of Indiana By command of Major General Curtis,
?H. Z.? Curtis
Assistant Adjutant General.

[back of paper]
8th Regt.
Asst. Surgeon
Bruce
Resigned

* * * * *

Camp West Plains, Mo
Feb. 1st 1863

Gov. Morton
Indianapolis
Ind
Sir –
The resignation of Dr. Bruce, Asst. Surg. 8th Ind., having been accepted and he mustered out of the service of the U.S. this date, I have the honor to recommend to you as successor Dr. J. K. Bigelow, late of the medical staff of the Regiment. And I hope that the pertinacity with which we urge the claims of Dr. Bigelow be sufficient assurance to you that in no way can you so indemnify us for his loss as by re-commissioning to the position from which he was so unjustly dismissed. I send you a petition of the line officers asking his appointment.

I am, sir, with great respect,
Your obt. servt.
D. Shunk
Col. comdg. 8th Ind.

[back of paper]
Dr. J. K. Bigelow
of Wabash Co.
Asst. Surg.

* * * * *

To his Excellency
Gov. O.P. Morton
Indianapolis
Indiana
Sir-
We would earnestly ask that you commission Dr. J.K. Bigelow, now of Wabash Co., Ind., lately upon the medical stuff of the 8th Ind., to the position of Asst. Surg. of our Regiment, made vacant by the resignation of Dr. Bruce and which we are notified takes effect this date.
West Plains Mo.

Feb. 1st 1863/
Andrew O'Daniel, Capt. Co. A 8th Ind. Infty
William D. Watson, 2nd Lt., Co. A 8th Ind. Infty
Wm G. Hill, 1st Lieut. Co. B " "
A.J. Kenny Capt. Co. C " "
J.A. Caho 2nd Lieut, Co. C " "
F.S. Wysong Capt. Co. D. 8th Ind. Inft
George W. Adams 1st Lieut. Co. D 8th Ind.
Isaac N. Smith, 2nd Lieut Co. D 8th Ind Inft
Benjamin F. Elwood Capt. Co. E 8th Ind. Infty
[can't read name] Lieut Co. E 8th " "
John R. Polk Capt. Co. F 8th Ind.
George W.H. Riley, Capt. Co. G 8th Ind.
Jacob Widaman 1st Lieut Co. G
Jesse W. Way 2nd Lieut Co. G
John Ruess Capt. Co. H. 8th Ind.
Luther H. Harman Lieut Co. H.
William W. Mather 2nd Lieut Co. H.
Joseph M. Thompson Capt. Co. I 8th Ind.
Robert E. Torrence 1st Lieut Co. I 8th Ind.
Elias B McPherson 2nd Lieut Co. I 8th Ind.
H.T. Vandevender Capt. Co. K 8th Ind.
L.D. McAllister, Lieut. Co. K 8 Ind. Vol
John H. Hicks Sec Lieut Co. K 8 Ind Vol.

[back of paper]
8
Dr. Ja. K. Bigelow
Asst. Surg.
vice Bruce

* * * * *

Head Quarters Med. Depart
Army S.E. Mo
West Plains February 2 1863.

Dr. Bruce Asst Surgeon 8th Regiment Ind Inft Vols has been in the Column of the Armies to which I have been attached for a Year. He has in the Field and Hospital performed his duties with diligence and Satisfaction.

Wm. C. Atlerson (?) Surg [can't decipher three letters]
Med. Director

[back of paper]
8
Dr. Bruce
Asst. Surg.

DESCRIPTIVE ROLL AND ACCOUNT OF PAY AND CLOTHING
If the books of the Company have been lost or destroyed, you will fill the Descriptive list to the best of your recollection; the special matter being to obtain the date of last payment correctly, and at least a full clothing account.

NAMES RANK WHERE BORN DESCRIPTION OCCUPATION
Town or county/State or kingdom
Years of age./Feet./Inches./Complexion./Eyes./ Hair
Robert Galbraith/ Priv./ Blackford/ Indiana/ 20/ 5/ 11 ½ / Blue/ Sandy/ Farm laborer

ENLISTED MUSTERED LAST PAID
By whom./ Where./ When. When./ Where./ Period. By paymaster/ To what time.
(Town and *State*.) (Town and *State*.)
Capt. Brady/ Muncie, Ind./ Aug.20, 1861/Sept. 5, 61/Indianapolis, Ind./
Maj. Chancy?/ June 30, 62

CLOTHING ACCOUNT

Last Settled April 30th 1862
Indebtedness for Clothing Now Given Last Settlement $10.50

OTHER STOPPAGES

Stoppages for *loss* or *damage* done to *arms*, or other *public property*, must be noted, and the *articles*, and *particular damage* to each specified.
When stoppages are due, under sentence of a Court Martial, *a transcript of the same* must be entered here, and the amount *already stopped* must be *carefully* stated.
If the soldier has brought his arms or accoutrements away from his command, you will state the kind, and their value, if known to you.

[back of paper]
DESCRIPTIVE ROLL
OF
Robert Galbraith [can't read]
[can't read]
of Co. (A) 8th Reg't, Ind. Vols.

REMARKS

The amount of any extra pay for which the soldier may be mustered, *ex.gr*. as *Acting Hospital Steward*, as *Saddler*, &c. and which may be *still due* him, must be carefully noted.
In *every case* of *desertion*, the *date*, and that of *delivery*, or *apprehension*, must be given, together with a correct transcript of the order of *sentence*, or *pardon*.
Should the man have been engaged in any *action*, or *skirmish*, it must be mentioned, together with *date* and *place*.
A *full and particular mention* will be made of any *wounds* he may have received in *action*, or *other injury*, whilst in the *line of his duty*.
A statement of all facts concerning disease, wound, or other disability, required by instructions to Company Commanders, set as forth in Form 13, Medical Department. (Consult these directions on page 325, Revised U.S. Army Regulations.)
You will also state your knowledge of the Soldier's absence from his command, whether by proper leave or otherwise.

If the soldier has lost any of his Clothing by the casualties of war, give the amount in Dollars and cents, or by articles, as well as the history of the loss.
Died in Hospital Keokuk, Iowa Nov. 1862.

* * * * *

Cardington, Morrow Co Ohio
Feb 11, 1863
To His Excellency
Oliver P. Morton
Dear Sir
The undersigned a citizen of Ohio, respectfully begs leave to call your attention to the military Servise and capacity of Col. David Shunk, of the 8th Indiana Regiment and to Solicit his promotion to Brigadier General on account of the following military Services to wit: -

First, He was one year in the Mexican War, as Capt., in the 5th Indiana. Col James H. Sand on the line from Vera Cruz to the city of Mexico and done much hard Service.

Second on the breaking out of this rebellion, in forty Eight hours after receiving your Excellency's proclamation he had an hundred and twenty men in Camp Morton at Indianapolis, a distance of Seventy five miles from his residence.

Third, was in the western Virginia Campaign with Gen. McClellan & Rosencrants, fought in the Battle of Rich Mountain as Major of the 8th Indiana.

Fourth, returned to Indianapolis at the end of ninety days, reorganizing the Regiment, was promoted to Lieutenant Col and Subsequently to Col. of the 8th Indiana.

Fifth, was out with Genl Fremont to Springfield last fall, next on the Black Water trip last winter, helped Capture the thirteen hundred prisoners accredited to Genl Pope In January 1862 Started from Springfield Mo. with Genl. Curtis, fought at the Battle of Pea Ridge for three days, and afterward made the eventful march down White River and Helena on which march daily skirmishes occured and a fight at the crossing of each River.

Sixth He is now commanding a Brigade composed of the 8th/18th Indiana and first Indiana Batery of 6 guns
Col. David Shunk is now in his Thirty Eight year in the full vigor of life has received his military education on the field of Battle in the various positions of private to acting Brigadier, of the most exalted character, unconditionally loyal, and good administrative abilities permit me therefore to say that my object in presenting you this petition is to Solicit from your excellency an endorsment of the Col. military character and of consent with your Sense of duty and recommendation for his promotion addressed to the proper authorities
You r Obt. Svt.???

W Shunk

The undersigned, although Entirely unacquainted with Col. David Shunk of the 8th Indiana we take pleasure in Saying that Wm Shunk Esq. whose name is Signed to this Miminal(?) is a highly Respected and worthy citizen, of Morrow, Ohio, whom recommendations and Statements are Entitled to the fullest consideration

Truly yours
Davis Miles Member
Of Ohio State Senator Morrow Co.
Jas. Grinsaulus? member of House

[back of paper]
Wm. Shunk
Ohio
In reference to promotion of Col David Shunk

* * * * *

STATE OF INDIANA
Adjutant General's Office,
Indianapolis, Feby 18th, 1863

Field officer of Inda Regt Resigned
8th Regt
Asst Surgeon, George W. Bruce Jany 26, 1863
Laz. Noble
Adj. Gen. Ind.
D.

[back of paper]
8
G.W. Bruce
Asst Surg
Resgd

* * * * *

WESTERN UNION TELEGRAPH COMPANY
[NO. 1.] TERMS AND CONDITIONS ON WHICH MESSAGES ARE RECEIVED BY THIS COMPANY FOR TRANSMISSION.

The public are notified that, in order to guard against mistakes in the transmission of messages, every message of importance ought to be repeated, by being sent back from the station at which it is be received, to the station from which it is originally sent. Half the usual price for transmission will be charged for repeating the message; and while this Company will, as heretofore, use every precaution to ensure correctness, it will not be responsible for mistakes or delays in the transmission or delivery of repeated messages, beyond an amount exceeding five hundred times the amount paid for sending the message; nor will it be responsible for mistakes or delays in the transmission of unrepeated messages from whatever cause they may arise, nor for delays from interruptions in the working of its Telegraphs, nor for any mistakes or omission of any other Company, over whose lines a message is to be sent to reach the place of destination. All messages will hereafter be received by this Company for transmission, subject to the above conditions.

A. STAGER, Gen. Sup't, Cleveland, Ohio. I.R. ELWOOD, Sec'y, Rochester,N.Y.

To L. Noble Feb 24 1863

By telegraph from Pilot Knob

Has S H Dunbar as Capt, Lieut Hills as first Lieut & Sergt Philander Smith as second [?] Lt of Co B 8th Ind Commissions been issued please answer immediately

S H Dunbar

rq[?] for 165 pd 1st Lt Co B 8th Ind.

Ansd 25th

* * * * *

Middle Brook Mo
March 9th 1863,

To his Excellency
Gov O.P. Morton
Indianapolis
Ind.
Sir,

To the vacancy in my company occasioned by the dismissal from service of 1st Lieut. Henry Rader, I have the honor to recommend for commission, -

1st Sergeant John R. Pearce.

To the vacancy occasioned by the dismissal of 2d Lieut Milton R. Dungan, I would recommend for Commission –

Sergeant Samuel Mitchell.

I am with much respect
Your Obt. Servt.
B.F. Elwood
Comd'g Co "E."
8th Ind. Infty.

* * * * *

Camp 8th Regiment Indiana Infty.
near Ste. Genevieve, Mo. March 13th/63

To His Excellency
Gov. O.P. Morton
Indianapolis,
Ind.
Sir.

To the vacancy in Co. "G" 8th Regiment Ind. Infty, occasioned by the Resignation of Capt. George W.H. Riley, I have the honor to recommend for promotion, as Captain.

1st Lieut. Jacob Widaman.

To the vacancy which will be created by above promotion, I have the honor to recommend for promotion, to 1st Lieut.

2nd Lieut. Jesse W. Way.

To the vacancy which will be created by the latter promotion, I have the honor to recommend for commission as 2d Lieut.

1st Sergeant Allan O. Neff.

Commissions all to date from March 5th, 1863.

[side] ? Noble

Very Respectfully
Your Obt. Servt.
David Shunk
Col. Com'd'g 8th Ind. Infty

[back of paper]
8th Regt.
From Co. G

* * * * *

8th Ind. Infty
St. Genevieve Mo.
March 15, 1863

Ex.
O.P. Morton
Gov. Indiana
Sir:

The undersigned officers of the 8th Ind. Infty take pleasure in commending to your consideration for promotion, James Coppock, 1st Sergeant of Co "H". We have known him since the organization of the regiment as a faithful and gallant soldier and an efficient non commissioned officer. We regard him as worthy of and fully capable to fill with __ __ to himself and to the service either of the three commissioned offices in a company. If he should receive a commission in any regiment that may here after be organized in our state, we would feel gratified, knowing that it could not be given to a more worthy man.

We are Sir with great Respect
David Shunk
Col. 8th Ind. Infty
Charles S. Parrish
Lt. Col. 8th Ind Infy
Thos. J. Brady
Maj. 8th Ind. Infty.
And. O'Daniel Capt. Co A 8th
W.D. Watson 2nd Lieut. Co. A 8th Ind. Infy
Sam H. Dunbar Capt. Co. B
Wm. G. Hill 1st Lt. Co. B 8th Ind.
Philander Smith – 2nd Lieut Co. B.
A. J. Kenny Capt. Co. C
J.A. Caho 2nd Lt. Co. C

F.S. Wysong Capt. Co. D.
Geo. W. Adams 1st Lieut.
Isaac N. Smith 2 Lieut Co. D
B. F. Elwood Capt. Co. E
John R. Pearce 1st Lieut E
S. Mitchell 2nd " E
Richard M. Smith 1st Lieut F
Stephen Wolf 2nd Lieut F
Joseph M. Thompson Capt. Co. I
Robert E. Torrence 1st Lieut Co. I.
E.B. McPherson 2nd Lt. Co. I
Jacob Widaman 1st Lt. Com'd'g Co. G ith Ind.
Jesse W. Way 2nd Lieut. Co. "G" 8th Ind.
John Ruess Capt. Co. H 8th Ind.
L.H. Harmon 1st Lieut 8th Co. H
William W. Mather 2nd Lieut Co. H
H.T. Vandevender Capt. Co. K
[back of paper]
James Coppock
1st Sergt. Co. H.
8th Regt.
Promotion.
[can't read]

* * * * *

Adjutant General Office
Washington, Mch. 15th 63,
Captain Richard F. Gardner
Co. "G" 8th Regt. Ind. Vol.
Resignation accepted, to take effect from Feby 24th, 1863.
[back of paper]
Capt. Rich'd F. Gardner
Resignation accepted Feby 24th, 1863.
Extract
Original filed with 7th Regt.

* * * * *

St. Genevieve Mo.
March 18th 1863
Gen. Noble
Indianapolis
Ind.
Dear Sir –

I am requested by Col. Shunk to ask you, in behalf of the Regt., to favor Dr. Bigelow for Commission as surgeon to the Regt., should Dr. Ford resigns as he contemplates doing. And also, Dr. Chas. S. Ellis of Wabash Co., formerly a Lieutenant in the 8th, as Asst. Surgeon.

And I may add, General, from my own knowledge of the --- of the Regt. that the appointment of these two will be highly gratifying to all concerned.

We are upon the insides of the River awaiting transportation to Vicksburgh or some other place "way down south." And I am suffering from "rheumatism" in my right shoulder, which many accept as an excuse for this scribbling.

I am, with much respect,
Your obt. servant,
Thos. J. Brady
Maj. 8th Ind.

[back of paper]
8
Dr. Bigelow for Surgeon
Dr. C.S. Ellis for asst. "
Recommendation of Major Thos. J. Brady.

* * * * *

___ ____ 8th Ind. Vol. Infty
April 15th 1863

Adj. Gen. Noble
Indianapolis, Ind.
Sir

___________ __________ ____________ ordering the description list has been read. __________ __________ will be promptly obeyed to the letter
But you will please allow me to say that I have been an upper(?) told by responsible men and women coming from his immediate neighborhood that he has attended School most of the winter, run jump and wrestle with other young men moreover that he will bring and hearing this 2 have from responsible men that could have no interest in letting it were it now – So this is the reason I have not sent this descriptive list before this. I have had to many men that have got away from the regt. played off until they would get a discharge and now they are at home preparing to make a large and laborious crop. If there is no way to put a stop to such things, it will prove very injurious to the army. I have allow a man to leave the company without his discriptive list unless when as it was in Allen's case. By order of L. Brock(?) Col I ordered Allen up to the Regt he refused to come. it appears to me if he can get to Indianapolis he could come to his Regt.
[side of next page] Jno W. Tucker Apl 15th 1863
I had one man who was slightly wounded at Springfield and went home and for more than two months he not reported to my men by Dr. Wilson of Hayshill Qubar's county, that he was not nor never would be able for duty any more besides his certificate was Sworn to Same time in Feb. I was detailed to go home, after deserters among the many, I got this man Harberson that had been reported to me by Dr. Wilson as being solely disabled. I brought him to camp and he is now as stout and hearing as any man that I

have. I then determined if any of my men was discharged again while absent from the company. It would not be by my consent, unless I was fully satisfied that that it was writ. But Jon have ordered it and I can do no more. Dr. Mitchell a good man and no doubt a skillful Dr. but the best of men may be discussed. Gen if in this letter I have said thing, that would lead to injury if feeling I hope to be forgiven have only done that which I regarded duty. and felt that Jon. ought to know. With feeling of high regard

I am yours truly
Jno W. Gedir. Capt.

* * * * *

Head Quarters 8th Ind. Infantry
Near Vicksburg, Miss. May 29th 63

To His Excellency. O.P. Morton.
Governor of the State of Indiana,

Sir: Having been through unofficial Sources informed that Surgeon James Ford of this Regt. has tendered or is upon the eve of tendering his resignation, and in the event that such be the case, I have the honor of recommending for your consideration the name of Assistant Surgeon James K. Bigelow, a worthy and efficient officer, for appointment and promotion to the office of Regt. Surgeon. Also, the name of Dr. Charles S. Ellis of Somerset, Wabash Co. Ind. for Assistant Surgeon to fill vacancy thus occasioned.

With Much respect
Your Obedient Servant
David Shunk, Col.
Comdg. 8th Ind. Infty.

[back of paper]
8
Col. D. Shunk
Names Charles S. Ellis
Appd. Asst. Surgeon

* * * * *

Extract. Head Quarters 14th Div. 13th Army Corps
May 31st 1863.

Colonel

In obedience to letter, dated at Headquarters 13th Army Corps, camp near Vicksburg Miss May 24th 1863, I have the honor to submit the following
Report
In conclusion while all have done their duty and men are intitled to special mention of whose names and deeds I am not yet informed, I would respectfully submit to the Government the following list of Officers and soldiers who from personal observation and official reports I know to be intitled to favorable notice

Lt. Col. C.S. Parrish 8th Indiana Infantry distinguished at Port Gibson though so ill that he could with difficulty stand upon his feet

I am very Respectfully

Your Obedt Servant
(Signed) E.A. Carr
Brig. Genl. Comdg 14th Div 13th A.C.

[back of paper]
Lieut Col. C.S. Parrish
8th Indiana Infantry
Application for Colonelcy
Extract from Report of Brig. Genl. Carr to Maj. Genl. McClerland? Comd'g 13th A.C.

* * * * *

To his Excellency
Gov. O.P. Morton
Indianapolis
Ind.

Sir –

To the vacancy occasioned by the acceptance of the resignation of Surgeon Jas. Ford, 8th Ind., I have the honor to recommend to you for Commission as Surgeon,

Dr. Jas. K. Bigelow,
present Asst. Surgeon
said Regt. –

And to the Asst. Surg. made vacant by the promotion of Dr. Bigelow,

Dr. Chas. S. Ellis, of Wabash Co, Ind. The latter appointment will be most acceptable to the Regt., Dr. E. having been with it for a long time as Lieutenant and at the same time most useful as Physician.

I am, with much respect,
your obt. Servt,
Thos. J. Brady
Maj. Comdg 8th Ind. Inft

Camp before Vicksburgh Miss
June 8th 1863.
[back of paper]
8 28
Major T.J. Brady
Condition of Regiment
and in regard to Surgeons

* * * * *

Head Quarters 14th Division
Medical Directors Office
June 10th 1863

Hon. O.P. Morton
Dear Sir:

I desire to bring to your notice Asst. Surgeon J.K. Bigelow of the 8th Ind. Infantry. Dr. Bigelow had been Division operating Board of Surgeons and in that capacity has demonstrated Superior judgment and attainments. As an operator he is excelled by my fur, and he is a faithful hard working competent physician. It would give me great pleasure to know that Dr. Bigelow, had received appointment and acknowledgement of his merit. Such men in the army should receive encouragement, and I hope that the way may be open Soon to bestow upon him in his own regiment what he So richly deserves.

I am Sir

Very respectfully yours

A.P. Strong?

Med. Director 14th Div.

[back of paper]

8

Dr. J.K. Bigelow

For Surgeon

* * * * *

Adjutant General's Office,

Washington, July 6th 1863.

To His Excellency,

The Governor of Indiana

Sir;

I have the honor to report, that the following names Officers of the Volunteer forces from the State of Indiana have resigned, to take effect at the dates set opposite their respective names, viz.:

First Lieut. Rich. M. Smith 8 Reg. F May 31, 1863

Captain Wm. A. Walker 1 Cav B Jany 26

Very respectfully

Your Obt. Servant

O.D. _____?

Asst. Adjt. General

[back of paper]

A.G.O.

Resignation

* * * * *

1[illegible]

2 " " for ? [8]

Middletown Henry Co. Ind. July 24/63

Rev. J. W. Montfort

Washington D.C.

DrSr?

Yours of 19th Inst. is before & in reply would say that the Soldiers spoken of are Joseph B. Gossett killed, June 16th 1863 and Henry Good killed May 22nd 1863 both killed in an attique on Vicksburg they both died unmarried & their Mothers are there hiers namely Temperance Gossett and Barbara Sheets (late Mrs. Good) They both live in Henry Co. Ind. & the soldiers both belonged to Co. E. 8th Ind. Infty.

In regard to getting pay for my service I have been getting about two dollars & I pay all expenses such as Notarial & Co. seal which-/ 1.00 then paper postage and time amountg to nearly the amt. Charged I do it mearly to keep attourneys from charging the poor relatives of deceased soldiers big fees as they always do. I am not a professional man I clerk in a dry goods store. If I am transending the laws or violating them in any way I will quit at once & turn the matter over to an attorney. I am merely doing to save poor folks money, I like would have some more blanks to fill in as I may need them.

Please inform me in regards to the legality of my proceedings

Respectfully Yours
W.W. Cotteral

[back of paper]
W.W. Cotteral
For Blanks
Ans. July 29th 1863
Joseph B. Gossett
& Henry Good

* * * * *

Vicksburg Miss
July 26th 1863

Laz. Noble
Adjt General
Indianapolis
Ind.

Sir:

I would respectfully recommend that the following promotions be made in Co. A 8th regt Ind Infty: -

To Captain – William D. Watson,
" 1st Lieut – Joseph W. Rigdon,
" 2nd Lieut – James Adams,

and that their commissions date from the 22nd of May 1863, since which time they have been acting in the several capacities for which they are recommended, with the exception of Sergt Rigdon, who was wounded and is now in Hospital at Evansville. And also that the promotions to be for "gallant and meritorious service" during "the campaign of Vicksburg".

Watson is now 2nd Lieut, Rigdon 1st Serg't and Adams Serg't.

The vacancies occur, in Captaincy by the death of Capt. O'Daniel, killed 22nd of May 1863 – by promotion of 1st Lieut Irwin to Capt. & A.C.

I am sir, with great respect
Your ob'd't Serv't
Thos J. Brady
Maj. 8th Ind. Inft.

[back of paper]

8
Company promotions

Approved and respectfully forwarded.
C.S. Parrish
Lt. Col. Comd'g
8th Ind. Infy.

Approved and respectfully recommended for Meritorious Conduct in the Battle of Port Gibson, Champion Hills, Blackriver and Vicksburg and uniformly good conduct as Soldiers
David Shunk
Col. 8th Ind. Infty
Comdg 1st Brig.

* * * * *

Camp 8th Ind. Inf.
Vicksburg, Miss, July 26th 1863.

O.P. Morton
Gov. Indiana,

I recommend the appointment of Sergeant William H. Keller ~~to~~ as 2d Lieutenant of Co. "G." 8th Regt. Ind. Vol. Inf. Vice Allen O. Neff resigned – Commission to date from

I am
With much respect
Your Excellency's
Obt Servt
Jacob Widaman Capt.
Com'dg Co. "G" 9th Ind. Inf.

[back of paper]
Promotion – Co. "G"
Approved and respectfully forwarded
C.S. Parrish
Lt. Col. Comdg 8th Ind. Infy
(Co. G.)
Respectfully forwarded
approved for meritorious conduct in the Battle of Pea Ridge Port Gibson Champion Hills Black River and Vicksburg and uniformly govd. conduct as a soldier
David Shunk
Col. 8th Ind. Infty
Comdg 1st Brig.

* * * * *

Head Quarters 8th Ind. Vols.

City Vicksburg Miss.

July 27, 1863

Laz Noble
Adjutant General
State of Indiana
Sir

I would respectfully recomend 1st Sergt Hampton Ellis Co. "K" Eighth Ind. Vols. to fill vacancy caused by promotion of 2d Lieutenant John H. Hicks Co. K. Eighth Ind. Vols.

Commission to date from 23d day May 1863.

L. D. McCallister
1st Lieut. Comd'g Co. "K"
8th Ind. Infy

[back of paper]
Approved and respectfully forwarded
C.S. Parrish
Lt. Col. Comd'g
8th Ind. Infy

Approved and appoint. Recommended for galantry and uniformly good conduct as officer in the Battles of Pea Ridge Port Gibson Champion Hills Black River and Vicksburg.

David Shunk
Col. 8th Ind. Infty.
Comd'g 1st Brig. 14th Div.

* * * * *

Vicksburgh Miss
July 28th 1863.

Laz. Noble
A.G.
Indianapolis
Ind.

Sir –

I would respectfully recommend for promotion in Co. "D" 9th Ind. Inft as follows –

To Captain, 1st Lieut. Geo. W. Adams -
" 1st Lieut., 2d Lieut. Isaac N. Smith -
" 2d Lieut., 1st Sergt. Joseph B. Hubbard –

These vacancies occur at the death of Capt. Wysong and the arrangement promotions in line.

I would also ask that the Commissions as above date from the 22nd May, 1863, since which time the above have been ---- and acting as recommended agreeably to orders from Camps Hd. Miss. and that the promotions mention for "gallantry and meritorious service in the Campaigns of Vicksburgh." I am, with great respect,

Your obt. servt.
Charles S. Parrish Lt. Col. Comd'g 8th Ind. Inf

[back of paper]
Respectfully forwarded
Approved
David Shunk
Col 8th Ind. Infy
Comd'g 1st Brig. 14th Div.
8th Regt.

* * * * *

Head Quarters, 8th Regt. Ind. Vol. Inf.
Vicksburg, Miss, July 28th, 63

His Excellency
Oliver P. Morton
Gov. State of Indiana

We cordially recommend William Short Q. Mr. Sergt. 8th Ind. Vol. Inf. as a man well qualified and in every way worthy of receiving a commission in one of the Regiments about being organized in our State.

See your Excellency see fit to commission him it will be a just acknowledgement of his merit, and will be received as a personal favor.

We are With much Respect
Your Excellency's
Very Obt. Servants

Sergt Short has been a very faithful and efficient and I heartily condone the above recommendation for promotion.

Charles S. Parrish
Lt. Col. Comd'g 8th Ind. Infy

[back of paper]
Approved and Respectfully forwarded Q.M. Sergt. has been with the 8th Ind. Infty since its reorganization and has proved himself a prompt and efficient officer his appointment is and fit to be made and has been abundantly earned.

David Shunk
Col. 8th Ind. Infty. Comdg
1st Brig 14th Div. 11th A.C.

I have known this Sergt. a long time. He is <u>honest</u> and <u>capable</u> and has well earned promotion.

W.P. Benton
Brig. Gen. Comdg. 14th Div. 13 A. C.

Wm. Short the above named Sergt. is a Citizen of Greenfield is a worthy young man and his promotion would generate satisfaction to our citizens.

A.T. Hart?
Q.M. Sergt. Short
For Quarter Master
new Regiment

* * * * *

Hd Quarters 8th Ind. Vols. Infty
City Vicksburg, Miss.
July 29?, 1863
Laz Noble
Adjutant General
State of Indiana
Sir

I would respectfully recomend 1st Lieut Lorenzo D. McCallister of Co. "K" Eighth Ind. Vols. to fill vacancy caused by the death of Capt. Hiram J. Vandevender Co. "K," Eighth Ind. Vols. May 23d 1863.

Commission to date from 23d day of May 1863.

C. S. Parrish
Lt. Col. Comd'g
8th Ind. Infy

[back of paper]
Approved and respectfully forwarded
C.S. Parrish
Lt. Col. Comd'g
8th Ind. Infy
8th Regt.
Prom. Co. K

Approved and appointment recommended, for galantry in the Battles of Pea Ridge Port Gibson Champion Hills Black River Vicksburg and Jackson this is an appointment fit to be made and has been abundantly earned.

David Shunk
Col. 8th Ind. Infty.
Comdg 1st Brig. 14th Div.

* * * * *

Head Quarters 8th Ind Vols Infantry
City Vicksburg Miss
July 29, 1863

Laz. Noble
Adjutant General
State of Indiana,
Sir

I would Respectfully recommend 2d Lieutenant John H. Hicks Co. "K." Eighth Ind Vols. To fill vacancy caused by promotion of 1st Lieut Lorenzo D. McCallister Co. "K." Eighth Ind vols.

Commission to date from 23d date May 1863.

L.D. McCallister
1st Lieut Comd'g Co
"K" 8th Ind Infy

[back of paper]

Approved and respectfully forwarded
C.S. Parrish
Lt. Col. Comd'g
8th Ind. Infy

Approved and appointment Recommended for galantry in the Battles of Pea Ridge Port Gibson Champion Hills Black River and Vicksburg this officer was also a soldier in the 2nd Regt in the Mexican War.
David Shunk
Col. 8th Ind. Infty
Comd'g 1st Brig. 14th Div.
[the back of the paper was microfilmed twice]

* * * * *

Middletown Ind Henry Co Aug 6/63
I N Montfort
Washington DC

Drss? You will please send me Blank for James A Brown late sargeant in Co. E. 8th Ind.

I send You his final statement Papers he died unmarried and his Mother Barbara Lambert (late Mrs. Brown) is the heir

Yours truly
W.W. Cotteral

[back of paper]
189
WW Cotteral
for Blank
ans. Aug. 10

James A. Brown
Serg't Co. E. 8th.

* * * * *

Inpolis
Ind.

Dear Sir –

I am informed that Mr. Meinsinger of my Co., lately commissioned asst. surg. 8th Inft., does not accept the position. If this – and the Dr. should join the Regt. if he intends to, for it is sadly in much need of its quota of Surgeons, - I would respectfully urge upon you the appointment to the vacancy of Dr. James Armstrong of this place. His recommendations are already in the hands of Governor or yourself, - I do, not know which, - and I am satisfied he will prove most acceptable to the Regt. –

Trusting to hear from you favorably
I am, with much respect,
your obt. servt.
Thos. J. Brady
Maj. 8th Ind. Inft

Muncie Ind.
Aug. 13th 1863.
[this letter was microfilmed two times]
[back of paper]
8th
Major T.J. Brady
As to Asst. Surgn.
Dr. James Armstrong
If Dr. Meinsinger does not accept wants Dr. James Armstrong app'd

* * * * *

To His Excellency
Gov. O.P. Morton

We, practicing Physicians of Muncie, Delaware Co. Indiana, would respectfully represent to your Excellency that Dr. James Armstrong of this place is a young man of unexceptional character and of considerable ability, and a regularly educated Physician & Surgeon giving promise during the short time that he has been practicing in our midst of Muncie in his profession; and would recommended him as a fine person to appoint to the Asst. Surgeoncy of the 8th Ind. Inft., to which he is recommended by many in the Regt., feeling confident he will give satisfaction to all concerned professionally and otherwise.

Muncie Ind. Respectfully,
Aug. 26th, 1863. James McCulloch, M.D.
William C. Hillard, M.D.
R. Minton, M.D.

[back of paper]
Dr. James Armstrong
Muncie
For Medical appt.

* * * * *

Col. Wm. R. Holloway
Print. Sect. ?
Indianapolis Ind.
Dear Sir –

You were gone to Cinc. when I called the last time, and my anxiety with reference to the matter of the Asst. Surgeoncy of the 8th leads me to this intrusion. I am sure my choice of Dr. Armstrong will be approved by Colonels Shunk & Parrish and by the Regt., and I not think I am asking too much in requesting his appointment. My anxiety in the matter, however, is to have his Commission issued immediately that he may return with me. If you can, then, will, in the absence of the Governor, please send me a Commission for the Doctor, and believe me,

your friend & obt. servt,

Thos. J. Brady

Muncie Ind.
Aug. 27th 1863
[back of paper]
8
Maj. T.J. Brady
Question to Asst. Surg. of Regt.

* * * * *

Middletown Ind. Sept 5/63

Revd I.W. Montford

Washington D.C.

Drss?

I throug Mr. D.W. Grubbs of Indianapolis Ind. applied for arears of pay & bounty of T.W. McCune for service in 8th Regt Ind Infty There is also pay due Mr. McCune for service in Miss Marine Corpse. Mr. McCune was transferred from 8th Ind to the Marine service sometime in the spring he was detailed as recruiting officer for the branch of the service with 2nd Lieut's commission & went into the service as first Lieut and was drowned off the steamer Baltic near Island no 35 on Miss River May 8/63 I send You required papers in letter from Auditor and also wish to apply for pay for service in marine service as you will see by inclosed letter from Auditor Also as Mr. Grubbs declined prosecuting the claim farther I wish to have it done in my name I inclose you Mr. Grubbs letter to show You what he says about it Hoping You will understand the matter

I remain Yours

W W Cotteral

[back of paper]
~~WW Cotteral~~
{Can't read two lines}
Sep 23 – Ans
T.W. McCune

* * * * *

Quarter-Master General's Department

Indiana Volunteers

Indianapolis, Ind. Sept. [can't read number] 1863

Capt. T. P. Buntin

Dear Sir.

You will remember that when your Co. was here on the 10th of July, on the Morgan Raid Expedition, you drew four guns to arm four members of your Co who were here, having left home before the Co. was called out, and not having time to go home and get their guns.

The enclosed Requisition is for the purpose of making that transaction regular. Please sign the Requisition and receipt and return it to me.

Yrs

A. Stone QMG

For James Greene

Asst.

The enclosed Circular is for distribution by us & may be useful to you.

[back of paper]

T.P. Buntin

p I now send you a ___ of evidence to comence with I will send you my comision if nesary pleas retern with your ___ ansor soon

* * * * *

Winchester, Randolph Co.

Sept. 19th-, 1863.

To his Excellency,

O.P. Morton

Gov. Indiana

We, the undersigned, respectfully recommend to your favorable notice Maj. Thomas J. Brady, 8th Ind. Infty Vols. as a proper person to command the Regt to be raised in this (the 5th) Congressional District. We believe his appointment would give general satisfaction to the many friends of the Union in this county, besides being, in our opinion a promotion richly ___.

Respectfully

Your obt servts

John B.Goodrich

Geo W. Monks

HLM Brown

John W. Jasnagin?

ES Watson

Thos? L. Scott

Simons Ramsey

Thos Ward

IW Williamson

James N. Temples

Jna Neff

Geo. H. Riley

Walter Mord

W.A. Pulle

Jno J. Cheney

* * * * *

Indiana Board of Agriculture

Secretary's Office

Indianapolis Sept. 19th 1863

Hon. O.P. Morton

Governor

Sir

I learn that there is a vacancy in the officer of Major of the 8th Regiment Indiana Volunteers And understand that in making promotions, your Excellency is governed somewhat by the reccommendation of the officers of the Regiment. And I Understand further that it is most likely that Capt. John R. Polk will desire? such recommendation and I wish to add my testimony in his behalf – I have known him long and well. He first went into the three month service as a private and then into the 3 years service as Lieut. Subsequently on the promotion of Capt. Parish become Capt. – He is a thorough Energetive ? business man and experience proves he has lots of fight in him – Thomas B. McCarty knows him better than any one else – and can give you reliable information –

Very Respectfully

S. Forbes?

[back of paper]
8th Regt.
Capt. J.R. Polk
for Major
Maj. Sternes? Fishers
recommendation

* * * * *

Indianapolis Sept 29th/63

Bro Holloway

This letter was rec by me this morning, and I conclude it was intended for your department. There may be a vacancy in the Reg that these officers want filled with Summers. – Say to the Gov. that John Summers is a premium young man, and will do credit to the "Great? Heart" of the man who promotes him –
Please place his Recommendation on file at any rate –

Yours truly

EB Martindale

[back of paper]
John Summers
Captain
1-32-A

* * * * *

Head Quarters 8th Ind. Infy.
Berwick City, La Oct. 1st 1863.

Governor,

We would respectfully recommend as worthy of promotion to a Field Officer Benjamin G. Ellwood. Captain of Co "E" 8th Indiana Infy Vol.

Captain Ellwood entered the ranks and served as a private soldier at the very commencement of the rebellion, and by his coolness, courage and energy, especially during the late campaign in Mississippi and the Siege of Vicksburg, he has evenced?

capacity for command, and we feel assured his promotion to a more important position would be conducive to the interest of the public service.

Hoping that the fine merits and claims of Captain Ellwood will not be overlooked by your Excellency in the distribution of Commissions.

We are Governor, Very Respectfully
You Obdt Servants,
David Shunk
Col. 8th Ind. Infty
C.S. Parrish Lt. Col. Commdg 8th Ind. Infy
H.D.Washburn, Col. " 18th "
Wm. Stanley Charles Lieut. Col. 18th Ind. Vol. Infty
[back of paper]
Capt. B. F. Elwood
8th Indiana
For promotion.

* * * * *

In the Field near Berwich City, La.
Oct. 2d 1863.

Hon. O.P. Morton.
Sir

I take pleasure in recommending to you for promotion in one of the new regiments forming in our state, Lieut. Colonel Charles S. Parrish, 8th Regiment Ind. Volunteers. We have been in the same Brigade since the reorganization of the 8th and I have ever found him prompt and active brave and energetic he has distinguished himself in several of the severe engagements it has been our lot to be in. His promotion would be immediately gratifying to his many friends in the army.

Very Respectfully
Your Obt. Servt.
H.D. Washburn
Col. 18th Ind. Vol.
[back of paper]
Lt. Col. C.S. Parrish
8th Indiana Infantry
Recommendation for Colonelcy
From
Col. Washburn
18th Ind. Regt.

* * * * *

Berwich City, La
Oct. 2nd 1863
To his Excellency
O.P. Morton

Gov. State of Indiana
Sir.
The undersigned have the pleasure in heartily recommending for the appointment as Colonel of the new regiment to be organized in the 11th Congressional District of Indiana, Lt. Col. Charles S. Parrish, of the 8th Indiana Infantry. He is a resident of Wabash County and a member of said District, has been in the service since the original organization of the regiment, and by his ability, faithfulness to duty and devotion to the cause, has risen from Captain to his present rank, in which capacity – he distinguished himself throughout the memorable campaign in the in Mississippi resulting in the surrender of Vicksburg nad the evacuation of Jackson, Miss. In every way we regard him as eminently fit for the colonelcy of a regiment and would be pleased to hear of his appointment.
Respectflully,
You obdt. Servts.
David Shunk Co. 8th Ind. Infty.
H.D. Washburn " 18th " "
Wm. Stanley Charles Lieut Col. 18th Ind. Vol. Infty
John H. Popp? R. L. M. 18th Ind. Vol.
E. Alerandall ? Maj 99th Reg. Ill Vol.
Samuel Parke Lt. Col. 99th Ill. Vol.
[back of paper]
Lt. Col. C. S. Shunk
8th Indiana Infantty
Recommendation for Colonelcy.
From C.S. Shunk, Washburn Parke? and others.

* * * * *

Head Quarters 33d Reg. Ill. Vol.
In the Field., La, Oct. 14th 1863
His Excellency O.P. Morton
Governor Indiana
I have learned through a friend that Lieut. Col. Chas. S. Parrish of the 8th Indiana Inf. would be glad to obtain the colonelcy of a new regiment to be raised in your state. I wish to say that I have served for nearly two years in the same division, as Col. Parrish. I have seen much of him on the march , in the bivouac, and on the field of battle. I wish to hear frank testimony to his worth as a gentleman and to his efficiency as an officer. The honor of your State – the success of our great Causes – cannot as well be entrusted to better hands that to Col. Parrish.
If it is in your power to place a regiment under command of Lt. Col. Parrish. I know
[back of paper]
You will be doing well for the service and for the command.
To say less than this would be to fail of my duty to a brave gentleman & faithful "brother-in-arms" – to say more would be to intrude upon your time.
I have the honor to be very resp'y
Your Obt. Servant
C. E. Lipincote Col

33d Regt. Ill. Infy
[back of paper]
Lt. Col. C.S. Parrish
8th Indiana Infantry
Recommendation for Colonelcy
From Col. Lippincott
33d Ills.

Head Quarters 2nd Brigade 3rd Divis 13th Corps?
New Iberia, La. Oct. 7th 1863

Gov. O.P. Morton
Sir

I take great pleasure in commending Lt. Col Charles S Parrish of the 8th Indiana, as a gentleman of efficiency & ability, and well worthy of promotion.

Col Parrish has been in the Army since the commencement of the rebellion, has seen a great deal of active service in the field, has been for a long time in command of the 8th Indiana Regt, and under old circumstances has acquainted himself with marked ability and efficiency. Is anxious to be in proved in command of one of the new Regts. Now in the process of formation in Indiana.

His promotion would be in more than a worthy tribute to his worth as an officer.

I have the honor to be sir
Very respectfully your
Obt. Servant
[illegible signature]
Col. Commdg 2nd Brigade

[back of paper]
Lt. Col. C.S. Parrish
8th Indiana Infantry
Recommendation for colonelcy
From Col. Shunk

* * * * *

Head Quarters 1st Brigade 1st Div 13 A.C.
Camped Near New Iberia, La.
Oct. 7th 1863

Governor

I take great pleasure in recommending Lieut Co. Charles S. Parrish of the 8th Ind. Infantry for promotion to Colonelcy of one of the new regiments being organized in our State. Col. Parrish has been a faithful officer from the beginning of the rebellion to the present time. And his promotion will undoubtedly give great satisfaction to his numerous friends at home as well as in the army. Knowing that it is an appointment to be made and has been well earned.

I have the honor to be
Very Respectfully your
Obt. Servt,
David Shunk

Col Comdg 1st Brig 1st Div
[back of paper]
Lt. Col. C.S. Parrish
8th Ind. Infty
Recommendation for Colonelcy
From Col. Shunk
Comdg 1st Brig.

* * * * *

Hd Qrs. 3rd Divn. 13th A.C.
New Iberia, La. Oct. 7th 1863
Hon O.P. Morton
Sir:

In addition to the recommendation made by me a few days since for a position in one of the new Regiments about to be organized in Ind., it gives me much pleasure to recommend to your favorable consideration for promotion to the position of Colonel, Lieut. Col. Charles S. Parrish, of the 8th Ind. as an officer well qualified to take charge of a regiment.

Col. Parrish entered the service at the beginning of the war, as Capt has remained in the service [unclear] since, and been twice promoted.

For nearly a year past, he has been in charge of his regiment, and his experience in the management of men, his knowledge of what is required to secure discipline, health and comfort, will fully qualify him, in my opinion, for such a position.

The appointment of Col Parrish to the command of one of the new regiments would be beneficial to the service,

Very Repy
Yr Obdt Servt
H.? F.McGinnis?
Brig. Ind Vols.
[back of paper]
Lieut. Col. C.S. Parrish
Recommendation for Colonelcy
From - Genl McGinnis

* * * * *

Head Quarters Med. Dept. 8th Ind. Infty
New Iberia, La. 7th Oct 1863
His Excellency
O.P. Morton
Gov. Indiana,
Sir: I am proud to recommend Lt. Col. C.S. Parrish of our Regt. for promotion to the Colonelcy of one of the new Regts. now being raised in Indiana. He has richly deserved

to be promoted long ago as a reward for merit. He having participation in all the battles in which we have been engaged most of the time commanding our Regt.
The honorable mention of him by his comdg. Officers does him but feeble justification I have been by his side on the field of battle and was proud of his bearing and bravery ~ I am sure the service would be benefited and a long list of friends be gratified if the Gov. would reward in a measure for his past present and prospective future services.
The universal expression of the rank and file of the 8th Ind. is that which I have expressed. Hoping that you will place us under renewed obligations

I am Sir, your obdt Srvt
J.K. Bigelow
Surgeon 8th Ind. Infty

[back of paper]
Lieut. C.S. Parrish
8th Indiana Infantry
Recommendation for Colonelcy
From Surgeon Bigelow
8th Ind. Infty.

* * * * *

8th Indiana Infantry
New Iberia La.
Oct. 7th 1863

Mr. Andrew Wilson
Indianapolis Ind.
Dear Sir,

I have frequently thought of writing to you, but from various causes and at various times I have been led to postpone it. Since I saw you last time, at your residence, I have been constantly in the service for 27 months, save a twenty day visit home last August. Our regiment has marched nearly four thousand miles and by steamboat and rail five more. The left wing of it was in the battle of Pea Ridge. In March last we were ordered to Vicksburg and was in all the engagement up to the final surrender of Vicksburg when we joined in the expedition against Jackson and forced its evacuation. I have thus far escaped all injury from battles and my health has far exceeded my expectations, only having the smallpox April a year ago, just after the battle of Pea Ridge.
After the campaign in Mississippi our corps was ordered to New Orleans and from thence with the 19th Army Corps we were ordered in the present expedition. We are going it is said to Texas, not so much to fight rebels I presume as to watch the operations of the french.
On our march from Brashear City [unclear] – a distance of sixty miles, we past through the richest and most beautiful country I ever saw. The people who are almost exclusively french, have lived in princely elegance, just going from their residences. Many of these people claim to yet be citizens of France, and claim protection under that Government. One particularly by this name of Sorrel[?] who owns two magnificent plantations and twelve hundred hogshead of fine sugar, all of which was preserved inviolate under the argis of the french flag. This man enrages our soldiers than to have to respect the property

of rebels. It being so notoriously humiliating to protect the property of a Government, which has the [unclear] and the wickedness to interfere against us and whose soldiers we may soon meet in bloody battle. In this event, I tell you we men will not be whipped but will fight french with a fury never before seen. If I could I would pity these french residents, should their country wage war against us. There would be no way for them to deceive us, they could not adopt the demure demeanor and clever tongue of the rebels, begging for the safety of himself and property, as their language would convict them, at once.

We heard last night through dispatches received from Head Quarters, that Rosecrans had defeated and routed Bragg. As the news was glorious the enthusiasm was intense. Men and officers joined in one long loud shout of joy. If it is time and we do not doubt it, the rebellion must be nearly at an end, and if Napoleon does not hurry he will not get into it.

I am somewhat interested in a matter Mr. Wilson in which you can help us should you see fit. I would like very much to receive the appointment of Lieutenant Colonel or Major, of this new regiment to be or being or organized in our district. This country has not a single field officer though it has furnished more than a regiment of men. My time will expire August next, but I am willing to fight on until peace and the flag are thoroughly restored. I can receive recommendations from my superior officers did I think it necessary. My capabilities can be judged of from the fact of my experience as an officer. My company is one of the largest and best disciplined in the regiment, though I have not had command of it from the beginning. Any influences that you exert with the Governor in my behalf will be fully appreciated and I shall be under lasting obligations to you.

It would gratify me very much to hear from [unclear]. It will give me great pleasure to communicate such items of interest writing my observation in this distant country.

For the present I am Yours Respectfully

S.H. Dunbar
8th Indiana Infantry
1st Brig. 1st Div.
13th Army Corps
New Orleans, La

[sideways on paper]
S.H. Dunbar
8th Indiana
For Field Appointment

* * * * *

Head Quarters 8th Regt. Ind. In'fy
In the Field La. October 9th 1863.

<u>Governor:</u>

I have the honor to apply for the Colonelcy of the new Regiment to be recruited and organized in the Eleventh Congressional District – I have held my present commission a long time; and to the best of my knowledge have discharged the duties of the position, in a field of active operations, in a manner entirely satisfactory to my superior officers, and

to my command. In my opinion this fact, other things being equal should secure for my application due consideration.
Hoping that you will find it consistant with Your duty to the public service to Grant my request.

I am Governor
Very Respectfully Your
Friend & Ob'dt Servant
C.S. Parrish
Lieut. Col. Commd'g
8th Ind. In'fy

To his Excellency }
O.P. Morton Gov. of the State of Indiana}
[back of paper]
Lt. Col. Chas. S. Parrish
8th Ind. Vols.
For Colonelcy of Regt. 11th Cong. Dist.
Special

* * * * *

Albert E. Lemon
8th Ind. Vols.

Richmond Ind.
Oct. 19th 1863

His Excellency
If affords me pleasure to endorse Corp. Albert E. Lemon of Co. K 8th Regt. Ind. Inf as a good and faithful soldier. He has performed his duty like a man from first to last. And I have no doubt that he would make a good Adjutant as he writes a good hand, and has much experience in the Adjutant office as clerk. He is a very sober well behaved young man.
I have the honor to be with great respect your obedient servant

W.P. Benton
Brig. [unclear]

Gov. O.P. Morton
Indianapolis, Ind.

* * * * *

Head Quarters 1st Brig. 1st Div.
13th Army Corps
Vermillion Bayou La
Oct. 11th 1863

To his Excellency
Gov. O.P. Morton
Sir:
I hereby take great pleasure in recommending to your favorable consideration for the appointment of Lieutenant Colonel or Major of one of the new regiments now forming in Indiana Captain Samuel H. Dunbar of the 8th Ind. Infty. He has been an officer

in said regiment since its organization in the "three year service". I have known him since that time and have ever found him faithful and efficient, devoted to the cause and zealous in the performance of duty. The position to which he aspires I am sure he could fill with credit to himself and to the service. I would be glad as would his numerous friends to hear of his promotion.

Your Obdt Svt.
David Shunk
Col 8th Ind Infty
Comdg 1st Brig 1st Div 13th A.C.

[back of paper]
Capt. Saml H. Dunbar
8th Indiana Infantry
Recommendation of promotion

* * * * *

Head Quarters 18th Ind. Infty
Vermillion Bayou, La.
Oct. 12th 1863

To His Excellency
Gov. O.P. Morton

Sir

I am pleased to recommend for the appointment of Lt. Col. or Major of one of the new regiments now organizing in Indiana, Capt. Samuel H. Dunbar of the 8th Indiana Infantry. I have been in the same brigade with him for two years and within that time have known him as Acting Adjutant of the 8th Indiana as Acting Asst. Adjt. Genl. of the Brigade and do not hesitate to testify to his qualifications as an Officer and soldier, would be pleased to hear of his promotion as he is deserving and would discharge the duties of a Field Officer with credit to himself and the service.

Your Obedient Servt.
H.D. Washburn Col
Comdg 18 Ind Vol

[back of paper]
Capt. Saml. H. Dunbar
8th Indiana Infantry
Recommendation for Promotion

* * * * *

Vermillionville Louisiana
October 12th 1863.

Hon. O.P. Morton
Governor of Indiana;

Allow me to recommend to your favorable consideration, Capt. Samuel H. Dunbar of the 8th Regiment of Indiana Volunteer Infantry and now Acting Assistant Adjutant General of this, first Brigade, first Division, 13th Corps [unclear] as an accomplished and efficient and gallant officer – well qualified to fill any position as Field

Officer, in any Regiment, and would especially recommend him for promotion in one of the Regiments about to be organized in our noble State.

I am Very Respectfully
Your Obedient Servant
Wm Stanley Charles
Lieut. Col. 18th Reg't
Ind. Vol. Infty.

[back of paper]
Capt. Saml. H. Dunbar
8th Indiana Infantry
Recommendation for promotion

* * * * *

Vermillion Bayou, La.
October 12th, 1863

To His Excellency the Governor of the State of Indiana. –

We the undersigned officers of the 1st Brigade 1st Division 13th Army Corps have served with Capt. Saml. H. Dunbar 8th Indiana Inf'y for more than two years and know him to be a brave and skillful officer. He conducted himself most gallantly in the battles in rear of Vicksburg and particularly in the charge on the enemies works on the 22nd of May; he has earned promotion and we earnestly ask that he may be appointed as Field Officer in one of the regiments now forming in the State of Indiana. He is iminently qualified to command a Regiment.

L.H. Potters, Lt. Col. 35 Ill. Inf.
I. H. Elliott Maj. 33d Ill. Infy
C.E. Lippincott Col. 33d Ill.

[back of paper]
Capt. Samuel H. Dunbar
8th Indiana Infantry
Recommendation for promotion

* * * * *

Head Quarters 99th Reg. Ill. Vol. Inf'y
Vermillionville La Oct. 12th 1863

To his Excellency
Governor Morton of the State of Indiana,

Having learned that new Regiments are being organized from the State of Indiana for the Volunteer service, and as a general thing newly recruited Regiments are not always supplied with competent officers to command a Regiment, therefore I would respectfully recommend for Colonel of one of the Regiments that is to be raised from your State, Capt. Samuel H. Dunbar of the 8th Indiana In'fty Vol. I have Known this Officer for five months, been with him during the Siege of Vicksburg Miss. and all the important battles, which have been fought since we crossed into the State of Miss. and I have no hesitancy in recommending him, as a Competent and deserving officer.

Respectfully,
Lemuel Parker
Lieut. Col. 99th Ill. Vol.
[back of paper]
Capt. Saml. H. Dunbar
8th Indiana Infantry
Recommendation for Promotion

* * * * *

Head Quarters 8th Ind. In'fy
Vermillion Bayou Oct. 14th 1863.
Governor,

It affords me much pleasure to be permitted to commend to your favorable notice Captain Saml H. Dunbar, and urge his claims for commission as a Field Officer in one of the new Regiments now forming in Indiana. As Adjutant of this Regiment and Brigade, and as Captain of a Company he has discharged the duties of his station with more than ordinary intelligence, skill and fidelity. Devoted to the cause, patriotic, highly Educated, brave and efficient, his appointment to a higher position would be to the interest of the service, and you would never have occasion to regret that you had selected him to lead the gallant soldiers from Indiana.

Hoping that you consider the claims, services and merits of this gallant soldier and gentleman favorable. I am Governor Very Respectfully Your Friend & Ob'dt Ser'vt
C.S. Parrish
Lt. Col. Comd'g 8th Ind. In'fy
[back of paper]
Capt. Samuel H. Dunbar
8th Indiana Infantry
Recommendation for promotion

* * * * *

Anderson Ind.
Oct. 14, 1863,
His Excellency –
Gen. O.P. Morton
Col. F.H. Stillwell informs me that a Certificate or Recommendation from some one of my Commanding Officers was desired by You before You would appoint [unclear]

I have obtained from Brig. Genl W.P. Benton, my command Genl, such recommendation, which I have the honor to present to Your Excellency.

I am Your Obt Servt. [unclear]
A.E. Lemon
Corp. Co. "K" 8th Regt Ind Vols,
[back of paper]
Corp. A.E. Lemon
"K" 8th Ind. Vols.

For promotion

* * * * *

8
Dr. James Beck
Mechanicsburg
Henry Co.
For appointment as Surgeon or ass't Surgeon.

Mechanicsburg Henry Co. Ind.
Gov. Morton Oct. 18th 1863

Dear Sir

I have been an applicant for a Situation as Asst Surgeon in some Regiment particularly the 8th Ind. Since the formation of the 8th after the first three months service petition after petition has been presented, signed by Senators & Representatives of our State who were acquainted with me, but to no effect, I have been Solicited by the Officers and privates if the 8th to make another application for the Asst. Surgeonship in that Regt., I had a Son with that Regiment that had been with them from the time they left Indianapolis he was mortally wounded on the 20th and died on the 21st of May in the battle of Vicksburg; I said mortally would not have been so with a little attention, a Spent grape shot stuck him between the Ankle & knee no bones broken the ligature Sloughed off and he was left to bleed to death, My anxiety when he was a member of the Regt was such that any Parent would have desired to have belonged to the medical Staff he was represented as a brave boy, and a good Soldier, and his loss regretted by his Comrades; and I now ask a Situation as an Asst Surgeon in the Regiment and do my duty, I had stated to them by letter and to some that were home on furlough particularly Capt. Elwood of Co. E. he requested me to go to Indianapolis to see you I done so, but you had gone to Ohio, I told him I would write and that was all I could do, I have discharged my duty and leave the matter with you, Should you think proper to give me the appointment I shall endeavour to do my duty,

I remain
Resp.
To
Gov. O.P. Morton Yours, Jas. Beck, M.D.

* * * * *

[8]

Carrollton, S.A.
Oct. 21st 1863

Governor

Having noticed in the New Orleans Times of this morning your plan as submitted to the war department for the purpose of filling up the old Indiana regiments, I am satisfied that your most sanguine expectations would be realized by the adoption of your plan. A plan something similar has been freely discussed among Indianians with who I have been associated. And has met with great favor among the officers and men. If the war department adopts your proposition I wish that the district of county assigned to my Regt (the 8th Ind) be the following counties in the 5th and 11th districts. All of which counties ennumerated [sic] in the accompaning [sic] list are at present and have been since organization of the regt represented by companies.

Over for list.

Counties	Companies
Wabash	2
Grant	1
Madison	1
Delaware	1
Randolph	1
Henry	1
Wayne	2
Hancock	1
	10 companies

Thus you will see that there are eight Counties represented in the regt and I think that the nearer that each Company Can recruit itself from in its own neighborhood the Sooner work Can be performed. hoping to hear Soon that your plan is adopted by the War Department, being satisfied it will be for the good of the Service.

I am Sir your Obt Servt
David Shunk
Col. 8th Ind Infty

Oliver P. Morton
Governor of the
State of Indiana
Indianapolis
[back of paper]
8th
Col. D. Shunk
Recruiting Plan

* * * * *

Wabash, Ind.
Oct. 31st 1863
To His Excellency
O.P. Morton Gov.

Sir,

In appreciation will be made to you for the appointment of Lieut. Col. Charles S. Parrish, Colonel, of the new Regiment to be raised in this Congressional District.

It will be gratifying to us as well as to his [unclear] friends in this County, if you will make the desired appointment.

We might, if deemed necessary, urge many considerations in favor of this merited application.

B.E. Davis I.D. Conner

H.F. Conner
John B. Tyes
B. Huffman P.M. Wabash
S. Clap
D. G. Thompson
Daniel Sayre
C. Cowgill
J. H. Pettit
J.B. Suman
John L. Knight
J.G. William
Thos. McKiffin
S.D. Sayre
Wm. Dillon
Elias Hubbard, Y.N.C. (?)
A.P. Ferry
Tim. M. Annoso (?)
Jas. Wilson
John C. Livey
Elijah Hackleman, clerk [note: not sure if all the above names were spelled right]
[back of paper]
Lt. Col. Chas. S. Parrish
8th Ind. Vols.
For Colonel

* * * * *

Head Quarters 8th Ind. In'fy
October 31st, 1863. New Iberia La.

Governor,
To fill vacancy, supposed to have occurred by promotion of Captain A.J. Kinney to the majority of this Regiment, I have the honor to recommend Second Lieut. John A. Caho for commission as Captain of Co. "C" 8th Ind. In'fy. Lieutenant Caho is recommended for this position on account of services rendered, distinguished gallantry and efficiency on the field and in camp.
I recommend him beyond the regular line of promotion for the reason that the First Lieutenant for two years last passed has been on detached service, and during that time has not performed company duty.

Very Respectfully
Your Ob'dt Servt
C.S. Parrish
Lieut Col. Comd'g 8th Ind In'fy

[back of paper]
8th Regt
Prom. Lt. Caho Co. A

* * * * *

Capt. B.F. Elwood
8th Ind.
For promotion

Muncie Nov. 1 1863.

Gov. Morton

Dear Sir,

I received the Enclosed recommendation of Capt. Ellwood , other papers, with the request that will (?) forwarded to you. I have made some inquiries and am satisfied that Capt. Elwood is a meritorious competent officer, and trust that his merits will be considered in making future promotions.

I received your communication in relation to volunteers, I have been absent from here for some days but will endeavor to give attention to the subject henceforth.

Yours truly

Walter March

* * * * *

Memphis Tenn

November 9, 1863

His Excellency

Hon. O.P. Morton

Governor of Indiana

Sir

I have the honor to recommend to your Excellency: Lieut-Col. C.S. Parrish 8th Ind. Vol. Infantry for appointment to a Coloncy.

Lieut Col Parrish has served with me for a considerable part of the war: he distinguished himself at Pea Ridge and was in my Division during the Vicksburg campaign where he distinguished himself though suffering from bad health consequent upon long and arduous services.

He is a good disciplinarian and tactician and a brave and gallant man.

Very Respy

Your obt Servt

E.A. Cain

Brig. Gen. U.S.V.

[back of paper]

Lt Col. C. S. Parrish

8th Ind. Vols.

For Colonel.

new regiment.

2-75

* * * * *

HEAD QUARTERS, CAVALRY DIVISION,

DEPARTMENT OF MISSOURI.

Little Rock Ark 1863

November 20th

To his Excellency

Governor Morton

Indianapolis

Sir.

Lieut. Colonel C. S. Parrish, 8th Indiana is an applicant for the appointment of Colonel of one of the new regiments authorized from your State.

He writes me to say to you what I know of his Capacity to fill the Commission. He served under me last winter when I commanded the Army of South East Mo., was thrown often on duty under my immediate Supervision and is in every respect well qualified to fill the position.

He was the most faithful and thoroughly posted Officer of our posts I had in my Army. I beg for him, your Kind Consideration What I say of Lt. Col. Parrish, I know.

I am, Yr. Excellency,
Mo Obt. Servant
J.M. Davidson
Brig. General

* * * * *

Greenfield, Ind. Dec. 9th, 1863
To his Excellency
Gov. O.P. Morton
Dear sir,

Enclosed please find papers recommending the promotion of Capt. Samuel H. Dunbar of the 8th Reg. Ind. Vol. I feel it to be my duty to urge his promotion &c he is (in my opinion) worthy in every respect, and as Hancock County has had but one Field officer since this rebellion began I am inclined to urge Mr. Dunbars promotion in view that he is worthy &c,

Yours truly
G.G. Atkison

[back of paper]
Capt. Sam. H. Dunbar
8th Ind. Vols.
Greenfield
For Lieut Col. or Major

* * * * *

Camp 8th Ind Infty
Malagorda Island Texas
December 8th 1863
To His Excellency
Gov OP Morton
Indianapolis
Ind:

Sir:

I have the honor to re~~e~~commend Serg't James W Lemon Co. "C" 9th Reg't Ind Infty for promotion. Reposing great confidence in his fidelity, Courage & Skill I take great pleasure in recommending him, as one of the many young men who have gone forth from our State to battle for her reputation and the integrity of our whole County, as well worthy a commission in any Reg't in the Service, or that may hereafter be brought into it.

I have specially noticed the Coolness and daring that Characterized him on the battle field of "Port Gibson" Miss. where he was wounded, and at other places where danger was on every hand. I earnestly rec~~e~~ommend him for promotion.

Respectfully
John A. Caho
Lieut Cmd'g, Co C 8th Ind. Infty

* * * * *

Head Qrs. 8th Ind. Infty
Matagorda Island Texas
Dec 9th, 1863

To His Excellency
O.P. Morton
Gov of Ind,

I would respectfully recommend Sergt. James W. Lemon of my Regt. that is now in the field or may hereafter be organized.

I <u>know</u> Sergt Lemon to be a young man not only worthy but well qualified to discharge the duties of a Commissioned Officer. He was one of the first to take up Arms in behalf of his Country, he served in the 8th Ind. Infty during the three months call, and reenlisted at its reorganization, since which time he has been in the field

Hoping your Excellency may see fit to give him an appointment

I remain very Respectfully
your Obedt Servt,
A.J. Kenny
Maj Comdg 8th Ind.

I Cheerfully acquiesce
in the above
H.D. Washburn, Col.
18th Regt Ind Vol Comg Brig (? ?)

I cheerfully concur in the foregoing recommendation, it is to such mean as Sergt J.W. Lemon that the credit is due for the proud reputation which Indiana holds in the Army.

I.W. Elliot
Major 33rd Ills Inft

I have known Sergt J.W. Lemon well for eighteen months. While I was acting adjutant of the 8th Ind, he was acting in Capacity of Sergt. Major. Of his literary qualifications I can but speak highly. I have seen his nerve tried in the hard fought battle and on the scout, and never saw it fail. His courage in unquestionable.

Saml. H. Dunbar
Capt. 8th Ind. Infty

[back of paper]
Sergt Jas. W. Lemon
8th Regt.
Commission

* * * * *

Wabash Ind
Dec 9th 1863

To His Excellency
Governor Morton
Sir,

I have the honor to lay before you the enclosed communication to you from Genl Davidson, which he has the kindness to send me, for the purpose; as a further testimony in behalf of my friend Co. C.S. Parrish, of whom I have had the pleasure of speaking to you heretofore, upon the subject mentioned in the enclosed communication.

Allow me, Governor, to avail myself of this opportunity to review my desire that you may find it for the interest of the public service to gratify our desire in the matter.

Very Respectfully
Your Obt Svt
I.D.Conner

[back of paper]
Lieut. Col. C.S. Parrish
8th Ind. Vols.
For Colonel
Other papers
Special.

* * * * *

Head Qrs. 8th Ind. Infantry
Ft. Esperanza Matagorda Island Tex Dec 10" 62
Maj. Wm H. Schlater

Sir. In compliance with a request from Gov. O.P. Morton, I have the honor to report as follows, to wit

Strength of Regiment

Present		
Commissioned Officers	22	
Enlisted men	469	
Absent		
Commissioned Officers	9	
Enlisted Men	190	
Aggregate		690.

Very Respectully Yours,
Alx. J. Kenny
Major 8th Ind. Infty
Comdg Regt.

[back of paper]
8
Strength of Regiment
Dec. 10, 1863

* * * * *

Port Cavalro ? Texas
Dec 18 '1863

His Excellency
Gov. OP Morton

The Glorious Old 8th Ind, will go as a unit in the veteran corps, provided they can get into the artillery service, and retain their number and present organization. Three fourths of them will remain in infantry service, they would rather their muster rolls show they have marched on foot over four thousand miles in the service, and some of them complain, they are worn out from marching, and therefore greatly prefer to ride here after. Will you please use your influence with the War Dept to get the 8th organized into a Regt of Art. or failing in that have them sent home, after the coming battle, to return home and fill up as a veteran regiment.

Your plan, is the favorite with all the officers and soldiers, if the Dept will adopt your plan you can get all the volunteers you want in my opinion. And I do know you will retain ¾ of the present forces.

We are all well here and ready for the next fight. In (?) tho troops were never in better health or spirits.

You may expect a good report from us, when you get the news of the next battle in Texas. Yours truly W.P. Benton

[back of paper]
8th Ind
W.P. Benton
Re to re-enlistment

* * * * *

Fort Esperanza, Matagorda Island, Texas
December 19th 1863

Mr. Andrew Wilson
Dear Sir,

Your very kind letter written Nov. 18th was received this morning. For the interest of my aspirations which it expresses I shall ever feel thankful to you. For placing my name and desire before the Governor I am very much obliged. I have some strong Unionists friends of mine in Hancock County, who assured me their influence and offices, should an opportunity for promotion present itself. Mr. G.Y. Atkson, Representative of the county seemed most anxious to assist, Consequently about the time I wrote you I forwarded to him from Vermillun Bayou, La. recommendations from all the Field Officers of our Brigade then present. I only applied to men who had known me well, who had seen me on drill, in camp, and in battle. I am fearful the recommendations never reached him, as I have not heard anything of them. In which event I do not know what I should do. To collect them again would be difficult as many of the officers who would willingly give me duplicates are not here. If Mr. Atkison has received them (?) the Gov. has doubtless

got them. I will write to him immediately. I dont know what better to do than to wait, until I can hear from you.
Since writing you, our Division Commanded by Maj. Genl. Washburn, quit the "Leche country" in La. and by way of New Orleans was suddenly transferred to this coast. Another Division of our corps having a short time previous landed at Brownsville opposite Matamoras Mexico. We landed fifty or sixty miles below here, (I mean our Brigade) and marched to this place under difficulties that made all others in the history of our service pale. We were without tents, but few blankets and indifferently clad. The northwinds so bitter on this coast, almost chilled the men to death. Wood was very hard to get, it being only such as had been borne upon the beach by the tide. Salt water in abundance but none fresh. This was somewhat oliviated? by digging wells, which afforded miserable stuff though better than if entirely salt. When on the march if a man wanted a drink he had to dig for it. At this place we had an interesting skirmish where we had anticipated a heavy battle. The enemy after two days sharp skirmishing evacuated, having a splendid Fort and eight or nice heavy pieces of artillery. Our Brigade did the fighting though Genl. Ransom's was present. We have been waiting since, I presume for supplies for campaigning and then will move forward into the country. The "Lone Star State" is menaced with East and south, how it will dispose its "Rangers" to keep us all out, I am at a loss to discover. In our Brigade there are four regiments 8 & 18th Ind, 33 & 99th Ills. The three first are anxious to enter the "veteran corps" accepting the proposition of the President. Our time is out in August next. You will see from this how our men feel about the prosecution of the war. A portion of our force are on Matagorda Peninsula which leads in to main land.
I will have letters from Cols. Brady, of the 117th Ind, who was lately our Major, and from Bennet of the 69th Ind. with whom I have been acquainted in college and in the army, and Gooding of the 31st Mass. with whom I was raised. They are in a different part of the army and it would be inexpedient to have their letters sent to me. I will therefore have them sent to Father. He will give them to you. Then if you will be so kind as to ascertain whether the Gov. has received the other recommendations, these can be filed as additional ones. However I would depend upon your judgment whether it would be best to file them alone without the others from my immediate command.
Hoping it will not be too long until the war is over soldiering no more and soldiers all at home and peace reigning all over the land.

I remain Very Repectfully
Your Friend
Saml. H. Dunbar
8th Ind. Vols. 1" Brigade
1" Divison 13" A corps
Texas.

[back of paper]
Saml H. Dunbar
Capt. 8th Regt.
Colonel

* * * * *

Marion Dec. 23d 1863

Gov Morton

In view of the appointments necessarily to be made, to Officer the new regiments, now organizing in our state, and without any desire, officiously to interfere in matters, which from necessity, must rest entirely with yourself I take the liberty very respectfully to suggest the name of Lt Col Charles S. Parrish of the 8th Ind. as meritorious and brave officer, whose promotion to the command of a regiment, would be a past tribute to his past military service, and would be gratifying to his numerous friends, in this part of the state.

I have the honor to be
Your obt Sevt
Jno M Wallace

[back of paper]
Lt. Col. C.S. Parrish
8th Regt.
Colonel

* * * **

Anderson January 18, 1864

Genl. Laz Noble

Dr Sir Our mutual friend Capt. S.D. McCallister wishes to recieve the position of Commander of the first Indiana Battery from the new recruits. He has been in survis from the commencement was lieutnant in the three months trip to Virginia has seen hard survis at Pea Ridge & Vicksburgh & quite distinguished himself at the fall of a Fort in Texas If I recollect right Fort Esperanza will you use your influence in his behalf with Govnor Morton any thing you can do for him will be properly regarded by myself and the Union men of Old Madison. He also disires? the promotion of Col. H.D. Washburn Col. of 18, Indiana Vol to that of Brigadier Genl. I hope and believe that our county will be right for the union cause in the next trial. I expect to be down at the union convention in February

I remain your old friend A.Jackson

Genl Laz Noble
Indianapolis
Ind

[back of paper]
297
Capt. McCallister
Co K, 8th Regt.
Ask Command of
Artillery Co.

* * * * *

Indianola, Texas,
January 25th 1864

His Excellency

Oliver P. Morton
Gov. State of Indiana
Sir.

I respectfully recommend to the favor of your Excellency, Sergeant Henry C. Lesson, of Co. "D." 8th Regt. Ind. Vol. Inf. as one worthy of promotion.

He has been with the regiment, since its organization in August, 1861, and has participated in the several engagements of Pea Ridge, Ark. and Port Gibson, Edwards' Station, and Black River Bridge, Miss. also the entire siege of Vicksburg. He has been with the regiment during the present Texas campaign.

We would especially recommend him to your notice, as one qualified to fill the position of Adjutant in one of the regiments now being formed in our State.

Very Respectfully
W.P. Benton
Brig Genl Comd'g
1st Div 10? A.C.
Fitz Henry Warren?
Brig Genl Commdg
1st Brigade 1st Div
David Shunk
Col 8th Ind Infty

Capt. George W. Adams
Co "D" 8th Ind. Vol. Inf.
8 A.C.S. 1st Brig. 1st Div.

A.J. Kenny
Maj. 8th Ind Infty
13 A.C.

John Ruess
Capt. Co. "H" 8th Ind. Infty.

W. C. Skinner
Chaplain 8th Regt. Ind.

W.B. Witt 1st Asst. Surg
69 Ind. Vol.

S.Clay Brown
Asst. Surg. 8th Ind. Vol. Inft.

Nathan Branson Q Master 8th Ind Infty
Isaac N. Smith 1st Lieut Co. "D" 8" Regt. Ind. Vol.

I have been intimately acquainted with Henry C. Leeson named in the foregoing recommendation for 8 years and take pleasure in recommending him as a truly worthy & honorable man.

Respectfully
B.F. Witt.

[back of paper]
Henry C. Leeson
Sergt 8th Regt
Adjutant

* * * * *

To all whom it may concern:

Know ye, that James Peacock a Sergeant of Captain Jacob Widaman's Company, ("G"), 8th Regiment of Indiana Infantry VOLUNTEERS who was enrolled on the twentieth day of August one thousand eight hundred and sixty=one to serve three years during the war, is hereby **Discharged** from the service of the United States this thirty-first day of December 1863, at Indianola Texas, by reason of re=enlistment in Veteran service. (No objection to his being re=enlisted is known to exist.*)
Said James Peacock was born in Kingston in the Province of Upper Canada, is 24 years of age, five feet 8 ½ inches high, florid complexion, blue eyes, sandy hair, and by occupation, when enrolled, a Private.
Given at Indianola, Texas this twenty seventh day of January 1864.

David Shunk
Col, 8th Ind. Vol. Inf.
Commanding the Reg't.

*This sentence will be erased should there be anything in the conduct or physical condition of this soldier rendering him unfit for the Army.
G.O. No 99
Chas McHold?
Lieut 3rd Cav. US Army
Asst. Com'sy of Musters
[back of paper – blanks were not filled in]
OATH OF IDENTITY

____
of the town of ____________________
County of ______________ in the State of _____________
On this _______________ day of ______________________ in the year
one thousand eight hundred and sixty ___________ personally appeared
before me, the undersigned, a Justice of the Peace for the county
and ________________ above mentioned, ______________
who, being duly sworn according to law, declares that he is the
identical _________________________ who was
a _________________ in the company commanded by
Captain ___________ in the regiment
____________ commanded by _________________
that he enlisted on the __________ day of ___________
for the term of _______________ and was discharged
at ________________ on the ____________ day
of _________________ by reason of _______________
____

____
Sworn and subscribed to before me the day and year above written.

____
I certify that _______________________ before
whom the above affidavit purports to have been made, is a Justice of the Peace duly authorized to administer oaths, and that the above is his signature.
In witness whereof, I have hereunto set my hand and affixed my

official seal, this __________ day of __________________
in the year _______________________

____
Clerk of the ____________________________

* * * * *

Indiana Military Agency
Nashville, Tenn., Feb 3", 1864
K. Bateman Esq.
Ind. Mil. Agent
Chattanooga, Tenn.
Sir
Enclosed I send Final Statements of William Young discharged from the 8th Indiana Battery. The Paymaster refuses to pay as they now stand without deducting about forty dollars for clothing. Please have Lieut. Maris state the ammount of clothing drawn since last settlement, date of last settlement on the new ones & send and sign them, and return them to this office as early as possible and oblige
Yours Truly
Edward Shaw
Ind. Mil. Agt
[back of paper]
Soldier
William Young.

* * * * *

Head Quarters 1st Brigade 1st Div. 13th A.C.
Indianola Texas M'ch, 3d 1864
His Excellency O.P. Morton
Governor of Indiana,
Sir:
The undersigned Surgeons in this Division would earnestly recommend Assistant Surgeon S. Clay Brown of the 8th Regiment Ind. Vet. Vols. for promotion to Surgeon of one of the new Regts. forming in Indiana. His experience and professional ability as a medical Officer – and his morality – with a constant application to duty since he entered the Army, entitles him to your favorable consideration in selecting and appointing Officers of the first Rank in the Medical Department. The 124th Regiment (Col. Kibbys) is organizing in his county and his preference would be for that Regt. if no one else has been selected. ~~for Surgeon of that Regt.~~
We have the honor to be sir your humble servts.
James K. Bigelow, 8th Ind. Sen. Surg. 1st Brig.
W.B. Witt, 1st Asst. Surg. 69 Ind. I.
David S. Evans Surg 69 Ind. V.I.
[back of paper]
Wm. L. Oir? Surg. 27th (unclear)

Alfred B. Lee Surg 22nd Iowa Vols.
O. Peadbody Surg 23 Iowa Vol
D: S. Clay Brown
Asst. Surg. 8th
Surgeon
Special

* * * * *

Medical Directors Office
(? ?) 1", Div 13" A.C.
Indianola Texas
March 7" 1864

I most cordially endorse the within application, thinking that a new regiment required just such a man; although I should regret his loss in the Division extremely
J.H. Ledlie
Surgeon in Chief 1" Div
13" A.C.

* * * * *

Office Med. Director
U.S. Forces, Texas
From an intimate personal and professional acquaintance with Dr. Brown, I take pleasure in saying that he is entirely qualified to take charge of a regiment in the capacity of surgeon.
B.B. Brashear,
Actg Asst. Director.
Indianola
Mch 7, 1864

* * * * *

Head Qrs 1st Brig 1st Div
Indianola Texas Mar 6" 64
From a personal acquaint. with Asst. Surgeon S. Clay Brown I most cordially endorce this recommendation he has Acted as Asst. Surgeon of my regt for Over one year and though I should regret to loose his valuable servis in the regt I think that this promotion has been well earned and one that is fit to be made.
David Shunk
Col 8th Ind. Vet Vols
Comdg 1st Brig 1st Div 13th AC

* * * * *

Special

* * * * *

Special Orders, No. 126.
WAR DEPARTMENT,
ADJUTANT GENERAL'S OFFICE,
Washington, March 24th, 1864.
(Extract.)

* * * * *

53. Lieutenant-Colonel C.S. Parrish, 8th Indiana Volunteers, having tendered his resignation, to accept an appointment as Colonel of another regiment, is hereby honorably discharged the service of the United States, to date March 11th, 1864.

* * * * *

By order of the Secretary of War:
E.D. TOWNSEND,
Assistant Adjutant General.

OFFICIAL:
E.D.Townsend
Assistant Adjutant General
[back of paper]
Lt Col Parrish
Resigned

* * * * *

Special Orders, No. 126.
WAR DEPARTMENT,
ADJUTANT GENERAL'S OFFICE,
Washington, March 24th, 1864.
(Extract.)

* * * * *

53. Lieutenant-Colonel C.S. Parrish, 8th Indiana Volunteers, having tendered his resignation, to accept an appointment as Colonel of another regiment, is hereby honorably discharged the service of the United States, to date March 11th, 1864.

* * * * *

By order of the Secretary of War:
E.D. TOWNSEND,
Assistant Adjutant General.

OFFICIAL:
E.D.Townsend
Assistant Adjutant General
[back of paper]
8 March 24, 1864
Adj. O. War Dept.
Lieut Col. Charles S. Parrish.
8th Ind. Vols. honorably discharged, to accept promotion.

* * * * *

Headquarters, Defences of New Orleans
New Orleans, March 26, 1864

Special Orders}
No. 72 } [EXTRACT.]
4

That portion of the 8" Indiana Vols. re-enlisted as Veterans will proceed to the state of Indiana, and report through the Governor, to the Superintendent of recruiting service for the state, for furlough, as provided in General Order No. 376, War Department 1863.

The Quartermaster Department will furnish necessary transportation.

By Command of Major General J.J. Reynolds

John Levering
Major and Assistant Adjutant General.

To the
Superintendent of Recruiting Service
for the State of Indiana
<u>thru</u> His Excellency
the Governor.

[back of paper]
8th
Re-enlisted
Ordered home.

* * * * *

Camp 8th Ind. Inf. Vet. Vols.
Indianapolis Ind. Apl. 19th 1864

His Excellency
Oliver P. Morton
Governor State of Indiana

I have the honor to recommend Cyrus Vanmatre, Sergeant, Co "E" 8th Ind. Inf. Vet. Vols. for promotion as 1st Lieutenant, vice John R. Pearce, resigned.

Commission to date from March 1st 1864.

Very Respectfully
Your Obt Servant
David Shunk

[back of paper]
8th Regt.
From Sgt. Vanmatre

* * * * *

[Side of paper]
8th Regt.
Prom. Sgt. Poindexter

Head Quarters Co. "K" 8th Ind. Vet. Vol.
Indianapolis Ind.
April 19th 1864

Col.

I would Respectfully recomend Sergt. James C. Poindexter Co. "K" 8th Ind. Veteran Volunteers as 1st Lt. to fill vacancy caused by Resignation of 1st Lt. John H. Hicks Jany 31 1864.

L.D. McCallister
Capt. Co. "K" 8th Ind. V.V.
apprd
David Shunk
Col Com'g Regt

(over)
[this portion is very faint and hard to read]
(?) 8 Ind. V.V.
Indianapolis Ind. April 19?
Orderly Sergt C. Ellis has declined to reenlist as a Lieut.?
David Shunk
Co. Comd'g 8" Ind. Inf.

* * * * *

Camp 8th Indiana Inf. Veteran Vols.
Indianapolis, Ind. April 19th 1864

His Excellency
Oliver P. Morton
Governor State of Indiana.

I have the honor to recommend for promotion as 1st Lieut. Co. "G" 8th Ind. Inf. Vet. Vols. Sergeant William H. Keller, <u>vice</u> Jesse W. Way resigned.
Commission to date from March 1st 1864

Very Respectfully
Your Obt Servt
David Shunk
Col. Com'd'g
8th Ind. Inf. Vet. Vols.

[back of paper]
8th Regt
From Co. G

* * * * *

Wabash May 11th, 1864.

Hon O.P. Morton,
Governor of Indiana,

The undersigned, citizens of Wabash respectfully recommend the appointment of Hon. Charles S. Ellis formerly Lieutenant of the 8th IndianaVolunteers, for appointment as Lieutenant Colonel or Major of the new regiment to be organized in this district.

We know him to be eminently qualified and deserving.

Very Respectfully
Your Obt. Servts.
E.S. Ross
J.C. Sivey?
Daniel Sayre
Henry Easterling?
Jon C. Tiller?
Sly Thomson
Constantine Lomas
Thos McNamie
Joseph Washburn
Tobias Beck
Aaron Markley
H.A. Markley
Dan'l B. Thurston
H.C. Skinner
Abt. Stitt
James V. Morgan
A. Fletcher
James Ford
Wm. Whiteside
J.H. Gamble
(too faint)
A. Stitt
(too faint)
Geor. Bruner?
[back of paper]
138
No. 241. 11th Div.
Hon. Chas. S. Ellis
Lieut Col. or Major
appd major

John M. Pettit
Daniel Wagoner
F.F. Weiner
C. Cowgill
Arthur G. Fosdyke
Jas. E. Mendenhall
I.D. Conner
I.L. Sailors
T.B. McCarty
A.P. Fenny
Elias Hubbard
Josiah Bowles
John Piper
Joseph Mackey
Gaunt Ping
A.V. Lee
Wm. R. Winton

* * * * *

Head Qrs 8th Ind Vet Vols
Camp Shanks May 29th 1864

Genl Laz Noble
Adjutant Genl.

I respectfully recomend for commission & Promotion in the 8th Ind Vet Vols the following persons, to wit

1st Lieut George W. Furrow for Capt of Company (F) Vice Capt Wolf Deceased

Sergt Wesley B. Ridgway for 1st Lieut Vice Furrow Promoted.
Respectfully yours
D Shunk
Col. 8th Ind Vet Vols
[back of paper]
8th Regt
Prom Co F

* * * * *

Indianapolis Ind
June 7 1864
To His Excellency
Gen O.P. Morton
I would respectfully recommend for promotion to the vacant surgeonship in my regiment Assistant Surgeon Clay Brown of the 8" Regt. Ind Vet Vols
Respectfully
Your Obt Servant
H.D.Washburn Col
Comdg 18" Regt Ind Vet Vols
[back of paper]
18th 165
Dr. Clay Brown
Asst. Surg. 8th Regt.
Surgeon
Col. Washburn

* * * * *

Head Quarters 8th Ind. Vet. Infty.
Terrebonne La. June 19th 1864
His Excellency
O.P. Morton
Gov. Indiana.
Sir.
I have the honor to recommend for 1st Lieutenant of Company "B" 8th Ind. Infty. 2 Lieut. Philander Smith, to fill vacancy occasioned by the death of 1st Lieutenant William G. Hill, which occurred at Vicksburg Miss June 3rd 1864.
Respectfully yours
David Shunk
Col. 8th Ind Vet Vols
[back of paper]
8th Regt.
For prom Lt Smith
Co. B.

* * * * *

[7]

Indianapolis, Indiana,
June 24, 1864,
Mr. W.H. Demotte,
Washington D.C.
Dear Sir:

On the 19th inst Private Issac P. Swafford Co I of the Ind. Vol. He was killed in battle front of Petersburg Va. His relatives are anxious to have him brought home. Can it be done? Please answer immediately

Yours Respectfully
Sam B. Corbaley

[back of paper]
From S.B. Cobaley in reference to removal of remains of Isaac D. Swafford –
Ans – Negative
June 28, '64,
Isaac P. Swafford.

* * * * *

Head Qrs 8th Ind Vet Vols
Terre Bonne July 6th 1864
Genl Laz Noble
Adjutant Gen of Indiana}

Permit me to recommend for promotion Sergt George W. Quay for 1st Lieut Company (C) 8th Ind Vet Vols Vice Lieut Jesse E. Scott promoted to A.Q.M. with rank of Capt.

Respectfully Yours
David Shunk
Col. Comdg 8th Ind. Vet. Vols

I want to come home to vote this fall cant you find some duty for me to perform about election time and get me ordered home to do it,
D.S.

[back of paper]
8th Regt.
For promotion Sgt. Quay
To Lieut Co. C

* * * * *

Indianapolis July 7th 1864
Gov. Morton
Dear Sir

If your Excellency has not appointed an Asst. Surg. for the 8th Ind. Vet. Vols, it is the wish of Col. Shunk, and Surg Bigelow, that Dr. Henry Minesinger by appointed or recommissioned. He was appointed some months since but at that time there was no vacancy as the Regiment is only entitled to one Asst. Surg. By making this appointment at your earliest convenience you will confer a favor on the Regiment.

Yours Respectully
S. Clay Brown
Surg. 18th Ind. Vet. Vols.

[back of paper]
8th
Dr. Henry Minesinger
Asst. Surgeon

* * * * *

SPECIAL ORDERS} No. 229. }
WAR DEPARTMENT,
ADJUTANT GENERAL'S OFFICE
Washington, July 7th, 1864.

(Extract.)

* * * * * *

45. To complete his record on the rolls, *Thomas J. Brady* is hereby mustered into service as Major, 8th Indiana Volunteers, to date May 10th, 1862.

* * * * * *

By order of the Secretary of War:
E.D. TOWNSEND,
Assistant Adjutant General.

OFFICIAL:
E.D. Townsend
Assistant Adjutant General.

[back of paper]
8.
Maj. Thos. J. Brady
Muster

* * * * *

WESTERN UNION TELEGRAPH COMPANY.
No. 1.] Terms and Conditions on which this and all Messages are Received by these Companies Respectively.

In order to guard against and correct as much as possible some of the errors arising from atmospheric and other causes appertaining to telegraphy, every important message should be *repeated*, but being sent back from the station at which it is to be received to the station from which it is originally sent. Half the usual price will be charged for repeating the message, and while this Company in good faith will endeavor to send messages correctly and promptly, it will not be responsible for our errors or delays in the transmission or delivery, nor for the non-delivery of *repeated messages*, beyond two hundred times the sum paid for sending the message, unless a special agreement for insurance be made in writing, and the amount of work specified on this agreement, and paid at the time of sending the message. Nor will the Company be responsible for any error or delay in the transmission or delivery or for the non-delivery, of any unrepeated message, beyond the amount paid for sending the same, unless in like manner specially insured, and amount of risk stated hereon, and paid for at the time. No liability is assumed for errors in cipher or obscure messages; nor is any liability assumed by this Company for any error or neglect by any other Company over whose lines this message may be sent to reach its destination, and this Company is hereby made the agent of the sender of this message to forward it over the lines extending beyond those of this Company. No agent or employee is allowed to vary these terms, or make any other or verbal agreement, nor any promise as to the time of performance, and no one but a Superintendent is authorized to make a special agreement for insurance. These terms apply through the whole course of this message on all lines by which it may be transmitted.

To. Laz Noble 10 Aug 1864

By Telegraph from Harpers Ferry, 9th A.G.

Have the Commission of Lt. Philander Smith of Co. B. Eighth (8) Indiana veteran volunteers Infantry as Capt. & Sergt. Jones as first Lieut been issued
answer

Philander Smith

26 P274 pd 2d Lt. Co. B 8" Ind Infy

* * * * *

[side of paper]
Concerning Mrs. Wilcoxen
Claim: Ans. Aug 19th
Edwin H. Wilcoxen
[8]
Greensburg Aug 11th – 1864
Indiana History Agent
Washington City

Dear Sir

Mrs. Wilcoxen has just learned through what (?) to be an official letter from the Surgeon of Armory Square Hospital of the death of her husband Edwin H. Wilcoxen Co B 8th Ind – Vol – from Typhoid fever No signature happened either to the notice of his death a to inventory of his effects – the last is in this (?) "Invoice of the effects of (?) – Edwin H. Wilcox Co B 8th Ind V 2 blankets 1 pair socks – shirts 2 Drawers 1 pair One Pocket book Then (?) the Printed materials.

"Surg. WSV
In Charge

If possible Mrs. W would like to know something more definite of her husband, his death – the circumstances of it of his effects &c Mrs. Wilcoxen gives you (?) however to act for her touching all these matters & asks for instructions also to obtain back pay ?c You will confer a favor upon a broken hearted one if you will furnish her all the information in your power at as early a moment as possible You may direct to Mrs. E.M. Wilcoxen.

Greensburg Ind.
Affectionately yours
David Marfert [unclear words are marked with question marks]

* * * * *

Mechanicsburg Henry Co Ind
Aug. 22. 1864.
Gov Morton
Dear Sir
I have returned from Nashville on account of sickness, in my family. There is a vacancy existing in the 8th Ind. in the Asst. Surgeonship by Dr. Brown being promoted to Surgeon of the 18th Ind, the reason I did not make application to you when I saw you, I understood that Mr. Minesinger was to have the position but Dr. Minesinger said he was not going into the Army, and did not expect to accept of any position, as I have stated to you in former communications there were a good many in the Regiment had solicited me to apply to you for the position, I am too old to come under the present draft therefore it is not on account of that that I am soliciting the position hoping you will look upon my application favourably I remain your obedient Servant
James Beck, M.D.
[back of paper]
Dr. Jas. Beck
Asst Surgeon
Other paper on file

* * * * *

[side of paper]
Asst. Surg. s- and the whole matter suposed to and planned for execution in hands of Dr. Blake
(initials unclear)
Capt. S.H. Dunbar.
Greenfield, Aug 24" 1864
Capt. Shaw,
Dear Sir,
I write to you concerning the removal of this place of the remains of Capt. Saml H. Dunbar.

I had addressed Mr. C.F. Trimball on the same business but having observed through the papers that you had been established at New Orleans in his stead, and moreover knowing the present uncertainty of the mails, I have concluded to write again.

Capt. Dunbar's relatives and friends are extremely anxious to succeed in this matter and want the remains by every consideration. I hope you may use your influence in that direction.

For fear our last did not reach its destination, I will restate in this portion of my letter. The remains were interred at Terre Bonne, La about one hundred yards north of the Railroad and water Tank – by a large live oak on the East bank of a small Bayou. His grave was marked by a headboard with name, rank and Regt. One other soldier was buried on the south side of him. Capt. Dunbar was buried in full uniform. Was a member of the 8" Regt. Capt. of Co. B.

Please let us hear from you as soon as possible.

Believe me to be Yours very truly,

A.K. Branham?

Capt. Ed. Shaw.

* * * * *

Head Quarters 8" Ind Vet Vols
Harpers Ferry Va. Aug 24" 1864,

Laz Noble
Adjt Genl State of Indiana,

Sir. I have the honor to recommend the following Com Officers and Enlisted men for promotion in the 8th Regt Ind Vet Vol Infantry. the same having been forwarded some time since but their commissions have not been received.

I. 2nd Lieut Philander Smith as Capt. Co "B" vice Capt. Samuel H. Dunbar deceased July 9th, 1864.

II. first Sergt Stephen A. Jones as 1st Lieut Co "B" Vice Lieut Wm G. Hill deceased June 3rd 1864.

III. Sergt George W. Quay as 1st Lieut Co. "C" Vice Lieut Jesse E. Scott promoted May 30" 1864.

IV Sergt Mathew Hughes as 1st Lieut Co. "A" Vice William D. Watson promoted May 23 1863.

Very Respectfully
Yours &c
A.J. Kenny
Lt. Col. Comd'g Regt.

[back of paper]
8th Regt.
For prom. Sept 1864

* * * * *

Head Qrs 8th Ind Vet Vols
Hall Town, Va. August 25th 1864

Genl Laz Noble
Adjutant Genl State of Ind

I wish you to commission and Send to the Regt. Doct C.S. Ellis as Assistant Surgeon of the 8th Regt. he is now Major of the 138 one hundred days Regt but will accept this appointment we want him because he was formerly associated with the Regt. as 1st Lieut of Company (I) and at times when medical officers was Scarce he done us much good. his address if at home is Somersett Wabash County Ind. we are here in line of battle under Genl Sheridan the enemy in our front in force we are daily skirmishing with him and are prepared for the attack when ever it Suits their convenience. the 8th 11th & 18th Ind Regts are here. I have the honor to command the 4th Brig 2nd Div 19th A.C.

We want to come home to vote Cant I be ordered to Indianapolis a few weeks prior to the election I am Shur that I could do Some good in the 11th dist for the State ticket, by giving this doctor matter Some attention you will much oblige

Yours Truly
David Shunk
Col. Comdg 8th Ind Vet Vols

[back of paper]
8th Regt
Col. Shunk wants
Dr. Ellis aptd Ass. Surg.

* * * * *

Head Qrs 4th Brig 2nd Div 19th AC
Camp Near Berry Ville Va
Sept 6th 1864

Adj Genl Laz Noble
Adjutant Genl of Indiana,

Genl Permit me to Introduce to You Capt John Ruess Company (H) 8th Ind Vet Vols Who is ordered home with the New Veterans of the regt. any favors Shown him will be duly appreciated by the Regt.

D. Shunk Col 8th
Comdg 4th Brig 2nd Div

[back of paper]
Capt. Jno Ruess
In charge of new veterans
Recd Sept 12, 1864

* * * * *

Head Qrs 4th Brig 2nd Div 19th AC
Camp of Cedar Creek Va.
October 25th 1864

Genl Laz. Noble

After consultation with the Officers of the Regt I have the honor to recommend for promotion And Commission the following named persons in the 8th Ind Vol Infty.
Sergt Mathew M. Hughs to Capt. of Company (A) Vice Capt. W.D. Watson killed Oct 19th 1864.
Sergt William Study to first Lieut of Company (C) Vice Lieut George W. Quay killed Oct 19th 1864
1st Sergt Stephen Jones to 1st Lieut Company (B) Vice Lt. William G. Hill deceased, this vacancy has existed Since June 3d 1864.
Recommendations for promotions have been forwarded for a Lieutenant for Sergt Hughs Some time ago but for Some Cause we have not heard from it he is inclined to think that

perhaps Col Brady of Muncie May have interfered in the Matter. In order to dispel any doubts that might be intertained in his case, permit me to Say that he is a brave man and will make a good officer, these recommendations cover all of the existing vacancies in the regt that we are entitled to fill except an Assistant Surgeon that Vacancy still exists. Made by the Appointment of Ast. Surgeon S. Clay Brown to the Surgeoncy of the 18th Ind Infty I sent recommendation for the Appointment of Major Charles S. Ellis of the 138th Regt to Asst Surgeoncy of the Regt. but have not heard any thing from it. by giving this matter Your early Attention you will Confer a great good to the Regt as three Companies are now without officers. We are again getting fitted up we lost all of our camp and garrison equipment on the 19th.

Very Respectfully Yours
David Shunk
Col 8th Ind Infty Comdg 4th Brig
2nd Div 19th A.C.

[back of paper]
8th Regt.
For prom.
Want asst Surg.
Dr. C.S. Ellis
138th.

* * * * *

[8]

Camden Street Hospital
Baltimore, Nov 18" //4

W.H. DeMott –
Indiana Military Agent.
Sir –

Will you do me the favor to present to Hon. E.M. Stanton Secratary of War, the accompanying application for leave of absence – and oblige

Yours most respectfully
A.J. Kenny
Lt. Col. 8th Ind. Inf.

[back of paper]
A.J. Kenny
App. leave of abs.
Nov. 19.

* * * * *

[8]

War Department
Adjutant General's Office,
Washington, D.C., December 1st, 1864.

Mr. W.W. DeMotte,

Military Agent, State of Indiana.
No. 332. "F" Street/
Washington, D.C.

Sir,

I have the honor to acknowledge the receipt of your letter of the 19th instant, requesting a leave of absence for Lieutenant Colonel A. J. Kenny, 8th Indiana Volunteers, and to inform you that from information recieved at this Office it appears this Officer died on the 26th ultimo.

I am Sir, Very Respectfully,
Your Obedient Servant,
Thomas M. Vincent
Assistant Adjutant General.

(F.1,34. (U.S.) 1864.)
[back of paper]
Adjt Genl
Ref. to (?) Received
Dec 2
A.J. Kenny.

* * * * *

Chestnut Hill Hospl. Philad.
Dec. 19th /64.
To Indiana Sanitary agency,
Dear Sirs

I desire to know whether I can not be transferred to my own state. I came here 18th of sept. and have been here since and as I am unfit for duty and am likely to be for some time, I would like to be transferred to my state, if tis possible. I belong the 8th Ind. Infty Co. B. any information from you will be most welcomely recieved. Yours Respectfully

Wm. S. Thomas

P.S. Direct to me,
C Ward 23. Chestnut Hill Hospt. Philadelphia Pa.
William S. Thomas
Please answer soon as convenient
[back of paper]
Thomas
abt Transfer
Dec 19
William S. Thomas

* * * * *

Headquarters 8 Ind Infty Vet Vols
Camp Russell West Va Dec 28" 1864.
Adjt Genl Terrell

State of Indiana.

General

I have the honor to report the following named Officers that have ceased to belong to this regiment. To wit:

/ Lt Col AJ Kenny died November 26" 1864 of wounds received at the Battle of Cedar Creek Va Oct 19" 1864.

/ Lt and Adjt Joe P Wiggins resigned on Surgeon certificate December 18" 1864

/ Capt. W. D. Watson Killed at the Battle of Cedar Creek Oct 19 1864

/ Capt B.F. Elwood mustered out by reason of Expiration of time of Service November 28" 1864.

/ Capt John Ruess mustered out by reason of Expiration of time of Service November 26" 1864.

Capt L.D. McCallister resigned November 26" 1864

Lieut L.H. Harmon mustered out by reason of Expiration of term of Service November 28" 1864.

/ Lt Cyrus Vanmatre resigned December 4" 1864, by reason of wounds received at the Battle of Cedar Creek Va Oct 19 1864;

Lieut Geo W. Quay Killed at the Battle of Cedar Creek Oct 19 1864

Very Respectfully
Your Obt Servt
John R. Polk
Maj Comg Regt.

[back of paper]

8th Regt

Vacancies in Officers.

Report of Maj. John R. Polk Comdg Regt.

* * * * *

[8] [Note: this letter is very faint and hard to read]

Camp Sheridan Jan 2 1865

Mr. Hannaman

(illegible) Ind Branch Inn (illegible)

Dear Sir

When at home in Wabash, Ind, I read & answered a letter from you in reference to John Jenkins, killed in the battle of Sept 19th, near Winchester, Va. I write you now to say that we are encamped in winter quarters, between two & three miles from where he fell, & if his friends wish to find & remove him, there are those here who can identify the graves, & will render any assistance necessary.

He was, I understand, wrapped in his blanket, with a green blanket around that, & a part of a tent cloth laid over him, & also his name written on a piece of paper, & pind to his breast I think he would be identified, if his friends wish to recover his body. There are in Manchester Undertakers, who will disinter the body, & furnish coffins at prices from 30 to $50 or more, as friends (illegible). The (illegible) charges will be from $25 to $35

If I should remain here, any assistance I can render will be cheerfully given, but the prospect now is that our Regt will be consolidated into a Battalion & I will be mustered out of the service, as a Battalion is not allowed a Chaplain.

I regret it for I love the service, & to (illegible) minister to our brave soldiers in the field & Hospital, but I see no help for it unless we can get some men to fill up our Regt.

If I should remain I will render the friends my assistance.

If you write me, direct to Camp Sheridan, care of Christian (illegible), & not to Winchester, as we have fallen back 5 miles in the rear of Winchester, toward Harpers Ferry, to the termination of the R.R.

Yours Dear Sir respectfully,
H.C. Skinner
Chaplain 8th Ind V. Infty
[on side of letter]
Chaplain Service
8 Inv.
Jan. 20, '65

* * * * *

Adjutant General's Office
Washington, D.C. Jan'y 5, 1865

Sir,

I have the honor to acknowledge the receipt of a Communication forwarded by you to this office for Sergt. J.W. Lemon. Co. "C." 8th Indiana, Vols., who claims his discharge by reason of expiration of period of enlistment, and to inform you in reply that the Chief Mustering Officer of Indiana has been directed to muster this man out of service if proper – on his making personal application for that purpose.

I am Sir Very Respectfully
(Over)
Your Obedient Servant
Sam Buck
Asst. Adjutant General

Col. Isaac W. Montfort
Mil. Agent State of Ind.
No. 70. West Washington St.
Indianapolis,
Indiana
[back of paper]
Adj. Genl, in regard
to J.W. Lemon
Jan. 19
Sergt. J.W. Lemon

* * * * *

Capt. Nathan Willard
Apptd Asst. Cav. Subsistence of Vols, by the President June 30, 1864
Dismissed Jan. 21, 1865
(See G.O. War Dept. A.G. O No. 15, Series of 1865. /
[back of paper]
Capt. Nathan Willard
A.C.S.
Dismissed Jan. 21, '65
Memorandum
for
Vol. 1 or 8 -

* * * * *

[side of paper]
Nottingham
for Disch
Feb. 11,
Appd to
Surg Genl.

Ex Dept. Indianapolis, Ind.
Febry 13, 1865,
Respectfully referred to Wm. H.D. Motte Ind. Milty agent Washington City for his attention with the request that a furlough or transfer may be granted in the within case.

By order of the Governor
J.M. Commons
Capt. A.D. C.

[8] B
U.S. Genrl. Hospital
Frederick, Md jan. 21st 65
Hon: OP Morton
Sir,
I have the honor to make an application for a discharge.

I have been in the US Service 3 years and five months and had the misfortune to get wounded in the Battle of Cedar Creek Va. Oct. the 19" – 64 in the left arm above the elbow which broke the bone entirely 8 pieces of bone came out since my arm appears to be of no use at all I was furloughed home to Grant County Indiana on a 20 days furlough my home is 20 miles from the Rail Road, I started from the hospital on the 27th day of Dec" arriving home the 4th of Jan" finding that my furlough could not be renewed under the late order I return to Hospital arriving the 17th of Jan"; I applied for a transfer to Indianapolis but nothing was done with it I wish to be Transferred to Indianap" or discharged; If I could do my country any service I would be willing to remain but as I cannot I wish to be discharged that I may Take care of my business at home I have a Kind Wife that needs my assistance as any means of support for her is poor, Hoping the above will meet up with your Approval

I am Sir your
Obt" Servant
Sergt. John C. Nottingham
Co. H 8" Regt. Ind. Vols. Infty
U.S. Genrl Hosptl
Frederick
Md.
P.S. If you feel disposed to assist me I would be thankful if you would

* * * * *

Anderson Jan. 26, 1865
Indiana State Agt
Indianapolis
Dr Sir
Benjamin Curtis Co G. 8 Regt. Ind. Vols was enlisted by Capt Vandervender and mustered into the U.S. service by Lt. Col. Wood Apr 26 1861, was wounded at Rich Mountain Va July 11, 1861 and was removed three days after to Beverly Va hospital when his regiment eleven months and thirteen days having been wounded in his left thigh in consequence of which his left leg in three inches shorter than right. He has drawn no pay or clothing allowance – nor has he been discharged

He is a poor man and deserves his money. Tell me how I can process his back pay and pension

Yours &c
S.D. McCallister
Lt. Co A. 153 Ind
Late Capt of his
Company

[back of paper]
Capt. McCallister
in regard to case of
B. Curtis
March 23, 1865
Benjamin Curtis

* * * * *

SPECIAL ORDERS,} WAR DEPARTMENT
No. 45. } ADJUTANT GENERAL'S OFFICE
Washington, January 28th, 1865.

(Extract.)

* * * * *

53. To complete his record on the rolls, *Andrew O'Daniel* is hereby mustered out of the service of the United States as 1st Lieutenant. Company "A," 8th Indiana Volunteers, to date May 9th, 1862, and in as Captain, same company and regiment, to date May 10th, 1862.

*   *   *   *   *

By order of the Secretary of War:

E.D. TOWNSEND,

Assistant Adjutant General.

OFFICIAL:
E.D. Townsend
Assistant Adjutant General.

[back of paper]
8th Regt.
Capt. Andrew O' Daniel
Co. A.
To complete record, ordered to be
Mustered out as 1st Lt. May 9 '62
and Mustered in as Capt. May
10. '62.   Date this order Jany. 28 '65
Rec'd A.G.O. Ind. Feby. 6 '65

* * * * *

Adjutant General's Office,
Washington. Feby 2nd 1865

Sir:

I have the honor to acknowledge the receipt, of your communication of the 21st ulto. requesting Descriptive List of Benjamin Curtis Priv Co "G" Indiana Vols (3 months service) to enable him to obtain his discharge & pay.

In reply I have the honor to inform you that this soldier should consider himself mustered out of service of the date of muster out of his Comp'y Aug 6th 1861. The Commdg. Officer of his Co. during his 3 months service should have his discharge papers, as the discharges of enlisted men were made out by the Co. commanders and upon their being signed by the mustering officers were returned to each Co Commander, to be given to the men.   (over)

Application for back pay should be made to the Pay Master General U.S.A. in accordance with enclosed circular, giving full particulars of the Case.

I am Sir Very Respectfully
Your Obedient Servant
Sam Buck
Ass't Adjutant General

Col. J.W. Montfort
Mil Agent State of Indiana
Indianapolis, Ind.

[back of paper]
Adjt General in
regard to B Curtis
Co G. 8 Ind Vols
Feb 2nd
Benjamin Curtis.

* * * * *

STATE OF INDIANA
Executive Department.
Indianapolis, February 6th, 1865.
Appointment and promotion.
8th Major John R. Polk to be Lieut. Colonel
Nov. 27, 1864, vice Alexander J. Kenney dec'd.
By order of the Governor
Wm. H. Schlater
Milt'y Sec'y

[back of paper]
8th Regt.
Maj. John R. Polk
to be Lt. Col. vice
Alex. J. Kenney dec'd
Com. (illegible) Feby 6, 1865
(Acctd 10?) Feby 6, 1865

* * * * *

[8]
[Back Pay & Bounty]
Office of Indiana Sanitary Commission,
Indianapolis, Ind., Feb 14th 1865

Wm. H. DeMotte,
Dr. Sir,

Please find enclosed power of attorney from Mrs. Mary E. Case, making you her agent to further prosecute claim No. 14,202, for Pension as widow of deceased Husband. the claim has been in the hands of McKernan, and she has already paid him some twelve dollars, but has receipt for only a part of that amount. he recd refusing to receipt for all she paid him, Her husband was a member of Co "E," 8th – Regt. Ind. Vol. and she has already drawn from his full amt. of back pay & bounty, yesterday she recieved the letter enclosed from this commission on the receipt of which I sent to the State Adjt. Genl. to ascertain to what Co. he did belong, but could find no such name in the Regimental record. Capt. Elwood of Co E. 8th Ind Regt. is now an A of P. She says by refering to him with proper explanation as to the purpose of information – he will readly give all information necessary to enable him to perfect her application. Mrs. C is Poor, works very hard when able to muster herself and is anxious to have the matter finally disposed of.

Respectfully C
Wm Hannaman ?
Genl. Mil. Agt.

[back of paper]
Hannaman

with Power of Atty
Mrs. Case
Feb 20

* * * * *

[8]
OFFICE OF THE
Indiana Military Agency,
332 F St., corner 10th St.,
Washington Feb 27 1865
Surgeon in Charge,
U.S.G. Hospital,
Frederick, Md.
Sir:
I respectfully beg your favor in the matter of an Examination with a view to Transfer to Hospital in Indiana for John C. Nottingham, Sgt. Co. H. 8th Regt. Ind. Vol. Inf'y.
Very Respectfully,
Yr. obt. Servant.
W.H. DeMotte,
Ind. Milt. Agt.
[back of paper]
Surg. Hos. Frederick
to transfer made
March 7
Respectfully returned with information that all applications for transfer of enlisted men must be made to the Surgeon General U.S. Army through the proper military channels
Tho. H. Velily?
Asst. Surgeon U.S. Army
In charge of General Hospital
U.S. A. General Hospital
Frederick Md March 6th 1865
John C. Nottingham.

* * * * *

SPECIAL ORDERS,} WAR DEPARTMENT
No. 106. } ADJUTANT GENERAL'S OFFICE,
Washington, March 3d, 1865.
(Extract.)
* * * * *
56. Leave of absence for thirty days is hereby granted the following officers, paroled Prisoners of War, at the expiration of which they will report in person to the Commanding Officer of Camp Parole nearest the Department or Army in which their regiments may be serving: -

2d Lieutenant Elias B. McPherson, 8th Indiana Volunteers.

*　　　*　　　*　　　*　　　*

By order of the Secretary of War:

E.D. TOWNSEND,

Assistant Adjutant General.

OFFICIAL:
E.D. Townsend
Assistant Adjutant General.

[back of paper]
8th Regt.
2d Lt. Elias B. McPherson
Paroled Prisoner of War
Leave of absence for 30 days
March 3d 1865

* * * * *

Executive Department of Indiana
ADJUTANT GENERAL'S OFFICE.
Indianapolis Mar 6th 1865

Col. W.H. Schlater
Mil. Sec'y.
Sir

The following is an Extract of Communication recd at this office recommending Promotions in the 8th Regt. Ind. Vols. of Field and Staff Officers viz:

"HdQrs 8th Regt Ind Inf. Vet. Vols.
Savannah, Ga. Feby 14th 1865.

"Sir: -
"　I have the honor to make recommendation and ask that you issue Commissions
"for the following named officers and Non-Commissioned officers of the 8th Regt. Ind.
"Inf. viz: -
"　Major John R. Polk to be Lt. Col. vice
" A.J. Kenny Wounded at Cedar Creek, Va. and died at Baltimor Md Nov. 26, 1864
" Sergeant Major Jacob Beshore to be Adjutant vice Joseph P. Wiggins resigned Dec'r 28th 1864.

*　　　*　　　*　　　*　　　*

I am Sir Very
respectfy Your Obt servt
John R. Polk.
Maj. Comdg Regt."

W.H.H. Terrell.
Adjt Genl Indiana.

Yours Very Respfy
W.H.H. Terrell
Adj. Gen. Ind.

[back of paper]

Maj. Jno R. Polk
For Lt. Col.
Jacob Beshore
Segt major
For Adjutant
Lt. Col. Polk appd
Col. Feby 27. 1865.
Adjt Jacob Beshore
Dec 29, 1864.

* * * * *

SPECIAL ORDERS, } WAR DEPARTMENT
No. 109 } ADJUTANT GENERAL'S OFFICE,
Washington, March 6th, 1865.

(Extract.)

* * * * *

51. Leave of absence for thirty days is hereby granted the following officers, paroled Prisoners of War, at the expiration of which they will report in person to the Commanding Officer of Camp Parole nearest the Department or Army in which their regiments may be serving: -

1st Lieutenant *James C. Pomdexter*, 8th Indiana Volunteers.

* * * * *

By order of the Secretary of War:
E.D. TOWNSEND,
Assistant Adjutant General.

OFFICIAL:
E.D. Townsend
Assistant Adjutant General.
[back of paper]
8th Regt.
1st Lt. James C. Pomdexter
(Poindexter)
Paroled Prisoner of War.
Leave of absence for 30 days
March 6, 1865.
Rec'd A.G.O. Ind. 13 Mar '65

* * * * *

[8]

To his Excellency O. P. Morton Governor of the State of Indiana:

Sir:

We the undersigned Officers of the Eighth Indiana Infantry hereby recommend to your notice as deserving promotion of a Commissioned Officer in one of the new

Regiments now forming in the patriotic State from which we hail; the name of Matthew Hughes, a Corporal of Captain O'Daniel's Company A, Eighth Indiana Infantry. He was a member of Colonel Lewis Wallace's Zouave Regiment, during the "Three Month's Service," from which he was honorably discharged. Afterward enlisted in Captain Brady's Company of the Eighth Indiana Infantry, in which he has served faithfully until the present time.

Middle Brook W.V.
March 9th 1865

Names Rank Co. Regt.

David Shunk Col 8th Ind
C.S. Parrish Lt. Col. 8th Ind. Infy
Tom J. Brady Maj. " " "
E.B. McPherson Lt. V.A.A. " "
And. ODaniel Capt. Co. A
William D. Watson 2nd Lieut Co. A 8th Ind.
(this name is too faint to read)
S.H. Dunbar Capt. Co. B
W.G. Hill 1st Lieut Co B
A.J. Kenny Capt. Co C
Jesse E. Scott 1st Lt C
John A Caho 2d Lt Co C
F.K. Wysong Capt Co D
George W. Adams 1st Lt.
J.N. Smith 2 Lieut Co. D
B.F. Elwood Capt. Co."E
Stephen Wolf 2nd Lt. Co. G
Jacob Widaman 1st Lieut Co. "G"
Jesse W. Way 2d Lieut. Co. "G"
John Ruess Capt. Co. H 8 Ind.
L.H. Harmon 1st Lieut Co "H"

Names Rank Co. Regt.
Joseph Thompson Capt. Co. I
H.T. Vandervender Capt. Co. K

John H. Hicks 2nd Lt Co. E
S. Clay Brown Asst. Surg
Charlie C Smith Hospital Steward
?Nathan Branson Q.M.S. 8th Ind Infty

[back of paper]
198
Matthew Hughes
Corpl Co. A. 8th Regt
For Promotion

* * * * *

Cambridge City Ind Mch 12th 1865

WHH Terrell
Adjt Genl State of Indiana

Sir: -

In reply to your communication of 6th inst, requesting a copy of muster out Roll of now veterans of Co. "G" 8th Ind. Inf. Vols., I would state that <u>all</u> the retained muster rolls were, on muster out of the regiment turned over to Brig. Genl. Pitcher Chf. Commissary of Musters State of Indiana,

Should you be unable to obtain it, or as I copy, I may from memory be able to furnish you

Very Respectfully &c
Jacob Widaman
formerly Capt. Com'd'g Co. "G."
8th Ind Inf Vet Vols

[back of paper]
8th Regt.
Co. "G"
Capt. Jacob Widaman
Cambridge City
Has no M.O. Roll, but will give information as to what became of the men from memory.
Blank return sent March 14, 1866
[seal]
REC'D ADJT. GENERAL OFFICE INDIANA
MAR 12 1866

* * * * *

Surgeon General's Office
Washington City, D.C.
March 15" 1865,

Sir,

In reply to your letter of the 16th ult, you are respectfully informed that Serg't John C. Nottingham, Co. "H" 8th Ind. Vols. at present in General Hospital Frederick, Md. has been Examined, and reported to be not a proper case for discharge.

Very Respectfully
Your Obd't Servant
By Order of the Surgeon General
W.A. Crane
Surgeon US Army.

Wm. H. DeMotte, Esq.
Indiana State Adj't
Washington D.C.

[back of paper]
Surg. Genl
Ref. to Disch.
Nottingham
Ans 3/15

* * * * *

SPECIAL ORDERS, } WAR DEPARTMENT,
No. 137. } ADJUTANT GENERAL'S OFFICE,

Washington, March 21st, 1865.

(Extract.)

*   *   *   *   *

43. Leave of absence for thirty days is hereby granted Captain *John A. Caho*, 8th Indiana Volunteers, a paroled Prisoner of War, at the expiration of which he will report in person to the Commanding Officer of Camp Parole nearest the Department or Army in whch his regiment may be serving.

*   *   *   *   *

By order of the Secretary of War:
E.D. TOWNSEND,
Assistant Adjutant General.

OFFICIAL:
E.D. Townsend
Assistant Adjutant General.
[back of paper]
8th Regt.
Captain John A. Cahoe
Paroled Prisoner of War
Leave of absence granted by order War Dept. Mar 21" 1865 at expiration of which he will report in person to Comdg officer of Camp Parole nearest Dept in which Regt. may be serving.
[seal]
RECEIVED A.G.O. IND.
MAR 27 1865

* * * * *

Filbert St. U.S. Hospital
Phil. Pa. March 21st 1863
Adjutant General.
State of Indiana.
Sir.

I have the honor to inform you in obedience to orders. Pro. Mar. Gen'l. that the following named men were this day discharged from my Company on Surgeon's Certificate of Disability.

Josephus Lacy, formerly of Co. A. 8th Regt. Ind. Vols. Transferred to 105th Co. 2nd Bat. V.R.C. by General Order No. 52 dated November 11th 1863. Discharged at Indianapolis Ind.

I am Sir, very Respectfully.
Your Obdt. Servt.
Jno. C. Hilton
1st Lt. V.R.C. Comdg 105 Co. Bat. V.R.C.
[back of paper]
8th Regt.
Joseph Lacy
(Co. A)

Dischg.

* * * * *

SPECIAL ORDERS,} WAR DEPARTMENT,
No. 137. } ADJUTANT GENERAL'S OFFICE
Washington, March 21st, 1865.

(Extract.)

* * * * *

6. The following officers, (published officially February 27th, 1865,) having failed to appear before the Military Commission, instituted by Special Orders, No. 53, series of 1863, from the War Department, within the prescribed time, the President directs that they be dismissed the service of the United States, to date February 27th, 1865, for the causes set opposite their respective names: -

Absence without leave.

1st Lieutenant Nathan Branson, Quartermaster 8th Indiana Volunteers.

* * * * *

By order of the Secretary of War:
E.D. TOWNSEND
Assistant Adjutant General.

OFFICIAL:
E.D. Townsend
Assistant Adjutant General.

[back of paper]
8th Regt.
1st Lieut & Qr. Mr.
Nathan Branson
Dismissed
By S.O. No. 137 War Dept. Mar 21 '65.
to date Feby 27 '65.
Absent without leave
Cause: Failing to appear before
Mil. Commission within prescribed time
[stamped]
RECEIVED A.G.O. INDA.
MAR 27 1865

* * * * *

[side of paper]
Tucker for Trans.
3/23
Ansd
appt for
[8] D [this letter is very faint]

HOMEWARD The U.S. CHRISTIAN COMMISSION furnished this Paper for the brave Soldiers and Sailors, that they may Write to their Friends at Home.

(too faint to read this line)

Frederick City, Md.

March 22nd 1865

To the military Agency of Indiana

Dear Sir

I seat my self to inform you of my situation I am here with the Chronic Diarrhea I have bin under medical treatment ever sence about the first of November I have made Aplications for furlough and cant get it and they Doctors told me I would be a fit Subject for the Invalid Corps I Now bin in my cuntry Servis ever sence the Rebelion first commenced and if I have to go in the Invalid corps I would like to be transfered to my own State if such a thing can be done I want to be transfered to Indinapolis but if I get well enough I would a great deal rather be with my regiment but if I dont get able for the front any more I would like to get nearer home if it is posible as I have a wife and two children and I can hear from them oftiner I rite this to See if you can do any thing for me my Regiment is at Savannah Ga,

Your Truly,

James A. Tucker, Private

Company I, 8,th Regt. Ind.

Vet. Vol.

* * * * *

Hd. qrs. 8th Regt. Ind. Inf. Vet. Vol.

Savannah Ga. April 11th 1865.

Sir:

I have the honor to make the following recommendation for promotion in the 8 Ind. Inf. Vols. viz: -

Joseph M. Thompson Capt. Co "I" to be Major, vice John R. Polk promoted.

I am sir, very
respectfully your obt Servt.
John R. Polk
Lt. Col. Comd'g. Regt.

W.H.H. Terrell.
Adj. Genl. State of
Indiana.

[back of paper]

8.
Joseph M. Thompson
Capt. Co. I.
For Major
vice Polk
promoted.
appd May 12, 1865
Respectfully forwarded to
Gov. Morton April 24, 1865

* * * * *

[side of paper]
T.W. Coffin
for D Roll
Ap 27, Ans
Thomas W. Coffin

U.S. General Hospital
Madison, Ind.
April the 18th /65
Sir I take the liberty of addressing you on a little business My Discriptive role is in your city some where at some of the offices and I have sent for it But get no answer to my letters there fore I have taken the liberty of applying to you hoping that you will attend to it for me and send the same to person to charge. I am a member of company G. of the 8th Ind. Regt. Vet. Vol. Inft.
Thomas W. Coffin
The same was ordered by Dr. New Commer to be sent from my Regt.
Yours with Respect

* * * * *

SPECIAL ORDERS,} WAR DEPARTMENT,
No. 205. } ADJUTANT GENERAL'S OFFICE
Washington, May 4th, 1865.
(Extract.)
* * * * *

47. Upon the report of a Board of Officers, convened by Special Orders, No. 285, June 27th, 1863, from this Office, 2d Lieutenant *P. Smith*, 8th Indiana Volunteers, is hereby honorably discharged the service of the United States, on account of physical disability, with condition that he shall receive no final payments, until he has satisfied the Pay Department that he is not indebted to the Government.

* * * * *

By order of the Secretary of War:
W.A. NICHOLS,
Assistant Adjutant General.
OFFICIAL:
Saml Buck
Assistant Adjutant General.
[back of paper]
8th Regt
2d Lieut
P. Smith
Co B.
Honorably Discharged
By order of the war Dept.

May 4" 1865.
Cause: Disability
/to B. 8

* * * * *

STATE OF INDIANA
Executive Department.
Indianapolis May 13th 1865
Appointments and Promotions
8th Regt. Capt. Joseph M. Thompson to be Major to date April 11, 1865
Major Joseph M. Thompson to be Lieut Col to date May 1, 1865
Capt. Jacob Wideman to be Major to date May 1, 1865
By order of the Governor
Wm. H. Schlater
Mil. Secy
[back of paper]
8th Regt.
Capt. Joseph M. Thompson to be Major vice Polk
Major Joseph M. Thompson to be Lt. Col. vice Polk
Capt. Jacob Widaman to be Major vice Thompson
Appointments
By Gov. Morton
Conferred & forwd
May 13, 1865

* * * * *

Madison Ind
June 1st 1865

Ser I have then the obertunity of Dropen you a few lines asken Informion of you about geting my Pay

I have ben discharged on a parsial role from Washington and I am disabeld and cannot work and stand In need of mony I have riten for my discriptdis role 3 diferent times and havent as yet Recieved any answer therefore I ask Informion of you whether you can do any thing toward geting It for me if not rite and instruct me how to go to work and get It

By you doing so you would obblige me vairy much
Hirem Allcom {Co. H. 8th Ind. Calvy
~~Thomas J. McManamon~~
~~Commanding offerser~~
~~of Co H~~
Address
Madison Ind
Jefferson Cou
Box No. 344

[back of paper]
(too faint to read top three lines)

George Allcom
private Co. H.
8th Ind. Cav. 39th Regt.
Ind. Vol.
Absent pay and
Descriptive list.
Respy referred to Isaac W.
Monfort Ind. Mil. Agt.
W.H.H. Terrell
Adjt. Gen.

* * * * *

Middletown Ind. June 13th 1865
W.H. Desnotte Esqr
Washington DC
DrSr

I want some information in regard to arrears of pay due Thompson W McCune who died April 8th 1863 in the Service of the Miss Marine Brigade. Mr. McCune was a member of Co E 8th Ind Infty and in Feby (7/63) was detailed to recruit for above named brigade with Lieuts Commission and raised some 80 men and took them to St. Louis Mo. and did or was to receive a regular Liets Commission and was assigned to duty on the Steamer Baltic then stationed at Island no 30 or 32 and went down the River on the Steamer R.F. or Genl Raines and came up with the fleet on the 8th day of April 1863 and in stepping from the Raines to the Baltic went down and was lost it being in the night, his Carpet bag went down with him & I am informed that he had his regular Com. with him in satchell I made application for arears of pay and bounty for his Father through Mess. Martindale & Grubbs of Indianapolis and I have just recd certificate for the amt due for service in the 8th Ind & I think there is some over <u>two months pay due him</u> in the service of Marine Brigade. he recd pay <u>to the first of Feby 1863</u>. And did not leave the service at all and died April 8th 63 and of course there is over two months pay due him in some service & I think it ought to be as Lieut in M.M. Brigade I would like for you to look into the matter The pay was for service in 8th Ind Infty and mention is made for service in Brigade.

Very truly
W.W. Cotteral

[written sideways on bottom of page]
W.W. Cotteral
about accts of McCune
ans June 23
Thompson W. McCune.

* * * * *

SPECIAL ORDERS,} WAR DEPARTMENT
No. 309. } ADJUTANT GENERAL'S OFFICE,
Washington, June 16th, 1865.

(Extract.)

* * * * *

26. By direction of the President, so much of Special Orders, No. 146, dated Headquarters, Department of the Tennessee, near Vicksburg, Mississippi, May 31st, 1863, as dismissed 1st Lieutenant *Richard M. Smith*, 8th Indiana Volunteers, for misbehavior in the face of the enemy, breach of arrest, and straggling, with forfeiture of all pay and allowances, is hereby confirmed.

* * * * *

By the order of the Secretary of War:
E.D. TOWNSEND,
Assistant Adjutant General.

OFFICIAL:
E.D. Townsend
Assistant Adjutant General.
[back of paper]
8th Regt.
1st Lieut
Richard M. Smith
(Co. F)
Dismissal Confirmed
By order War Dept. June 16 '65.
Dismd May 31" 1865 for misbehavior in face of enemy, breach of arrest and straggling with forfeiture of pay &c.

* * * * *

[side of paper]
Chas. W. Sewart
Fairfax Seminary
Descptv Lst appld, as by
Surg. in Chg.
Jne 22nd 1865

[8]
U.S. Christian Commission
"For God so loved the world, that he gave his only begotten Son, that whosoever believeth in him should not perish, but have everlasting life." – JOHN III, 16.

June the 19 1865 Fairfax Seminary Hospital Alexandria
W.H. DeMotte Dear Sur

I set down to Drop you a fue lines to informe you that the Boyes are guiting vary impatient for they think the time long for to guit thare Discriptive lists and to guit of you cant guit now information here eaven if your Discriptive list was here and I wright to you to know If my Discriptive role has not come to Washington or whare it would guit to from Alexandria for it come with mea from Savannah thare and that is the last oI can here from it and I wish you to se to the matter for I am vary tuching to be at home with my familey and to guit some money to help them in time of nead and weather you belong to Brother hood ore not I ask you to take (unclear) notices and governer your self acording I shal wate with patience for your answer to tell mea what is best to be done we cant guit now tobaco nor nothing else that we want answer this as soon as Can and Oblige money
Ancious friends
yours as ever
Charles W. Stewart Co
L the 8 Indiana Covelry
To WH DeMotte

* * * * *

War Department,
Adjutant General's Office,
Washington, June 24" 1865

His Excellency
The Governor of Indiana
Indianapolis Ind.

Sir,

I have the honor to acknowledge the receipt of papers, in reference to the dismissal of Richard M. Smith late 1"Lieutenant, 8" Indiana Vol Infty, now Private C.E., Illinois Cavalry, forwarded by you, by endorsement, drafted 7th inst, with the recommendation, that the disability resulting from his dismissal, be removed in order that he may be recommissioned.

In reply, I am instructed to inform you, that upon an examination of the charges upon which said dismissal was based, it is found that the interests of the service will not permit the request to be granted.

I have the honor to remain
Very Respectfully
Your Servant,
Thomas W. Vincent
Asst adjt Genl.

(illegible)
[back of paper]
8th Regt
A.G.O.
June 24, 1865
Rich. M. Smith
Late Lt. 8th
(Co. F)

Disability not removed

* * * * *

War Department,
Adjutant General's Office,
Washington, June 24" 1865.

His Excellency
The Governor of Indiana.
Indianapolis, Indiana.
Sir,

I have the honor to acknowledge the receipt of your letter of the 19th instant, requesting that the entire organization of the 8" Indiana Volunteers be mustered out of service.

In reply, I am directed to inform you, that the request cannot be favorably considered consistently with the public interest.

The dates at which troops shall go out of the service are fixed and departing therefrom, create dissatisfaction in the Army.

I have the honor to remain
Very Respectfully,
Your Obedient Servant
Thomas W. Vincent
Assistant Adjutant Genl.

(I. 341. (V.O.) 1865.)
[back]
8.
A.G.O.
June 24, 1865
Reply to request
for muster out of
8th Regt

* * * * *

[note written on top of this]
Paid June 28/65
Extra pay only
Henry W. Scovel
Punya
[stamped]
MILITARY TICKET OFFICE
COLUMBUS, OHIO
June 28 1865
G.H. WALDO,
Agt.

TO ALL WHOM IT MAY CONCERN.
Know Ye, That Hilton Lineford
Private of Captain
Company (A) "8" Regiment of Indiana Cavalry
Volunteers, who was enrolled on the day of
one thousand eight hundred and to serve years
during the war, is hereby Discharged from the service of the United States
this 28 day of June 1865, at Camp
Chase, O. by reason of G.O. No. 77 dated April 28" 1865
(No objection to his being re-enlisted is known to exist.*)
Said Hilton Lineford was born in Floyd
in the State of Va is 26 years of age,
5 feet 4 inches high, fair complexion, Blue eyes,
Dark hair, and by occupation, when enrolled, a Farmer
Given at Camp Chase O this 28 day
of June 1865.
T.F. Huntington
Capt. VRC and Cvy
Commanding the Regiment.
*This sentence will be erased should *there be anything in the conduct or physical condition* of the soldier rendering him *unfit for the Army.*
[A.G.O. No. 99.]
[back of paper]
[written on side]
Hilton Lineford
A 8th Cav Ind
[this part was not filled in]
OATH OF IDENTITY

of the town of County
of in the State of
On this day of in the year
one thousand eight hundred and sixty personally appeared
before me, the undersigned, a Justice of the Peace for the county
and above mentioned
who, being duly sworn according to law, declares that he is the
identical who was
a in the company commanded by
Captain in the regiment
commanded by
that he enlisted on the day of
for the term of and was discharged
at on the day
of by reason of

Sworn and subscribed before me the day and year above written.

I certify that , before
whom the above affidavit purports to have been made, is a Justice of the Peace duly authorized to administer oaths, and that the above is his signature.
In Witness Whereof, I have hereunto set my hand and affixed my official seal, this day of
in the year
at in the State of

Clerk of the

* * * * *

Discharged from Co. "A" 5th V.R.C.
Grovendyke Montgomery formerly of Co "A" 8th Ind. Vol; discharged July 5th1865
Extract: Original filed with 84th Regt.
[back of paper]
8th Regt.
Montgomery Granendyke
Co. "A" 5th V.R.C.
formerly of
Co "A" 8th Ind Vols
Discharged July 5th 1865
Extract
Original filed with 84th

* * * * *

CERTIFICATE
TO BE GIVEN TO VOLUNTEERS AT THE TIME OF THEIR DISCHARGE TO ENABLE THEM TO RECEIVE THEIR PAY, &c.

NOTE. – Two of these certificates (or duplicates) are to be given to each volunteer soldier who may be discharged previously to the discharge of his company, that he may at once receive from the Paymaster the pay, &c., due him, and the Captain or other officer commanding the company, will certify to the act of the delivery of the duplicate certificates; on these certificates the soldier is "entitled to" his DISCHARGE, and should also present his discharge to the Paymaster to have the payment endorsed on it. The discharge is to be given back to the soldier, by the Paymaster, the latter only retaining as his voucher the duplicate certificates.

NOTE. – When Descriptive Roll has been given to a soldier, no FINAL CERTIFICATES should be given until he returns his Descriptive Roll.

I Certify, on honor, that Henry Johnson a Private of Captain [scribble] Company G of the Eighth Regiment of Cavalry Volunteers, of the State of Indiana born in Schuikill Co. State of Pennsylvania aged 23 years; 5 feet 8 inches high, light complexion blue eyes dark hair, and by occupatiov a Farmer was enrolled or enlisted at Indianapolis State of Indiana by Capt. Blake on the twelfth day of December 1863, and mustered in service by Capt Locke at [scribble] State of ind on the twelfth day of December 1863, to serve in the regiment for the term of three years; and having served honestly and faithfully with his Company in   to the present day, is now entitled to a discharge by reason of *
[*State particularly the cause of discharge; if for disability, whether the disability existed prior to the date of muster, or was contracted after it.]
SURGEON'S CERTIFICATE OF DISABILTY,
Gunshot wound received in action near Pulaski Tenn Sept 27th 1864 one ball passing through the deltoid muscle of left arm resulting in partial loss of use of arm the after passing through the left hip causing lameness He is unfit for the Veteran Reserve Corps. Disability one half
The said Henry Johnson was last paid by Paymaster Huffman to include the thirtieth day of June 1864 and has pay due him from that time to the ~~present~~ date of discharge and he is entitled to pay subsistence for traveling to place of enrollment, and whatever other allowances authorized to volunteer soldiers, or militia, so discharged.
He has received One Hundred and Forty Dollars, advanced bounty.
He is entitled to One Hundred and Fifty Dollars bounty.
He has received Clothing from the United States, not paid for, amounting Thirty five and 53/100 Dollars.
He is entitled to Clothing pay from the twelfth day of December 1863, to the time of discharge.
He is indebted for other stoppages than above Transportation to the amount of thirteen and 57/100 Dollars.
He is indebted [scribble] Sutler, [scribble] /100 Dollars
GIVEN in duplicate, at St. Louis, Mo., this Eighteenth day of July 1865.
Ben M. Pall?
Ass't Adj't Gen., Hd. Qrs. Dep't of the Mo.
[back of paper]
P.35 Hd. Qrs. Dept. Mo. 1865.
Henry Johnson

* * * * *

[8]
[Back Pay & Bounty]
INDIANA MILITARY AGENCY.
Indianapolis, Ind. July 18th 1865
Mr. Henry P. Case
Ind. Mil Agt.
Dear Sir,
Will you please enquire at the Pension Office as to the situation of the claim of Mrs. Mary E. Case for Pension as widow of Danl E. Case Co. "E" 8th Ind. Vol. do not

know the Mrs. as it was a claim not originally made by us, but the agency was transfered to Mr. DeMotte by power of attorney executive by Mrs. Case, We sent to you 12th of April the Certificate of Adjt. Genl. of Ind. as to Co. & Regt. to which Case belonged at that time that appeared to be the only difficulty. Mrs. C. health is very poor and she is in very great need of the money, if any thing further is wanting please see what, and we will try and have it attended to.

Respectfully

W. Hannaman

Mil. Agt.

[back of paper]

176

~~Wm Hammaman~~

Con claim of Mrs. Case

Ans July 24

David E. Case

Co. E. 8th Ind.

* * * * *

(copy) Hd.Qrs. 8th Ind Inf. V. Vols.

Hawkinsville Ga July 19, 1865.

Recommendations for promotions to fill vacancies in Line and Staff officers of 8th Indiana

Names	To be commissioned	To date from	Remarks
James C. Poindexter	Capt.	Nov. 27. 64	vice McCallister discharged.
William H. Keller	do.	May 1. 65	vice Widaman promoted
Stephen A. Jones	do.	May 5. 65	vice Smith discharged
Robert E. Torrence	do.	May 22. 65	vice Thompson promoted
Chas. W. Wynn	1st Lieut.	Nov. 27. 64.	vice Poindexter promoted
William Hamilton	do.	Oct. 19. 64	vice Hughes promoted.
William Perry	do.	Dec. 1. 1864	vice Tarkleson promoted.
Benjamin P. Williamson	do.	Jany 1. 1865	vice Harmon discharged
Swain Marshall	do.	May 1. 1865	vice Keller promoted.
George H. Black	do.	May 5. 1865	vice Jones promoted.
Flavius I. Brewer	do.	May 22d. 65	vice Torrence promoted.
John Harton	2d Lieut.	May 23d. 63	vice Smith promoted.
Geroge W. Dubois	2d Lieut.	Mch 15/64	vice Keller promoted
Samuel Woods	do.	Feby 8/64	vice Mathers dischgd.
Ambrose Whitecotton	do.	Feby '/64	vice Hicks dischgd.
George Britton	do.	Jany 1 64	vice Caho promoted
Levi P. Shoemaker	do.	Feby 23/64	vice Mitchell resigned
Joseph C. Milliron	do.	Apl. 8/65	vice McPherson dischgd
Nicholas Miller	do.	May 5/65	vice Smith promoted
David A. Long	do.	May 24/65	vice Smith promoted.

(over)

James Peacock	1st Lt. and Adjt.	Dec 29. 64.	vice Wiggins dischgd.
Robert S. Knode	Asst. Surgeon	July 7. 64.	vice Brown promoted

Also prior to the above but no commissions recd.
John A. McConnell. 1st Lieut. & Regt. Qr. Mr. to date from January 1, 1865 – vice Branson dismissed

* * * * *

[on side of paper]
Hd Qrs. 8th Ind. Inf. V. Vols.
Hawkinsville Ga
July 19, 1860.
Recommendations forwarded this day to His Excellency O.P. Morton Gov. State Ind for promotions to fill vacuum in line & staff officers
[the next portion was in two colums with two lines per person but will be listed in one line per person instead one column at a time]

8th Regt

1st Lt. James C. Poindexter to be Capt. "K" vice McCallister
1st Lt. Wm. H. Keller to be Capt. "G" vice Widaman
1st Lt. Robert E. Torrence to be Capt. "I" vice Thompson
1st Lt. Stephen A. Jones to be Capt. "B" vice Smith
Charles W. Wynn to be 1st Lt. "K" vice Poindexter
William Hamilton to be 1st Lt. "A" vice Tarkleson
Benj. P. Williamson to be 1st Lt. "H" vice Harmon
Swain Marshall to be 1st Lt. "G" vice Keller
George H. Black to be 1st Lt. "B" vice Jones
Flavius J. Brewer to be 1st Lt. "I" vice Torrence

8th Regt

John Wharton to be 2d Lt. "D" vice Smith
Geo. W. Dubois to be 2d Lt. "G" vice Keller
Samuel Wood to 2d Lt. vice Mather
Ambrose Whitecotton to be 2d Lt. "E" vice Hicks
George Britton to be 2d Lt. "C" vice Caho
Levi P. Shoemaker to be 2d Lt. vice Mitchell
Joseph C. Milliron to be 2d Lt. vice McPherson
Nicholas Miller to be 2d Lt. vice Smith
David R. Long to be 2d Lt. vice Smith
(over)
Copy
Hd. Qrs. 8th Ind. Inf. V. Vols
Hawkinsville Ga. July 19. 1865.
Recommendations for promotions to fill vacancies in Line and Staff officers of 8th Indiana.

* * * * *

James Peacock to be commissioned 1st Lt. and Adjt. vice Wiggins dischgd.

Robert S. Knode, Assistant Surgeon vice Brown promoted.
also prior to the above, but no commission received,
John A. McConnell, 1st Lieut. and Regt. Qr. Mr. vice Branson dismissed.
A true Extract
W.H.H. Terrell
Adjt. Gen. Indiana
[back of paper]
James Peacock to be 1st Lt. & Adjt. v. Wiggins dismissed
Robert S. Knode to be Asst. Surgeon v. Brown
John A. McConnell to be 1st Lt. & Qr. Mr. v. Branson resigned.

* * * * *

[side of paper]
C.C. Mikesell
For Trans or dischg
Ans. July 21
[8] [the first portion of this letter is very faint and difficult to read]
[cannot read the first three lines of this letter]
Sir
I herein a soldier from Indiana I believe it my duty to let you know my Situation I am a Member at Co I 8th Indiana Vet. Vol. Infty I came to Baltimore last Nov sick & have been Sick the most of the Winter & Spring but am sound again at this present time & would like to have My Discharge or go to My Regt. which is at Savannah Georgia & have been ever since last fall that is they were there that last I heard
[next four lines are too faint to read]
I have been in the army ever Since Aug 1861 I never missed a campaign & the first time I have been in the Hospl & I hope it May be the last for am not doing any thing only as we call it [unclear next two words] this does not suit my style for My Services ar needed very bad at home & should have been home Ear. this had not that little Ward Vet been attacking [too faint next two words] to know whether we ar going to be Discharged or sent to our Regt [illegible] that is going to be home with Vets in Hospl I am the only one from my State in this Hospl if we ar not going to be Discharged I should like to hunt for My Regt. for I have not been Paid for Seven months & I stand in need of Money this is all at present I hope I shall hear from you soon
Very Respectfully your
Obedient Servant
Sergt Christopher C. Mikesell
McKines Mansion Hospl ?
2nd Section Ward
Baltimore Md.

* * * * *

"Soldiers Home"
Indianapolis Ind. Aug 1, 65

I.W. Montfort
Ind. Mil. Agent.
Sir
By order of the Capt. Comdg I enclose Descriptive List. of Priv. Simon D. Brady 8th Regt. Ind. Infty. You will please attend to his pay and return roll to these Hd Qrs
Very Respy.
Your Obt Servt.
Richard Rahn
Clerk.
[back of paper]
In regard to Roll of Brady Ret. Aug. 2,
Simon D. Brady
8th Reg't.

* * * * *

[side of paper]
Jas. A. Tucker
M.S. Hospl
Grafton, Va
Regt. not mustered and he'll be entitled to dis. soon as it is.
Aug. 7th, 1865.
[8]
D
General Hospital
Grafton, W. Va. Aug. 2nd / 65
To the Hon. Military Mil. Agent for the State of Indiana. Sir –

I take the liberty of addressing you for the purpose of gaining a little information.

I will state my case as briefly as possible, and perhaps you can better direct me as to the proper course to pursue. I was sent to Frederick City Hospital in Nov. last transferred thence to Gallipolis, Ohio, and from there to this place in June last.

I have endeavored time & again to get to my Regt. but have not been able to succeed, and now I do not know where my Regt. is, but have understood that it was mustered out, and if such is the case, I think it no more than right that I should be mustered out also; if they are not mustered out, I would like to be transferred to Indianapolis, and then perhaps I can get to my Company.

I have served four years and more, and have drew no pay for eleven months; I have a family who deserve my care and attention instead of wasting my time about Hospitals, and under the circumstances, I think it hardly fair treatment, and if you can serve me in any way, you will confer a lasting obligation upon your obedient servant
Jas. A. Tucker
Priv. Co. I 8th Regt. Indiana V. V. Infy.
[side of paper]
Office, Indiana Mily Agency
Washington D.C. 1863
Aug. 7th, 1865

* * * * *

U.S. Army ~~General~~ Post Hospital,
Harpers Ferry Va. August 2nd 1865

Sir

I have to report that Private Wm. D. Stayman of Company F, 8th Regiment Ind. Vet. Vol. was transfered from this Hospital to Hospital Indianapolis Ind. on the 22nd July 1865 for muster out.

Very Respectfully,
Your obedient servant,
Lincoln R. Stine?
Surg. U.S. Vol.
In Charge.

[back of paper]
Ind. Mil. Agency?
Transfer order of Wm. D. Stayman
Co. F, 8" Ind. Inf.
To Home

* * * * *

Anderson August 7" 1865

W.H.H. Terrell –

Sir – Your letter addressed to Capt. H.F. Vandevender is at hand. God only knows how deeply I regret that he is not here to comply with your request. he was one of Indianas noblest sons & how proud I am of his history. how glad that his perishing was not in vain. The books muster roll and muster out rolls are not in my possession.

Respectfully his wife
C. Vandevender

[back of paper]
Mrs. C. Vandevender
Anderson, Ind
Announcing death of her husband, Capt. Hiram T. Vandevender
Co. E. 8th Reg.

* * * * *

Office Chief Commissary of Musters
Department of the East
New York City, Augst. 21, 1865

I have to report that private John S. Hendricks of Co. C. 8th Regt. Indiana Vols, is this day mustered out of the United States service, in compliance with telegraphic instructions from War Department of may 3d, 1865.

Very respectfully
Your obedient servant

(signed) Wilson Barstow
Capt. and A.D.C.
Chief Commissary of Musters
To the Chief Mustering Officer,
State of Indiana
War Department, A.G.O. Ind.?
Washington, D.C. July 3d 1864
A true copy
Jno. Elcott
Capt. 24 Infy
In charge Br.
[back of paper]
(H) 54
John S. Hendricks,
Priv. Co. C "8" Ind Vols.
Muster out

* * * * *

Depot Camp Hartford Conn
Sept. 8th 1865.
Adjutant General.
State of Indiana
Sir.

In compliance with instructions from the Provost Marshal General. I have the honor to report the following named enlisted men, Volunteers from the state of Indiana, discharged from Company "K" 3d Regiment Veteran Reserve Corps prior to this date.

* * * * *

Hillburt, Daniel R. Private – enlisted Aug. 20. 1861 at Indianapolis in Co. "K" 8" Ind. Vols. Discharged Aug. 19. 1865 at Washington. D.C. by reason of expiration of term of service.

* * * * *

Very Respectfully
Your Obedient Servant
(signed) Nelson Branson
1st Lieut Comdg Company
[back of paper]
8th Regt.
Private Daniel R. Hurlburt. Co. "K" 3d Regt. V.R.C.
formerly of Co. "K" 8" Regt. Ind. Vols
Discharged August 19, 1865 Term expired
Notification of such discharge from the Comdg officer Co. "K' 3d Regt V.R.C.
Copy
Recd. A.G.O. Ind. Sept. 19, 1865

* * * * *

SPECIAL ORDERS,} WAR DEPARTMENT,
No. 491. } ADJUTANT GENERAL'S OFFICE,
Washington, September 13th, 1865.

(Extract.)

* * * * *

13. So much of Special Orders, No. 87, February 23d, 1863, from this Office, as accepted the resignation of 2d Lieutenant *Milton R. Dungan*, 8th Indiana Volunteers, is hereby amended so as to honorably discharge him, to date March 6th, 1863, he having returned to his regiment and performed duty up to that date.

* * * * *

By order of the Secretary of War:
E.D. TOWNSEND,
Assistant Adjutant General.

OFFICIAL:
E.D.Townsend
Assistant Adjutant General.

[back of paper]
8th Regt.
2d Lieut Milton R. Dungan
Co. E
Honorably discharged
By order of War Dept. to date Mar 6" 1863. and order of Feby 23. 63 accepting resignation is amended

* * * * *

Head-Quarters "53d" Co., Second Bat., Vet. Res. Corps,
MOWER U.S.A. GEN. HOSPITAL,
Philadelphia, October 30 1865.

SIR:

In obedience to the directions in Circular Letter dated "War Department, Provost Marshal General's Bureau, Washington, D.C., February 10th, 1865, "I have the honor to inform you that W.S. Thomas a Private of my Company, was this day discharged from the military service of the United States, by reason of G.O. No 116 dated War Dept A.G. Officer Washington D.C. June 17, 1865.

Said W.S. Thomas enlisted in Co. B 8 Reg't, Ind Vols on the twenty third day of January 1864, and was musterd into service on the twenty third day of January 1864 at Indianapolis Ind. He was transferred to the 53d Co., Second Battalion, Veteran Reserve Corps, by ~~Special~~ Order ~~No.~~ from dated War Dept. A.G.O. Washington D.C. May 15 1865

Very respectfully, your obedient servant,
Thos Mathews
2d Lieut., 53d Co., 2d Batt. V.R.C.,
Commanding the Co.

Adjutant General

State of Indiana
[back of paper]
8th
Head-Quarters 53d Co., 2d Bat. V.R.C.
MOWERS U.S.A. GEN. HOSPITAL,
Philadephia, Pa. 1865.
THOMAS MATHEWS,
2D LIEUT., 53D CO., SECOND BATT., VET. RES. CORPS.
Discharge of Priv. W.S. Thomas
8th Regt.
Co. B
Private W.S. Thomas
Discharge
Ho8B

* * * * *

Dayton Ohio Nov 18th / 65
To his Excellency
Gov O.P. Morton
Indianapolis
Ind
Kind Sir

I am under the painful necessity of informing you of the death of our dear boy Capt John A. Caho, after being presented with your very kind leter, to Mr. Rice of Minn. he came & took leave of his home, & kind friends, believing that he might be benifitted physically, by going to Minn. he Reached St. Paul, and was kindly treated by Mr. Rice, but finding his health Rapidly failing, he Resolved to make an attempt to Reach Home, but ere he Reached La Crosse, Wis, his Spirit had taken its flight his body was taken from the Steamer, and burried there notwithstanding, his dying Request that his body be Sent Home, to his friends. I, have no means of going after his body, being poor and physically a wreck, as well financially. I lost my health through Exposure, in the Army, having Served all through Gen'l Sheridans Campaigns, in Va, myself at an advanced age, and my one boy dead, and my other boy, by wounds Received in Battle, made a cripple for life. I feel that I with my Two Boys, haved Served my Country well, therefore Gov Morton, I send this to you, Requesting you, to grant me a pass, from Dayton to La Crosse, Wis. for the purpose of getting the body of my Son, and back again. Knowing you to be a man of feeling, and the Friend of the Soldier, I thus appeal to you. Knowing that you are familiar with the Services of my boy, of the 8th Regt Ind V. Vol. and, I feel that this Request would be listened to by you, our boy had Some money along with him, but It was missing upon Reaching LaCrosse, therefore we have Nothing left us, of any hope of every Seeing our boy, except this meets with your approbation, thanking you very kindly for the favors shown our boy heretofore & hoping you will favor me in this last Request. Anxiously awaiting your Reply.

I remain your Humble servant C.H. Caho
[back of paper]

8.
Capt. John A. Caho.
Letter from his father
Ansd Jany 1 1866

* * * * *

Muncie Ind
Dec. 12th 1865

Mr. W. Montfort
Ind. Milty. Agt.
Indolis –
Dear Sir –

There is already in the case of Mrs. Mary A. Stultz, widow of Allen Stultz, formerly of Co. "A" 8th Ind. Infty a certificate from myself and from others on file in Washington. The difficulty in the way, I believe, is that the Surgeon General cannot be convinced that he came to death "while in the line of his duty," but inclines to the opinion it was through his own negligence. He was a weak-lunged man and through carelessly building a charcoal fire in a closed tent suffocated, bled at the lungs and so died.

I am, with respect,
Your obt. Servt.
Thos. J. Brady
formerly Captain 8th Ind.

[back of paper]
~~Thos J Brady~~
In regard to the cae of Mrs. Stultz
Dec 13
Allen Stultz

* * * * *

Adjutant Generals Office
Washington January 3. 66.

Capt. L.D. McAllister 8th Regiment Ind. Volunteers
Honorably resigned November 26, 64.

[back of paper]
8th Regiment
McCallister L.D.
Captain
Honorably resigned November 26. 64
Official order filed with papers of 8th Regiment

* * * * *

SPECIAL ORDERS,} WAR DEPARTMENT,

No. 24 } ADJUTANT GENERAL'S OFFICER,
Washington, January 18th, 1866.

(Extract.)

* * * * *

8. By directions of the President, so much of Special Orders, No. 146, May 31st, 1863, from Headquarters, Department of the Tennessee, (confirmed by Special Orders, No. 309, June 16th, 1865, from this Office,) as dismissed 1st Lieutenant *Richard M. Smith*, 8th Indiana Volunteers, is hereby revoked, and he is honorably discharged the service of the United States, to date May 31st, 1863, with condition that he shall receive no final payments, until he has satisfied the Pay Department that he is not indebted to the Government.

* * * * *

By order of the Secretary of War:
E.D. TOWNSEND,
Assistant Adjutant General.

OFFICIAL:
E.D. Townsend
Assistant Adjutant General.

[back of paper]
8th Regt.
1st Lt. (Co. F) Richard M. Smith
Order of dismissal revoked
Special Order War Dept.
January 18, 1866

* * * * *

Marion, Ind.
March 8th, 1866

Gen. Terrell,
Indianapolis, Ind.
Sir,

Yours of the 6th has been received, the Muster out Roll of ~~the~~ Co. "H" of the nonveterans is not in my possession. I think it was left with Capt. John L. Hummell, he lives in this County, will see him and if he has it, will have it forwarded to you. Maj. Stevenson has Copy of the nonveterans of the whole Regiment.

Respectfully Your
Obdt. Servt
John Ruess

[note at bottom]
Maj. C.S. Stevenson cashr Oceans Nat. Bk [illegible]
[back of paper]
8th Regt.
Co. "H"
Capt. John Ruess
Has no copy of roll

Will see Capt Hummell who has
Maj. Stevenson, Pay master has all the Rolls of Regt.
March 10, 1866
Note Maj. Stevenson
[seal]
REC'D ADJT. GEN'S OFFICER, IND'A
MAR 10, 1866

* * * * *

Wabash Ind
March 11th 1866
Gen. W.H.H. Terrell
It is impossible for me to furnish you the Muster out roll of the non Vetrans of Co. I 8th Ind Vols the officer that mustered them out never returned to me a copy to retain.
I am Very Respectfully your Obt Servt
Joseph M. Thompson
N.B. The history of the time of the discharge will be found at the bottom of the final muster out roll of the company of Aug. 28th, 1865
J.M.T.
[back of paper]
8th Regt.
Co. "I"
Capt. Jos. M. Thompson
Wabash Ind.
Has no M.O. Roll

* * * * *

Milton, Wayne County, Indiana
March 11th, 1866,
W.H.H. Terrell
Ajt. Genl" Indiana
Sir
Your letter Dated March 6th was Receved Several Days ago. in Reply I would Respectfully State that the muster-out Roll of the non-Vetrans of co" "D" 8" Ind. Vet. Vol." Inft. was togeather with other Rolls. Papers, company Books, and all Records, Pertaining to the co" turned over to Capt. J.M. Tompson, co" "I" 8" Ind. Vet. Vol. at Darian Ga. to Be taken By him to Indianapolis, Indiana, and there turned to the chief must" offic" of the State. There was also four copys turned over to the asst" comd" of must" 2" Div" 19th A.C. at Winchester Va. on or about the 4th of Sept" 1864. One copy to Be sent to Ajt" Genl." U.S.A. one to asst" Indiana, and two to the Pay Mst. Genl. So I am of the opinion that you will find a copy of the Roll, eather in your own office, or at the chief must" offic" of State, or at the Ajt" Genl" U.S.A. there is no Rolls in My Posesion, if there was I would Gladly Send them.
I am with Respect,

George W. Adams,
Late Capt. Co. "D" 8th Ind. Vet. Vol. Inft.

[back of paper]
8th Regt.
Co. "D"
Capt. Geo. W. Adams
Milton, Ind
Says he turned over his copy M.O. Roll – non-vet.

* * * * *

[8]

Post Hospital 19th A.C.
Savannah, Ga. March 16th, 1865
Dear W.H.D.? Mott
Dear Sir

Believing that you are interested in hearing from our Ind. troops, wherever they may be, of the conditions & prospects of our army here, & being am willing that our correspondence, am presently command in this valley of the Shenandoah should lose I take the liberty of addressing you a few lines

There are but two Ind Regts, the 8th & 18th Both are encamped out on the works in the rear of the town, or rather starting from the river shore, encircling the city, & stiking it again below

They have five pleasant camps, in chrg surely said, & am in excellent health the entire Brig is also pleasantly situated, & in good health

Our State Branch of the In. Com. sent Dr. Woods, Col. Shunk & Mr Hannaman here with goods, fruit, & stationary, which will very ---plable in our present conditions, not having been paid in more than six months as we arrived here Jan 18th, I found a number of Regts in & out of our Brig. destitute of Chaplains, - some having resigned in Va & one died & one or more resigned after we arrived here. I immediately enjoyed in the work of supplying them reading from the Chris. Com. & am still engaged in the same work, having to carry my bundles of religious papers, tracts, &c, from one to 1 ½ miles thru the sand.

One of these is a "city Regt" & almost entirely catholic, but receive my papers, &c eagerly & I think read them. I have also supplied them with the Catholic List, with a few of the common translations.

Some time since, at the earnest request of Dr. J.K. Bigelow, I removed to the Post Hospital of the 19th A.C. supplying the U.S. Barracks there, in addition to my other work, I am supplying the patients with religious reading, conversing with them, holding religious meetings & burying the dead. We have religious meetings from four to six times per week A part of thse we hold in the Dining Hall, having no other room for that purpose But as there are many unable to attend these, we go from ward to ward several evenings in the week, & hold a short service in each, which is well, & often thankfully rec'd by the patients

Then between the two branches of labor, I find my hands full, but my health has generally been excellent, & I am not only happy in my work, but thankful that I am able to perform it.
March 21st Have been very much pressed with business since writing the above, so as to impair my health somewhat, but there are so few Chaplains or laborers here, & so many Regts. with no one to supply them, that I have tried to supply the deficiency. If I should confine myself to the Hospital, I could get along very well but I have been over three years in the service, without intermissions, except an occasional visit home, & have never exempted myself from any toil of hardship, & at my age it is beginning to task seriously on my health, & I now think I should soon retire from the field to a more quiet life
If I could attain the position of Chaplain to some of the post or permanent Hospitals, I should like it much, & think I could be useful, but that requires an amount of political influence & backing which I cannot command here, & know very little about at home, in my state.

Those appointments I believe are made by the Presdt or Secy of War

Pardon Dear Sir this very very long letter I had no intention of writing half as much when I commenced

I am glad the friends Geo Ridfinkel? have removed his body I witnessed so many hearts needing service in the valley, of friends looking for friends, fathers for sons, sisters for bros, wives for husbands, mothers for sons, &c that the assistance is exceedingly painful, & I hope never to be repeated.

Pardon once more this long letter & write me I should sure be please to hear from you

Yours Dear Sir Respectfully
H.C. Skinner
Chaplain 8th Ind Infty

[side of paper]
Chaplain Skinner

* * * * *

[side of paper]
8th Regt
Co. "G"
Capt. Jacob Widaman
Cambridge City
Send company Return
Ackngd Mch. 27, 1866
[seal on paper]
REC'D AJDT. GEN'S OFFICE IND'A
MAR 27 1866

Cambridge City Ind
Mch 26 1866

Gen. W.H.H. Terrell
Adjt Genl State of Indiana

Sir.

Herewith I transmit for Muster Roll of Co. "G" 8th Ind Inf. Vols. including Veteran organization, from Aug. 20, 1861, to Aug. 28, 1865 final discharge from U.S. Service.

Having very imperfect data in my possession in consequence of having turned over all the records of the veteran organization to Brig Gen. Pitcher at muster out I have been unable to make it as complete as desirable, but I have given final disposition of every man who belonged to the company. In a very few instances, I have no dates nor can I obtain them.

Hoping the Roll will prove satisfactory.

I am
Sir
Your Obt Servt
Jacob Widaman
Formerly Capt. Comdg Co "G"
8th Ind Inf. V. Vols.

* * * * *

Galena Delaware County, Ohio
April 3rd 1866

General Terrell

Your communication has been received calling for the muster out roll of non veterans of Co. "A" 8th Indiana Vet. Vol. Inft.

The Rolls are in position of Capt John M Thompson at Wabash Ind. turned over to him by me, in Obedience to Orders from Lt. Col. John R. Polk Late Lt. Col. 8th Ind vet Vol Inft At Darrien Ridge Georgia My Address has been Changed from Muncie Ind. and from this reason your Letter has been Some time in reaching me.

I Am Sir
Your Obt.
Servt. M.M. Hughes
Lt. Capt. Co A
8th Ind. Vet
Vol. Inft.

[back of paper]
8th Regt.
Co. "A"
Capt Levi M. Hughes
Galena, Ohio
Has no M.O. Roll.
[seal]
REC'D ADJT. GEN'S OFFICE IND'A
APR 7 1866

* * * * *

Richmond August the 7th 1866

Mr. Hannanan Dear Sir

I saw by the paper there was a pension allowed to Soldiers Children 2 dollars A month would you please to inform me how to get it and also inform me if I cant get my pension with out paying Mr Payne two dollars every six months I have five Children all the way I have to get A liveing is by sewing am I entitled to an hundred dollars more bounty Mr. McMinn enlisted 3 times never received but one hundred dollars bounty that I got after his death he enlisted in Co D 8th reg Ind vol infantry April 1861 for 3 month was in the battle of Rich Mountain was discharged at expiration of term reenlisted in Co B 37 reg Ind vol inf Nov 1861 for 3 years was in the battle of Pittsburg landing other hard battles discharged on account of physical disability Feb 1863 reenlisted in Co. F 6th Reg Ind Vol. Cav June 1864 was taken sick and died at Camp Nelson he was in the Service one year the last time when he died

Yours respectfully

Virginia McMinn

* * * * *

Colfax Clinton Co. Ind. Aug 14, 1866

Hon Wm Hannaman

Sir I am requested by Mrs. Sarah Darne Widdow of Andrew Darne deceased late of the 8th Ind. Infantry to call your attention to her application for pension (which I believe passed through your hands) and to enquire whether she will obtain the additional bounty provided by the late law or whether she will have to forward a separate application, and if so please send her the necessary blanks

If you can send me several such blanks I can probably be of service to soldiers in this vicinity I never have charged or received any thing for such services nor do I know very well when to obtain them

Very respectfully

M.V. White

[back of paper]
Sarah Darne
Andrew Darne

* * * * *

Dublin Aug 15th 1866

Mr. William Hannaman Esq

I have noticed in the Papers that you have been appointed by Gov Morton to attend to getting the extra Bounty to Soldiers of the last Congress.

Joseph H. Conklin My Son belonged to Company D, 8th Regt I.V.I. under Capt Wysong & was killed in the Battle of Magnotin on the 1st May 1863 I wish you would be kind enough to send me a blank & I will have it filled out properly attested & then return to you please find enclosed stamp to prepay answer

Yours Truly

M.M. Conklin

N.B. Perhaps you had better fill out all except Signature, VR

M.M.C

Merric M Conklin
[back of paper]
M M Conklin
Joseph H. Conklin

* * * * *

[side of paper]
Martin McFarland
Mt Etna
Ind
Edward McFarland

Mt Etna
Huntington Co Ind
August the 16th 1866
Col Hanniman Dear Sir
I Recvd a Sercular from you the other day Conserning soldiers back pay and bounty I wish you to attend if you please to the geting of the back or aditional bounty of My Son Edward that died in the Servise. He belonged to the 8 Ind Regt. Comp H He died at Oterville Masouria about the 23 of Dec 1861 I made application to the Department at Washington and I have Recvd $1.00 hundred dollars bounty He volunteered for three years or during the War If I am to make out another Set of papers (I wish you to Send me the nessary blanks, and I will have them filed up and Send them to you amedially - - I also want to know if you have heard any thing of my papers conserning my own case that I left with you when I was down to the State Convention last Febuary I would like to get My back pay if posable that was due me before or up to the time they wheare made out as myself and three Sons have all been in the Service as three years Soldiers Without but very litle bounty and as on the day of our State Election two years ago Whar the misfortun of having my dwelling house and all ajoining buildings burned up by Some of the Buternuts in this cuntry and have in a great measure lost my health by being Broke down while in the Service, and having a large family to take cair of it has been a very hard time with me. I do not want to loose my papers that I left with you and if theare is any thing Rong or any thing that I am to do yet I am redy to try to do what is Wright please wright to me conserving these if you have Recvd any Word from them yet

Yours Respectfully
Martin M. Garland

* * * * *

Headquarters Department of the Lakes,
OFFICER CHIEF COMMISSARY OF MUSTERS,
Detroit, Mich., 20th July 1867
Wm Hanniman Esq. &
Sir.

Herewith, please find the Discharge of Jacob Dingle Compny B, 8" Indna Vols. Mite you please acknowledge the receipt of the Document, and hand to the War

Truly yours

J.R. Smith

Br. Brig. Gen'l USA

Adt C.W.D.L.

[back of paper]
J.R. Smith
[illegible]
Concerning discharge
of Jacob Dingle
Co. "B" 8th Ind

* * * * *

[8]

Anderson Ind Sept 25" 1869,

Capt. Broise,
U.S. Pension Agent
Indianapolis Ind
Dear Sir

I am the brother of Carrie Vandevender deceased and also the Administrator on her estate. She was the widow of Capt Hiram T. Vandevender of Co. "K," 8th Ind Vol Infty who was killed in May 1863, At Champion's Hills Miss. She has had a Pension Certificate and has been drawing 20$ per Month for several years past. She died of Consumption 7th July 1869. Since her death, we have been unable to find her Certificate. In August 1868 she went to Topeka Kansas and remained there until April 1869. Her father and Mother are both living also four brothers, and three Sisters. These are the facts that I presume are pertinent to the case. Will you be kind enough to give the information necessary to draw the balance due her.

And Oblige yours Very Respectfully

W.R. Myers

Anderson, Indiana

[back of paper]
W.R. Myers
Anderson
US Pension Agent
11 Oct 1869
Respectfully referd
to Wm Hanniman
State Agent Mil)
Respectfully
C.W. Brown
Pen. Agt.
Oct. 12, 69.
[illegible] for arrears

[cannot decipher this line]
Att
91564 com May 23 '63 $20. Mo.
paid to Mar
[illegible] Vandevender
Widow
Hiram T. Capt.
Hiram T. Vandevender.

* * * * *

June 18 84 New Winchester
Hendrick Co Ind
Dear Sir I recieved of you a leter in regard to the Morgan Raid claim on recit of Saim I inclo you My pay role will-ly and my one promotion I must explain I was Capton of home Gard Co and when Morgan invaded the Soil of Ind I was called by the Governor of the State I responded to the call and took my co to Indianapolis and was receve and plaised in Reg no 80 Comanded Torance Shular as Coparl but thru a blunder they got part of the rocord 8-20 for Capton of the 80 hoo was aproved in the [too faint to read] and handed comision and was [illegible] Sword in as Capton of the Company [illegible section] comition sworn in as Capton of the Company I are the full proof in my possion made and more I never recieved my pay now if you [illegible] to help me rite to me and tell me we may have to go to Indianapolis and I [unclear] the record if you think so rite to me I mean business if you intende to help me to inform me if no to return my pay role
Theodore P. Bunter

* * * * *

SPECIAL ORDERS,} HEADQUARTERS OF THE ARMY,
No. 26. } ADJUTANT GENERAL'S OFFICE,
Washington, January 31, 1889.

Extract.

* * * * *

7. By direction of the Secretary of War paragraph 5, Special Orders, No. 22, current series, from this office, relating to 2d Lieutenant *James H. Adams*, Company A, 8th Indiana Infantry Volunteers, is revoked.

* * * * *

BY COMMAND OF MAJOR GENERAL SCHOFIELD:
R.C. DRUM
Adjutant General.

OFFICIAL:
J Melton
Assistant Adjutant General.
[back of paper]
Record of
James H. Adams

2" Lieut Co "A" 8" Regt. Ind. Vol.
Par. 5 – S.O. No 22
Revoked

* * * * *

[picture and inscription on side of heading of paper]
GRAND CENTRAL DEPOT UNDERGROUND RAILROAD
SOL WOODY,
SOLE AGENT FOR THE
HISTORY OF THE UNDERGROUND RAILROAD.
3300 Slaves passed through this Depot.
Agents Wanted in Every County
in the United States.

OFFICE OF
M.M. LACEY,
Justice of the Peace,
Fire and Tornado Insurance Agent.
COLLECTIONS PROMPTLY MADE.
Fountain City, Ind., Aug 29" ~~189~~ 1900

Genl J.K. Gore
Indianapolis.
Dear Sir,

Your letter of Yesterday at hand, and I am not at all surprised that you find the records of the 8th Ind. three months Service somewhat tangled up. Jacob Dewald was a private in my Company, but the particular letter of that Company is some what mixed, and in the light of subsequent events I am of the opinion that we did not know much about the proper Organization of a Regt in the early sixties. When the 8" was Organized the Cos. were arranged "A,"B."C" & D" &c. and not A.F.D. & so on. and my Co was called and known as Co "D." during the entire Service, and my position in the line was 4" from the right. Capt Brady was 3rd and Co "B" was 2nd Co. instead of the Extreme left. When I think of it Now I am the more surprised from the fact that our Adjt. A.I. Harrison was a graduate from the Lexington Military Col. and Col Benton, Major Shunk and Capt Carey were Mexican War Veterans.

Promotions followed swift & fast during the first few days of our Military experience, and A.I. Harrison (a brother of the Ex-President) was grafted into our Regt because of his Military Experience. At the request of Col Benton he was Elected 1st Lieut of my Company, and at Once promoted to be Adjutant, and a Splendid man and soldier he was, though he did not remain with us long, was detailed by Genl Rosecrantz As A.A.A.G.

Shall be glad at any time to render any aid I can and have no hesitency in calling on me. My kindest regards to Col Walker,

Fraternally Yours
M M Lacey

* * * * *

[side of paper]
Co D 8th Regt 3 mos.

Form 24, A.G.D.

STATE OF INDIANA,
Adjutant-General's Office,
INDIANAPOLIS.
July 21, 1913.

FROM: The Adjutant General, State of Indiana.
TO: The Adjutant General, U.S. Army.
SUBJECT: Company commanded by Capt. Reuben A. Riley of the 8th Indiana, - three months service.

In order to correct our records, information is desired as to the correct designation of the company commanded by this officer.

Geo. W. McCoy
JUL 23 1913

2060783 1st Ind.
War Dept., A.G.O., July 24, 1913. – To the Adjutant General, State of Indiana, Indianapolis.

The records show that Captain Reuben A. Riley commanded Company I, 8th Indiana Infantry (three months, 1861).

F.J. Korsten
Adjutant General.

[stamp of back of paper]
ADUTANT GENERAL'S OFFICE
JUL 23 1913
2060783
WAR DEPARTMENT

* * * * *

To his excellency O P Morton Gov of the State of Indiana
we the undersigned take pleasure in recommending Francis Williams a citizen of Del. County Ind to a position of Capt in the so called Drafted militia we think him in every respect capable to fulfill every duty enjoined upon said Officers he having served two years in the first U.S. Cavalry under Gen. Wood, formly mustering Officer of this State, and the term of three months in the 8th Regiment Indiana volunteers and three months in the 41st Regiment Ind. Vol.

List of names	list of names
G.W.Thomas	Jacob [illegible]
Jno. H. Rutter	John Frey
J.G. Williams.	Jesse Hullman
J.G. Kigdon	Wm. H. Sanders

A.B. Dillon
G.C. Saunders
N. Lyons
[back of paper]
Draft
Francis Williams
Delaware Co
Captain
Drafted militia

IB Hall
Eli Rigdon   T.M. Wheeling Ind

* * * * *

[side of paper]
8th Regt.
Prom. Co. E

Respectfully Forwarded to Adjutant Gnl Laz Nobel, approved David Shunk Col 8th Ind Infty
Enclosed pleased find three dollars enclosed to pay for Commisions.

* * * * *

To Gov. Morton

Orderly Sergeant William W. Mather, Co. H. 8th Reg't Ind Vols. was unanimously elected by the members of the company to fill the vacancy in the office of 2nd Lieutenant in said Co. occasioned by the dath of 2nd Lieut. James R. Smith who was killed in the battle of Pea Ridge Ark. on the 7th of March last, and was thereupon recommended by Capt. Ruess commanding the company for appointment, which recommendation was approved by Col. W.P. Benton com'dg said regiment and by him forwarded for mail to your Excellency on the 3d day of the present month from Camp Cross Timbers Ark. – Owing to the time already elapsed since it was dispatched and the known uncertainty of mails from that locality I fear that it is lost.

The impaired health of the Capt. and 1st Lieut. render the speedy filling of the vacancy important.

Respectfully submitted
A.W. Sanford
Chaplain 8th Ind

Refer to Col. A. Stone
[back of paper]
8th Regt.
Co. "H"
Prom
Ho8H
Adjt Gen
L. Noble
Present,

* * * * *

Col. IS Williams [this letter is hard to decipher, so this may not be correct]

I certify that I was this 2 [illegible] 1862 mustered into the reg been in an for the 8" Vet. Ind. Vols. the following named person George W. Quay

Quay

Charles S. [illegible]
[illegible line]

[back of paper]
8th Ind. Vols.
1-68

* * * * *

Co. E 8th Ind service

The Roll of commissioned and non commissioned officers Mucians and Privates of the Madison County Guards, Madison Co. Indiana.

1st Hiram T. Vandevender	Captain
2nd John T. Robinson	1st Lieutenant
3 James Fergus	Ensign
st Orderly Sergeant	L.D. McCallister

[rest of paper appears to be torn]
[strip of paper]
Capt. Vandevender
Commissions issued April 20 / 61
[back of paper]
3 mos. 8th Regt.
Capt. H.T. Vendevender
Co. "E"
Madison County
Election of Officers

* * * * *

Eighth regiment.
Captain Widaman
" Carey
" Lee.
" Brady.
" Vandeventer
" Riley
" Howard
" Lacey
" Parrish.
[back of paper]

45
John W. Andrews
(Druggist
Appt. in Hospital

* * * * *

[8]
To his Excellency
O.P. Morton
The undersigned officer & soldiers of Co. I 8 Regt. Ind Vols from Hancock Co. Ind. State to your Excellency, that we have just learned with surprize that there are efforts being made to appoint one James R. Bracken formerly of our County as a Major in one of the Regts of State troops. Most of us have know him long as well. Our objections to such appoint are not and could not be petitioned for the reason that he was "boxed [illegible] the political campaign. He is unstable as water, and utterly wanting in integrity and the manly and soldierly qualities necessary for such position as we verily believe.

Newton Pope	G.W.H. Riley Capt. Co. I
John H. Duncan	8 Regt. Ind. Vols.
A.W. Brown	[too faint] 1st Lieut
[too faint to read]	[too faint] 1st Lieut
[too faint to read]	Henry [too faint]
T.L. Horne	Wm H. Short
[too faint to read]	[too faint]
[too faint to read]	[too faint]
Seth Marsh	Henry Jones
Samuel Marsh	P.E. Harrison [too faint]
Jas. S. Reuss	Jacob Hock
Geo. L. Lipscomb	J. W. Allison

[rest of names on back are extremely faint and difficult to read]
[note of side of back]
James R. Bracken

* * * * *

To all whom it may concern, [most of this letter is very faint and hard to read]
The undersigned officers of the 8th Indiana [illegible section] write to recommend [illegible section] of Company G 8th Indiana as a soldier worthy an appointment in the [long illegible section]
David Shunk
Col 8th Rgt Ind Vols
Saml H. Dunbar
Le & A Adjutant.
N Branson QM 8th Regt
H T Vandevender
Capt Comandg 8th Reg

L.D. McCallister 1 Lieut Co K
Joseph M Thompson Capt Co. I
Robert E. Torrence 1st Co I
John R. Polk Capt Co F. 8th Ind Infty
Frank Daily 1st Lt Co F
Wm. R. Walls Capt Co B. 8th Ind
G.W. Bruce ass Surgeon 8 Reg Ind. Vol
W.D.Watson 1st Lt. Commdg Co. A, 8th Regt.
Geo W. Adams
1st Lieut Com Co D
Isaac N Smith 2nd Lieut Co D, 8th Ind. Vol.
John Ruess Capt. Co. H, 8th Ind.
Willaim W. Mather 2nd Lieut Co. H 8th Ind. Vol
[illegible]
[illegible]
A.J. Kenny Capt Co C 8th Ind Comd'g Fort Curtis Mo
John A Caho Lieut Co C 8th Ind
Jesse E Scott Qr Master 1st Div ASW
J.R. Pearce Comdg Co E 8th Ind
[back of paper]
133
Sgt. Allen O. Neff.
(8th Regt. Ind. Vols.)

* * * * *

To His Excellency
Gov O.P. Morton
Sir

Having learned that the Office of Major of the 8th Indiana Regiment is vacant by the occasioned by the promotion of Major Brady, we the undersigned citizens of Wabash County desire to recommend Capt J.R. Polk of Co F. of the 8th as a suitable person to fill the vacancy.

B Cowgill
E.S. Ropleushn?
EP Peters
W.H. Whitende
CD Sayre
Geo. J. Stephenson
Jas Whitende
John M. Pettit

I.D. Conner
John L. Knight
William L. Russell
Madison Whiteside
William J Ford
David Coble
IB Suman
Mason J. Thomas

[back of paper]
8th
Capt. J.R. Polk
For Major

* * * * *

Eighth Regt
Captain Milton M Lacy
" Widdeman (Cambridge
" C.O. Howard
" T.J. Brady
" Tykle
" Vandevender (Anderson
" Charles S. Parrish
" Reuben A. Riley
" Thos. J. Lee (Winchester
" O.H.P. Carey (Marion

* * * * *

[8]

To his Excellency
Gov O P Morton
Indiana
Sir.

I would communicate the following statement of facts with reference to a matter of deep importance to this Regiment, in the hope that some action may be taken by which our Regimental organization may be more complete viz

During the months after last, while at Springfield Mo, 1st Lt and Q Master Nathan Branson was detached from the 8th as actg Brigade Quarter Mr, to Col (now Brgd Genl) Jeff C Davis, comdg Brigade – In this, and as Division Qr Mr, he has been continued since, Genl Davis's command having been detached from this corps, Lt Branson, continues with him in the same capacity, Query cannot the QuarterMastership of this Regt be treated as vacant and another commissioned as such?

I would add the interest of companies suffer in the absence of their full corps of Officers, and that it will be returned a favor if such action may be taken in this matter that will enable me to make recommendations for a successor to Lieut Branson

I am Sir
Your Most Obt Servt
David Shunk
Col 8th Infantry
Charles S Parrish
Lieut Col 8th Rgt

Tom J. Brady
Maj. 8th Ind.
[back of paper]
8th Regt. Quarter Master place.
The field officers of the Regt. ask if the place of the Q.M. is not vacant, the former Q.M. having been on detached duty as acting Brigade & Division Q.M.
David Shunk,

Col.
Ans. July 5th & copied.

* * * * *

J.H Long
William Adsit
William Dunlap
Co A. Hirpe?
Walter March
[too faint to read]
John Brady
E Bumer
PH Pangan
Joel W. Long
William Abbott
L. Hathaway, M.D.
G. H. Baxter
Thomas Jonson

Geo W Spilker Clk D.C.C.
D.I. Hunter
Alfred Kilgore
John Marsh
[too faint to read]
Thomas J. Sanifile
D.J.T. Leellevere?
L.P. Everett?
Henry Kirby Capt 84 Reg
George Jones Lieut 84?
J.A. Riley Capt. Co. G 5 Cav.?
N.B. Gregory Lieut 84 Regt

* * * * *

Casualties at Port Gibson

Name	Rank	Regt.	Co.	Date of Death	Cause	Remarks
Hess, W.D.	Prt	8th Regt.	C	May 1 63	Killed	
Conklin Jos	"	"	D	" 20 63	"	
Hampson Jas.	"	"	F	" " "	"	
Duck Jno	"	"	H	" " "	"	
						Millikens Bend La
Clevenger Joshua	"	"	"	" " "	"	"
Strown Moses	"	"	D	June 8 "	"	---
McCollough?	"	"	?	[can't read]		St. Louis, Mo
Davis, J.	Priv.	8th Regt.	H	July 13 63		Memphis Tenn
Jackson Jno.	"	"	B	Mar 22 "		"
Jones James	"	"	E	Jan 23 64 Died Delaware [unclear]		"
Skinner Jno	"	"	"	Aug 30 63		"
Norton Henry	P.	Co. A. 8th		Dec 7 64		Salisbury N.C. Louisville Sem.

[note: there are several notes on the side that are not very clear]
[the above was copied again on the next page]

* * * * *

Regiment Indiana Volunteer Co.
ROSTER OF ENLISTED MEN

NAME AND RANK.	Residence.		Mustered Into U.S. Service.	REMARKS.
King D	8th ..	A	Sept 13 64	8621 Andersonville Ga
Packett T.C. Corp.	" ..	E	Oct. 1 64	10128 Andersonville Cemetery Ga
Whiteman Albert pvt	"	A	July 26/65	Evansville Ind
~~Robinson R. pvt~~	~~"~~	~~G~~	~~Jan 14 65~~	~~12404 Andersonville Ga.~~
Wilcoxen, Edwin H	" "	B	Aug 3 64	National Cemetery Arlington Va
~~Rhinehart Elias~~	~~" "~~	~~G~~	~~Mar 12 65~~	~~US Genl Hospl Div. Annapolis Md~~.
Trentleman Chas	" "	H	Aug 20 63	Indianapolis Ind.
Gordon John	8th			" "
Overman Calvin J.	8th	B 3 mos	----	" "
McGuire James	prt	K	Feb 16 65	Nat. Cem. Alexandria Va
Hale Alexander		I	Oct 20/62	Oakland Cemetery Keokuk Ia
Reeve Cephas		H	" 21 / 63	"
Holdron Dudley		A	" 22 "	"
Miller John		"	" 27 62	"
~~Forward, S Priv~~		~~I~~	~~Sept 14 64~~	~~Died Andersonville Prison~~
Jenkins John		G		Died on Battlefields of Shenandoah Val
Hoffman J		G	Oct 1 64	" Andersonville
Adams David P		B	" 29 62	St. Louis, Mo
Benjamin Wm "		I	Dec 13 61	"
Brickel George "		F	Nov 18 "	"
Brown Wm "		D	" 1 62	"
Colvin Bennett "		"	Feb 17 "	"
Daniels Isaiah "		K	Nov 16 61	"
Ellsberry Fredrick C "		B	Dec 20 "	"
Shower John H	8th Private	E	Aug 16 63	St. Louis Mo. Chronic Diarr
Vanoleit Martin	"	C	Sept 20 63	" " " " "
Underwood John M	"	B	Oct 13 "	New Orleans La Chron Diarr
Pittser A		E	" 7 "	" " "
Walker John H	"	A	" 18 "	" " " Diarrhea
~~Mullenhair Charles~~	~~"~~	~~G~~	~~Nov 11 "~~	~~" " "~~
Jones James	"	E	Jany 23 64	Memphis Tenn.
Wilcox E. H.	"	B	Aug 3 "	Washington D.C.
Rinehart Elias	8th Cav	G	Mch 12 65	Annapolis Md
Robisson Power	8th Cav	F	Jany 14 "	Andersonville Ga
Filson Chas	"		Dec 6 65	[cannot read]
Burris Henry H	"	G	Died at Millikens (Bend) La.	

8th

[on side of paper]

Hospl or Sanitary Reports

Garrison Oliver	P.	D	Dec 7 61	St. Louis Mo
Hale Ezra	"	I	Nov 28 "	"
Harvey Daniel	"	F	Dec 10 62	"
Hendricks Joel P.	"	D	Nov 2 61	"
Hendricks J.H.	"	C	" 6 "	"

Heinshaw Abner	“	G	Jan 7 63	“
Hipes Joel	“	D	Nov 13 “	“
Horitz Wm H.	“	F	Dec 18 61	“
Jones Isaac T.	“	B	Oct 14 62	“
Kelly John	P.	I	Nov. 5 62	“
McCarthey Wm S.	“	K	“ 20 61	“
Neal John A	“	K	“ 13 61	“
Overman Uriah	“	I	“ 8 “	“
Pearson Isaiah	“	C	“ 15 62	“
Runyon Jonathan	“	E	Oct. 24 “	“
Skinner Elias	“	I	Nov. 7 “	“
Stalker Geo	“	C	“ 24 62	“
Stevenson Anderson	“	K	Oct. 31 61	“
Vanbuskirk W.A.	“	F	Dec. 9 62	“
Warner Henry T	“	G	Oct. 10 62	“
Wilson Saml	“	G	Nov. 13 61	“
Woods James	“	C	“ 4 “	“
Woolworth Solomon	“	A	Dec 22 “	“
McGuire Chas. P.	“	G	Feb 21 63	“
Jenkins Rich’d	“	“	Apr 16 “	“ Small Pox or Arsenal Island
Foster Jeremiah	“	K	“ 5 “	“ Jefferson Barracks
Melick Thos	“	C	July 18 “	“ “
Snyder Jacob	“	E	Aug 11 “	“ Ch Dir “
Showers Jno A	“	“	“ 16 “	“ “
Garrison W.A.	“	I		Pea Ridge Ark.
Hardbarger Henry	“	F		“
Potter --	Capt.			“
Smith J.R.	Lieut	C		“
Salisbury W.	P	G		“
Wagner J.		K		Sherman’s Army from Chatt to Atlanta
~~Davis Benj~~				~~“~~
Leonard Jas	P	D		Buried at Lewisville Henry Co. Ind.
Filson Chas	“	“	Dec 6 65	“ Dublin Wayne Co. Ind. by wife of two mo
Burris Henry H	“	G		Died at Millikins (Bend) La.

8th
[back of paper]
8th
Dead Lists
Made up from National Cemetery Records
Records Ind Milty Agency &c

* * * * *

[news clipping]
Campaign of the 8th Indiana in Texas
Correspondence of the Daily Journal.

CAMP ON MATAGORDA ISLAND, TEXAS,
December 10, 1863.

Soon after our return from the campaign up the Bayou Teche, we embarked, with seven companies of the 18th I.V.I., on the steamer St. Mary's, for Brazos Santiago, Texas, on the 12th ult., and arrived on the 15th ult. Toward evening of the same day we were ordered, with six steamers and gunboats, to return to Corpus Christi Pass, where, after reconnoitering and sending several shot and shell ashore, a part of our force, including the 18th I.V.I., was landed. The 8th was ordered to Aransas Pass, some 12 miles, and landed on Mustang Island, where they met the force landed at Corpus Christi Pass, who had marched through during the night, surprising and taking a battery of three guns, 120 men, and two small schooners.

From this point our regiment, with other forces, was ordered to march to the attack of Fort Esperanza, on a point of this island, with nothing but blankets, guns, ammunition and cooked rations. On this march of more than 60 miles, they suffered much from the want of provisions, hard marching through the sand, and the severe cold prevalent in this climate, called "Northers." – They arrived here on the 28th ult., and on the morning of the 29th, the 8th, under the command of Major Kinney, was ordered to report to Gen. Washburne and hold themselves in readiness for an armed reconnoissance of the enemy's works, and soon after to file to the right 200 yards and lie down to avoid the enemy's fire. Col. Washburne, in command of the brigade, then ordered Major Kinney to move the regiment to, and cautiously up the beach, and detach three companies to take possession of the rifle pits constructed by our men the night previous, and to move by companies till all were in, to avoid presenting a large mark for the enemy's guns in the fort. Capt. Elwood, with company E, was then sent forward to the enemy's outer works, and company B ordered to his support. Capt. Elwood then sent word to Major Kinney that he could deploy two companies as skirmishers to advantage in front of these works, and companies D and H were immediately sent forward for that purpose. At this time Col. Lippincot of the 34th Illinois, came up and ordered Major Kinney to move the remainder of his regiment forward to the first line of the enemy's works, and he would occupy our line of works with his regiment, which was immediately done. In this position we remained till 3 P.M., when Col. Washburne came up, and Major Kinney asked and obtained leave to move to, and occupy an earth-work erected by the enemy. This was assigned to company K, Captain McAllister, while company I, Captain Thompson, was ordered to their support. As soon as these companies had obtained position, Maj. Kinney, on order of Col. Washburne, sent forward companies B, D, and H, some 250 yards to gain the next chain of sand hills, which they gallantly did, supported by five companies of the 33d Illinois, driving in the enemy's sharp shooters, until they took shelter under cover of the fort. In this position we remained till half past twelve A.M. of the 30th ult, when an explosion of one of the magazines of the fort notified us that the enemy had evacuated it. Col. Washburne then ordered the advance companies, B, D and H, of the 8th, supported by five companies of the 33d Illinois, to move forward cautiously, when they found that the enemy had abandoned the fort, leaving behind his ammunition, stores, and personal baggage of the officers. They had, however, piled a large quantity of cotton around magazines, scattered gunpowder among it and set it on fire. Finding no enemy here, except those left to fire the magazines (who were made prisoners) they immediately started in pursuit. When a mile distant they came to the floating bridge, on which the enemy had crossed to McHenry's Island, and the ropes of which they had cut, allowing it to swing round so as to prevent pursuit. They also attempted to burn the bridge by placing cotton upon it and setting it on fire; but our advance was too close in pursuit and extinguished the flames. As soon as it was ascertained that the rebels had fled, Col. Washburne ordered Major Kinney to move the remainder of the 8th forward, and at one o'clock A.M. we took possession of Fort Esperanza. Five of the seven magazines blew up, wounding four men of the 8th, one of whom died, belonging to company I, Capt. Polk.

The Fort mounted eight guns – seven 24-pounders and one 128-pounder – all of which were spiked, but in such a manner that all have been removed.

On entering the fort, Adjutant McPherson, of the 8th, discovered a line of torpedoes on the outside, with strings extending inside, to be exploded beneath our feet in an attempt to take it by storm. We carefully cut the strings and ordered the prisoners to dig up and remove them, which was done without accident, and thus valuable lives were saved.

I may here remark that the movements above described were made amid more or less firing from sharpshooters and the guns of the fort; but our regiment, and indeed all the men and officers in the field conducted themselves with a coolness and courage deserving great praise. It has been the subject of frequent remark that our forces approached the outer works, and the fort itself, with the coolness and discipline of a dress parade, although they knew not what moment the enemy might rise in their works and fire point-blank into their approaching ranks. Major Kinney, in command of the 8th in the absence of Col. Shunk and Lieut. Col. Parrish, though recently commissioned, acquitted himself with honor, and gave promise of an able, brave and efficient officer. But it would be unjust to make invidious distinctions, where all, both officers and men, acquitted themselves so well.

In this communication I have not aimed to give a description of the part taken by the different regiments in our approaches to and capture of this fort, but only so much as related to the 8th regiment and those immediately connected with its movements. The rest I leave to other and abler pens.

Fort Esperanze is a beautiful work and capable of strong defense, but having been constructed mainly with reference to an attack from the water, by gunboats, and forces landed from them in its immediate vicinity, it was not sufficiently guarded in the rear against a land force as large and determined as ours; therefore it fell an easy prey to our arms.

The 8th, and, indeed, all our forces here are in fine health and spirits, and ready for any further service their country may demand. Our greatest prevailed against men from other parts of the world. We seem to be cut off in a great degree from, other parts and know little of what is going on around us.

R.O.L.

[back of paper]
Campaigns 8th Ind. in Texas
Letter to Indpls Journal Dd Dec 10th 1863

* * * * *

[newspaper article]

Was organized April 20, 1861, for three months' service, in an engagement at Rich Mountain, Va., July 11, 1861, returned home and mustered out, August 6, 1861, reorganized August 20, 1861, for three years, arrived in St. Louis September 11; September 3d marched en route for Springfield, Mo., under command of General Fremont, arriving October 29th; returned to Otterville, Mo., arriving November 13, 1861; December 17th marched to Warrensburg, Mo., and assisted in the capture of 1,300 rebels; returned to Otterville January 24, 1862, marched for Springfield under command of General Curtis; continued the march to Cross Timbers, Ark, and participated in the battle of Pea Ridge, Ark., March 6th, 7th and 8th, and 8th, and April 6, 1852; marched for Helena, arriving July 13, 1862. The command suffered severely on this march by reason of scarcity of provisions, there being but a scanty supply with the command and little in the country; very often they subsisted on parched corn; August 1862, was in a skirmish at Austin, Mississippi; October 11, 1862, proceeded to Ironton, Missouri, and marched and counter-marched through the southwestern portion of that State, until March 5, 1863, when the regiment embarked on a steamer to join General Grant's army, then organizing at Milliken's Bend, Louisiana, where it arrived March 26; crossed the Mississippi river April 29; participated in the engagements at Port Gibson May1; Champion Hills, May 15; Black River Bridge, May 17, and from the 19th of May to the 4th of July, was in the siege of Vicksburg; July 5th marched for Jackson, which, after a few days' siege, was evacuated by the rebels; returned to Vicksburg; August 20, embarked on a steamer for Carrollton, Louisiana, and made a campaign through the Teche country, under General Banks, November 12, embarked on a steamer for Texas; Nov. 17, in the attack and capture of a fort on Mustang Island; Nov. 27, in the attack and capture of Fort Esperanza; Dec 31st, Regiment mustered out, and organized as veterans; April 22d, 1864, arrived at Indianapolis; remained one month and returned to New Orleans; July 27th, embarked at Algiers, La., for Morganza Bend, arriving on the 28th; 28th marched to Atchafalaya; engaged the rebels, and returned to Morganza Bend; August 14th, embarked on steamer, and arrived at Washington, August 12th; Marched to Berryville, and assigned to the 19th corps; participatied in the campaign of the Shenandoah Valley, under General Sheridan, from August 14, 1864; was in the engagement at Opequan, September 19, "Fisher's Hill" September 22d, and "Cedar Creek" October 19th; left the Valley January 6th, 1865, and arrived at Savannah, Ga., January 16th, 1865; remained in Georgia until August 28th, 1865, when mustered out; the regiment arrived home on the 17th, Lieutenant Colonel Polk commanding, with 14 officers and 245 men.
[back of paper]
8th
History of Regiment

* * * * *

[newspaper article]
Histories of the Regiments.

Yesterday morning the clouds were forbidding, and the air chilly and raw. Yet despite all, the ladies were out in force at the Home, and prepared such a dinner as even Polyphemus would have given up his "brace of Greeks" for, to the veterans of the four regiments who were to receive, at the hands of the State, the meed of a public welcome.

When dinner time came, the clouds lifted, and the air was pleasantly warmed, so that among the whole volumes of receptions, there is not a pleasanter page than this last. After dinner the regiments formed around the reception stand in the State House yard, and were briefly addressed by General Mansfield, the old soldier, whose eye is always lit with a warm welcome for the returning braves. The General's remarks were short, pithy and soldierly, and were well received by the men to whom they were addressed.

After the General, followed Governor Morton, who, though still suffering from feeble health, did not deny the regiments the pleasure of receiving their thanks from the mouth of their honored Executive. The Governor would have been glad to have spoken more at length than he did, but prudence forbid him. He was doubly gratified to meet and to speak a few words of welcome to the body of men before him. The soldiers have done their duty, and come home victorious and full of honor. He had always believed that the rebellion would be suppressed, and it afforded him peculiar pleasure to greet those who had contributed so materially to the final triumph of the Government. The Governor concluded by returning his own thanks, and the gratitude of the State, and the loyal people for the services of the regiments before him. The remarks were received with marked applause.

Major General Grose was then introduced and made an excellent and interesting address. After prefacing his remarks with a few introductory phrases, he reviewed the bare possibility of the defeat of the Government in the late struggle. Had history recorded such an humiliation, he would have been ashamed of himself, of his country, and of his fellow-men. The Government was no play thing, but had been bought by the blood of the patriot fathers, and by them bequeathed to us in the faith that we had patriotism and honor sufficient to maintain and preserve it. There were times when things looked dark, when the political horizon was black and lowering; but he had never doubted the final issue. The citizen who stood at the back of the soldier, with heart and money; to cheer, with supplies and stores to sustain him in the field and in the hospital, are entitled to the meed of praise. He would always remember them, and he would also always remember those who stood upon the other side of the question. The soldiers knew the rebels had been helped by Northen traitors. The prisoners they had taken had taunted them with the fact that the North was upon the eve of a revolution. He would never forget such men. Probably he might forgive them, in deference to a command from a higher power than himself; but he didn't know how to go to work to forget them. He referred to the efforts of the Northern Copperheads; the letters they had written to the army, urging their sons and brothers to desert. Had we always been united, as the country appeared to be in 1861, the rebellion would not have last twelve months, and the returning regiments would have brought home thousands of men they have left upon the field of battle, or in the dismal pens of Southern prisons. These dead men are now clinging to the skirts of these Northern traitors, and will do so forever.

The General continued his remarks at some greater length, humorously referring to the disloyal chickens and pigs which the soldiers ball turned into loyal flesh and sinew, and cautioned the soldiers to let no minor questions disrupt the ranks of the great Union party, which had saved the country, and which alone was fit to be trusted with the administration of the government in the years to come.

General Washburned, Colonel Brady and Hon. Delana E. Williamson, Attorney General of the State, all made short and interesting addresses, extending the welcome of themselves individually, and of the loyal people of the State, to the returning regiments.

Chaplain Lozier, whose absence at the few last receptions has been so marked, fortunately came in just in time to give us a bit of song, in the shape of a humorous, rythmical history of the meeting of a Johnny Blue-coat, and a regular Southern female, high-strung, high-blooded, and awfully "snuffed up." The Chaplain's efforts pleased the boys so well, that he was compelled to favor them with his "Loyal Dixie."

The following is the histories of the regiments, as well as an account of the casualties by death of the commissioned officers of the 44th:

EIGHTH REGIMENT.

Was organized April 20, 1861, for three months' service, in an engagement at Rich Mountain, Va., July 11, 1861, returned home and mustered out, August 6, 1861, reorganized August 20, 1861, for three years, arrived in St. Louis September 11; September 3d marched en route for Springfield, Mo., under command of General Fremont, arriving October 29th; returned to Otterville, Mo., arriving November 13, 1861; December 17th marched to Warrensburg, Mo., and assisted in the capture of 1,300 rebels; returned to Otterville January 24, 1862, marched for Springfield under command of General Curtis; continued the march to Cross Timbers, Ark, and participated in the battle of Pea Ridge, Ark., March 6th, 7th and 8th, and 8th, and April 6, 1852; marched for Helena, arriving July 13, 1862. The command suffered severely on this march by reason of scarcity of provisions, there being but a scanty supply with the command and little in the country; very often they subsisted on parched corn; August 1862, was in a skirmish at Austin, Mississippi; October 11, 1862, proceeded to Ironton, Missouri, and marched and counter-marched through the southwestern portion of that State, until March 5, 1863, when the regiment embarked on a steamer to join General Grant's army, then organizing at Milliken's Bend, Louisiana, where it arrived March 26; crossed the Mississippi river April 29; participated in the engagements at Port Gibson May1; Champion Hills, May 15; Black River Bridge, May 17, and from the 19th of May to the 4th of July, was in the siege of Vicksburg; July 5th marched for Jackson, which, after a few days' siege, was evacuated by the rebels; returned to Vicksburg; August 20, embarked on a steamer for Carrollton, Louisiana, and made a campaign through the Teche country, under General Banks, November 12, embarked on a steamer for Texas; Nov. 17, in the attack and capture of a fort on Mustang Island; Nov. 27, in the attack and capture of Fort Esperanza; Dec 31st, Regiment mustered out, and organized as veterans; April 22d, 1864, arrived at Indianapolis; remained one month and returned to New Orleans; July 27th, embarked at Algiers, La., for Morganza Bend, arriving on the 28th; 28th marched to Atchafalaya; engaged the rebels, and returned to Morganza Bend; August 14th, embarked on steamer, and arrived at Washington, August 12th; Marched to Berryville, and assigned to the 19th corps; participatied in the campaign of the Shenandoah Valley, under General Sheridan, from August 14, 1864; was in the engagement at Opequan, September 19, "Fisher's Hill" September 22d, and "Cedar Creek" October 19th; left the Valley January 6th, 1865, and arrived at Savannah, Ga., January 16th, 1865; remained in Georgia until August 28th, 1865, when mustered out; the regiment arrived home on the 17th, Lieutenant Colonel Polk commanding, with 14 officers and 245 men.

* * * * *

[newspaper article from Indianapolis Daily Journal, Sept. 19, 1865.]
Horses and Mules.
QUARTERMASTER GENERAL'S OFFICE,
WASHINGTON D.C., August 15, 1865.
WILL BE SOLD AT PUBLIC AUCTION, To the highest bidder, at CHICAGO, ILLINOIS and INDIANAPOLIS, INDIANA, (150 Horses and Mules alternately each day), superior lots of public animals, as follows:

AT CHICAGO, ILLINOIS,

Under the direction of Colonel J.A. Ellison, Depot Quartermaster, commencing MONDAY, September 4th, 185, and continuing each second week thereafter, until FRIDAY, September 29, and thenceforward daily until the whole are disposed of,

2,000 HORSES AND 1,600 MULES.

At INDIANAPOLIS, INDIANA, under the direction of Captian James Wilson, A.Q.M., commencing MONDAY, September 11, 1865, and continuing the second week thereafter until sold.

1,000 HORSES AND 500 MULES.

An opportunity to purchase a superior class saddle and draft animal, at far less than their true value, is now offered to the public.

Though the majority of them are sound and serviceable, they are no longer required in the army and must be sold.

Many of the mules were bought in the beginning of the war, when young, accompanied the armies in all their marches and camps, and are thoroughly broken, hardened by exercise, gentle and familiar from being so long surrounded by the soldiers.

Animals will be sold singly.

Sales to commence at 10 A.M.

Terms: Cash in United States currency.

JAMES A. EKIN,
Brevet Brigadier-General in charge First Division
Q.M.G.O. aug19dtitlsep28

STATE OF INDIANA,
EXECUTIVE DEPARTMENT,
Indianapolis, Nov. 12th, 1864.
GENERAL ORDERS.

WILLIAM H.H. TERRELL, heretofore Colonel and Aid de Camp on the staff of the Commander-in-Chief, has been appointed and commissioned Adjutant General of Indiana, and will be obeyed and respected accordingly, *vice* LAZARUS NOBLE, elected and commissioned Clerk of the Supreme Court.

OLIVER P. MORTON,
Governor of Indiana.

[back of paper]
8th Regt.
Reception Sept. 18th 1865

* * * * *

1. Sanford Preston
2. John Summers
3. Andrew Perdue
4. Edwin Bournye
5. Joseph Wiseacre?
6. Jackson Windsor
7. John Carter
8. John Mannig
9. Joseph B. Gossett
10. David Coffman
11. A.C. Neff
12. Joseph Speakman
13. Nat Potter
14. John Loven
15. Robert Commons
16. Ben West
17. Lorenzo Study
18. Thomas A. Bell
19. Wm Roberts
20. S. Bowers
21. Wm Skinner
22. James L Moor
23. Abner Vanmetre
24. Cyrus Pitser
25. George Starbuck
26. Henry W. Jack
27. Ruben Miller
28. David S Scott
29. Samuel Miller
30. ~~Thomas Bell~~ Henry Luce
31. Wm H Keller
32. Job Ginn
33. John Hodson
34. Joel Hendricks
35. M. Graham
36. Jessy Williams
37. John Clevenger
38. Richard Brown
39. Joe Hawkins
40. John Fisher
41. M.M. Conklin
42. Thomas Leakey
43. Daniel Miller
44. J.R. Paltia?

45. James McCabe
46. George Dennis
47. Harvey Berry
48. ~~Wm Gates~~ W Gates
49. L H Miller
50. George Packson
51. Thomas Packson
52. George Albun
53. TB Harper
54. John Hardin
55. David Coble
56. Ben Wimer
57. Edward Shafer
58. Wm Smith
59. Grimes Holcom
60. Andrew Robinson

[back of paper]
List of returning Vols.
Reg[illegible]

* * * * *

8th Ind. Inf. Vols. was organized April 20, 1861 – in service for three months - In engagement Rich Mountain, Va., July 11, 1861. - Returned home and mustered out, August 6, 1861. Re-organized Aug. 20, 1861, for three years. Arrived St. Louis Sep. 11, 1861. Sep. 23d Marched <u>en route</u> for Springfield, Mo., under command of General Fremont, arriving October 29th - Returned to Otterville, Mo., arriving November 13, 1861. - Dec 17,1861, marched to near Warrensburg, Mo., and assisted in capture of 1,300 rebels - Returned to Otterville - January 24, 1862, Marched <u>en route</u> for Springfield under command of Gen Curtis. continued on to Cross Timbers, Ark, and participated in battle of Pea Ridge, Ark., Mch 6 – 7 – 8. 1862. Apl .6. 1862. Marched <u>en route</u> for Helena, arriving July 13, 1862. The command suffered severely on this march by reason of scarcity of provisions, there being but a scanty supply with the command and little in the country. Very often they subsisted on parched corn – Aug. 1862 - In skirmish at Austin, Miss. Oct. 11, 1862 - proceeded to Ironton, Missouri, and marched and counter-marched through the South Western portion of that State, until M'ch 5 / 63, when the regiment embarked on Steamer to join Gen. Grant's army then organizing at Milliken's Band, La. where it arrived M'ch 26. - Crossed Miss. river Apl. 29. participated in the engagements at Port Gibson May 1. Champion Hills, May 15. Black River Bridge, May 17. and from the 19th of May to 4th July in the siege of Vicksburg. July 5 – marched <u>en route</u> for Jackson which after a few days' siege was evacuated by the rebels. Returned to Vicksburg - Aug 20. Embarked on Steamer for Carrollton La and made campaign through the Teche country under Gen Banks –
Nov. 12. Embarked on Str. for Texas - Nov. 17 in attack and capture of Fort on Mustang Island Nov. 27. In attack and Capture of Fort Esperanza Dec. 31. Regt. mustered out and reorganized Jany 1, 1864, in Veteran organization –

Apl 22d, 1864, arrived at Indianapolis remained one month and returned to New Orleans July 27. Embarked at Algiers La. for Morganza Bend La arriving 28th 29th Marched to Atchafalaya - in engagement with rebels and marched back to Morganza Bend.
Aug. 4. Embarked on Str. and arrived at Washington Aug. 12. Marched to Berryville and assigned to 19th Corps. participatied in Campaign of Shenandoah Valley under Gen. Sheridan from August 14, 1864. In engagements of Opequan Sep. 19. Fisher's Hill Sep 22d. and Cedar Creek Oct. 19. Left the Valley January 6, 1865, and arrived at Savannah, Ga., January 16, 1865.
Remained in Georgia until August 28th, 1865, when mustered out.
[back of paper]
8th Regt. Inf.
Historical Mein.
[back of paper]
8th
History of Regt.

* * * * *

[8]
Adjutant Generals Office
Washington Feb 15 1867
Colonel William Hannaman.
Military Agent of Indiana.
Indianapolis, Indiana.
Sir:

In reply to your communication of March 7th, 1866, requesting the honorable discharge of Simon Cumming, Philip Killan and James Gray all are Co "K" 8th Indiana, Vols. I have to inform you that the application is not favorably considered, there being sufficient evidence of the guilt of the men to justify their dishonorable discharge.

In view of which fact no change can be made in the records of this Office.

I am, Very Respectfully,
Your obdt Servant,
Simon Buck?
Asst Adjutnat General.
[unclear] General WHH Terrell
Adjt General of Indiana
[back of paper]
A.G.O. Indiana
Indpls. Feb. 18. '67
Reply forwarded to Wm Hannaman Esq Gen. Mil. ?an Agent Indiana
W.H.H. Terrell
Adj. Gen. Ind
[seal]
REC'D ADJT. GEN'S OFFICE IND'A.
FEB 18 1867

Phillip Killan
James Gray
and
Simon Cumming.
3-32

* * * * *

Office of Commissary of Musters,
DEPARTMENT OF THE LAKES,
Adjutant General State of Indna.
Sir: Detroit, Mich., 20th July 1867

I have the honor to report that I have this day discharged from the service of the United States, pursuant to instructions from War Department, A.G.O., dated 11th July 1867, and Paragraph 1, Special Orders No. 114, current series, Headquarters Department of the Lakes, the following names enlisted men

No.	NAMES	Rank.	Co.	Regiment.	REMARKS.
1.	Dingle (or Dinkel) Jacob	Private	B	8th Indiana Vols.	

A partial Disc. Listg the above named soldier dated June 27th 1867 War Dept. A.G.O. says – "It is stated on the Muster Rolls of his company for the months of Sept & Oct 1862, that he was last paid by Pay Master [illegible two words] – to the 31" day of Dec 1862; clothing acct last settled Nov. 1st 61, and to be stopped for clothing $32.11/100 – Later account of pay and clothing.

Muster Roll of company dated Augt 28th 1865 reports him "was taken up from Desertion Sept 13th 1864, and discharged by order of I.G.M. Augt 6th 1865, at Hawkinsville Ga"

Sp. Order, No. 106, par. 1 – HdQrs Dept of the Lakes, of July 5th 1867, says.. "The charge of Desertion against private Jacob Dinkel, compy B, 8th Regt Indna Vols, with all penalties incident thereto is removed, satisfactory evidence having been furnished that the same was erroneously performed," and sp. order no. 114, par. 1, H.Qrs. District of the Lakes, July 15th 1867 says "In accordance with instructions of July 11th 1867, from the Adjutant Generals office, [illegible] on papers in the case private Jacob Dinkel, compy B 8th Indna Vols, will be honorably discharged from the date of muster out of his compny With forfeiture of pay and allowances from March 10th 1862 to Sept 17th 1864, for which period we will be considered as absent from proper authority." Pursuant older foregoing instructions and W. orders private Jacob Dinkel, is this day Honorably discharged as of date of muster out of his compny Aug. 28th 1865, with forfeiture of pay and allowances from March 10th, 1862 to Sept. 17th 1864. He will apply to the Pay Master General USA for a detilement? of his awards.

Very Respectfully,
Your obedient servant,
J.R. Smith
Brevet Brigadier General U.S. Army,
Chief Commissary of Musters, Department of the Lakes.

[back of paper]
Office Chief Commissary of muster

Department of the Lakes Detroit
July 20th, 1867
Smith J.R.
Bvt. Brig. General U.S.A.
Reports to the discharge of one enlisted man without descriptive list.
Co. B 8th
Jacob Dinkle.
Change of Desertion removed and mustered out July 20th 1867, to Date Augt, 28, 1865.

* * * * *

SPECIAL ORDERS,} HEADQUARTERS OF THE ARMY,
No. 282. } ADJUTANT GENERAL'S OFFICE,
Washington, December 2, 1884.

Extract.

* * * * *

4. By direction of the Secretary of War, under the act approved June 3, 1884, and to complete his record, the discharge of 1st Sergeant *George W. Tarkleson*, Company E, 8th Indiana Volunteers, August 28, 1865, is amended to take effect December 14, 1864; he is mustered into service as 1st lieutenant, same company and regiment, to date December 15, 1864; mustered into service as captain, same company and regiment, to date January 1, 1865; mustered out and honorably discharged as captain, to date August 28, 1865; and he is mustered for pay in said grades during the periods embraced between the aforesaid dates.

* * * * *

BY COMMAND OF LIEUTENANT GENERAL SHERIDAN:
R.C. DRUM,
Adjutant General.

OFFICIAL:
Thomas Ward
Assistant Ajutant General.

[back of paper]
1st Sergt. Geo. W. Tarkleson
8th Ind. Infty. Co "E"
Amended Record.

* * * * *

SPECIAL ORDERS,} HEADQUARTERS OF THE ARMY,
No. 34. } ADJUTANT GENERAL'S OFFICE,
Washington, February 10, 1885.

Extract.

* * * * *

8. By direction of the Secretary of War, under the act approved June 3, 1884, and to complete his record, the discharge on September 7, 1864, of 1st Sergeant *Joseph W. Rigdon*, Company I, 20th Regiment Veteran Reserve Corps (to which he was transferred

from Company A, 8th Indiana Infantry Volunteers), is amended to take effect May 22, 1863; he is mustered into service as 1st lieutenant, Company A, 8th Indiana Infantry Volunteers, to date May 23, 1863; mustered out and honorably discharged as 1st lieutenant, same company and regiment, to date September 7, 1864, and he is mustered for pay in said grade during the period embraced between the aforesaid dates.

* * * * *

BY ORDER OF LIEUTENANT GENERAL SHERIDAN:

R.C. DRUM,

Adjutant General.

OFFICIAL:

Thomas Ward,

Assistant Adjutant General.

[back of paper]
Jos. W. Rigdon
Co. A 8" Regt. I. Vol.
Vol. 2
Page 49 - - -

* * * * *

SPECIAL ORDERS,}
No. 258. }

HEADQUARTERS OF THE ARMY,
ADJUTANT GENERAL'S OFFICER,
Washington, November 9, 1885.

Extract.

* * * * *

10. By direction of the Secretary of War, under the act approved June 2, 1884, and to complete his record, the discharge of Sergeant Major *Jacob W. Beshore*, 8th Indiana Infantry Volunteers, June 14, 1865, is amended to take effect December 28, 1864; he is mustered into service as 1st lieutenant and adjutant, same regiment, to date December 29, 1864; mustered out and honorably discharged as 1st lieutenant and adjutant, to date June 14, 1865, and he is mustered for pay in said grade during the period embraced between the aforesaid dates.

* * * * *

BY ORDER OF LIEUTENANT GENERAL SHERIDAN:

R.C. DRUM,

Adjutant General.

OFFICIAL:

Wm. I. Volkman

Assistant Adjutant General.

[back of paper]
Jacob S. Beshore
Maj. 8th Ind Infty
Amended Record.
Vol. 2
P 48.

* * * * *

SPECIAL ORDERS,} HEADQUARTERS OF THE ARMY,
No. 64. } ADJUTANT GENERAL'S OFFICE,
Washington, March 18, 1886.

Extract.

* * * * *

7. By direction of the Secretary of War, under the act approved June 3, 1884, and to complete his record, *Philander Smith* is mustered into service as 1st lieutenant, Company B, 8th Indiana Infantry Volunteers, to date July 1, 1864, and as captain, same company and regiment, to date September 30, 1864; his discharge as 2d lieutenant, by paragraph 47, Special Orders, No. 205, May 4, 1865, War Department, Adjutant General's Office, is amended to read captain; and he is mustered for pay in said grades during the periods embraced between the aforesaid dates.

* * * * *

BY COMMAND OF LIEUTENANT GENERAL SHERIDAN:
R.C. DRUM
Adjutant General.

OFFICIAL:
Wm. I Volkman
Assistant Adjutant General.

[back of paper]
Philander Smith
Company B. 8 Regt.
Record Amended
Vol 2 page 50
to B8

* * * * *

SPECIAL ORDERS,} HEADQUARTERS OF THE ARMY,
No. 64. } ADJUTANT GENERAL'S OFFICE,
Washington, March 18, 1886.

Extract.

* * * * *

8. By direction of the Secretary of War, under the act approved June 3, 1884, and to complete his record, the discharge of 1st Sergeant *Steven A. Jones*, Company B, 8th Indiana Infantry Volunteers, June 10, 1865, is amended to take effect September 29, 1864; his muster into service as 1st lieutenant, same company and regiment, June 11, 1865, is amended to date September 30, 1864; his discharge as 1st lieutenant, August 28, 1865, is amended to date July 18, 1865; he is mustered into service as captain, same company and regiment, to date July 19, 1865; mustered out and honorably discharged as captain, August 28, 1865; and he is mustered for pay in said grades during the periods embraced between the aforesaid dates.

* * * * *

BY ORDER OF LIEUTENANT GENERAL SHERIDAN:

R.C. DRUM,
Adjutant General.

OFFICIAL:
Wm. I Volkman,
Assistant Adjutant General.

[back of paper]
Stephen A. Jones.
to 8B

* * * * *

SPECIAL ORDERS,} HEADQUARTERS OF THE ARMY,
No. 74. } ADJUTANT GENERAL'S OFFICE,
Washington, March 30, 1886.

Extract.

* * * * *

3. By direction of the Secretary of War, under the act approved June 3, 1884, and to complete his record, the discharge of Sergeant *Matthew M. Hughes*, Company A, 8th Indiana Infantry Volunteers, February 28, 1865, is amended to take effect September 30, 1864; his muster into service as 1st lieutenant, same company and regiment, March 1, 1865, is amended to date October 1, 1864; and he is mustered for pay in said grade during the period embraced between the aforesaid dates.

* * * * *

BY ORDER OF LIEUTENANT GENERAL SHERIDAN:
R.C. DRUM,
Adjutant General.

OFFICIAL:
Wm. I Volkman,
Assistant Adjutant General.

[back of paper]
Matthew M. Hughes
(Co. A.)

* * * * *

SPECIAL ORDERS,} HEADQUARTERS OF THE ARMY,
No. 31. } ADJUTANT GENERAL'S OFFICE,
Washington, February 7, 1887.

Extract.

* * * * *

1. By direction of the Secretary of War, under the act approved June 3, 1884, and to complete his record, the discharge of 1st Sergeant *John L. Hummell*, Company H, 8th Indiana Infantry Volunteers, April 15, 1865, is amended to take effect December 31, 1864; his muster into service as captain, same company and regiment, April 16, 1865, is amended to date January 1, 1865; and he is mustered for pay in said grade during the period embraced between the aforesaid dates.

*   *   *   *   *

BY ORDER OF LIEUTENANT GENERAL SHERIDAN:
R.C. DRUM,
Adjutant General.

OFFICIAL:
J C Kelton,
Assistant Adjutant General.

[back of paper]
8th Reg
Amended Record
John L Hummell.
Co. H 8" Ind. Vol.
Vol 2 page 53.

* * * * *

SPECIAL ORDERS,} HEADQUARTERS OF THE ARMY,
No. 201. } ADJUTANT GENERAL'S OFFICE,
Washington, August 30, 1887.

Extract.

*   *   *   *   *

10. By direction of the Secretary of War, under the act approved June 3, 1884, and the act amendatory thereof, approved February 3, 1887, and to complete his record, the discharge of 1st Sergeant *William Study*, Company C, 8th Indiana Infantry Volunteers, August 28, 1865, is amended to take effect October 19, 1864; he is mustered into service as 1st lieutenant, same company and regiment, to date October 20, 1864; mustered out and honorably discharged as 1st lieutenant August 28, 1865, and he is mustered for pay in said grade during the period embraced between the aforesaid dates.

*   *   *   *   *

BY ORDER OF LIEUTENANT GENERAL SHERIDAN:
R.C. DRUM,
Adjutant General.

OFFICIAL:
J C Kelton,
Assistant Adjutant General.

[back of paper]
Amended. Record.
William Study
Co. C 8. Regt. Ind. Vol.
Vol. 2 page 51

* * * * *

1194 A. A.G.O. (E.B.), 1882.
War Department,
ADJUTANT GENERAL'S OFFICE,

Washington, Aug. 4th, 1888.

Adjutant General,
State of Indiana,
Indianapolis, Ind.

Sir:

I have the honor to inform you that the charge of desertion of Sept. 27, 1863, standing against William S. Griffy, as of Co. "C," 8th Ind. Vols. has been removed from his record in this office. He is supposed to have been drowned Sept. 27, 1863, at Brashear City, La., while absent without permission.

Very respectfully,
Your obedient servant,
O D Grrue?
Assistant Adjutant General.
(325)

[For the files of the office of the Adjutant General State of Indiana.
[back of paper]
Co. C 8"
Vol 4
P. 114
3-42

* * * * *

SPECIAL ORDERS,} HEADQUARTERS OF THE ARMY,
No. 22. } ADJUTANT GENERAL'S OFFICE,
Washington, January 26, 1889.

Extract.

* * * * *

5. By direction of the Secretary of War, under the act approved June 3, 1884, and the act amendatory thereof, approved February 3, 1887, and to complete the record, the discharge of Private *James H. Adams*, Company A, 8th Indiana Infantry Volunteers, August 28, 1865, is amended to take effect May 22, 1863; he is mustered into service as 2d lieutenant, same company and regiment, to date May 23, 1863, and to read sergeant; mustered out and honorably discharged as 2d lieutenant August 28, 1865, and he is mustered for pay in said grade during the period embraced between the aforesaid dates.

* * * * *

BY ORDER OF MAJOR GENERAL SCHOFIELD:
R.C. DRUM,
Adjutant General.

OFFICIAL:
J C Kelton,
Assistant Adjutant General.

Adjutant General
State of Indiana
[back of paper]
Record of

James H. Adams
Private Co. "A" 9th Regt Ind. Vol.
Amended
Vol. 4
P. 110

* * * * *

SPECIAL ORDERS,} HEADQUARTERS OF THE ARMY,
No. 26. } ADJUTANT GENERAL'S OFFICE,
Washington, January 31, 1889.

Extract.

* * * * *

8. By direction of the Secretary of War, under the act approved February 3, 1887, amendatory of the act approved June 3, 1884, and to complete the record, the discharge of Private *James H. Adams*, Company A, 8th Indiana Infantry Volunteers, August 28, 1865, is amended to take effect May 22, 1863, and to read sergeant; he is mustered into service as 2d lieutenant, same company and regiment, to date May 23, 1863; mustered out and honorably discharged as 2d lieutenant August 28, 1865, and he is mustered for pay in said grade during the period embraced between the aforesaid dates.

* * * * *

BY ORDER OF MAJOR GENERAL SCHOFIELD:
R.C. DRUM,
Adjutant General.

OFFICIAL:
J C Kelton,
Assistant Adjutant General.
Adjutant General
State of Indiana

[back of paper]
Record of
James H. Adams
Priv. Co "A" 8" Regt Ind. Vols.
Amended

* * * * *

SPECIAL ORDERS,} HEADQUARTERS OF THE ARMY,
No. 30. } ADJUTANT GENERAL'S OFFICE,
Washington, February 5, 1889.

Extract.

* * * * *

2. By direction of the Secretary of War, under the act approved June 3, 1884, and the act amendatory thereof, approved February 3, 1887, and to complete the record, the discharge of 1st Sergeant *Hampton Ellis*, Company K, 8th Indiana Infantry Volunteers,

September 4, 1864, is amended to take effect May 23, 1863; he is mustered into service as 2d lieutenant, same company and regiment, to date May 24, 1863; mustered out and honorably discharged as 2d lieutenant September 4, 1864, and he is mustered for pay in the advance grade during the period embraced between the aforesaid dates.

*   *   *   *   *

BY ORDER OF MAJOR GENERAL SCHOFIELD:
R.C. DRUM,
Adjutant General.

OFFICIAL:
J C Kelton,
Assistant Adjutant General.

Adjutant General
State of Indiana
[back of paper]
Record of
Hampton Ellis
1st Sergt. Co "K" 8th Regt I.Vol.
Amended & Corrected
Vol 4 p 126

* * * * *

Address: "Chief of Record and Pension Office, War Department, Washington, D.C.
Subject: True name. 494,170

Record and Pension Office,
War Department,
Washington City,
February 18, 1898.

The Adjutant General,
State of Indiana,
Indianapolis.

Sir:

I am directed by the Secretary of War to inform you that it has this day been determined, upon evidence before this Department, that James D. McWhorter is the true name of the soldier who served as James D. Smith in Company D, 8th Indiana Volunteers (3 Months).

A discharge certificate as of the former name has been granted under the provisions of the acy of Congress approved April 14, 1890.

Very respectfully,
F.L. Arnimond?
Colonel, U.S. Army,
Chief, Record and Pension Office.

[back of paper]
8th
3 mos

* * * * *

Form 24, A.G.D. STATE OF INDIANA,
Adjutant-General's Office,
INDIANAPOLIS.
July 30, 1913.

FROM: The Adjutant General, State of Indiana.
TO: The Chief, Division of Militia Affairs.
SUBJECT: Company Commanders of the 8th Indiana, three months service.

Since your report of the record of Captains Lacey, Riley and Parrish of the 8th Indiana Regiment, three month's service has raised some question as to the enrollment and final mustering out of other companies in the three month's service of the 8th Indiana Regiment, we respectfully request that you furnish us with information concerning the Captains of all companies in the three month's service of the 8th Indiana Regiment.

Geo. N. McCoy

RECEIVED D.H.A. .... AUG 1 1913
Received A.G.O. AUG 1 1913

1ST Indt.

War Department, A.G.O., August 2, 1913, -- To the Adjutant General, State of Indiana, Indianapolis.

1. Official records in this Department show that the following named served as captains of the various companies of the regiment not referred to hereinbefore: Jacob Widaman, mustered in as Company B and mustered out as Company A; Frederick Tykle, mustered in as Company F and mustered out as Company B; Thomas J. Brady, mustered in as Company D and mustered out as Company C; Thomas J. Lee, mustered in as Company E and mustered out as such; Charles O. Howard, mustered in as Company C and mustered out as Company F; Hiram T. Vandevender, Mustered in as Company H and mustered out as Company G; and Olvier H.P. Carey, mustered in as Company G and mustered out as Company K.

Hos Heinstand
Adjutant General.
F

[stamp on back of paper]
ADJUTANT GENERAL'S OFFICE
AUG 1 1913
2063776
WAR DEPARTMENT

* * * * *

Form 24, A.G.D. STATE OF INDIANA,
Adjutant-General's Office,
INDIANAPOLIS.
July 21, 1913.

FROM: The Adjutant General, State of Indiana.
TO: The Adjutant General, U.S. Army.

SUBJECT: Company commanded by Capt. Chas. S. Parrish, 8th Indiana, - three months service.

In order to correct our records, information is desired as to the correct designation of the company commanded by this officer.

Geo. N. McCoy
JUL 23 1913

2060784 1st Ind.

War Dept., A.G.O., July 24, 1913. – To the Adjutant General, State of Indiana, Indianapolis.

The records show that Captain Charles S. Parish's Company, 8th Indiana Infantry (three months, 1861), was mustered into service as Company I of that regiment, but that the designation of that company was afterwards changed to Company H, as of which latter designation it was mustered out of service.

F.J. Korsten
Adjutant General.

[stamp on back of paper]
ADJUTANT GENERAL'S OFFICE
JUL 23 1913
2060784
WAR DEPARTMENT

* * * * *

Form 24, A.G.D.

STATE OF INDIANA,
Adjutant-General's Office,
INDIANAPOLIS.
July 21, 1913.

FROM: The Adjutant General, State of Indiana.
TO: The Adjutant General, U.S. Army.
SUBJECT: Company commanded by Capt. M.M. Lacey of the 8th Indiana, - three months service.

In order to correct our records, information is desired as to the correct designation of the company commanded by this officer.

Geo. N. McCoy

JUL 23 1913
2060782 1st Ind.

War Dept., A.G.O., July 24, 1913. – To the Adjutant General, State of Indiana, Indianapolis.

The records show that Captain Mayberry M. Lacey's Company, 8th Indiana Infantry (three months, 1861), was mustered into service as Company A of that regiment, but that the designation of that company was afterwards changed to Company D, as of which latter designation it was mustered out of service.

F.J. Korsten
Adjutant General.

[stamp on back of paper]
ADJUTANT GENERAL'S OFFICE

JULY 25 1913
2060782
WAR DEPARTMENT

* * * * *

ROSTER of Capt. Co., Indiana Continued

NAME. RANK. RESIDENCE. DATE OF SERVICE. Days Served.

Wiggins, Lawson "B" Greenfield Dischgd Indpls 7th Augt 62 for Genl Debility &c
Derry, James " " " " 13th " " accidental Injury
Thompson, Isaac P " Hancock Co. " " 17th Sept. " Ph. Pul.
Hawkins, James (Corpl) " Mt Comfort " " 19 " " "
Helmer, Henry A. C. Fairfield, Ohio " " 31st July " Broken leg – thrown from horse while on duty.
Spealman, Joseph (Corpl) " Williamsburg " " " " Disease
Hamilton, David S. " Wilmington " " " " "
Jenkins, George " Anderson " " 16th " " Frostbite
Van Buskirk, Martin D Bentonville " " 25th June " Cannon wd right side, Pea Ridge
Shelly, Christian H " E. Germantown " " 21st July " Disease
Boyer, Amandus (Sergt) " " " 18th Aug " Inj. Left foot – run over by R-
Burr, Chauncey S (Sergt) " Middletown " " 1st July " Ph. Pulm.
Moore, George S. " Greenfield " " 17th " " Disease – only 17 years age
Gray, John M. (Corpl) " Middletown " 5th Aug " Poisoned by charcoal fumes
McAlister, Alexr " Daleville " 11th Apr " Ch. Dyspepsia
Finkle, John P. H Warren " 14th June " Cannonball ws left elbow Pea R
Lytle, Thomas " Grant " 28th Augt " Poisoned.
Carr, Mills " Bloomington " 27th " " Ph. Pulm.
Swank, James K Anderson " 25th June " Rheumatism left foot
Bowman, Henry Sergt Maj. Rensselaer " 18th Feby 63 Disease (as Private)
Nixon, Azor M. B Henry Co. " 2d Apr " Genl Debility
Craw, David A Wheeling " 27 Apr 64 Gun shot wd right forearm
Welling, Wm. W. (Corpl) B Marion Co. " 8th June " " " " "
Curry, Robt C Alexandria " " 20 Sept 63 " " " arm
Kunkle, Cyrus E Indpls " " 11th " " Ch. Diar. Contd in Service
[back of paper]
8th
Discharges compiled from Genl Services and Discharge Registers.

Bibliography

ELECTRONIC SOURCES:

The Civil War CD-ROM. Carmel: Guild Press of Indiana, 1997.

This CD-ROM contains many of the records found in the National Archives in the following books:

Aimone, Alan C. and Barbara A. *A User's Guide to the Official Records of the American Civil War.* White Mane Publishing Company, 1993.

Dyer, Frederick H. *A Compendium of the War of Rebellion.* Des Moines: Dyer Publishing Company, 1908.

Fox, William F. *Regimental Losses in the American Civil War (1861-1865).* Albany: Albany Publishing Company, 1889.

National Archives historians, eds. *Military Operations of the Civil War: A Guide Index to the Official Records of the Union and Confederate Armies.*

The War of the Rebellion: A Compilation of the Official Records of the Union and Confederate Armies. Washington: Government Printing Office, 1880.

Websites:

"28th Regiment, United States Colored Troops." Accessed July 22, 2001. http://www.in.gov/iwm/2397.htm.

"Abner Hinshaw." Accessed May 23, 2012. http://www.rawbs.com/~hishaw/cgi-bin/id?965.

"American Civil War Research Database." http://www.civilwardata.com.

"Bethel Cemetery." Accessed January 5, 2009. http://www.rootsweb.ancestry.com/~ingrant/bethel.htm.

"Brevet Brigadier General Charles Sherman Parrish." Accessed April 13, 2013. http://www.electriccemetery.com/ecPARRISHC.html.

"Carroll County, Arkansas Civil War Union Soldiers." Accessed April 13, 2013. http://www.rootsweb.ancestry.com/arcchs/ccunion.html.

"Cemetery History – September 2012." Accessed April 13, 2013. http://www.greenfieldin.org/residents/history-of-greenfield/852-cemetery-history-september-2012.

"Census and Voter Lists." http://search.ancestry.com/search/category.aspx?cat=35.

"Civil War." http://www.civilwar.com.

"Civil War: Governor Morton Telegraph Books and Slips." *The Digital Collections of IUPUI University Library*. Accessed February 3, 2012. http://www.ulib.iupui.edu/digitalscholarship/collections/Telegraph.

"Civil War Indiana." http://www.civilwarindiana.com.

"Civil War Pensions." Accessed March 22, 2012. http://www.civilwarhome.com/pensions.htm.

"The Civil War: The Origins of Veterans' Health Care." *United States Department of Veterans Affairs*. Accessed March 22, 2012. http://www.va.gov/health/NewsFeatures/20110413a.asp.

"Congressional Medal of Honor Society." http://www.cmohs.org/.

Davis, Mark and Karen Marshall. "Civil War Soldiers of Grant County, Indiana." http://www.ingenweb.org/ingrant/CivilWar/CWSa.htm.

"Family Tree For James Barlow RUMSEY / Mary DALZELL (MRIN:168)." Accessed April 15, 2013. http://www.geneandsue.com/genealogy/fam168.html.

"Fayetteville National Cemetery." Accessed January 16, 2009. http://www.cwc.lsu.edu/cwc/projects/dbases/ncfayett.htm.

"Find A Grave." http://www.findagrave.com/.

"Forest Cemetery: Lincoln County, Oklahoma." Accessed April 15, 2013. http://www.okcemeteries.net/lincoln/forest/forest.htm.

"Frederick Purgett, 1843-1900." Accessed April 15, 2013. http://freepages.genealogy.rootsweb.ancestry.com/~hutch/PURGETT/frederick2.htm.

"G. A. R. Roster." *Henry County Genealogical Services*. Accessed August 18, 2003. http://www.hcgs.net/gar.html.

"Government Military Memorial Markers." Links found on *Wabash County Genealogy*. http://www.rootsweb.ancestry.com/~inwabash/index.html.

"Grand Army of the Republic (GAR) Records Project." *Sons of Union Veterans of the Civil War*. Accessed May 26, 2015. http://www.garrecords.org/.

"Greenfield Glimpses 2." Accessed April 15, 2013. http://www.hancocknews.com/greenfield_glimpses_2.htm.

"Headstones Provided for Deceased Union Civil War Veterans, 1879-1903." *Ancestry.* http://search.ancestry.com/search/db.aspx?dbid=1195.

"Henry County's First Civil War Volunteers." Henry County Genealogical Services. Accessed February 7, 2012. http://www.hcgs.net/civilvolunteers.html.

"Historical Obituaries." http://www.daytonmetrolibrary.org/research-a-databases/history-a-genealogy/resources/hobits.

"History of the National Home for Disabled Volunteer Soldiers." *Veterans Affairs National Home for Disabled Volunteer Soldiers*. Accessed April 27, 2012. http://www.nps.gov/nr/travel/veterans_affairs/History.html.

"Hospitals part 3." Accessed March 4, 2013. http://www.cincinnativiews.net/hospitals_part_3.htm.

"Illinois Genealogy Trails, Welcome to Richland County, Biographies R." Accessed November 20, 2012. http://genealogytrails.com/ill/richland/Bios_R.html.

"Index of /public_html." www.publicbookshelf.com/public_html.

"Ira Hough." *Home of Heroes*. Accessed December 8, 2006. http://www.homeofheroes.com/gravesites/states/pages_go/hough_ira_fl.html.

"Ira Hough: Henry County, Indiana Medal of Honor Recipient." *Henry County Genealogical Services*. Accessed February 7, 2012. http://www.hcgs.net/ira.html.

"Jeremiah O'Sullivan and Hanora (Annie) O'Brien Family Information." Accessed April 30, 2010. http://www.osullivanfamilytree.com.

"Kansas History and Heritage Project – Ford County Obituaries." Accessed April 15 2013. http://www.rootsweb.ancestry.com/~ksfordhp/obituaries/obituaries.html.

Marten, James. "Exempt from the ordinary rules of life: Researching postwar adjustment problems of union veterans." *Civil War History* 47, no. 1 (March 2001), 57-70. Accessed April 27, 2012. http://muse.jhu.ed/journals/cwh/summary/v047/47.1marten.html.

"Medal of Honor." *Center of Military History: United States Army*. http://www.army.mil/cmh-pg/mohciv.htm.

Miner, Mark. "Who's Who Bios: Last names beginning with 'B'." *Minerd – Minard – Miner – Minor Archives*. http://www.minerd.com.

"National Graves Registration Database." *Sons of Union Veterans of the Civil War*. http://www.suvcwdb.org/home/.

"Nationwide Gravesite Locator." http://gravelocator.cem.va.gov.

"Notes for Samuel Bumpus." http://freepages.genealogy.rootsweb.ancestry.com/~judysstuff/burials/bumpus_desc.htm.

Plante, Trevor K. "Genealogy Notes: The National Home for Disabled Volunteer Soldiers." *Prologue* 36, no. 1 (Spring 2004). Accessed April 27, 2012. http://www.archives.gov/publications/prologue/2004/spring/soldiers-home.html.

"Poinsett Veterans of the Civil War." Accessed April 13, 2013. http://www.bscn.com/~harryv/civilwv.htm.

Roll of Honor, Vol. XVIII. http://search.ancestry.com/search/db.aspx?dbid=48626.

"Samuel Bumpus, Co. G 8th Indiana Volunteer Infantry." http://freepages.genealogy.rootsweb.ancestry.com/~judysstuff.burials/Bumpus.htm.

"Sesquicentennial | Arbor Familiae." Accessed April 15, 2013. http://arborfamiliae.wordpress.com/2011/04/13/sesquicentennial/.

"Soldiers and Sailors Database." *National Park Service*. www.itd.nps.gov/cwss.

"U.S. Army, Register of Enlistments, 1798-1914." http://search.ancestry.com/search/db.aspx?dbid=1198.

"U.S., Burial Registers, Military Posts and National Cemeteries, 1862-1960." *Ancestry*. http://search.ancestry.com/search/db.aspx?dbid=3135.

"U.S. Civil War Draft Registrations Records, 1863-1865." *Ancestry*. http://search.ancestry.com/search/db.aspx?dbid=1666.

"U.S., Civil War Pension Index: General Index to Pension Files, 1861-1934." *Ancestry*. http://search.ancestry.com/search/db.aspx?dbid=4654.

"U.S. National Homes for Disabled Volunteer Soldiers, 1866-1938." *Ancestry*. http://search.ancestry.com/search/db.aspx?dbid=1200.

"Vandevender Cemetery." Accessed January 5, 2009. http://www.cemeteries-madison-co-in.com/vandevender_cemetery.htm.

"Vigo County Indiana Obituaries." Accessed April 15, 2013. http://genealogytrails.com/ind/vigo/vigoobits.html.

Whipple, Henry P., 1906. *Henry P. Whipple's The Diary of a Private Soldier*. Wisconsin Historical Society, 2011. Accessed May 15, 2014.

http://content.wisconsinhistory.org/cdm/ref/collection/quiner/id/24846.

"William Clement Scott Jr. Civil War Service." Accessed November 2, 2016. http://bjsgenealogy.com/Scott/WCScottJrCivilWar.htm.

"Widow's Pensions." *Fold 3*. http://www.fold3.com/title_24/civil_war_widows_pensions/.

"Yost Bios." *Henry County Indiana Biographies, Genealogy Trails History Group*. Accessed April 13, 2013. http://genealogytrails.com/ind/henry/yostbios.html.

MEMORIALS AND MUSEUMS

Colonel Eli Lilly Civil War Museum

Medal of Honor Memorial

Soldiers' and Sailors' Monument

World War Memorial

MICROFILM

Indiana State Archives

Eighth Indiana Volunteer Infantry regiment correspondence. Records of the Adjutant General of Indiana: Roll No. 3.

Hospital Records (six reels)

IMA1. Indiana Military Agency Roll No. 1, AAIS #023219.
IMA2. Indiana Military Agency Hospital Register: Nashville, Tennessee #2.
IMA3. Indiana Military Agency Hospital Registers: Evansville, Indiana, Out of State Troops, L733 023244.
IMA4. Indiana Military Agency Hospital Register: Murfreesboro, Tennessee, 1863-1864, L729 023212.
AGOIFA9. Adj. Gen. Record of Hospitalization of Soldiers, 1862-1865, Vol. 1.
AGOIFA10. Adj. Gen. Record of Hospitalization of Soldiers, 1862-1865, Vol. 6.

Index to Muster Rolls (multiple reels for all Indiana soldiers).

MANUSCRIPTS

Anthony Meeks

Sanford, Chaplain Arthur. Pension file and six transcribed letters January to July 1862 published in the *Indianapolis Daily Journal*.

Ball State University

Smith, Philander. "Philander Smith Papers." U.S. Civil War Resources for East Central Indiana Collections. MSS 216/ PSC 225, Box 1.

Cedar Creek Battlefield Foundation

Hixon, Robert Tracey. "Battle of Ceader Creek."

Dorothy Jones (family member)

Gregg, Ira T. "A Brief Sketch of my parents, Stephen and Hannah Gregg; Genealogy and Biography of Ira T. Gregg," Photocopy of unpublished memoir.

Dr. James Ford Historic Home

Civil War Correspondence, 1861-1863 between James Ford, U.S. Surgeon 8th Regiment Volunteer Infantry, and America Holton Ford, Wabash, Indiana. Manuscript published July 2004 for the Ford Family Reunion by the Charley Creek Foundation.

Eric Lowman

Company I death and burial information.

Indiana Historical Society

Burget, Erastus G. "Diaries, 1862." SC 2701.

Burris, Johnson. "Johnson Burris letter." SC 156.

Conley, Henry C. "Henry C. Conley letter." Found in Robert G. Conley letters. SC 272.

Kinney, J.S. "J.S. Kinney letter." SC 920.

Marshall, Swain. "Swain Marshall letters." Found in Thomas Marshall Papers, 1821-1920. M 199.

Melick, Thomas. "Thomas Melick letters." Found in Jacob W. Bartmess Civil War letters. M 0012.

Pollock, Lizzie. "Lizzie Pollock letters." Found in Robert G. Conley letters. SC 272.

"Regimental Records, Company K." M 164.

Savage, C.A. "Battle of Cedar Creek, Oct. 19, 1864." SC1310.

Scott, David S. "Civil War letters, 1862-1865." SC 0447.

Thuma, Valentine. "Valentine Thuma diary." SC 1458.

Van Buskirk, William A. "Papers, 1846-1858." SC 2580.

Indiana State Library

John Coburn collection. L34. Manuscript Section.

Charles Lawson collection. L163. Manuscript Section.

Daniel Roberts collection. S1123. Manuscript Section.

Mark Frye and Robert Grant

Pension file for William Collins Dove.

National Archives

Military record for James W. Alexander.

Nikki Schofield

Burial records from Crown Hill Cemetery for Conrad Shellhouse.

Transcribed letter from Daniel Roberts collection. S1123.

Sons of Union Veterans of the Civil War – Ben Harrison Camp #356

Grave photos.

1939 WPA Veterans' Grave Registration cards for Marion County.

Tony O'Sullivan

Information and grave photos for Jeremiah Sullivan family.

Truman State University

"Ira P. Humphreys GAR Application." Archives of Corporal Dix Post No. 22, Grand Army of the Republic, 1882-1934 (D1). Special Collections – University Archives. Pickler Memorial Library.

U.S. Army Military History Institute, Carlisle Barracks, Pennsylvania

Samuel P. Herrington diary. Haerle Collection.

Winfield Mayne

Mississippi Marine Brigade.

NEWSPAPERS

Abilene Daily Chronicle. https://www.newspapers.com/title_3405/abilene_daily_chronicle/.

Abilene Daily Reflector. https://www.newspapers.com/title_3372/abilene_daily_reflector/.

The Albany Democrat. https://www.newspapers.com/title_3634/albany_democrat/.

The Akron Beacon Journal. https://www.newspapers.com/title_4267/the_akron_beacon_journal/.

The Albemarle Press. https://www.newspapers.com/title_2404/the_albemarle_press/.

The Alexandria Times-Tribune. https://www.newspapers.com/title_3383/the_alexandria_timestribune/.

The Alton Democrat. https://www.newspapers.com/title_85/the_alton_democrat/.

Alton Evening Telegraph. https://www.newspapers.com/title_19/alton_evening_telegraph/.

Anderson Daily Bulletin. https://www.newspapers.com/title_24/anderson_daily_bulletin/.

Anderson Herald. https://www.newspapers.com/title_22/anderson_herald/.

The Argos Reflector. https://www.newspapers.com/title_4057/the_argos_reflector/.

Arizona Silver Belt. https://www.newspapers.com/title_1290/arizona_silver_belt/.

Arkansas City Daily Traveler. https://www.newspapers.com/title_1989/arkansas_city_daily_traveler/.

The Bakersfield Californian. https://www.newspapers.com/title_8/the_bakersfield_californian/.

The Baltimore Sun. https://www.newspapers.com/title_4466/the_baltimore_sun/.

The Belleville Telescope. https://www.newspapers.com/title_98/the_belleville_telescope/.

Boston Post. https://www.newspapers.com/title_2068/boston_post/.

The Bremen Inquirer. https://www.newspapers.com/title_4044/the_bremen_enquirer/.

The Brook Reporter. https://www.newspapers.com/title_4062/the_brook_reporter/.

The Brookville Democrat. https://www.newspapers.com/title_4058/the_brookville_democrat/.

The Brownsville Herald. https://www.newspapers.com/title_351/the_brownsville_herald/.

Burlington Republican. https://www.newspapers.com/title_3968/burlington_republican/.

The Call-Leader. https://www.newspapers.com/title_3510/the_callleader/.

The Cambridge City Tribune.

https://www.newspapers.com/title_201/the_cambridge_city_tribune/.
The Chanute Daily Tribune. https://www.newspapers.com/title_2051/the_chanute_daily_tribune/.
Chicago Daily Tribune. https://www.newspapers.com/title_839/chicago_daily_tribune/.
The Chillicothe Constitution-Tribune. https://www.newspapers.com/title_128/the_chillicothe_constitutiontribune/.
The Cincinnati Daily Star. https://www.newspapers.com/title_4395/the_cincinnati_daily_star/.
The Cincinnati Enquirer. https://www.newspapers.com/title_844/the_cincinnati_enquirer/.
Cleveland Daily Leader. (*Cleveland Morning Leader*). https://www.newspapers.com/title_1465/cleveland_daily_leader/.
The Coffeyville Daily Journal. https://www.newspapers.com/title_2060/the_coffeyville_daily_journal/.
The Columbus Republican. https://www.newspapers.com/title_3998/the_columbus_republican/.
The Courier Journal. https://www.newspapers.com/title_845/the_courierjournal/.
The Daily Free Press. (Carbondale, Illinois). https://www.newspapers.com/title_580/the_daily_free_press/.
The Daily Gazette. (Colorado Springs, Colorado).
Daily News-Democrat. https://www.newspapers.com/title_990/daily_newsdemocrat/.
Daily Ohio Statesman. https://www.newspapers.com/title_1780/daily_ohio_statesman/.
The Daily Reporter. (*Greenfield Daily Reporter*). https://www.newspapers.com/title_4272/the_daily_reporter/.
The Daily Republican. (Cherryvale, Kansas). https://www.newspapers.com/title_3373/the_daily_republican/.
The Daily Republican. (Rushville, Indiana). https://www.newspapers.com/title_3421/the_daily_republican/.
The Daily Review. https://www.newspapers.com/title_381/the_daily_review/.
Decatur Daily Republican. https://www.newspapers.com/title_432/decatur_daily_republican/.
Decatur Weekly Republican. https://www.newspapers.com/title_449/decatur_weekly_republican/.
The Des Moines Register. https://www.newspapers.com/title_86/the_des_moines_register/.
Eau Claire Leader. https://www.newspapers.com/title_627/eau_claire_leader/.

Edinburg Daily Courier. https://www.newspapers.com/title_3967/the_edinburg_daily_courier/.

The Elwood Call-Leader. https://www.newspapers.com/title_3510/the_callleader/.

The Elwood Daily Press. https://www.newspapers.com/title_3508/the_elwood_daily_press/.

The Elwood Free Press. https://www.newspapers.com/title_3512/the_elwood_free_press/.

The Eureka Herald and Greenwood County Republican. https://www.newspapers.com/title_4485/the_eureka_herald_and_greenwood_county/.

Evening Star. https://www.newspapers.com/title_1353/evening_star/.

The Evening Telegraph. https://www.newspapers.com/title_1623/the_evening_telegraph/.

The Evening Times. https://www.newspapers.com/title_3440/the_evening_times/.

The Fairmount News. https://www.newspapers.com/title_4048/the_fairmount_news/.

Fort Scott Weekly Tribune and the Fort Scott Monitor. https://www.newspapers.com/title_2188/fort_scott_tribune_and_the_fort_scott_monitor/.

Fort Wayne Daily Gazette. https://www.newspapers.com/title_434/fort_wayne_daily_gazette/.

Fort Wayne Daily News. https://www.newspapers.com/title_439/fort_wayne_daily_news/.

The Fort Wayne Journal-Gazette. https://www.newspapers.com/title_643/the_fort_wayne_journalgazette/.

The Fort Wayne Sentinel. https://www.newspapers.com/title_404/the_fort_wayne_sentinel/.

Fort Wayne Weekly Gazette. https://www.newspapers.com/title_463/fort_wayne_weekly_gazette/.

Freeport Journal-Standard. https://www.newspapers.com/title_105/freeport_journalstandard/.

The Fulton County News. https://www.newspapers.com/title_1405/the_fulton_county_news/.

Garnett Journal. https://www.newspapers.com/title_3006/garnett_journal/.

Garrett Clipper. https://www.newspapers.com/title_4061/garrett_clipper/.

The Girard Press. https://www.newspapers.com/title_3410/the_girard_press/.

The Globe Republican. https://www.newspapers.com/title_1510/the_globerepublican/.

Greeley Daily Tribune. https://www.newspapers.com/title_819/greeley_daily_tribune/.

The Greenfield Daily Reporter. https://www.newspapers.com/title_3640/greenfield_daily_reporter/.

Hagerstown Exponent. https://www.newspapers.com/title_1240/hagerstown_exponent/.

The Hancock Democrat. https://www.newspapers.com/title_3639/the_hancock_democrat/.

The Herald-Despatch. https://www.newspapers.com/title_906/the_heralddespatch/.

The Herington Headlight. https://www.newspapers.com/title_4754/the_herington_headlight/.
The Holt County Sentinel. https://www.newspapers.com/title_1487/the_holt_county_sentinel/.
The Hood River Glacier. https://www.newspapers.com/title_3662/the_hood_river_glacier/.
The Houston Post. https://www.newspapers.com/title_1549/the_houston_post/.
The Huntington Democrat. https://www.newspapers.com/title_972/the_huntington_democrat/.
The Huntington Herald. https://www.newspapers.com/title_1241/the_huntington_herald/.
The Huntington Press. https://www.newspapers.com/title_1236/the_huntington_press/.
Huntington Weekly Herald. https://www.newspapers.com/title_1261/huntington_weekly_herald/.
The Hutchinson News. https://www.newspapers.com/title_37/the_hutchinson_news/.
Independence Daily Reporter. https://www.newspapers.com/title_3595/independence_daily_reporter/.
The Independent Record. https://www.newspapers.com/title_151/the_independent_record/.
The Indiana Herald. https://www.newspapers.com/title_1239/the_indiana_herald/.
The Indiana State Sentinel. https://www.newspapers.com/title_4156/the_indiana_state_sentinel/.
The Indianapolis Journal. https://www.newspapers.com/title_4073/the_indianapolis_journal/.
The Indianapolis News. https://www.newspapers.com/title_919/the_indianapolis_news/.
The Indianapolis Star. https://www.newspapers.com/title_384/the_indianapolis_star/.
The Iola Register. https://www.newspapers.com/title_36/the_iola_register/.
Iowa City Press-Citizen. https://www.newspapers.com/title_393/iowa_city_presscitizen/.
Jackson County Banner. https://www.newspapers.com/title_4585/jackson_county_banner/.
Journal and Courier. https://www.newspapers.com/title_5090/journal_and_courier/.
The Junction City Weekly Union. https://www.newspapers.com/title_3338/the_junction_city_weekly_union/.
Kokomo Daily Tribune. https://www.ingenweb.org/ingrant/CivilWar/obitgwa.htm.
Lancaster Daily Intelligencer. https://www.newspapers.com/title_1351/lancaster_daily_intelligencer/.
Lansing State Journal. https://www.newspapers.com/title_3758/lansing_state_journal/.
Lead Daily Call. https://www.newspapers.com/title_3581/lead_daily_call/.
The Leavenworth Times. https://www.newspapers.com/title_621/the_leavenworth_times/.
The Leavenworth Weekly Times. https://www.newspapers.com/title_1640/the_leavenworth_weekly_times/.

Lincoln Evening Journal. https://www.newspapers.com/title_1093/lincoln_evening_journal/.

The Lincoln Star. https://www.newspapers.com/title_1094/the_lincoln_star/.

The Logan Republican. https://www.newspapers.com/title_4774/the_logan_republican/.

Logansport Pharos-Tribune. (*Logansport Daily Tribune*). https://www.newspapers.com/title_4/logansport_pharostribune/.

The Logansport Reporter. https://www.newspapers.com/title_18/logansport_reporter/.

Los Angeles Herald. https://www.newspapers.com/title_1278/los_angeles_herald/.

The Los Angeles Times. https://www.newspapers.com/title_4312/the_los_angeles_times/.

Memphis Daily Appeal. https://www.newspapers.com/title_1252/memphis_daily_appeal/.

Modesto Evening News. https://www.newspapers.com/title_2061/modesto_evening_news/.

The Monett Times. https://www.newspapers.com/title_4230/the_monett_times/.

The Monroeville Breeze. https://www.newspapers.com/title_992/the_monroeville_breeze/.

Morning Daily Herald. https://www.newspapers.com/title_3597/morning_daily_herald/.

Muncie Evening Press. https://www.newspapers.com/title_4976/muncie_evening_press/.

Nashville Union and American. https://www.newspapers.com/title_1558/nashville_union_and_american/.

National Republican. https://www.newspapers.com/title_1344/national_republican/.

The National Tribune. https://www.newspapers.com/title_1345/the_national_tribune/.

The New North-West. https://www.newspapers.com/title_4115/the_new_northwest/.

The New York Times. https://www.newspapers.com/title_395/the_new_york_times/.

The News. https://www.newspapers.com/title_458/the_news/.

Oakland Tribune. https://www.newspapers.com/title_2/oakland_tribune/.

The Olathe Mirror. https://www.newspapers.com/title_2293/the_olathe_mirror/.

The Ottawa Daily Republic. (1902-1914). https://www.newspapers.com/title_3347/the_ottawa_daily_republic/.

The Ottawa Herald. https://www.newspapers.com/title_38/the_ottawa_herald/.

The Oskaloosa Independent. https://www.newspapers.com/title_2707/the_oskaloosa_independent/.

The Palladium-Item. Richmond, Indiana. April 3, 1958.

Perrysburg Journal. https://www.newspapers.com/title_1378/perrysburg_journal/.

The Petaluma Argus-Courier. (1899-1993). https://www.newspapers.com/title_4734/the_petaluma_arguscourier/.

The Piqua Daily Call. https://www.newspapers.com/title_195/the_piqua_daily_call/.

The Pittsburg Daily Headlight. https://www.newspapers.com/title_3632/the_pittsburg_daily_headlight/.

The Pittsburgh Daily Commercial. https://www.newspapers.com/title_3672/the_pittsburgh_daily_commercial/.

Public Ledger. https://www.newspapers.com/title_1801/public_ledger/.

Randolph Journal. https://www.newspapers.com/title_4142/randolph_journal/.

Reading Times. https://www.newspapers.com/title_1325/reading_times/.

The Republic. https://www.newspapers.com/title_4056/the_republic/.

The Republican-News. (Hamilton, Ohio). May 13, 1919.

The Richmond Item / The Evening Item. https://www.newspapers.com/title_4965/the_richmond_item/.

Richmond Weekly Palladium. https://www.newspapers.com/title_4964/richmond_weekly_palladium/.

Rolla Herald. https://www.newspapers.com/title_4000/rolla_herald/.

San Francisco Chronicle. https://www.newspapers.com/title_835/san_francisco_chronicle/.

St. Joseph Herald. https://www.newspapers.com/title_1085/st_joseph_herald/.

St. Louis Post-Dispatch. https://www.newspapers.com/title_4064/st_louis_postdispatch/.

The Saint Paul Globe. https://www.newspapers.com/title_1544/the_saint_paul_globe/.

The Salina Evening Journal. https://www.newspapers.com/title_3600/the_salina_evening_journal/.

The Salt Lake Tribune. https://www.newspapers.com/title_373/the_salt_lake_tribune/.

The Sandusky Star-Journal. https://www.newspapers.com/title_444/the_sandusky_starjournal/.

Santa Ana Register. https://www.newspapers.com/title_3160/santa_ana_register/.

The Star Press. https://www.newspapers.com/title_3757/the_star_press/.

The Stark County Democrat. https://www.newspapers.com/title_1473/the_stark_county_democrat/.

Steuben Republican. (Angola, Indiana). May 16, 1894.

The Tennessean. https://www.newspapers.com/title_3707/the_tennessean/.

The Times-Picayune. https://www.newspapers.com/title_824/the_timespicayune/.

The Tipton Daily Tribune. https://www.newspapers.com/title_186/the_tipton_daily_tribune/.

The Topeka Daily Capital. https://www.newspapers.com/title_2577/the_topeka_daily_capital/.

The Topeka State Journal. https://www.newspapers.com/title_2716/the_topeka_state_journal/.

The Valley Falls Vindicator. https://www.newspapers.com/title_4579/the_valley_falls_vindicator/.

The Vicksburg American. https://www.newspapers.com/title_4615/the_vicksburg_american/.

The Vidette-Messenger. https://www.newspapers.com/title_1176/the_videttemessenger/.

Wabash Times / Wabash Plains Dealer. (Wabash, Indiana).

The Waco News-Tribune. https://www.newspapers.com/title_1268/the_waco_newstribune/.

Walnut Valley Times. https://www.newspapers.com/title_3614/walnut_valley_times/.

The Washington Herald. https://www.newspapers.com/title_1374/the_washington_herald/.

The Washington Times. https://www.newspapers.com/title_1607/the_washington_times/.

Waukesha Daily Freeman. https://www.newspapers.com/title_779/waukesha_daily_freeman/.

The Wellington Daily News. https://www.newspapers.com/title_2510/the_wellington_daily_news/.

The Wichita Beacon. https://www.newspapers.com/title_3324/the_wichita_beacon/.

The Wichita Daily Eagle. https://www.newspapers.com/title_1364/the_wichita_daily_eagle/.

Wichita Eagle. https://www.newspapers.com/title_1486/wichita_eagle/.

Wilmington News-Journal. https://www.newspapers.com/title_2115/wilmington_newsjournal/.

The Worthington Advance. https://www.newspapers.com/title_1736/the_worthington_advance/.

The York Daily. https://www.newspapers.com/title_2764/the_york_daily/.

PUBLISHED WORKS

Adams, Henry C., Jr. *Indiana at Vicksburg*. Indianapolis: William B. Burford, 1911. Reprint. Lexington, KY: Forgotten Books, 2012.

The Annals of the War Written by Leading Participants North and South, Originally Published in the Philadelphia Weekly Times. Vol. I. Philadelphia: Times, 1879. Reprint. National Historical Society, 2012.

The Annals of the War Written by Leading Participants North and South, Originally Published in the Philadelphia Weekly Times. Vol. II. Philadelphia: Times, 1879. Reprint. National Historical Society, 2012.

Arguimbau, Ellie. "The Mystery of Valentine Thuma, or Why I Love My Job So Much." *Northwest Archives Easy Access* 34, no. 3 (October 2008): 3-4.

Arnold, James R. *Grant Wins the War: Decision at Vicksburg*. New York: John Wiley & Sons, 1997.

Baker, Sue. *Hancock County, Indiana Civil War Soldiers Plus Related Facts*. Westminster, MD: Heritage Books, 2006.

Baldwin, Edgar M. *The Making of a Township, Being an Account of the Early Settlement and Subsequent Development of Fairmount Township, Grant County, Indiana, 1829 to 1917, Based upon Data Secured by Personal Interviews, from Numerous Communications and Various Other Reliable Sources of Information Concerning Local History*. Fairmount, IN: Edgar Baldwin, 1917. Reprint.

Bearss, Edwin C. *Fields of Honor: Pivotal Battles of the Civil War.* Washington, D.C.: National Geographic, 2006.

Berkin v. Marsh et al. Supreme Court of Montana, April 13, 1896. *The Pacific Reporter,* 44.

Berry, Rev. Chester D. *Loss of The Sultana and Reminiscences Of Survivors*. Lansing, Michigan: Darius D. Thorp, 1892. Reprint, San Bernardino, CA: Old South Books, 2014.

Bigelow, James K., M.D. *Abridged History of the Eighth Indiana Volunteer Infantry, from its Organization, April 21st, 1861, to the date of Re-enlistment as Veterans, January 1, 1864*. Indianapolis: Ellis Barnes, 1864.

Boatner, Mark M., III. *The Civil War Dictionary*. New York: Vintage Books, 1987.

Bock, Gene. "Man About Town – Samuel Hicks Family Came to Ovid in 1838." *Anderson Daily Bulletin*, September 2, 1970.

Bodenhamer, David J. and Robert G. Barrows, eds. *The Encyclopedia of Indianapolis.* Bloomington: Indiana University Press, 1994.

Booth, Benjamin F. and Steve Meyer. *Dark Days of the Rebellion: Life in Southern Military Prisons*. Garrison, Iowa: Meyer Publishing, 1995.

Brash, Sarah, ed. *The American Story: War Between Brothers.* Alexandria: Time-Life Books, 1996.

Brown, Louis A. *The Salisbury Prison: A Case Study of Confederate Military Prisons 1861-1865.* Wilmington: Broadfoot, 1992.

Callen, Cathy. "Reconstituting Allen: Finding a Family Member Lost in History." *Connections: The Hoosier Genealogist* 52, no. 2 (Fall/Winter 2012): 47-55.

Civil War Times Illustrated, eds. *Great Battles of the Civil War*. New York: Gallery Books, 1989.

Cohen, Stan B. *A Pictorial Guide to West Virginia Civil War Sites and Related Information*. Charleston: Quarrier Press, 2003.

Commager, Henry Steele, ed. *The Civil War Archive: The History of the Civil War in Documents*. New York: Black Dog and Leventhal, 2000.

Commemorative Biographical Record of Prominent and Representative Men of Indianapolis and Vicinity. Chicago: J.H. Beers, 1908.

Davis, Barbara Butler. *Affectionately Yours: The Civil War Home-Front Letters of the Ovid Butler Family*. Indianapolis: Indiana Historical Society Press, 2004.

Davis, William C. *First Blood: Fort Sumter to Bull Run*. Alexandria: Time-Life Books, 1983.

Documents of the General Assembly of Indiana, at the Forty-third Regular Session, Begun on the Fifth of January, A.D. 1865. Part II. Indianapolis: W.R. Hollingway, State Printer, 1865.

Eicher, David J. *The Longest Night: A Military History of the Civil War*. New York: Simon and Schuster, 2001.

Ewald, Erich L., ed. "A Letter from the Front: Vicksburg, 1863." *Indiana Magazine of History* 41, no. 3 (September 1995): 321-325.

---------------------. "War at the Crossroads." *Indiana Magazine of History* 42, no. 4 (December 1996): 346-359.

The Fight For Chattanooga: Chickamauga to Missionary Ridge. Alexandria: Time-Life Books, 1985.

Foote, Shelby. *The Civil War: A Narrative*. Vol. 6, *Charleston Harbor to Vicksburg.* Alexandria: Time-Life Books, 1999.

Ford, James. *Genealogy of the Ford Family*. Wabash, 1890, e-book.

Forkner, John L. *History of Madison County Indiana: A Narrative Account of Its Historical Progress, Its People and Its Principal Interests*. Vol. I. Chicago: Lewis, 1914.

"Fort Recovery Bicentennial History, 1791-1991." The Bicentennial Committee.

Gallagher, Gary W., ed. *The Shenandoah Valley Campaign of 1864*. Chapel Hill: University of North Carolina Press, 2006.

Gallman, J. Matthew, ed. *The Civil War Chronicle: The Only Day-by-day Portrait of America's Tragic Conflict as Told by Soldiers, Journalists, Politicians, Farmers, Nurses, Slaves, and Other Eyewitnesses*. New York: Gramercy Books, 2000.

Harden, Samuel. *History of Madison County, Indiana From 1820 to 1874, Giving a General Review of Principal Events, Statistical and Historical Items, Derived from Official Sources*. Markleville: Samuel Harden, 1874. Reprint. Lexington: Forgotten Books, 2012.

---------------. *Those I have met, or Boys in Blue; in which is remembered those I have met along the road of life*. N.p.: W. Mitchell, 1888.

Harrison, Ned. "Civil War Surgeon Treated Wounded Under Primitive Conditions." *Greensboro News and Record*, August 9, 2000.

Hazzard, George. *Hazzard's History of Henry County, Indiana 1822-1906, Military Edition*. Vol. I. New Castle: George Hazzard, 1906.

--------------. *Hazzard's History of Henry County, Indiana 1822-1906, Military Edition*. Vol. II. New Castle: George Hazzard, 1906.

Henry County Indiana W.P.A. Index to 10 Histories, Atlases and Other Source Books. Indianapolis: Indiana State Library, 1941. Reprint, Knightstown: Bookmark, 1979.

Hess, Earl J. *The Union Soldier in Battle: Enduring the Ordeal of Combat*. Lawrence: University Press of Kansas, 1997.

Hicks, Roger W. and Frances E. Schutz. *Battlefields of the Civil War*. Topsfield, Massachusetts: Salem House, 1989.

History of Henry County, Indiana. Chicago: Inter-State, 1884.

History of Madison County, Indiana with Illustrations and Biographical Sketches of Some of Its Prominent Men and Pioneers. Chicago: Kingman Brothers, 1880.

History of Medicine in Nebraska. 1928.

History of Wabash County, Indiana. Chicago: John Morris, 1884.

Hoehling, A. A. *Vicksburg: 47 Days of Siege*. Mechanicsburg, PA: Stackpole Books, 1969.

Holzer, Harold. *Witness to War: The Civil War 1861-1865.* New York: Berkley, 1996.

Howe, Henry, LL.D. *Historical Collections of Ohio in Two Volumes*. Vol. II. Cincinnati: C.J. Krehbiel, 1888.

Hughes, Michael A. "A Forgotten Battle in a Region Ignore…Pea Ridge, or Elkhorn Tavern Arkansas – March 7-8, 1862: The Campaign, the Battle, and the Men Who Fought for the Fate of Missouri." *Blue & Gray Magazine* 5, no. 3 (January 1988): 8-36.

Hunter, Lloyd A. *For Duty and Destiny: The Life and Civil War Diary of Hoosier Soldier and Educator William Taylor Stott*. Indianapolis: Indiana Historical Press, 2010.

Indiana in the War of Rebellion: Indiana Historical Collections. Vol. XLI. Indianapolis: Indiana Historical Bureau, 1960.

"Indiana's 28th Regiment: Black Soldiers for the Union." *The Indiana Historian* (February 1994): 2-15.

Jones, Wilbur D., Jr. *Giants in the Cornfield: The 27th Indiana Infantry*. Shippensburg, PA: White Mane, 1997.

Journal of the American Medical Association 14, no. 11 (March 13, 1920): 751.

Julin, Suzanne. "National Home for Disabled Volunteer Soldiers: Assessment of Significance and National Landmark Recommendation."

Katcher, Philip. *The Civil War Source Book.* New York: Facts on File, 1992.

Kiper, Richard L., ed. *Dear Catherine, Dear Taylor*. Lawrence: University Press of Kansas, 2002.

Knight, Rena Marie. *Civil War Soldiers Buried in Arkansas National Cemeteries*. Conway, Arkansas: Arkansas Research, 1996.

-----------------. *Union Soldiers Buried in Arkansas: A Compilation Representative of Union States.* Jacksonville, Arkansas: R. M. K., 2000.

Kollbaum, Marc E. *Gateway to the West: The History of Jefferson Barracks from 1826-1894,* Volume I. St. Louis: Friends of Jefferson Barracks, n.d.

Letters Home IV: Life at the Front, Original Civil War Soldiers' Letters & Photographs. Gettysburg: Alan Sessarego Collection, 2003.

Lewin, J.G. and P.J. Huff. *Witness to the Civil War: First-Hand Accounts from Frank Leslies' Illustrated Newspape*r. New York: Collins, 2006.

Lewis, Thomas A. *The Guns of Cedar Creek*. New York: Laurel, 1988.

------------------. *The Shenandoah in Flames: The Valley Campaign of 1864.* Alexandria: Time-Life Books, 1987.

Macy, William M. "The Civil War Diary of William M. Macy." *Indiana Magazine of History* 30, no. 2 (June 1934): 181-197.

McCormick, David I. *Indiana Battle Flags.* Indianapolis: The Indiana Battle Flag Commission, 1929.

McMullen, Judith Q. "Hoosiers in Oregon." *The Hoosier Genealogist* 41, no. 2 (June 2001): 123-125.

Marius, Richard, ed. *The Columbia Book of Civil War Poetry.* New York: Columbia University Press, 1994.

Mathless, Paul, ed. *Voices of the Civil War: Vicksburg.* Alexandria: Time-Life Books, 1997.

McSpadden, Jennifer. *A Leaf of Voices: Stories of the American Civil War in the Words of Those Who Lived and Died, 1861-65*. Indianapolis: Indiana Historical Society Press, 2014.

The Medal of Honor of the United States Army. Washington: U.S. Govt. Printing Office, 1948.

Merrill, Catharine, ed. *The Soldier of Indiana in the War for the Union.* Indianapolis: Merrill, 1869.

Monghan, Jay. *Civil War on the Western Border, 1854-1865*. Lincoln: University of Nebraska Press, 1955.

The Nebraska State Medical Journal V, no. 2 (February 1920): 62.

Nelson, Jacqueline S. "The Military Response to the Society of Friends in Indiana to the Civil War." *Indiana Magazine of History* 81, no. 2 (June 1985): 101-130.

Nevin, David. *The Road to Shiloh.* Alexandria: Time-Life Books, 1983.

Northcott, Dennis. *Indiana Civil War Veterans: Transcription of the Death Rolls of the Department of Indiana, Grand Army of the Republic, 1882-1948*. St. Louis: Dennis Northcott, 2005.

----------------. *Iowa, Kansas and Nebraska Civil War Veterans: Compilation of the Death Rolls of the Departments of Iowa, Kansas and Nebraska, Grand Army of the Republic, 1883-1948*. St. Louis: Dennis Northcott, 2007.

Northcott, Dennis and Thomas Brooks. *Grand Army of the Republic Department of Illinois:*

Transcription of the Death Rolls, 1879-1947. St. Louis: Dennis Northcott, 2003.

O'Hair, Mary C. *The Great War: Wabash County, 1860-1861*. 1962.

Phillips, Herb. *Champion Hill!* Clinton, Mississippi: Phillips, n.d.

Pond, George E. *Campaigns of the Civil War XI: The Shenandoah Valley in 1864.* First published in 1883; Reprinted Edison, NJ: Castle Books, 2002.

Porter, Horace. *Campaigning with Grant.* New York: The Century Co., 1987. Reprint, Alexandria: Time-Life Books, 1981.

Power, J. C., ed. *Directory and soldiers' register of Wayne County*. Richmond: W. H. Lanthurn, 1865.

Presidents, Soldiers, Statesmen. Vol. II. New York: H.H. Hardesty, 1899.

Radiches, Lora. *History of Delaware County*. N.p.: T. B. Helm, 1881.

Riley, James Whitcomb. *The Complete Poetical Works of James Whitcomb Riley*. Indianapolis: The Bobbs-Merrill Company, 1937.

Rose, Ernestine Bradford. *The Circle: "The Center of Indianapolis."* Indianapolis: Crippin Printing Corporation, 1971.

Rose, Melissa. *Indiana and the Civil War.* Mooresville: Mooresville Park and Recreation District, 1994.

"Roster of Veterans of the Mexican, Civil, and Spanish-American Wars Residing in Nebraska in 1915." *The Hoosier Genealogist* 38, no. 3 (September 1998): 129-145.

Shea, William L. and Earl J. Hess. *Pea Ridge: Civil War Campaign in the West.* Chapel Hill: The University of North Carolina Press, 1992.

Sheridan, Philip. *Civil War Memoirs.* New York: Bantam Books, 1991. Original edition, *Personal Memoirs of P.H. Sheridan.* Charles L. Webster, 1888.

Sigel, Franz. "The Pea Ridge Campaign." *Battles and Leaders of the Civil War: Grant-Lee Edition*. Vol. I, Part I. New York: Century Co., 1884-1887. Reprint, National Historical Society, 2005, 314-334.

Smith, David M., ed. *Compelled to Appear in Print: The Vicksburg Manuscript of General John C. Pemberton*. Cincinnati, Ohio: Ironclad Printing, 1999.

Smith, Timothy B. *Champion Hill: Decisive Battle for Vicksburg.* New York: Savas Beatie, 2004.

The Soldier of Indiana in the War for the Union. Vol. I. Indianapolis: Merrill, 1866.

The Soldier of Indiana in the War for the Union. Vol. II. Indianapolis: Merrill, 1866.

Spies, Scouts and Raiders: Irregular Operations. Alexandria: Time-Life Books, 1985.

Stempfel, Thedore. *Artist's Life: Rudolf Schwarz and Karl Bitter.* Nashville, Ind.: NCSA LITERATUR, 2002.

Stevens, Robert Allan. *The Bracken Rangers, Co. K, 28th Regiment, 1st Indiana Cavalry and essays on the American Civil War*. Miami: Three Stars Press, 2010.

Stevenson, David, A. M. *Indiana's Roll of Honor*. Vol. I. Indianapolis: A. D. Steight, 1864.

------------------. *Indiana's Roll of Honor*. Vol. II. Indianapolis: A. D. Steight, 1866.

Symonds, Craig L. *A Battlefield Atlas of the Civil War.* Annapolis: Nautical and Aviation Publishing Company of America, 1983.

Terrell, W. H. H. *Indiana in the War of the Rebellion: Report of the Adjutant General*. Vol. 1. 1869. Reprint, Indianapolis: Indiana Historical Society, 1960.

-----------------. *Report of the Adjutant General's Office.* Vol. 2. Indianapolis: W.R. Holloway, State Printer, 1865.

----------------. *Report of the Adjutant General, Indiana*. Vol. 4. Indianapolis: Samuel M. Douglass, State Printer, 1866.

Thomsen, Brian M., ed. *The Civil War Memoirs of Ulysses S. Grant*. New York: Tom Doherty Associates, 2002.

Thornbrough, Emma Lou. *Indiana in the Civil War Era 1850-1880: The History of Indiana*. Vol. III. Indianapolis: Indiana Historical Bureau & Indiana Historical Society, 1965.

Trostel, Scott D. *The Lincoln Funeral Train: The Final Journey and National Funeral for Abraham Lincoln*. Fletcher, Ohio: Cam-Tech, 2002.

Tucker, Phillip Thomas. *Cathy Williams: From Slave to Buffalo Soldier*. Mechanicsburg, PA: Stackpole Books, 2009.

Uggen, Orville, Jr. *Indiana Civil War Veterans Blackford County, 1861-1865*. N.p.: Blackford County Civil War Re-enactment Club, 2004.

Volo, Dorothy Denneen and James. *Daily Life in Civil War America.* Westport,Connecticut: Greenwood Press, 1998.

Warner,Ezra J. *Generals in Blue.* Baton Rouge: Louisiana State University Press, 1964.

Webster's New World Dictionary, 3rd College Edition. New York: Simon and Schuster, 1988.

Weesner, Clarkson W. *History of Wabash County Indiana: A Narrative Account of Its Historical Progress, Its People, and Its Principal Interests*. Vol. I. Chicago: Lewis, 1914.

Wheeler, Richard. *Voices of the Civil War.* New York: Thomas Y. Crowell, 1976.

Whitehorne, Joseph W.A. *The Battle of Cedar Creek.* Washington, D.C.: Center of Military History, 1992.

Williams, Richard Brady. "Chicago's Battery Boys." *Hallowed Ground* 5, no. 3 (Fall 2004): 36-37.

Winschel, Terrence J. *Triumph & Defeat: The Vicksburg Campaign*. Vol. 2. El Dorado Hills, CA: Savas Beatie, 2006.

------------------. "Unvexing the Father of Waters: The Fall of Vicksburg." *Hallowed Ground* 5, no. 3 (Fall 2004): 21-28.

Woodward, Ron and Gladys Harvey. *Wabash County Chronicles: Raucous Quirky and Essential Tales.* Charleston, SC: History Press, 2010.

Worsham, John H. *One of Jackson's Foot Cavalry*. New York: Neale, 1912. Reprint, Alexandria: Time-Life Books, 1981.